# CHALLENGES
# OF
# URBAN
# EDUCATION

# CHALLENGES OF URBAN EDUCATION

## Sociological Perspectives for the Next Century

*edited by*

KAREN A. McCLAFFERTY
CARLOS ALBERTO TORRES
THEODORE R. MITCHELL

State University
of New York
Press

Chapter 1 appeared previously with the same title in the *British Journal of Sociology of Education* 17.2 (1996): 125–44. Copyright by Carfax Publishing, Ltd., 1996. Reprinted here with the kind permission of the publisher, Carfax Publishing (U.K.).

Chapter 8 comprises approximately forty-two pages from *Revolutionary Multiculturalism: Pedagogies of Dissent for the New Millennium*, ed. Peter McLaren. Copyright 1997 by Westview Press. Reprinted here with the kind permission of Westview Press.

Published by
State University of New York Press, Albany

Production by Susan Geraghty
Marketing by Patrick Durocher

Printed in the United States of America

For information, address State University of New York
Press, State University Plaza, Albany, N.Y., 12246

Library of Congress Cataloging-in-Publication Data

Challenges of urban education : sociological perspectives for the next
  century / Karen A. McClafferty, Carlos Alberto Torres, Theodore R.
  Mitchell, editors.
    p.    cm.
  Includes bibliographical references and index.
  ISBN 0-7914-4433-3 (alk. paper). — ISBN 0-7914-4434-1 (pbk. :
alk. paper)
    1. Education, Urban—Social aspects—United States. 2. Children
of minorities—Education—United States. 3. Educational change-
-United States. I. McClafferty, Karen A. II. Torres, Carlos
Alberto. III. Mitchell, Theodore R.
  LC5131.C38  2000
  370'.9173'2—dc 21                                     99-24397
                                                           CIP

10  9  8  7  6  5  4  3  2  1

# CONTENTS

# TABLES AND FIGURES

# ACKNOWLEDGMENTS

In June 1996, sociologists from across the United States—as well as from Canada, Spain, South Africa, Hungary, and England—gathered at the University of California, Los Angeles. At that time, a three-day meeting of the Research Committee on Sociology of Education of the International Sociological Association was held to address the challenges that urban education presents to sociologists of education. This project could not have come to fruition without the support of the International Sociological Association. One individual, Ken Hale, also deserves mention here. We are grateful for his generous assistance and support in the preparation of the final version of this manuscript.

Two chapters have been reprinted here with the generous permission of the original publisher. Specifically, Michael Apple's piece, "Power Meaning and Identity: Critical Sociology of Education in the United States," originally appeared in the *British Journal of Sociology of Education* (1996, vol. 17, no. 2). Peter McLaren's piece, "Gangsta Pedagogy and Ghettocentricity: The Hip Hop Nation as Counterpublic Sphere," originally appeared in the Westview Press text, *Revolutionary Multiculturalism: Pedagogies of Dissent for the New Millennium* (1997).

The balance of the chapters contained in this volume represent a sampling of the papers presented at the 1996 conference, all of which were important contributions to the sociology of urban education. The editors are deeply indebted to each of the conference participants, whose determination and commitment to improving urban education should serve as an inspiration to educators everywhere.

PART I

# Critical Issues in Urban Education and Challenges for the Sociology of Education

INTRODUCTION

# Challenges of the New Sociology of Urban Education

## Karen A. McClafferty, Carlos A. Torres, and Theodore R. Mitchell

According to a report by the National Center for Education Statistics (NCES), the proportion of all public school students in the United States who attend urban schools has been increasing slowly over time, to the point where the proportion of students in urban schools was at 28 percent in 1990. The report also points out that urban schools tend to be larger, with fewer resources, and located in areas with higher poverty rates. The student populations in urban schools are also more likely to be comprised of people of color[1] or of students who have difficulty speaking English. In addition, children in urban areas are more often exposed to conditions that endanger their health and well-being, such as limited access to medical care and increased exposure to violence and crime.[2]

Each of these factors alone presents a challenge to the student who must cope with it. These factors compounded present an even greater challenge. Hence, the perception that students in urban schools are "disadvantaged" or "at-risk" is not surprising. Indeed, the NCES found that even after controlling for poverty, students who attend urban schools are less likely than their suburban or rural counterparts to complete high school. Those who do graduate are more likely to be unemployed or living in poverty. Given these findings, the characterization of urban schools as in a "state of crisis"[3] seems reasonable and even necessary. This perception has been reinforced recently by works such as Jonathan Kozol's *Savage Inequalities*, which, through rich description and disturbing statistics, emphasizes the enormous inequities that exist in many urban schools.[4] The media attention received by Kozol's book and others like it has served to heighten awareness of the often drastic conditions of urban schools in the United States.

Another important point of the NCES report, however, is that the "often-cited bleak perceptions of urban schools and students may be overstated."[5] Indeed, the tendency in urban educational research to focus on problems and weaknesses is being challenged on many fronts, as researchers and practitioners alike realize the importance of highlighting both strengths and triumphs. In response, many researchers have begun to wrestle the spotlight away from the deficiencies of education, to shine it on the successes. Gloria Ladson-Billings, for example, describes the triumphs of teachers of African American students, calling them "dreamkeepers" because of their ability to enable their students to keep their dreams alive. She concludes her book by asserting her belief and hope that "if we can dream it, we can surely do it."[6] Similarly, Mike Rose argues that our criticism of public schools has become "one-dimensional . . . the humanity drained from it." In his contribution to a critique that "encourages both dissent and invention, fury and hope,"[7] Rose sets out on a journey to document the successes of public education. His rich descriptions of classrooms across the country highlight the greatest strengths of our efforts. It is in the voices of students and teachers—heard in works such as these—that an alternative vision of education can be found. Because these voices are often not easily heard through traditional positivistic research, the field of the sociology of education has begun to shift as well.

Viewed through a sociological lens, an analysis of contemporary urban education is increasingly an analysis of tensions, contradictions, and complexity. While both cities and the students in city schools have always been challenging and important subjects of inquiry, we are at a point in social history that increases this challenge enormously. More specifically, as the bodies of sociological theory for understanding cities become more complex, so too do the geographic and demographic structures of the cities themselves. As we begin to focus our theoretical frameworks more closely on making connections between the local and the global and the individual and the structural, these connections and characteristics become even more confounding.

## CHANGING URBAN STRUCTURE

According to the U.S. Census, the proportion of people living in urban areas in the United States has been steadily increasing over the past fifty years.[8] Indeed, American cities—like cities everywhere—have been expanding and increasing in population and size since the end of World

War II. But as the cities change, so too do the ways in which we define them. To be sure, the definition of "urban" has never been simple or straightforward.

Urbanicity is perhaps most often discussed in terms of numbers. Frequently, this simply means population levels, with those of a certain size being deemed urban. Other distinctions have been based on population densities, with figures ranging from 1,000 to 10,000 persons per square mile serving as the line of demarcation. Although this type of analysis is important for many types of sociological inquiry that examine cities in broad scope, Louis Wirth, in a now classic discussion of the topic, notes its arbitrariness. He argues that this way of defining cities does not account for many of their significant social characteristics, and that attention to the many particularities of urban areas is necessary. With that in mind, he contends that "for sociological purposes a city may be defined as a relatively large, dense, and permanent settlement of socially heterogeneous individuals."[9] The result of this particular social structure, in his view, is the replacement of primary-group relationships with more impersonal, secondary relations, leading to lives more solitary and isolated than those of non–city dwellers.

In a response to Wirth's article, Herbert Gans makes an important, further distinction between "inner city," "outer city," and "suburban." He notes that Wirth's analysis seems to apply only to those residents of the inner city—the area that surrounds the central business district. It neglects the surrounding residential areas (or, the outer city) and the less population-dense suburbs. Gans notes both the importance of and difficulty in distinguishing between these different types of areas, because it may be economics, interpersonal relations, or something else entirely that sets them apart.[10]

Researchers must make distinctions somewhere, however, and in such instances, the criteria used by the U. S. Census are of some value. The Bureau of the Census defines "urban" as any area populated by 2,500 people or more. Clearly, this definition is still too vague to be of use to the sociologist studying urban education, but the broader Census category of "Metropolitan Statistical Area" (or MSA) is useful and applicable in this context. This refers to a city with 50,000 or more inhabitants or an urbanized area (defined by the Census bureau) with at least 50,000 inhabitants and a total metropolitan population of 100,000 (or 75,000 in New England). Using these criteria, "urban" can be understood as the central city of the MSA, suburban as the towns and cities outside of the central city, but still within the MSA. Any area outside of an MSA is considered rural.

The use of the Census category "MSA" is particularly relevant at this point in social history because it more fully captures a very significant shift in our city structures—the development of the megalopolis. As Robert Fishman notes, the largest cities at the beginning of the twentieth century typically measured one hundred square miles. The "new city" (the megalopolis) generally covers up to three thousand square miles. Encompassing both urban centers and suburban neighborhoods, these cities lack "what gave shape and meaning to every urban form of the past: a dominant single core and definable boundaries."[11] The difficulty in defining "urban," combined with this dramatic change in city structure, presents a great challenge to researchers. The city is no longer definable by geographic boundaries. Instead, it must be understood within the context of the surrounding region, which typically has characteristics quite distinct from the urban core.

The decentralization of cities, particularly evident in North America, is simultaneous with the gradual loss of the economic and political importance of the urban core (or "inner city").[12] The implications for urban education are enormous, as attention and resources shift away from the "city proper" and are dispersed to more affluent suburbs. Englert notes that this type of change results in a "severe concentration of poverty and social isolation of the inner-city from the mainstream of American life."[13] As more affluent residents depart for the outlying suburbs, the economy of the city becomes even more depressed. As a result, tax-supported services—such as schools—are at a great detriment. This is only compounded by problems with crime and violence, which are more common in cities than in suburbs or rural areas.[14]

As a result of the departure of the middle class from urban areas, some argue, the city is left with an impoverished "underclass." Often, this underclass is discussed in relation to people of color, most often blacks, because residential segregation is such a strong enforcer.[15] Residents of the ghetto, argues W. J. Wilson, have no ties to members of the middle and upper classes, because as individuals (in his analysis, blacks) move up the social ladder, there is an out-migration.[16] The end result is a lack of role models and "feelings of resignation originating from bitter personal experiences and a bleak future."[17] Massey and Denton echo this thought, arguing that "what set ghetto blacks apart from other Americans was not their lack of fealty to American ideals but their inability to accomplish them."[18] This concentration of "poor and minority children in inferior inner-city schools," it is argued, makes it difficult "for urban schools to respond effectively to the altered social context."[19]

Alternative analyses of urban life portray the city as space that is essentially at the mercy of dominant interests. For instance, Stephen Haymes argues that consumer capitalism "imposes structures of meaning on black narratives, consequently regulating how blacks come to know who they are as blacks."[20] The important aspect that these two perspectives share is the distinction between urban and nonurban, and the consequent weakness of the former when compared to the latter. Clearly, these issues of race and class become issues of power as well.

Another considerable factor related to the characteristics of urban areas is the significant demographic shift in recent years.[21] The almost constant flow of new residents has contributed to the development of the megalopolis, described above. Most recently, the accompanying demographic shift has been characterized by the relative increase in numbers of people of color. Englert, for example, notes that between 1993 and the year 2000, the overall growth rate of the Mexican American population in the United States is expected to be 46%. The growth rate in the African American population is projected to be 23%. In sharp contrast, the white population is expected to increase by only 7%.[22] Kretovics and Nussel paint the following picture of urban demographics:

> The minority population of Washington, DC is 73%; 66% of which are black. Detroit has 79% minorities; 76% of which are black. In these cities there are virtually no white children attending public schools. Those that remain are usually from economically depressed families. . . . Hispanic concentrations are noteworthy in other cities. In New York City, the total minority population is 56.8%; 29% black and the remainder mostly Hispanic. In San Antonio, the minority population is 64% of which 56% is Hispanic. In El Paso, the minority population is 74% of which 69% is Hispanic.[23]

Certainly, a portion at least of this demographic shift stems from increasing immigration—a phenomenon occurring worldwide. OECD reports the United Nations' estimate that, in 1993, "100 million people—almost one in fifty of the world's population—were living outside their native country, double the number in 1990."[24] Because the majority of immigrants arriving today settle in urban areas, cities are experiencing particularly dramatic population shifts.[25] The impact of these changes on one school district is described by Dworkin and colleagues in this volume.

The relationship between immigration and education has historically been a difficult one. As is often the case, schools have been seen as an antidote to the perceived related problems. Toward the end of the nineteenth century, for example, when immigration from non–northwestern European countries was on the rise, American schools took on the task of "Americanization." In 1909, Professor Ellwood P. Cubberley of Stanford University described the new wave of immigrants as "illiterate, docile, lacking in self-reliance and initiative, and not possessing the Anglo-Teutonic conceptions of law, order, and government . . . their coming has served to dilute tremendously our national stock, and to corrupt our civic life."[26] While it would be surprising to hear it in such crass terms today, similar sentiments relating to the need to "Americanize" the immigrant population still exist. The issue of language—a strong indicator of national identity—is a particularly relevant and poignant example of this persistence.

Consider, for example, the debate concerning bilingual education. Conservative supporters of bilingual education do not see it as a means to maintain the ethnic identity of a particular group (as liberal supporters often do), but rather as "a means to speed the assimilation of non-English speakers."[27] Thus, students are often forced to surrender a vital part of their culture if they are to succeed in school. Similarly, Antonia Darder argues that schools serve to "civilize" marginalized students as they are taught their appropriate roles in the economic hierarchy.[28] They must find a way to mediate the differences between their home culture and the culture of the school in order to negotiate their education with any success. Thus, although the terminology and techniques may have evolved into something a bit more subtle, the "Americanizing" function of primary and secondary schools remains and, as a result, students of color "learn" their roles and experience increasing marginalization from the curriculum.

Bilingual education reforms are but one example of the many reform initiatives that characterize American urban education today. Politicians, policy experts, practitioners, and community members all contribute to the ongoing effort to allow city schools to thrive and succeed. Their energies are directed to all levels, from the notion of a national curriculum to the emphasis on the importance of the individual student's engagement with her work. The following section provides a brief overview of some of these efforts.

## CURRENT EDUCATIONAL REFORM

In recent years, a variety of educational reforms have addressed the problems with urban education in various ways. Curriculum, school governance, and teacher training—among others—have each received attention. Public interest in the topic has been increasing, arguably as a result of the release more than a decade ago of "A Nation At Risk: The Imperative for Educational Reform."[29] At the time, the report was the subject of intense media attention, as the "failure" of American schools was brought to our attention. By some estimates, more than six million copies have been circulated through direct distribution and journal reprints.[30] The report continues to receive attention as support for more recent reform initiatives such as Goals 2000 is sought.[31]

The goals laid out in "A Nation at Risk" address a wide range of factors including standards, curriculum, teachers, and school funding. It was a true "clarion call" for this country, appealing to the fears and concerns of public officials, educators, parents, and students. It warned that if something was not done, America was at risk of losing its stature as a world superpower. But the authoring committee's methods of fixing the schools served a particular purpose and, "all in all," Hlebowitsh argues, the report "was more of a political treatise than a thoughtful statement for the reform of American public schools."[32] Nevertheless, it had grabbed the nation's attention and created a framework for understanding educational reform. This framework is still evident in more current reform initiatives such as President Bush's America 2000 and President Clinton's Goals 2000. Both of these are rooted in top-down reform strategies and both, to varying degrees, push for a national curriculum. Despite widespread political support, the notion that standardization of curricula will make education more rigorous for both students and teachers is nevertheless problematic.

Many arguments for a standardized curriculum are clearly tied to those found in "A Nation at Risk"—education must be improved in order to maintain (or improve) this nation's stature. Michael Apple rightly argues that this push must be understood within the larger context if its implications are to be sufficiently appreciated. To be more specific, "a national curriculum and national testing needs to be situated within larger ideological dynamics in which we are seeing an attempt by a new hegemonic bloc to transform our very ideas of what education is." More precisely, Apple notes the current political context that prizes the market over the individual and "in which democracy becomes an economic, not a political, concept and where the idea of the public good withers at its very roots."[33] Indeed, this neoliberal ideology has enormous implications for urban education, some of which deserve attention here.

The call for more clearly defined standards comes simultaneously with a push for decreased federal intervention and increased privatization in schooling. Amy Stuart Wells and Jeannie Oakes refer to this as "simultaneous centralization and decentralization," noting that many believe freeing schools "of bureaucratic constraints while assuring that all students meet the same standards will lead to greater equality of opportunities across schools and districts."[34] At the root of today's reform efforts is the idea that if market principles are applied to education, schools will be forced to improve in order to survive. Most often, this manifests itself in debates concerning school choice, a principle which encompasses vouchers as well as magnet and charter schools.

The debate surrounding school choice is a heated one. The preface to a 1995 issue of *Daedalus*—devoted to the issue of equity in American schools—points out that there is a strong belief that public schools are expendable: "if schools do not quickly measure up to what are perceived to be yesterday's standards, parents will be invited to send their children to private facilities, helped to do so by some form of governmentally-supported voucher system."[35] In contrast, there are many who believe that the market is a biased system which cannot solve social, economic, and educational problems and, in fact, will only increase inequality.[36]

Chubb and Moe are strong supporters of the push for school choice. They, like many other neoconservative theorists and policymakers, see the choice as the impetus to school improvement. Specifically, they assert that

> schools of choice tend to be more informal, professional, and unified around a common mission than regular schools of assignment are. Their teachers are more autonomous, more excited about their work, more influential in decision-making, and happier with their overall situations. Students are more satisfied with their chosen schools; dropout and absenteeism rates are down; achievement scores are up. Parents are better informed, more supportive, and participate more actively.[37]

But as rosy as this picture sounds, critics and skeptics of school choice point to the inherent inequities in a market-driven educational system.

Opponents of school choice worry, for example, about the implications for those students not traditionally served by public education. Jonathan Kozol, for instance, worries that if we "strip away the fancy language" that schools will become "a triage operation that will filter off the fortunate and leave the rest in schools where children of the 'better' parents do not need to see them."[38] As Cookson warns, "markets as power structures are ill-suited to providing the kinds of human services that are needed in a stratified and deeply unequal society."[39]

Roslyn Mickelson (in this volume) draws attention to the importance of recognizing both the dangers and opportunities of one form of privatization—corporate interest in school reform. Through her description of one community's experience with these issues, the ways in which these more macrotrends manifest themselves at the local level become clear. Her analysis reveals that it is not a simple issue, and that it must be examined from all aspects before accepted or dismissed. Indeed, as Amy Stuart Wells (also in this volume) makes clear, the neoliberal agenda of privatization and market-driven policy plays differently in different contexts. Her comparative analysis of charter schools in the United States and grant-maintained schools in England highlights the struggle over the very meaning of these political contexts.

Inherent in many of the school choice reform movements is the idea that individual schools can and should be better-suited to local needs. Local control of schools (or decentralization) can be found in many successful cases including the recent school reform in Chicago. There, political leaders seeking to improve the city's public schools drew on "a well-established network of community-based organizations" and "opted for an unparalleled level of parent and community control."[40] The goal and result was that "the distance between the site of political activity and its consequences was radically reduced. Individual political accountability is now personal, immediate, and sharply drawn."[41] As Mirel notes, "no other reform effort has so clearly targeted the central bureaucracy as the source of the system's educational problems nor has any governance change given so much power to parents to oversee the education of their children."[42] The issue of decentralization, then, is obviously complex and worthy of careful attention.

Two chapters in this volume pay particular attention to issues of local control and reform. The first is a conversation with Ted Mitchell, who serves as advisor to Los Angeles Mayor Richard Riordan on educational matters. His insights into programs such as LA's LEARN (Los Angeles Educational Alliance for Restructuring Now), which emphasizes the importance of local control and school autonomy, bring these issues to a very concrete level. Similarly, a conversation with three former superintendents of schools in Los Angeles about their experiences and thoughts on urban education is presented in another chapter. Their ideas about educational research and practice—based on years of first hand experience as practitioners and policymakers—highlight the importance of critical reflection from the national policy level to the classroom.

Indeed, classroom-level urban educational reform, focused on curricular issues, is a critical component that must not be overlooked. Often, these initiatives take the form of multicultural education, a concept rooted in ideas about teaching students of color that has been expanded to include gender, sexual orientation, and a myriad of other student characteristics.[43] The concept has taken many forms through the years, often according to the political perspective of he or she who is advocating it. Sleeter and Grant, for example, have identified five categories of interpretation, ranging from teaching to bring students into the mainstream to preparing them to question and challenge the status quo.[44] The former is more acceptable to neoconservatives, who advocate a common culture and are therefore often skeptical of (or even adverse to) multicultural movements. The latter is more popular with those who perceive education as a means to social change. Each of these extreme positions is discussed in slightly more detail below.

Norman Podhertz, an early and notable neoconservative, referred to the integration of women and minorities into the curriculum as a "brazen assault on the entire concept of the classics." Furthermore, he called multiculturalism a "'vulgar' plot to undermine Western civilization itself."[45] Similarly, a 1992 article in *National Review* described multicultural education as "a systematic dismantling of America's unitary national identity in response to unprecedented ethnic and racial transformation."[46] According to Dorrien, the very term "multicultural" is rejected by neoconservatives who believe that this type of education is actually a rejection of all culture (i.e., the common culture) in favor of an empty "diversity." Many neoconservatives argue that the addition of these "other" voices overloads educators and thereby threatens the quality of education.

Neoconservative Diane Ravitch makes a distinction between pluralistic and particularistic forms of multiculturalism. Pluralistic multiculturalism, she argues, rejects the notion of the "melting pot" (which essentially erases ethnic differences) and rather emphasizes the idea that "we must listen to a diversity of voices in order to understand our culture, past and present."[47] Particularistic multiculturalism touts the idea of a "national culture," and posits that this culture is comprised of a diverse mix. Multicultural education allows for a richer, broader interpretation of that culture.

Pluralistic multiculturalism is typically acceptable to neoconservatives, who are amenable to highlighting differences and accepting diversity, provided those who are outside the mainstream assimilate and reshape themselves according to hegemonic ideals.[48] As noted above, neoconservatives advocate an "official knowledge" or a common culture to which others should be exposed, maintaining their own culture only for its folkloric character. In this sense, multicultural education does little to empower individuals, and a great deal to create conformity. Perhaps because there is room for such varied reconceptualization, multiculturalism has been criticized for being "mired in liberal ideology" and offering "no radical change to the current order."[49]

As noted above, however, there are numerous other theorists who do not perceive the potential of the curriculum as simply limited to elaboration on a canon. Educational theorists such as Paulo Freire,[50] Michael Apple,[51] and others warn that unless the curriculum encourages critical reflection, students merely serve as depositories of whatever "knowledge" the teacher chooses to impart. The curriculum, according to Apple, should be "a complicated and continual process of environmental design."[52] A concrete illustration can be found in the work of Ladson-Billings, who describes successful teachers in urban schools. Through culturally relevant teaching, she argues, students are empowered "intellectually, socially, emotionally, and politically by using cultural referents to impart knowledge, skills, and attitudes."[53] In order to be effective, the curriculum must be co-constructed, not prescribed from above, as in the case of reform initiatives such as the push for a national curriculum, for example.

What is clear from the initiatives described above is that educational reform is now being approached from a variety of perspectives and on numerous levels. At the national level, standards and testing are proposed as a means of "restoring rigor" to our educational system. At the state and community levels, school choice programs such as vouchers and charter schools are intended to decentralize control of the system. And at the classroom level, new curricula are being explored to engage and empower individual students and teachers. And just as reform efforts recognize and address numerous levels and perspectives, so too do the sociological theories that frame them.

## THE NEW SOCIOLOGY OF URBAN EDUCATION

Like much social theory, the sociology of education has adopted and incorporated many of the tenets of what has come to be called postmodernism. As Henry Giroux has articulated, postmodernism is largely a reaction to the modernist notion that there is a referent point (or meta-narrative) from which all individuals work and that truth exists independently of these individuals.[54] This idea is challenged by postmodernists as restrictive and totalizing. The claim is that in a diverse society such as ours, the wide range of cultures cannot possibly be explained or guided by a single, absolute truth. Essentially a challenge to the positivistic notion that there is an answer for us to work toward in one correct way, postmodernism has been instrumental in reshaping the direction of the sociology of urban education.

In recent years, sociologists of education have called not only for the incorporation and recognition of both qualitative and quantitative approaches, but also for the bridging of the two.[55] Apple (in this volume), in his in-depth discussion of the theoretical tendencies of the sociology of education in the United States, refers to the bridging of various traditions in theory, noting that "a little trespassing may be a good thing here." Similarly, Raymond Morrow (also in this volume) argues that we must develop a critical theory of methodology in order to allow for critical-emancipatory knowledge. Hence, in both theory and research, the trend toward making connections between what were previously seen as dualisms or oppositional concepts is increasingly common. As Wallerstein explains, "If we are to be serious about utopistics, we must stop fighting about nonissues, and the foremost of these nonissues is determinism versus free will, or structure versus agency, or global versus local, or macro versus micro."[56] Instead, if we are to work toward a more just society, our research must not be limited to one or the other, but dedicated to a broader, more all-encompassing scope.

Hence, the new sociology of education has an important role to play in the improvement of our urban schools. In his chapter included in this volume, for example, Geoff Whitty argues that sociology can and should be used to understand current educational policy. Through an analysis of contemporary social theory and current educational reforms such as school privatization and the reconceptualization of the teaching profession, Whitty argues that "sociologically informed studies of education policy can . . . help to provide lenses which are at some variance with the taken-for-granted assumptions of much contemporary education policy." And it is through these lenses that we may begin to perceive hope and, in turn, change.

Ayers and Ford argue that if city schools are to be improved (in their words, "saved"), we must "create the collective capacity to imagine a dramatically different world, and summon the collective courage to sustain that vision as we work toward making that imagined world real."[57] Indeed, this hope can be found in the voices of students, teachers, and administrators who have the power to bring about the change. This hope can also be found in research that respects these voices and seeks to understand them within a larger context.

Many of the chapters in this volume are presented within the framework of the incorporation of a plurality of voices and the bridging of gaps between research and practice, school and community. For instance, Dworkin and colleagues present an excellent example of the potential for universities to contribute to local school reform. Through their ongoing project assisting school districts with forecasting their changing demography, they have been able to help local school leaders better understand the implications of these important changes. Similarly, Fenning, Wilczynski, and Parraga conclude that if high school violence policies are to be effective and relevant, they must be formulated with a greater degree of input from both parents and students.

In slightly different ways, the chapters from David Keiser and Peter McLaren also give voice to the students of urban schools. Keiser's rich description of his students' lives and writing offers a compelling lens through which to understand the potential of critical pedagogy for combating nihilism in urban schools. Similarly, McLaren offers a thorough analysis of a very particular aspect of many urban students' lives—gangsta rap. Through his labeling of this genre as an oppositional practice, McLaren allows us to more fully understand the connections between the individual, culture, and society in the urban context.

Education is a source of both hope and frustration. Alternately portrayed as saviors and as scapegoats, schools are expected to please the body politic, serve individual students, and often work within unreasonable parameters, with insufficient funding and resources. This is particularly the case with urban schools, where political strength is often minimal, student populations are particularly diverse, and resources are especially scarce. Unless the conditions within these schools are better understood so that all of our students are being served, we will deny them their own successes and deny ourselves this vast and critical resource.

Recent sociological theory provides additional, useful lenses for understanding the issues particular to urban education. With increased attention to individual voice and to understanding the interconnectedness between the individual and society at large, sociologists of education have the potential to contribute to a project aimed at more equitable, just, and rewarding experiences for the students in our urban schools and the creation of more productive and prosperous members of our urban societies.

With this volume we seek to contribute to the evolving conversation surrounding these issues. Through the inclusion of sociological inquiry that is as diverse as it is rigorous, it is our intention to illustrate how critical it is that we begin to view urban education through a more complex and rich set of theoretical and empirical lenses. As we move into the next century, it is imperative that we recognize that it is only from this more comprehensive perspective that the sociology of urban education can sufficiently contribute to the improvement of our cities' schools and the empowerment of our cities' students.

## NOTES

1. No terminology that differentiates between ethnic and/or racial categories is wholly acceptable. Ethnic or racial "minority" implies a numerical underrepresentation that is not necessarily accurate; use of the term "nonwhite" implies that "white" is a norm; and the phrase "people of color" implies that white is not, in fact, a color. We have chosen the phrase "people of color," however, because we believe it has greater political poignancy than the alternatives.

2. Laura Lippman et al., *Urban Schools: The Challenges of Location and Poverty* (Washington, D.C.: National Center for Education Statistics [Report 96–184], 1996).

3. H. Kantor and B. Brenzel, "Urban Education and the 'Truly Disadvantaged': The Historical Roots of the Contemporary Crisis, 1945–1990," *Teachers College Record* 94.2 (1992): 278–314.

4. Jonathan Kozol, *Savage Inequalities: Children in America's Schools* (New York: Harper Perennial, 1992).

5. Lippman et al., *Urban Schools*, p. xii.

6. Gloria Ladson-Billings, *The Dreamkeepers: Successful Teachers of African-American Children* (San Francisco: Jossey-Bass, 1994), p. 143.

7. Mike Rose, *Possible Lives* (New York: Houghton Mifflin, 1995), p. 4.

8. U.S. Bureau of the Census, *1990 Census of Population, Social and Economic Characteristics, United States* (Washington, D.C.: U.S. Government Printing Office, 1993).

9. Louis Wirth, "Urbanism as a Way of Life." 1938 essay reprinted in *Metropolis: Center and Symbol of Our Times,* ed. Philip Kasinitz (New York: New York University Press, 1995), p. 64.

10. Herbert J. Gans, "Urbanism and Suburbanism as Ways of Life: A Reevaluation of Definitions," 1991 revision in *Metropolis: Center and Symbol of Our Times,* ed. Philip Kasinitz (New York: New York University Press, 1995), pp. 170–95.

11. Robert Fishman, "Megalopolis Unbound," in *Metropolis: Center and Symbol of Our Times,* ed. Philip Kasinitz (New York: New York University Press, 1995), p. 398.

12. Philip Kasinitz, *Metropolis: Center and Symbol of Our Times* (New York: New York University Press, 1995).

13. Richard M. Englert, "Understanding the Urban Context and Conditions of Practice of School Administration," in *City Schools: Leading the Way,* ed. Patrick B. Forsyth and Marilyn Tallerico (Newbury Park, Calif.: Corwin Press, 1993), p. 20.

14. David C. Berliner and Bruce J. Biddle, *The Manufactured Crisis: Myths, Fraud, and the Attack on America's Public Schools* (Reading, Mass.: Addison-Wesley, 1995).

15. Douglas Massey and Nancy Denton, *American Apartheid: Segregation and the Making of the Underclass* (Cambridge: Harvard University Press, 1993).

16. William J. Wilson, *The Truly Disadvantaged: The Inner City, the Underclass, and Public Policy* (Chicago: University of Chicago Press, 1987) and William J. Wilson, *The Declining Significance of Race* (Chicago: University of Chicago Press, 1980).

17. Wilson, *The Truly Disadvantaged,* p. 159.

18. Massey and Denton, *American Apartheid,* p. 171.

19. Kantor and Brenzel, "Urban Education," p. 29.

20. Stephen Haymes, *Race, Culture, and the City: A Pedagogy for Black Urban Struggle* (Albany: State University of New York Press, 1995), p. 41.

21. Thomas J. La Belle and Christopher R. Ward, *Multiculturalism and Education: Diversity and its Impact on Schools and Society* (Albany: State University of New York Press, 1994).

22. Englert, "Understanding the Urban Context," p. 8.

23. Joseph Kretovics and Edward J. Nussel, *Transforming Urban Education* (Boston: Allyn and Bacon, 1994), p. 44.

24. Mike Duckenfield, *Schools for Cities* (Paris: Organisation for Co-Operation and Economic Development, 1995), p. 14.

25. See, for example, Dennis Carlson, "The Politics of Educational Policy: Urban School Reform in Unsettling Times," *Educational Policy* 7.2 (1993):

149–65 and A. Portes and R. G. Rumbaut, *Immigrant America* (Berkeley: University of California Press, 1990).

26. Lawrence Cremin, *The Transformation of the School* (New York: Vintage Books, 1964), pp. 67–68.

27. J. Citrin, B. Reingold and D. P. Green, "American Identity and the Politics of Ethnic Change," *Journal of Politics* 52.4 (1990): 1126.

28. Antonia Darder, *Culture and Power in the Classroom: A Critical Foundation for Bicultural Education* (Westport, Conn.: Bergin & Garvey, 1991), p. 6.

29. National Commission on Excellence in Education, *A Nation at Risk: The Imperative for Educational Reform*. [On-line.] Available: http://www.ed.gov/pubs/, 1983.

30. G. Holton, "A Nation at Risk Revisited." *Daedalus* 113.4 (1984): 1–27.

31. D. Tanner, "A Nation 'Truly' at Risk." *Phi Delta Kappan* 75.4 (1993): 289–97.

32. P. S. Hlebowitsh, "Playing Power Politics: How *A Nation at Risk* Achieved its National Stature," *Journal of Research and Development in Education* 23.2 (1990): 88.

33. Michael Apple, "The Politics of a National Curriculum," in *Transforming Schools*, ed. Peter W. Cookson Jr. and Barbara Schneider (New York: Garland, 1995), pp. 364–65.

34. Amy Stuart Wells and Jeannie Oakes, "Tracking, Detracking, and the Politics of Educational Reform: A Sociological Perspective," in *The Sociology of Education: Emerging Perspectives*, ed. Carlos A. Torres and T. R. Mitchell (Albany: State University of New York Press, 1998), p. 161.

35. American Academy of Arts and Sciences, "American Education: Still Separate, Still Unequal," *Daedalus*, Fall 1995, p. ix.

36. Gary Orfield and Carole Ashkinaze, *The Closing Door: Conservative Policy and Black Opportunity* (Chicago: University of Chicago Press, 1991).

37. John E. Chubb and Terry M. Moe, *Politics, Markets, and America's Schools* (Washington, D.C.: Brookings Institution, 1990), p. 209.

38. Jonathan Kozol, "The Sharks Move In," *The New Internationalist*, October 1993.

39. P. W. Cookson, *School Choice: The Struggle for the Soul of American Education* (New Haven: Yale University Press, 1994), p. 499.

40. Anthony S. Bryk, David Kerbow, and Sharon Rollow, "Chicago School Reform," in *New Schools for a New Century: The Redesign of Urban Education*, ed. Diane Ravitch and Joseph P. Viteritti (New Haven: Yale University Press, 1997), p. 168.

41. Ibid., p. 169.

42. Jeffrey Mirel, "School Reform, Chicago Style: Educational Innovation in a Changing Urban Context, 1976–1991," *Urban Education* 28.2 (1993): 117.

43. Gloria Ladson-Billings and William F. Tate, "Toward a Critical Race Theory of Education," *Teachers College Record* 97.1 (1995): 47–68.

44. C. E. Sleeter and C. A. Grant, "An Analysis of Multicultural Education in the U.S.A.," *Harvard Educational Review* 57 (1987): 421–44.

45. Gary Dorrien, *The Neoconservative Mind: Politics, Culture, and the War of Ideology* (Philadelphia: Temple University Press, 1993), p. 355.

46. Lawrence Auster, "The Forbidden Topic," *National Review* 44.8 (April 27, 1992): 43.

47. Dorrien, *The Neoconservative Mind*, p. 359.

48. Carlos A. Torres, "State and Education Revisited: Why Educational Researchers Should Think Politically about Education," *Review of Educational Research* 21 (1994): 255–331.

49. Ladson-Billings and Tate, "Toward a Critical Race Theory of Eduation," p. 62.

50. Paulo Freire, *Pedagogy of the Oppressed* (New York, Continuum, 1970).

51. Michael Apple, *Official Knowledge: Democratic Education in a Conservative Age* (New York: Routledge, 1993).

52. Ibid., p. 144.

53. Ladson-Billings, *The Dreamkeepers*, p. 18.

54. See, for example, Henry A. Giroux, *Living Dangerously: Multiculturalism and the Politics of Difference* (New York: Peter Lang, 1993), and Henry A. Giroux (ed.), *Postmodernism, Feminism, and Cultural Politics: Redrawing Educational Boundaries* (Albany: State University of New York Press, 1991).

55. See, for example, Scott Davies, "Leaps of Faith: Shifting Currents in Critical Sociology of Education," *American Journal of Sociology* 100.6 (1995): 1448–78; Hugh Mehan, "Understanding Inequality in Schools: The Contribution of Interpretive Studies," *Sociology of Education* 65 (1992): 1–20; and Immanuel Wallerstein, "Social Science and the Quest for a Just Society," *American Journal of Sociology* 102.5 (1997): 1241–57.

56. Wallerstein, "Social Science and the Quest for a Just Society," p. 1255.

57. W. Ayers and P. Ford (eds.), *City Kids, City Teachers: Reports from the Front Row* (New York: The New Press, 1996), p. 87.

CHAPTER 1

# Power, Meaning, and Identity: Critical Sociology of Education in the United States

## Michael W. Apple

### INTRODUCTION

I trust that it comes as no surprise that answering the question "What is the state of sociology of education in the United States?" is not an easy task. The reasons for this are varied. First, surveying a field is itself an act of cultural production.[1] Like social and cultural activity in general, any field encompasses multiple dynamics, multiple and partly overlapping histories, and is in constant motion. Second, and equally important, what actually *counts* as the sociology of education is a construction. Academic boundaries are themselves culturally produced and are often the results of complex "policing" actions by those who have the power to enforce them and to declare what is or is not the subject of "legitimate" sociological inquiry. Yet, as Bourdieu reminds us, it is the ability to "trespass" that may lead to major gains in our understanding.[2] For these very reasons, I shall construct a picture of the state of sociology of education that is broad and that cuts across disciplinary boundaries—including important work in education in curriculum studies, history, gender studies, cultural studies, postcolonial studies, critical race theory, and so on.

Because of limitations of length, I shall only be able to give a sense of the multiple traditions and the constitutive tensions and agendas that are currently having an impact in the United States. Indeed, *each* of these traditions would require a book length investigation to do justice to the internal controversies and conceptual, empirical, and political assumptions and arguments contained in them.[3]

Further, the development of any field is not linear. Rather, it is characterized by untidiness and unevenness. Thus, what is important in the development of a field are the breaks in which previous traditions are disrupted, displaced, and regrouped under new problematics. It is these breaks that transform the questions to be asked and the manner in which they are answered.[4] In assessing these breaks, in some ways my contribution here by necessity will take the form of something like an enhanced bibliographic essay, in essence a series of snapshots specifying what I take to be particular examples of some of the most interesting work being done. It will also require that I say something about the current political situation in the United States.

## MULTIPLE TRADITIONS

There are very real tensions within the multiple traditions of sociology of education in the United States, in part because of the historical trajectory of what might be called the "academic/scientific project." The attempt over time to make sociology of education into something other than "educational sociology"—that is, to gain recognition as a "science"—meant that quantitative, "value-neutral" orientations dominated here in very powerful ways. For some current interpreters, this had a chilling effect on those sociologists of education whose major interest was not a generalizable understanding of all schools but instead the development of thick descriptions of particularities.[5]

It also had other effects, some of which still are embodied as constitutive tensions within the field. Thus, the academic/scientific project:

> also generated the tension between knowledge production, the legitimated activity of the professorate in academe, and knowledge use as exemplified by social intervention to change and improve educational practice. . . . These tensions are at the very heart of rethinking the sociology of education. [Furthermore], questions of how best to understand how education works for different people in various settings, how best to evaluate educational outcomes, and how best to restructure schools to maximize the educational benefits for all students, must now begin with discussions concerning (a) whose knowledge is privileged most . . . and on what basis these competing knowledge bases are constructed . . . and (b) which role (observer vs. [active] participant) is most appropriate for the sociologist to adopt.[6]

In their own attempt to portray how these constitutive tensions are worked through—or ignored—Noblit and Pink point to five traditions existing simultaneously: empirical-analytic, applied policy, interpretive, critical, and postmodern.[7] These, of course, are no more than ideal types, since some of these can at times "trespass" onto the others' terrain. Yet it is the first two that characterize much of the sociology of education in the United States. That this is so is evident in the contents of the "official" journal of the field here, *Sociology of Education*. While the journal is a forum for some of the most technically sophisticated empirical work, and even though in the last decade and a half it has had editors such as Philip Wexler and Julia Wrigley who have themselves been part of the interpretive, critical, or postmodern traditions, it has been much less apt to publish ethnographic, theoretical, and critical material than, say, the *British Journal of Sociology of Education*. It has been an outlet for the empirical-analytic and applied policy perspectives, although more than before there will be an occasional interpretive study. (It would be even more unusual to find a serious article organized around more critical or postmodern frameworks.)

Speaking very generally, then, following a path that first came to wide public attention in the research of Coleman and Blau and Duncan, a large portion of research in the sociology of education continues to focus on the problematics of social stratification and status attainment. Its questions center around "the extent to which students from different social backgrounds have access to school experiences that foster academic and social success and on how success or failure in school affects later life chances."[8]

Further, a considerable portion of sociological research on education in the United States continues to devote its attention as well to systematic attempts at policy initiatives at the federal, state, and local levels, including such areas as the reform of finance, school "restructuring," accountability and assessment, and governance.[9]

Elsewhere, Lois Weis and I have engaged in an analysis of the strengths and weaknesses of these traditions and of the interpretive research that partly grew in response to them.[10] My critical evaluation of their basic orientations remains the same. Therefore, I shall spend less time on them here.[11]

Even though I shall not spend much time discussing the empirical-analytic, applied policy, and interpretive perspectives here, it is important to state that I do not wish to dismiss these traditions. Take the first two as examples. Weis and I have raised crucial theoretical, political, and empirical questions about their agendas—for example, their equating of socioeconomic status (SES) with class, their focus on the atomistic individual, their sometimes acritical stance on multiple relations of power, their vision of the disinterested researcher, their neglect of what actually counts as school knowledge and of cultural politics in general, their tendency to ignore or radically simplify issues of the state, and their neglect of what actually happens in the daily lives of teachers and students inside and outside of schools.[12] Yet, having said this, it is still crucial that we recognize the importance of their analytic and empirical sophistication.

All too many critical and postmodern researchers, for example, have too easily assumed that *any* statistical questions and representations by definition must be positivist, thereby giving over this terrain to conservatives or to methodological "experts for hire" who lend their technical expertise to any policy group willing to pay for it. This has proven to be disastrous in terms of our ability to raise and answer critical questions about the large-scale effects of the conservative reconstruction of education. It has also led to a partial deskilling of an entire generation of critically oriented researchers who, when confronted with quantitative analyses, simply reject them out of hand or do not have the analytic skills to deconstruct and criticize their specific arguments or their technical competence. While I have no wish at all to return to the days of unbridled positivism (there were *reasons* for the decades of critiques against it), we may need to take much more seriously the losses that accompanied the largely progressive move toward, say, qualitative work.

Having raised these cautions, however, I shall devote the rest of this article to recent developments within what I take to be some the most interesting movements in the sociology of education that have occurred following the breaks with the dominant traditions. I shall begin with a discussion of representative examples within the sociology of curriculum and its concern with the politics of meaning. In essence, the issue of the politics of meaning will be the thread that guides my entire analysis of the recent development of certain tendencies in the field and of the breaks that have been made. In order to accomplish this, I shall then take up work on critical discourse analysis, identity politics, political economy and the labor process, and racial formation. Finally, I shall conclude with a discussion of the continuing tensions within and between the critical and postmodern communities methodologically, conceptually, and politically.

## OFFICIAL KNOWLEDGE AND POPULAR CULTURE

In the Noblit and Pink statement quoted above, a major question they point to is "Whose knowledge is privileged most and on what basis [are] these competing knowledge bases constructed." This involves complex issues of cultural politics, of the relationship between cultural legitimacy and state regulation, and of the power/knowledge nexus. It has also involved tensions between different models of understanding these issues from neo-Marxist, world-system, and poststructural/postmodern perspectives. In the sociology of curriculum, the relationship between culture and power has continued to receive considerable attention, with what counts as "official knowledge" being one of the foci and what does *not* receive the imprimatur of legitimacy also being subject to attention. Thus, the tradition represented in *Knowledge and Control* in the United Kingdom[13] and first articulated in coherent form in *Ideology and Curriculum* in the United States[14] has been widened and deepened, not only both in its scope and sophistication but in the number of ways in which the relationship between knowledge and power is interrogated. One of the prime emphases has been on that most common "pedagogic device," the textbook and other commodities actually found in classrooms. Influenced in part by Basil Bernstein's work on the processes of "recontextualization" of knowledge,[15] by the long European and American traditions of sociological studies of culture, and by newer models of textual analysis, considerably more sophisticated investigations of the political economy of texts (of various sorts), of the form and content of knowledge, and of readers' constructions of meanings have been produced.[16]

These issues have been examined historically in Teitelbaum's exceptional analysis of the development of socialist alternatives to the knowledge that was declared by the state to be official knowledge.[17] Olneck's series of studies on the symbolic crusade of "Americanization" and its influence on what was taught and on the larger politics of what schools were to do are very useful here.[18] David Labaree's investigation of class politics, credential markets, differentiated course offerings, and the contradictory pressures on schools provides an insightful discussion of the connections between curricular organization and larger political struggles in the development of secondary schools.[19] A growing concern with the role of the state is evident as well in Apple's treatment of the growth of state intervention into the process of the regulation, organization, and control of knowledge in textbooks. Here the activist state is seen as the contradictory result of social movements organized around class and race antagonisms and around regional politics.[20]

While a focus on textbooks as the embodiment of official knowledge is but one example of a much larger concern for the politics of culture in schools, there are a number of reasons why such things have been seen as important. First, textbooks and other curriculum material provide levers to pry loose the complex connections among economy, politics (especially the state), and culture. They are *simultaneously* commodities produced for sale, representations of what powerful groups have defined as legitimate knowledge that are at least partly regulated by the state, and they speak to ongoing struggles over cultural legitimacy. In the absence of an officially recognized national curriculum, though there are such proposals now being argued for,[21] they provide the material basis for the construction of legitimate content and form in schools. Further, they are the results of hegemonic and counterhegemonic relations and social movements involving multiple power relations, including but not limited to race, class, gender/sexuality, and religion.[22] Finally, they are subject to processes of interpretation as they are used and read by teachers, students, parents, and other community members. Thus, they are subject to multiple readings—in dominant, negotiated, or oppositional ways—depending on their form and content, the ways they position the reader, and on the person doing the reading.[23] In this way, such material provides one of the best examples for illuminating what Richard Johnson has called the circuit of cultural production.[24]

Yet the analysis of official knowledge has not only proceeded along such "critical" lines. Part of the research agenda in the sociology of curriculum has centered around a more world-system perspective. Thus, John Meyer and his colleagues have argued that most critical sociological studies of educational systems and of their curricula have overly emphasized the determining role of specific national or local needs and interests, assuming too readily that the curriculum "reflects" particular social histories, problems, and requirements that are the embodiments of entrenched powers. While recognizing that such research has contributed a good deal to our understanding of the relationship between power and school knowledge, Meyer and his colleagues emphasize the worldwide power of the idea of modernity as a distinctive project or vision.[25] In Meyer's words, "the overall structure of this vision—organized around great conceptions of the nation-state as moving toward progress and justice—is entrenched on a worldwide basis. Both the nation-state model, and the particular professions that define the nature and content of mass education within this model, have had worldwide hegemony throughout the modern period."[26]

Thus, for the tradition that Meyer and his colleagues wish to advance, the characteristics of mass education, and especially the curriculum in nations throughout most regions of the world, reflect worldwide forces. Local determinants and interests "tend to be filtered through such wider world cultural forces." For this very reason, the general outline of mass education and the curricula found in most nations are remarkably homogeneous around the world.[27]

This kind of approach is partly flawed by its unfortunate stereotyping and lack of knowledge of some of the best work within the more critical tradition, by its neglect of national and international class relations, and by its treatment of the state in undertheorized ways. Yet Meyer's analyses do raise a number of interesting issues about the internationalization of ideological visions that may cut across political economies.

Though less theoretically elegant than, say, Basil Bernstein's formulations, it is similar in some ways to Bernstein's emphasis in his later work on the similarities of pedagogic devices across economic systems.[28]

A third tendency represented in the United States is that organized around poststructural and postmodern forms of analysis of the power/knowledge nexus. Grounded in anti-essentializing tendencies, in a mistrust both of "grand narratives" and of calls for "emancipatory" curricula and pedagogy, and in broadening the traditional concern with particular kinds of power relations (in particular class, but also gender and race), these kinds of arguments have become increasingly influential. For example, Ellsworth's (1989) analysis of the politics of meaning and pedagogy in a college classroom[29] and of the ways in which multiple relations of power are constructed in that specific site, draws heavily on postmodern and feminist poststructural theories of multiplicity and difference. It suggests that previous critically oriented curricula and teaching smuggled in hidden assumptions about power as a zero-sum game that in actuality served to reproduce existing hierarchies and continued to privilege particular kinds of knowledge and experience centered around the power/knowledge relations of the academy and largely white, male, heterosexual assumptions.

This was an important intervention into the debate over "the" emancipatory project in critical educational activity, one that generated considerable debate.[30] Also representative of some of these tendencies is Popkewitz, who employs one particular reading of a Foucaultian approach to the study of the politics of educational reform and the relationship between power and knowledge.[31] While I have a number of concerns about what is lost as well as gained in the recent turn to postmodern and poststructural theories—for example, the tendency by *some* postmodernists and poststructuralists to see *any* focus on political economy and class relations to be somehow reductive, to analyze the state as if it floats in thin air,[32] to expand the linguistic turn until it encompasses everything, to embrace overly relativistic epistemological assumptions, and the stylistic arrogance of some of its writing[33]—and shall say more about this later on in this essay, it is important to note the emerging emphasis on these approaches and to recognize that there are a number of advances in them.

By and large, the orientations to curricula I have just discussed see official knowledge in two general ways. In the first, it is seen as the commodified result of a complex historical and political process in which particular knowledge, ways of knowing, and perspectives are made available. Hence, "legitimate" culture is seen as an object. In the second, culture is seen as lived.[34] A lived curriculum, a curriculum-in-use, that embodies multiple and contradictory power relations is produced in the bodily and linguistic interactions among texts, students, and teachers in educational institutions and between these institutions and other sites. Among the most significant ways of understanding such productions is critical discourse analysis, which is itself the result of the tensions, and sometimes the merger, of the interpretive, critical, and often poststructural tendencies I noted.

## CRITICAL DISCOURSE ANALYSIS

Like sociolinguistics and ethnomethodology, critical discourse analysis begins with the assumption that language plays a primary role in the creation of meaning and that language use must be studied in social context, especially if we are interested in the politics of meaning. In a manner similar to interpretive research, it sees human subjects as constantly engaged in the negotiation of knowledge, social relations, and identity. However, it goes well beyond "mainstream" ethnographic research in that its primary focus is on how power, identity, and social relations are negotiated, are legitimated, and are contested toward political ends. In Luke's words, "Such an analysis attempts to establish how textual constructions of knowledge have varying and unequal material effects, and how these constructions that come to 'count' in institutional contexts are manifestations of larger political investments and interests."[35]

The focus here is on "systematic asymmetries of power and resources." Such asymmetries between speakers and listeners and between, say, writers and readers are then linked to the processes of the production and reproduction of stratified economic and political (in the broadest sense) interests. In essence, discourse in institutional life is viewed in a particular way. It is seen as "a means for the naturalization and disguise of power relations that are tied to inequalities in the social production and distribution of symbolic and material resources."[36]

Speaking broadly, Luke puts it this way.

> This means that dominant discourses in contemporary cultures tend to represent those social formations and power relations that are the products of history, social formation and culture (e.g., the gendered division of the workforce and domestic labor, patterns of school achievement by minority groups, national economic development) as if they were the product of organic, biological and essential necessity. By this account, critical discourse analysis is a political act itself—an intervention in the apparently natural flow of talk and text in institutional life that attempts to 'interrupt' everyday commonsense.[37]

The Bakhtinian influences here should be clear. Behind this position is the sense that critical discourse analysis should be involved in the destabilization of "authoritative discourse."[38] In the process, its task is to place at the very center of attention relations of domination, subordination, and inequality.[39]

This critical moment in critical discourse analysis is accompanied by a positive or constructive moment as well. Unlike some of the more aggressively postmodern positions that even deny its existence, one of the major aims of such critical research is to "generate agency." It wishes to provide tools to students, teachers, and others that enable them to see "texts"[40] as embodying both particular "representations"[41] of the social and natural world and particular interests. It wants to enable people to understand how such "texts" position them and at the same time produce unequal relations of institutional power that structure classrooms, staffrooms, and educational policies.[42]

Thus, some of these analyses are not only concerned with the active production of institutional power through a particular politics of meaning-making. They are also concerned with the ways in which knowledge is reconfigured, how new meanings are produced that challenge institutional regimes of power, not only in the classroom but in the structuring of daily economic and political relations. To take but one classroom example, in an insightful study Dyson analyses how young children in an urban primary school who are learning how to read and write construct and reconstruct stories to reveal and transform images of gender and power in their classrooms. The children constantly mediated and transformed images of gender relations that did not stand alone, but "were interwoven with race, class, and physical demeanor."[43] They reworked the material of the official curriculum and reworked material from popular culture (e.g., "superheroes" such as Ninja Turtles and the X-Men) that usually privileged male-dominated meanings and relations in ways that provided the possibility for counterhegemonic roles to be established in their classrooms.

There are many strengths in these kinds of approaches to the study of the politics of knowledge in schools, not the least of which is the activist component that takes a position on one of the tensions Noblit and Pink noted are deeply ingrained in the sociology of education in the United States. Yet there are a number of cautions that need to be taken seriously. Seeing the world as a "text" has a number of dangers if taken too far. It can lead to the neglect of the gritty materiality of the social world, of the materiality of the state, economy, and class/race/gender relations. It can ultimately embody what Whitty earlier called a "romantic possibilitarianism" in which changes in meaning and consciousness are the "new engines" of social transformation.[44] And it can make everything into a discursive construction.[45] On the other hand, used well such a research agenda and perspective can be extremely insightful in illuminating and acting on the complexities of the relationships between power and meaning in education.

The continuing attempt to think through the complex issue of the socio/cultural "determinants" of commodified and lived culture is not limited to official knowledge or discursive relations in schools. In fact, some of the most insightful advances have occurred in the area of popular culture. Though Giroux has recently called for more attention to be paid to popular culture,[46] an interest in this area predates this recognition and some of the best of current work goes well beyond his call in analytic and empirical sophistication.

Perhaps the best example of such work is Weinstein's analysis of the ways the "texts" of popular culture at a popular tourist museum are produced, made available, and then "read" by youth.[47] This investigation takes Johnson's earlier intuitions about the circuit of cultural production and Willis' interrogation of the multiple uses of popular culture to a new level by examining the processes by which culture is constructed, deconstructed, and "performed."[48] Its integration of material in cultural studies, political economy, and critical poststructuralist theory enables Weinstein to give us an analysis both of the ways in which popular culture is produced and consumed and of the sense-making practices of youth in and out of schools. Koza's recent discussion of rap music in schools and the larger society is also useful here,[49] as is Giroux's deconstruction of the popular cultural productions of Walt Disney.[50]

## IDENTITY POLITICS AND SOCIAL MOVEMENTS

The intuitions that lie behind critical discourse analysis and the study of the politics of official and popular culture also underpin the recent growth of interest in various forms of narrative research in the United States. These include life histories, oral histories, autobiographies, largely feminist or antiracist "testimonies," work on popular memory, and narrative interviews. These approaches are distinctly interdisciplinary. While socially critical in intent, they selectively integrate elements from literary, historical, anthropological, psychological, sociological, and cultural studies.

As Casey documents in her recent review of such narrative approaches, what links these together is again a powerful interest in the ways people make meaning through language. While tracing out the history and contradictions of narrative research in education, and being duly cautious of some of its possible roots in the "bourgeois subject" and in the new middle-class's seeming infinite need for self-display, Casey demonstrates how such social and cultural research attempts to defy "the forces of alienation, anomie, annihilation, authoritarianism, fragmentation, commodification, depreciation, and dispossession."[51] In her words, those forms of narrative research that are culturally and politically *committed* "announce 'I am'('we are')."[52] Perhaps one of the best examples of such work is her own research on the collective biographies of politically active women teachers engaged in struggles over curricula, teaching, and larger relations of power inside and outside of schools.[53]

The issue of "I am" ("we are") speaks directly to the study of identity politics. While Casey's synthetic review of the emergence of narrative approaches is largely devoted to methodological and political issues, a considerable portion of the newest critical sociocultural work deals with the role of the school as a site for the production of identities. Here too there are benefits and problems. The poststructural emphasis on identity politics is visible in a number of areas, with for example Bromley arguing for much more attention to be paid to it and Wexler criticizing its evacuation of class dynamics as *the* primary determinant of identity formation.[54]

Wexler's ethnographic study of the "moral economy" of identity creation in different American secondary schools is a partial return to structural forms of analysis by him, but still within a partly poststructural understanding.[55] His argument that class is primary in the production of student identities is provocative, but his volume is too brief to fully develop his arguments about this. It is not just the issue of brevity that has been a concern here. Lois Weis, whose own research on the politics of identity formation provides important connections among political economy, identity in gender, class, and race terms, and social movements,[56] has raised a number of cautions about the centering of class as *the* fundamental dynamic.[57]

Weis's argument about Wexler's position is instructive in this regard. Both have some major concerns about the loss of a structural understanding of identity formation within some of the recent poststructural material. Yet, for Weis, rather than seeing race and gender as things that students bring in after their identities are structured in class terms by schools, the very structure of these institutions compellingly reflects raced and gendered—as well as classed—practices that are deeply implicated in identity formation.[58] I have sympathy with both positions here. It is unfortunate but clear that all too often class relations have been marginalized in much of the recent work on identity politics, in part because a concern with it is seen as somehow "too reductive." This position speaks more to the researcher's unfamiliarity with the best of class analysis and of the ways we might think through the contradictory tensions both within class and among multiple relations of power with class being one of them, than to the necessarily reductive nature of a concern with class itself. There is a world of difference between taking class as seriously as it deserves and reducing everything down to it.[59]

The Wexler/Weis discussion points to an important movement in the multiple critical communities within the sociology of education in the United States. It speaks to an attempt to widen the dynamics of power considered important, to look at the contradictory histories and relations within and among them, and at the same time to not ignore class dynamics—when thought about more elegantly—as truly constitutive.[60] In my mind, this is a crucial movement. There is perhaps a widening divide epistemologically, empirically, and at times politically between the "neos" and the "posts," with unfortunate stereotypes on both sides. Some of this is caused by, but not limited to, the rejectionist impulses, partial loss of historical memory, overstatements, and stylistic peculiarities of some postmodern and poststructural writings and some of it is caused by an overly defensive attitude on the part of some neo-Marxists.[61] In the midst of this, however, a tendency has begun to grow that seeks to let these traditions "rub against each other." The attempt is to let each one correct the emphases of the other and to see the tensions caused by their differences as *productive*—always provided that there is a clear political commitment behind each and always provided that the interest is not cynically deconstructive only.

Let me say more about this, since I believe it provides a context for one of the more significant breaks that I noted earlier were important. There have been attempts at combining neo-Marxist (specifically neo-Gramscian) and poststructural theories together. Thus Bruce Curtis, in a book that should be required reading for anyone involved in the history and sociology of education, integrates these two perspectives to illuminate the complex politics of state formation and the growth of school bureaucracies over time.[62] He examines the collective biographies of the groups of people who populated the newly emerging state, demonstrates the power of the conflicts over meaning and control and over the local and the more global, and insightfully shows the ethical and political nature of the search for centralization, standardization, and efficiency.

Perhaps some of my own recent works can also be useful here in providing an instance of the search for more integrative strategies. In *Cultural Politics and Education*, I demonstrate how a neo-Gramscian perspective—with its focus on the state, on the formation of hegemonic blocs, on new social alliances and the generation of consent, all within an economic crisis—and poststructuralism—with its focus on the local, on the formation of subjectivity, identity, and the creation of subject positions—can creatively work together to uncover the organizational, political, and cultural struggles over education.[63]

This work analyzes how authoritarian populist social movements are formed during a time of economic and ideological crisis and when the state engages in "policing" official knowledge. By examining a textbook controversy in a polarized local community undergoing an economic crisis and changes in class relations, it demonstrates how people can be pushed into rightist identities through their interactions with the state. Research such as this represents not only an attempted integration of neo and post positions, but an extension and reorientation of the material involving identity politics so that it focuses on the formation of *oppositional* identities and oppositional politics—the growth of rightist social movements.

In *Social Analysis of Education*, Wexler urged critical sociological work in education to devote more of its attention to the formation and power of social movements.[64] These social movements—both emergent and residual[65]—provide crucial elements in determining the stability and instability of the policies and practices involved in curricula, teaching, and evaluation and of beliefs about schooling, the state, and the economy in general. This insight is what has been taken up in work on the dialectical relationship between conservative cultural, religious, and economic movements on the one hand and schooling on the other. Struggles over schooling both participate in the formation of oppositional social and religious movements and are the subjects of these social and religious movements.

The research on the role of struggles over meaning in the formation of authoritarian populist movements represented in my own work is an attempt to take these issues seriously. It argues that most analyses of "the Right" assume (wrongly) a number of things. Too often they assume a unitary ideological movement, seeing it as a relatively uncontradictory group rather than a complex assemblage of different tendencies, many of which are in a tense and unstable relationship with each other. Even more importantly, many analyses also take "the Right" as a fact, as a given. This takes for granted one of the most important questions that needs to be investigated. How does the Right get *formed*? Thus, this research demonstrates how conflicts over state supported schooling—in particular the struggle over official knowledge and over the bureaucratic state—can lead to the formation of rightist movements that combine authoritarian populist religious elements (which in the United States are growing extremely powerful) and economic conservatism. In essence, oppositional political and cultural identities are formed among community members in interaction with local institutions such as schools, identities that are sutured into conservative movements in powerful ways.[66]

The Gramscian moment—his dictum that one must look to the role of commonsense in the formation of ideologies that organize and disorganize "a people"—is more than a little visible here in these analyses, as are the poststructuralist moments surrounding issues of identity and subjectivity. It is here where the sociology of curriculum and theories of state formation meet the sociology of identity, where a concern with the politics of meaning and the formation of new conservative hegemonic blocs meets the realities of the formation of subject positions and identity at a local level.

While I have focused on the building of oppositional identities and social movements, in no way do I wish to slight the research on identity politics inside schools in the lives of students and teachers. Although some of this research, like other elements of the postmodern and poststructural positions, is at times in danger of underplaying the very real structurally generated conditions of this society, as my comments on the Wexler/Weis positions indicate important work indeed is being done on the role of the school as a site of contested student and teacher identities along multiple dynamics such as race, class, gender, sexuality, and ability. Perhaps some of the best places to turn for examples of such research is in work by McCarthy and Crichlow, Weis and Fine, and Fine, Weis, and Wong.[67] Of considerable interest here as well is Bourgois, a detailed and sensitive study of the complex educational, economic, and personal lives of Latino drug dealers.[68] These issues are not only related to questions such as "I am" ("we are") among students, but also have surfaced in important ways in terms of the identities of researchers as classed, raced, gendered, sexed, and differently abled people as well, though at times in ways that again marginalize class issues a bit too much.[69]

## POLITICAL ECONOMY AND THE LABOR PROCESS

The fact that there has been a growing interest in cultural politics and in the area of identity politics and an increasing influence (some of it warranted and some of it rather too trendy) of poststructuralist/postmodern theories and cultural studies does not mean that research on issues surrounding political economy and the labor process have not also had a significant presence. Exactly the opposite is the case.

Even though neo-Marxist sociology of education—especially the sociology of curriculum—advanced fairly sophisticated arguments against the reductive tendencies in base/superstructure models and developed alternatives to them, the current neoliberal attempts at reorganizing schooling around its ideological and economic agenda has stimulated a return to an emphasis on economic arguments. At times, this has meant a "return" in negative ways. That is, the material sounds not unlike the positions of an earlier generation influenced by Bowles and Gintis, *Schooling in Capitalist America*.[70] In this situation, there has been something of a loss of collective memory of the very real conceptual and empirical advances that were made surrounding such issues as the dialectical and contradictory relationships among the economic, political, and cultural spheres, on the nature of the state, on the "relative autonomy" of cultural practices, and so on.[71]

Yet, at other times, the reemergence of political economy has been accomplished through the incorporation of some of the best newer material in critical urban studies and on the social organization of class and race in spatial terms. Thus, Rury and Mirel provide an insightful discussion of the political economy of urban education that draws on David Harvey's analysis of the transformations of the political geography of space in advanced capitalism.[72] This is crucial. Rury and Mirel demonstrate how previous traditions of analyzing urban contexts are weakened in the extreme by their inability to situate the transformations of cities in the histories of class and race dynamics and by their lack of sophistication in *political* economy.[73]

A return to political economy,[74] and an increasing focus on the tensions and conflicts related to the crisis in the paid labor market and in income distribution, is also visible elsewhere. Thus, there have been comparisons of the claims made by neoliberals about the connections between schooling and the economy with demographic evidence about the current and future structuring of paid employment and the distribution of benefits. They show that such claims are at best based on very shaky evidence and at worst are simply incorrect.[75]

At the same time, approaches based on political economy have been used with counterintuitive results. For example, Gintis has recently argued in support of particular marketized voucher and choice plans for schools. He claims that there are political and economic justifications for such marketized initiatives, when they are incorporated into a larger program for the redistribution of economic assets.[76] As you would imagine, this suggestion has proven to be exceptionally contentious. It may document the fact that critical studies in the political economy of education may lead to surprising results. Or it may signify the loss of faith in democratic socialist alternatives among a number of scholars who were leaders in the early years of the political economy of education. It is not totally clear at this time which direction this kind of analysis will take. My own position is that such arguments may ultimately lend support to those marketized initiatives proposed under the conservative restoration that expressly *do not* have economically redistributive ends.

While analyses of political economy have once again gained momentum—in part stimulated by the evident crisis and the climate of conser-

vative triumphalism here—there has also been a continuation and deep-
ening of research on the labor process of teaching. This has followed up,
expanded, corrected, and made more empirically substantial previous
research on intensification, deskilling, reskilling, the contradictions of
professionalism, and the daily lives of teachers.

Gitlin and Margonis may serve as an example here.[77] Taking
account of previous work on intensification, resistance, and the contradictory elements of "good sense" and "bad sense" in teachers' understanding of their daily practices,[78] and situating their work within the
past efforts at understanding the classed and gendered nature of teaching,[79] they examine the processes by which teachers interpret administrative attempts at "school reform." Gitlin and Margonis engaged in an
intensive study of a site-based management reform and teachers' resistance to it. They demonstrate how what they call "first wave" research
on such reforms and second wave investigators fundamentally miscon-
strue what is happening.[80] Both of these groups of social researchers
"overlook the good sense embodied in teachers' resistant acts, which
often point to the fundamental importance of altering authority relations and intensified work conditions."[81]

While there indeed is a recognition that teaching is a gendered occupation in Gitlin and Margonis, as Acker notes in her important synthesis
of the literature on gender and teachers' work in the United States,
Canada, the United Kingdom, Australia, and elsewhere, the increase in
feminist scholarship in education over the past three decades has led to a
significant body of recent work that makes gender central to the study of
teaching.[82] She cautions us about the dangers of employing simple
dichotomies (male/female) and urges us to think through the complexity
that lies at the heart of teaching. Thus, there is a growing recognition here
that not only do we need to integrate class and race into our discussions
of gender, but we need to recognize the diversity *within* each of these
groups. The research challenge facing those interested in teachers' work is
clear in Acker's words: "how to keep gender considerations paramount,
while simultaneously deconstructing the concept of teacher and still managing to achieve some generalizability about teachers' work."[83]

While less overtly connected to political economy and to studies of
the labor process, the complexities of the racial structuring of teaching
have provided important insights into the historical and current construction of teaching around racial dynamics.[84] Further, Ladson-
Billings's recent ethnographic study of racial dynamics at the level of
teaching and curricula—a study that highlights the potential of socially
committed, largely African American, teachers to connect with students
of color—gives us a sense of possibility in a literature that is too often
characterized by a sense of defeat.[85]

## RACIAL FORMATIONS

My previous section concluded with a statement about race and teaching. Yet it would be hard to overstate the constitutive role played by overt and covert racial dynamics historically and currently in the construction of teaching, evaluation, official knowledge, popular culture, identities, economic divisions, public policy, and the state itself in the United States. A sociology of education that does not recognize this lives in a world divorced from reality. For race is not an "add on." The realities and predicaments of people of color are neither additions to nor defections from American life. Rather, they are *defining* elements of that life.[86] In Omi and Winant's words, in what is considered to be one of the most impressive analyses of race and the state in the United States, "Concepts of race structure both state and civil society. Race continues to shape both identities and institutions in significant ways."[87]

Race is not a stable category. What it means, how it is used, by whom, how it is mobilized in social discourse, its role in educational and more general social policy—all of this is contingent and historical. Of course, it is misleading to talk of race as an "it." "It" is not a thing, a reified object that can be tracked and measured as if it were a simple biological entity. Race is a set of fully social relations.[88]

If race is not a thing, but what critical cultural analysts have called a "performance," neither is it an innocent concept. Real people's histories and collective memories, languages, and futures are at stake here. Understanding what race is and does has required a multidisciplinary approach including studies of popular culture, literature, the state, national and international political and economic structures, and the cultural politics of imperialism and postcolonialism, to name but a few areas.[89]

In fact, it has become abundantly clear that much of the conservative discourse about education—the supposed decline in standards, the call for a return to the "Western tradition," a reassertion of toughness and discipline, the call for privatization and marketization—lies a vision of "the Other." It symbolizes an immense set of anxieties, including cultural and economic ones, that are used to build a new hegemonic alliance around conservative policies.[90]

The increasing circulation of racial subtexts is heightened by the visibility of racist and racial discourse in the popular media and in (supposedly) academic books that receive widespread publicity. The recent popularity of the genetic arguments found in Herrnstein and Murray's volume, *The Bell Curve* (of which nearly 400,000 copies were sold) is an indication of this phenomenon.[91] This has occasioned a series of critical interrogations of its conceptual, empirical, and social assumptions and of the historical reasons behind its wide circulation and acceptance as plausible.[92] The fact that there have been a considerable number of such engaged critical social and historical analyses of positions such as Herrnstein and Murray's provides yet another example of the critical sociologist as "public intellectual" during a time of conservative restorational politics.

The growing acceptance of genetic arguments about race or of conservative restorational positions in general has led to even greater emphasis on the issue of the politics of race in the sociology of education, especially on the issue of "whiteness," that bears on my earlier discussion of identity. An assumption that has underpinned much of the research on racial identity is the belief that "white racial hegemony has rendered whiteness invisible or transparent."[93] Thus, whiteness becomes the unarticulated normative structure. It becomes so naturalized that "European-Americans" do not even have to think about "being white." It becomes the absent presence, the "there that is not there." As Roman puts it, race becomes a "reified synonym" that is applied only to racially subordinate groups.[94]

Yet the assumption of such invisibility is now more than a little problematic. Racial identities among, say, white students—partly formed out of a politics of commonsense during a period of conservative restructuring—are becoming increasingly powerful and volatile. Gallagher's research on the construction of white identities among university students provides an important example here, one that is worth examining.[95]

For many white working-class and middle-class students, there is now a belief that there is a social cost to being white. Whites are the "new losers" in a playing field that they believe has been levelled now that the United States is a supposedly basically "egalitarian, colorblind society."[96] These students constructed identities that avow a "legitimate, positive narrative of one's own whiteness . . . that negated white oppressor charges and framed whiteness as a liability."[97] Since "times were rough for everybody," but policies such as affirmative action were unfairly supporting "nonwhites," these students now claimed the status of victims.[98] As Gallagher puts it,

> Ignoring the ways in which whites "get raced" has the makings of something politically dangerous. A fundamental transformation of how young whites define and understand themselves racially is taking place. [They] have generally embraced the belief that the U.S. class system is fair and equitable. [They argue] that individuals who delay gratification, work hard, and follow the rules will succeed regardless of their color. . . . For many whites the levelled playing field argument has rendered affirmative action policies a form of reverse discrimination and a source of resentment. White students who believe social equality

has been achieved are able to assert a racial identity without regarding themselves as racist, because they see themselves as merely affirming their identity through language and actions—something racially defined groups do frequently.[99]

These arguments point to something of considerable moment in the politics of education in the United States and elsewhere. As it is being shaped by the political Right, whiteness as an explicit cultural product is taking on a life of its own. In the arguments of the conservative discourses now so powerfully circulating, the barriers to social equality and equal opportunity have now been removed. Whites, hence, have no privilege. Thus, "this ostensibly non-racist white space being carved out of our cultural landscape allows whites to be presented as just another racial contender . . . in the struggle over political and cultural resources and self-definition"—but always with an underlying belief that history has shown the superiority of "Western" political and cultural institutions and values.[100]

The implications of all this are profound politically and culturally. For, given the Right's rather cynical use of racial anxieties, given the economic fears and realities many citizens experience, and given the historic power of race on the American psyche, many members of the next generation now in school may choose to develop forms of solidarity based on their "whiteness." This is not inconsequential in terms of the struggles over meaning, identity, and the very characteristics and control of schools, to say the least. It underscores the movement toward marketized schooling in the United States and points toward a crucial terrain of research for socially committed sociological inquiry.

## CRITICAL POLICY RESEARCH

While not totally explained by racial dynamics, the issue of the characteristics and control of schools has played an important role in one particular part of the sociology of education. Even though I have not gone into detail about the policy oriented tradition in the sociology of education in the United States, it should be noted that there has been an emerging focus on *critical* policy research.[101] As in the United Kingdom, the conservative restoration has attempted to redefine what is public as necessarily bad and what is private as necessarily good. The effects of this emphasis in educational policy have been predictable. This has included opening schools to even more corporate control and influence. The most powerful example is Channel One, in which schools sign contracts with a large corporation that gives them "free" equipment and a "free" news broadcast in return for converting their students into a captive audience for advertisements also broadcast over Channel One and which must be seen by the students in their schools. More than 40 percent of all private and public middle and secondary school students are currently enrolled in schools that receive Channel One. In reaction to this, research has critically examined the history, policy formation process, and ideological effects of such "reforms."[102]

Another major effect of such marketization initiatives has been the development of voucher and choice plans. While many of the empirical assessments are still being completed, there is growing evidence that such policies do not lead to higher achievement on the part of poor children and children of color. As Whitty has concluded in his review of what the American evidence has shown, "The stronger claims of choice advocates cannot be upheld . . . and choice needs to be carefully regulated if it is not to have damaging equity effects."[103] A number of analyses of the neoliberal project of marketization, and of the academic discourse that supports it, have been carried out. By and large, these too raise serious questions about its ideological vision and its differential effects.[104]

The neoliberal emphasis on the weak state has been accompanied by a neoconservative emphasis on strong state control over values, culture, and the body.[105] While there have been analyses of the cultural agendas of neoconservatives—especially of their visions of what and whose knowledge is legitimate[106]—it is only recently that investigations of their educational policies have been linked specifically to the ways in which they construct the meanings and histories of social problems and to the question of whether the empirical evidence supports such constructions.

Perhaps one of the more interesting examples of such an investigation is Burdell's analysis both of the social and cultural construction of the problem of teenage pregnancy and of the educational responses to it.[107] Using critical feminist tools, Burdell contextualizes the growth of teenage pregnancy as a *public* problem. She shows how these largely conservative constructions take on the power of "truth" and increasingly dominate discussions of the causes, effects, and solutions to the "problem of pregnant teens." In the process, she brings together historical and current evidence to counter the commonsense views of these causes, effects, and solutions, and suggests an alternative agenda for research and for educational policy and practice. Burdell's discussion provides another interesting example of the model of engaged research I noted earlier.

## CONCLUSION

In this essay, by necessity I have had to be selective both in my discussion of the multiple traditions within the sociology of education and related areas in the United States and in my choice of research that exemplifies some of these traditions. I have sought to show how concerns with the politics of meaning, identity formation, the state, political economy, and the labor process intersect with concerns with multiple and contradictory dynamics of power such as race, gender, and class.

After reviewing the vast amount of material within these multiple traditions, especially within the critical and postmodern/poststructural elements of them, certain things become more obvious. There were clear silences, areas that were in considerable need of critical analyses of various kinds. For example, while a focus on identity politics is growing, it is much harder to find work on the best of recent theories of class. The *state* remains undertheorized and does not surface enough within critical analyses. Further, while the perspectives growing out of, say, cultural studies are growing, there is still a relative neglect of non-reductive theories of the political economy of culture. Consumption practices now too often "eat" production practices. And, even though there has been a partial "return" to political economy, in my opinion this is still too neglected and at times is less sophisticated than it might be. Finally, it is clear that there has been a growth of interest in postmodern and poststructural approaches in the United States.

In other places, I have raised a number of questions concerning this turn.[108] Yet, while I have real worries about the relatively uncritical acceptance of some aspects of these theories—and have noted a few of them briefly here—as I also indicated amongst the most positive signs on the horizon are the attempts at integrating the perspectives of the neo and post traditions and letting them interact with each other. At a time when we face a period of conservative triumphalism in the United States, too many neos and posts wind up arguing with each other rather than enabling the critical impulses of each to inform the other.

A good deal of the postmodern and poststructural emphases now emerging in "critical educational studies" has had a positive effect. It has increased the number of "voices" that need to be made public. It has helped legitimate or generate a welcome return to the concrete analysis of particular ideological or discursive formations, as well as the multiple sites of their elaboration and legitimation in policy documents, social movements, and institutions.[109] This focus on the concrete historical instance, without always having to search for "hidden" sets of determinations, in part does free us to understand the complexities of "the local" and contingent.

Yet, this said—and it must be—some of these studies suffer from the same silences as one of the major figures from whom they have often borrowed their emphases—Michel Foucault. As Hall reminds us, it has proven all too easy in scholarship and theory to accept Foucault's epistemological position whole and uncritically. There is a world of difference (and no pun is intended here) between emphasizing the local, the contingent, and non-correspondence and ignoring any determinacy or any structural relationships among practices. Too often important questions surrounding the state and social formation are simply evacuated and the difficult problem of *simultaneously* thinking about both the specificity of different practices and the forms of articulated unity they constitute is assumed out of existence as if nothing existed in structured ways.[110]

In my mind, it is exactly this issue of simultaneity, of thinking neo and post together, of actively enabling the tensions within and among them to help form our research, that will solidify previous understandings, avoid the loss of collective memory of the gains that have been made, and generate new insights and new actions. A little trespassing may be a good thing here.

## NOTES

This article originally appeared as "Power Meaning and Identity: Critical Sociology of Education in the United States," in *British Journal of Sociology of Education* 17.2 (1996): 125–44. It is reprinted here with the generous permission of the original publisher (Carfax Publishing Limited, PO Box 25, Abingdon Oxfordshire, OX14 3UE, United Kingdom).

The author would like to thank Geoff Whitty for his perceptive comments on earlier drafts of this article.

1. G. Noblit and W. Pink, "Mapping the Alternative Paths of Sociology of Education," in *Continuity and Contradiction: The Futures of the Sociology of Education*, ed. W. Pink and G. Noblit (Cresskill: Hampton Press, 1995), p. 8.

2. P. Bourdieu, *In Other Words* (Stanford: Stanford University Press, 1990).

3. See, for example, R. Morrow and C. Torres, *Social Theory and Education* (Albany: State University of New York Press, 1995).

4. S. Hall, "Cultural Studies: Two Paradigms," in L. Grossberg, C. Nelson, and P. Treicher, eds., *Cultural Studies* (New York: Routledge, 1992), p. 520.

5. Noblit and Pink, "Mapping the Alternative Paths of Sociology of Education," p. 27.

6. Ibid., p. 27.

7. Ibid., p. 25.

8. B. Rowan, "Research on School Effects and Status Attainment," in *Continuity and Contradiction*, ed. Pink and Noblit, p. 34.

9. See the section on "The Policy Path," in *Continuity and Contradiction*, ed. Pink and Noblit, pp. 233–303.

10. M. W. Apple and L. Weis, "Ideology and Practice in Schooling," in *Ideology and Practice in Schooling*, ed. M. W. Apple and L. Weis (Philadelphia: Temple University Press, 1983).

11. For those readers who wish to examine the recent empirical and social agendas of such research programs, clear discussions can be found in the sections on "The Empirical-Analytic Path" and "The Interpretive Path," in *Continuity and Contradiction*, ed. Pink and Noblit, pp. 33–100 and 103–73.

12. Apple and Weis, "Ideology and Practice in Schooling."

13. M. F. D. Young, ed., *Knowledge and Control* (London: Collier-Macmillan, 1971).

14. M. W. Apple, *Ideology and Curriculum* (New York: Routledge, 1979; second edition 1990).

15. B. Bernstein, *The Structuring of Pedagogic Discourse* (New York: Routledge, 1990).

16. See, for example, M. W. Apple, *Teachers and Texts* (New York: Routledge, 1988); M. W. Apple, *Official Knowledge* (New York: Routledge, 1993); M. W. Apple, and L. Christian-Smith, eds., *The Politics of the Textbook* (New York: Routledge, 1991); L. Christian-Smith, ed., *Texts of Desire* (London: Falmer, 1993); A. Luke, *Literacy, Textbooks, and Ideology* (London: Falmer Press, 1988); and A. Luke, "The Secular Word," in *The Politics of the Textbook*, ed. Apple and Christian-Smith.

17. K. Teitelbaum, *Schooling for Good Rebels* (New York: Teachers College Press, 1995).

18. See M. Olneck, "Americanization and the Education of Immigrants, 1900–1925," *American Journal of Education* (1989): 398–423; M. Olneck, "The Recurring Dream: Symbolism and Ideology in Intercultural and Multicultural Education," *American Journal of Education* 98 (1990): 147–74; and M. Olneck, "Terms of Inclusion: Has Multiculturalism Redefined Inequality in American Education?" *American Journal of Education* 101 (1993): 234–60.

19. D. Labaree, *The Making of an American High School* (New Haven: Yale University Press, 1988).

20. Apple, *Official Knowledge*, and C. Cornbleth, *The Great Speckled Bird* (New York: St. Martin's Press, 1995).

21. Apple, *Cultural Politics and Education* (New York: Teachers College Press, 1996; London: Open University Press, 1996) and E. Eisner, ed., *Hidden Consequences of a National Curriculum* (Washington, D.C.: American Educational Research Association, 1995).

22. J. Delfattore, *What Johnny Shouldn't Read* (New Haven: Yale University Press, 1992).

23. Apple, *Official Knowledge*, and Luke, *The Secular Word*.

24. R. Johnson, "What is Cultural Studies Anyway?" *Social Text* 16 (1986/1987): 38–80.

25. J. Meyer, D. Kamens, and A. Benavot, *School Knowledge for the Masses* (London: Falmer Press, 1992).

26. Ibid., pp. 1–2.

27. Ibid., p. 2.

28. Bernstein, *The Structuring of Pedagogic Discourse*. It is unfortunate that Bernstein's work is now less well known in the United States among students and sociologists in education. As I have argued elsewhere for a largely American audience, it provides some of the most important elements of a serious and disciplined sociology of education. Given the popularity—and at times trendiness—of an all too often uncritical acceptance of postmodern and poststructural approaches in a number of areas in the United States, too many individuals have turned away from such work. I shall have more to say about this later. See M. W. Apple, "Education, Culture, and Class Power," *Educational Theory* 42 (1992): 127–45.

29. E. Ellsworth, "Why Doesn't This Feel Empowering?" *Harvard Educational Review* 59 (1989): 297–324. The focus on *pedagogy*, rather than *teaching*, in much of the new literature on "critical pedagogy," is an interesting case of the politics of linguistic usage I believe. Since teaching is seen as a low status occupation and taking it as worthy of scholarly criticism, hence, is also usually seen as low status within the academy and confined to low-status areas such as the field of education, higher-status academic inquiries into one's teaching must be reconfigured and reorganized around more "elegant" linguistic forms. In my mind, it is not an accident that much of the newer attention being paid to "critical pedagogy" (whatever that means, since it is a sliding signifier that shifts around the linguistic map) as a theoretical enterprise is to be found among academics in the humanities (see, e.g., D. Morton, and M. Zavarzadeh, eds., *Theory/Pedagogy/Politics*. [Urbana: University of Illinois Press, 1991]). All of this proceeds as if it was a new topic and as if the field of education and the very long tradition of dealing with the politics of teaching and curriculum did not exist. This would make a fascinating study in the politics of academic discourse and the construction of "new" fields.

30. C. Luke and J. Gore, eds., *Feminisms and Critical Pedagogy* (New York: Routledge, 1992).

31. T. Popkewitz, *A Political Sociology of Educational Reform* (New York: Teachers College Press, 1991).

32. For one example of this tendency, see I. Hunter, *Rethinking the School* (Boston: Allen and Unwin, 1994).

33. M. W. Apple, *Education and Power*, 2nd ed. (New York: Routledge, 1995); Apple, *Cultural Politics and Education*; and L. Zipin, "Emphasizing 'Discourse' and Bracketing People," in T. Popkewitz and M. Brennan, eds., *Foucault's Challenge* (New York: Teachers College Press, 1998).

34. Apple and Weis, "Ideology and Practice in Schooling."

35. A. Luke, "Text and Discourse in Education," in M. W. Apple, ed., *Review of Research in Education Volume 21* (Washington, D.C.: American Educational Research Association, 1996), p. 9.

36. Ibid.

37. Ibid.

38. M. Bakhtin, *Speech Genres and Other Essays* (Austin: University of Texas Press, 1986).

39. Luke, "Text and Discourse in Education," p. 9.

40. In this tradition, a "text" is not only a textbook, but is defined as language use—that is, as any instance of written and spoken language that has coherence and coded meanings. See Luke, "Text and Discourse in Education."

41. Of course, the very concept of representation and how it is used, and overused, is contentious. See ibid.

42. Ibid. See also K. Gutierrez et al., "Script, Counterscript, and Underlife in the Classroom," *Harvard Educational Review* 65 (1995): 445–71.

43. A. H. Dyson, "The Ninjas, the X-Men, and the Ladies," *Teachers College Record* 94 (1994): 219–39.

44. G. Whitty, "Sociology and the Problem of Radical Education Change," in *Educability, Schools and Ideology*, ed. M. Flude and J. Ahier (London: Halstead Press, 1974).

45. B. Palmer, *Descent into Discourse* (Philadelphia: Temple University Press, 1990).

46. H. Giroux, "Doing Cultural Studies," *Harvard Educational Review* 64 (1992): 278–308. See also P. McLaren, *Critical Pedagogy and Predatory Culture* (New York: Routledge, 1995).

47. M. Weinstein, "Robot World," Ph.D. dissertation, University of Wisconsin, Madison, 1995.

48. Johnson, "What is Cultural Studies Anyway," and P. Willis et al., *Common Culture* (Boulder, Colo.: Westview, 1990).

49. J. Koza, "Rap Music," *The Review of Education/Pedagogy/Cultural Studies* 16 (1994): 171–96.

50. H. Giroux, "Animating Youth," *Socialist Review* 94 (1994): 23–55. Giroux's analysis here does prove that he can write more clearly when he works hard enough at it. It is unfortunate that this is found much less often in the rest of the corpus of his work and in his overly defensive dismissal of such efforts to develop a less arrogant writing style.

51. K. Casey, "The New Narrative Research in Education," in *Review of Research in Education, Volume 21*, ed. M. W. Apple.

52. Ibid.

53. K. Casey, *I Answer with My Life* (New York: Routledge, 1993).

54. H. Bromley, "Identity Politics and Critical Pedagogy," *Educational Theory* 39 (1989): 207–23, and P. Wexler, *Becoming Somebody* (London: Falmer Press, 1992).

55. Wexler, *Becoming Somebody*.

56. L. Weis, *Working Class Without Work* (New York: Routledge, 1990).

57. L. Weis, "Qualitative Research in the Sociology of Education," in *Continuity and Contradiction*, ed. Pink and Noblit.

58. Ibid., p. 164.

59. See Apple, "Education, Culture and Class Power," and E. O. Wright et al., *The Debate on Classes* (New York: Verso, 1989).

60. See L. Weis and M. Fine, eds., *Beyond Silenced Voices* (Albany: State University of New York Press, 1993).

61. See Apple, *Education and Power,* and Apple, *Cultural Politics and Education.*

62. B. Curtis, *True Government by Choice Men?* (Toronto: University of Toronto Press, 1992).

63. Apple, *Cultural Politics and Education.* See also M. W. Apple and A. Oliver, "Becoming Right: Education and the Formation of Conservative Movements," *Teachers College Record* 97 (1996): 419–45.

64. P. Wexler, *Social Analysis of Education* (New York: Routledge, 1987).

65. R. Williams, *Marxism and Literature* (New York: Oxford University Press, 1977).

66. See Apple, *Cultural Politics and Education*; Apple, *Official Knowledge*; and Apple and Oliver, "Becoming right."

67. See C. McCarthy and W. Crichlow, eds., *Race, Identity and Representation in Education* (New York: Routledge, 1993); Weis and Fine, eds., *Beyond Silenced Voices*; and M. Fine, L. Weis, and W. Wong, eds., *Off White* (New York: Routledge, 1997).

68. P. Bourgois, *In Search of Respect* (New York: Cambridge University Press, 1995).

69. A. Gitlin, ed., *Power and Method* (New York: Routledge, 1994).

70. S. Bowles and H. Gintis, *Schooling in Capitalist America* (New York: Basic Books, 1976).

71. See, for example, Apple, *Education and Power* and M. Carnoy and H. Levin, *Schooling and Work in the Democratic State* (Stanford: Stanford University Press, 1986).

72. J. Rury, and J. Mirel, "The Political Economy of Urban Education," in *Review of Research in Education Volume 21*, ed. Apple and D. Harvey, *The Urban Experience* (Baltimore: Johns Hopkins University Press, 1989).

73. See also J. Mirel, *The Rise and Fall of an Urban School System* (Ann Arbor: University of Michigan Press, 1993).

74. Actually, "return" is not the appropriate word since while the tradition of political economy was never dominant in the United States in sociology of education, it also was never abandoned and continued to grow and to become increasingly nuanced.

75. See Apple, *Cultural Politics and Education*, especially chapter 4, and A. Sherman, *Wasting America's Future* (Boston: Beacon Press, 1994).

76. H. Gintis, "The Political Economy of School Choice," *Teachers College Record* 96 (1995): 492–511.

77. A. Gitlin and F. Margonis, "The Political Aspect of Reform," *American Journal of Education* 103 (1995): 377–405.

78. See Apple, *Teachers and Texts*; Apple, *Official Knowledge*; and Apple, *Education and Power.*

79. See, especially, S. Acker, "Gender and Teachers' Work," in *Review of Research in Education Volume 21*, ed. Apple.

80. They particularly and appropriately refer to A. Hargreaves, *Changing Teachers, Changing Schools* (New York: Teachers College Press, 1994).

81. Gitlin and Margonis, "The Political Aspect of Reform," p. 379. See also J. Anyon, "Teacher Development and Reform in an Inner-City School," *Teachers College Record* 96 (1994): 14–31; J. Anyon, "Race, Social Class, and Education in an Inner-City School," *Teachers College Record* 97 (1995): 69–94;

and D. Carlson, *Teachers and Crisis* (New York: Routledge, 1992).

82. Acker, "Gender and Teachers Work."

83. Ibid., p. 79. See also J. Rury, "Who Became Teachers?" in *American Teachers*, ed. D. Warren (New York: Macmillan, 1989).

84. See L. Perkins, "The History of Blacks in Teaching," in *American Teachers*, ed. Warren; and M. Fultz, "African-American Teachers in the South, 1880–1940," *Teachers College Record* 96 (1995): 544–68.

85. G. Ladson-Billings, *The Dreamkeepers* (San Francisco: Jossey-Bass, 1994).

86. C. West, *Race Matters* (New York: Vintage, 1993), p. 6. See also G. Ladson-Billings and W. Tate, "Towards a Critical Race Theory of Education," *Teachers College Record* 97 (1995): 47–68.

87. M. Omi and H. Winant, *Racial Formation in the United States* (New York: Routledge, 1995), p. viii.

88. Ibid.

89. Among the more interesting works of note here are E. Said, *Culture and Imperialism* (New York: Vintage, 1993); McCarthy and Crichlow, eds., *Race, Identity, and Representation in Education*; Weis and Fine, eds., *Beyond Silenced Voices*; and Fine, Weis, and Wong, eds., *On Whiteness*.

90. Apple, *Official Knowledge*, and Apple, *Cultural Politics and Education*.

91. R. Herrnstein and C. Murray, *The Bell Curve* (New York: The Free Press, 1994). This volume basically argues that African-Americans are genetically "less intelligent" on average. It had an immense advertizing budget and was given considerable resources to bring its case to the public by conservative foundations. It has also been reported in the national press that the authors received as much as $1,000,000 from conservative foundations to support the writing of the book. No reputable geneticist would make such arguments. But, as is often the case, conservative movements must find ways of explaining the destructiveness of their social policies that distance their own decisions from these consequences. Social Darwinist and biological arguments are often turned to here consciously or unconsciously as part of a legitimation strategy.

92. See, e.g., J. Kincheloe and S. Steinberg, eds., *Measured Lies* (New York: St. Martin's Press, 1996). Of considerable importance in situating these positions within larger historical dynamics is N. Fraser and L. A. Gordon "Genealogy of Dependency," *Signs* 19 (1994): 309–36.

93. C. Gallagher, "White Reconstruction in the University," *Socialist Review* 94 (1994): 167.

94. L. Roman, "White is a Color!" in McCarthy and Crichlow, eds., *Race, Identity, and Representation in Education*, p. 72. See also B. Hooks, *Black Looks* (Boston: South End Press, 1992).

95. Gallagher, "White Reconsruction in the University."

96. Ibid., pp. 175–76.

97. Ibid., p. 177.

98. Ibid., p. 180.

99. Ibid., pp. 182–83.

100. Ibid., p. 183.

101. The basis of both "mainstream" and critical policy research has been critically analyzed, using largely Bourdieuian and postmodern perspectives, in J. Ladwig, *Academic Distinctions* (New York: Routledge, 1996). While at times Ladwig overstates his case and is not always accurate chronologically, he does make a number of interesting arguments.

102. See Apple, *Official Knowledge.*

103. This evidence is clearly synthesized in G. Whitty, "Creating Quasi-Markets in Education," in *Review of Research in Education Volume 22*, ed. M. W. Apple (Washington, D.C.: American Educational Research Association, 1997).

104. Among these are J. Henig, *Rethinking School Choice* (Princeton: University Press, 1994); A. Wells, *A Time to Choose* (New York: Hill and Wang, 1993); and K. Smith and K. Meier, eds., *The Case against School Choice* (Armonk, N.Y.: M. E. Sharpe, 1995). Henig, in particular, shows the importance of technical and quantitative sophistication in his critical analysis of the empirical claims of research on marketization and choice plans.

105. Apple, *Cultural Politics and Education.*

106. S. Aronowitz and H. Giroux, "Textual Authority, Culture, and the Politics of Literacy," in Apple and Christian-Smith, eds., *The Politics of the Textbook.*

107. P. Burdell, "Teen Mothers in High School," in *Review of Research in Education Volume 21*, ed. Apple.

108. See Apple, *Official Knowledge*; Apple, *Education and Power*; and Apple, *Cultural Politics and Education.*

109. Hall, *Cultural Studies*, p. 537.

110. Ibid., pp. 537–38.

CHAPTER 2

# Social Theory and Educational Research: Reframing the Quantitative-Qualitative Distinction through a Critical Theory of Methodology

## Raymond A. Morrow

### INTRODUCTION

*The Problematic*

As Robert Dreeben has noted, "In the 1960s and 1970s, the sociology of education, hitherto a sleepy and empirically underdeveloped subspecialty of the larger discipline, became embroiled in controversies over social stratification to an unprecedented extent. Education found itself at the center of them. . . . The subfield . . . grew in volume of research and in conceptual salience. It also moved out of its subdisciplinary backwater to become integrated into the larger sociological enterprise."[1]

The direct participation of critical social theory in the integration of education and sociology can only be dated in the Anglo-American context from the late 1970s.[2] In the context of educational research, critical theory—and here I refer to a theoretical program originating in the Frankfurt School tradition, but now ranging widely beyond it—is most often associated with critical pedagogy and related forms of curriculum theory.[3] Most recently, critical theory has also been defined in terms of a particular strategy for appropriating postmodernism for a theory of cultural politics.[4] In this context, critical theory is largely identified with critical pedagogy as an approach to curriculum theory and teaching practice, and the implications for empirical research largely restricted to a conception of ethnographic participatory action research.[5]

My task here is not to question directly these strategies of engagement and theorizing, which do indeed represent an important manner of extending the insights of the critical theory tradition. But I will contest the assumption that this *comprehensively* portrays the implications of critical theory for methodology, here with reference to educational research. Rather, I will be concerned with developing another—yet largely complementary—face of critical theory, one that more directly joins up with questions posed by empirical research in the sociology of education.[6] Though some of these issues have been addressed in the book written with Carlos Torres on *Social Theory and Education*,[7] which focuses on the problematic of social and cultural reproduction, here I would like to develop the more specific *methodological* issues involved. In particular I will attempt to justify the importance of social theory for the methodological concerns of the sociology of education today. To this end, I will sketch the way in which a critical theory of methodology, based on the metatheory of what I have termed in my *Critical Theory and Methodology*[8] as *interpretive structuralism*, provides a basis for reframing the quantitative-qualitative distinction. As well, this strategy opens the way for a more expanded conception of qualitative research, the primary focus of the present discussion.[9]

This essay will develop a position with respect to the notion of a critical theory of education that may take those familiar with critical pedagogy by surprise. The overidentification of the tradition of critical theory with two phases of its development (its origins in the 1930s and 40s; the antipositivist debates of the late 1960s), has culminated in a consistent stress on its antipositivism and anti-empiricism. But this antipositivist image of critical theory begs the question of its conception of the alternative, especially in a postmodernist context where there has been a proliferation of antipositivist standpoints.[10] The present essay might be read accordingly as a fraternal rejoinder and counterweight to the current postmodernist variants of critical theory associated with critical pedagogy. In the process, I attempt to sketch the framework for a more productive and inclusive methodological account of the actual and potential relationship between critical theory and educational research.

I found it instructive in developing this essay to return—with the vantage point of two decades—to the illuminating introduction by Karabel and Halsey to their *Power and Ideology in Education*.[11] On the one hand, one is struck by the continuity of the debates and issues. Even more true today is the general claim that "over the last generation educational research has come from the humblest margins of the social sciences to occupy a central position in sociology, as well as to receive considerable attention from economists, historians, and anthropologists."[12] Also familiar is their agenda of five "outstanding trends, theories and preoccupations":

1. Functionalist theories of education
2. The economic theory of human capital
3. Methodological empiricism (within which we attach a special importance to empirical studies of educational inequality)
4. Conflict theories of education
5. The interactionist tradition in educational research and the challenge of the "new" sociology of education.[13]

Equally striking, however, are the *additional preoccupations* that would inevitably also be a part of a similar agenda today:

- The revitalization and revisions of neofunctionalism and systems theory
- Gender inequalities and their epistemological ramifications in social science and culture in general
- The specific aspects of the interplay between race, gender, and class in educational reproduction
- The problematic of critical pedagogy and its intersection with postmodernist debates
- The emergence of cultural studies as an interdisciplinary space for rethinking culture, ideology, and educational knowledge in relation to class, gender, race, and so on
- Critical social theory as a conflict orientation increasingly distinct from neo-Marxist theory

Yet most of these shifts were prefigured in the agenda of two decades ago. Perhaps the revitalization of functionalism was most surprising given the mood of the mid-1970s. The gender and race questions were apparent in conflict theories of education, but what was missing here was the remarkable radicalization of these standpoints as epistemological interventions. Similarly, the problematic of critical pedagogy lurks in the background of various sections, for instance, references to the confrontational strategies of the New Left; the identification of a British form of "action-research";[14] and the problematization of school knowledge outlined by the "new sociology of education." Yet the radicalization of curriculum theory associated with critical pedagogy was just emerging despite the long-standing interest in Freire in adult education circles.[15] The diffusion of Freirean themes to education generally is a phenomenon of the 1980s, though a "reconceptualist" curriculum theory can be traced to the late 1970s.[16] Nor was there any hint of the remarkable explosion of one of the themes of the new sociology of education: its radical, relativist constructionism; or how these issues would be connected up with standpoint theories by feminist and postcolonial theorists. Paradoxically, aspects of the epistemological critiques of the new sociology of education have resurfaced and been reincarnated in a new and fleshed out form under the heading of postmodernism.[17]

Finally, neither the problematics of cultural studies nor critical theory are explicitly addressed in the Karabel and Halsey volume. The most obvious reason of course is that education was not an explicit part of the agenda of early critical theory[18] and education was just emerging as a site of cultural studies under the influence of Gramsci's theory of hegemony.[19] Further, the Anglo-American reception of Frankfurt critical theory had just got underway.

But, I would argue, it would have been only through engaging cultural studies and especially critical theory that Karabel and Halsey could have found some direction with respect to the metatheoretical and methodological dilemmas that underlie their introductory discussion, but do not get explicitly articulated. Such issues come to a head in their ambivalent critique of the "new sociology of education":

> What, then, is one to make of the claim that the "interpretative paradigm" that marks the beginning of a "scientific revolution" in educational research? . . . when the transformation of a discipline is announced *before* the event, there is reason to suspect that one is witnessing not a scientific revolution but a more familiar phenomenon of an attempt by an emergent school of thought to legitimate its approach. . . . Only if the "new" sociology of education were able to incorporate into its framework the contribution of "traditional" educational research could it lay claim to scientific revolution. This it has been unable to do.[20]

Though I would hesitate to use the somewhat grandiose terminology of "scientific revolutions" here, I would argue that now, a quarter century later, there has indeed been something like a paradigm shift in educational theory and research which has been documented indirectly in Carlos Torres' and my *Social Theory and Education* (1995). What I would like to address more directly and explicitly here, however, is the basis of the metatheoretical shifts underlying the reconfiguration of education around the problematic of social and cultural reproduction.

The frame of reference for developing this metatheoretical problematic is indicated by the title of my essay: "Social Theory and Educational Research: Reframing the Quantitative-Qualitative Distinction through a Critical Theory of Methodology." Let me anticipate my argument at the outset in somewhat oversimplified terms. From the later 1960s onward, metatheoretical and related methodological debates get formulated in terms of two basic, though overlapping polarizations: initially the confrontation of quantitative and qualitative research; and somewhat later—under the influence of European social theory—the parallel oppositions of "positivist social science" versus "interpretive social science," or "positivist social science" versus "critical social science." Though there were always voices that challenged these simplifications, there were things about the deep structure of the fields of social science—in the English-speaking world at least—that tended to reproduce these often unproductive and intellectual superficial characterizations. Whatever their theoretical deficiencies, such labels served to describe the actual splits that dominate training and research.

This essay will explore the origins and some of the problems of the way in which a critical theory of methodology reframes the problematic in terms of a threefold classification between *postpositivist empiricism*, *critical theory*, and *radical constructionism*. But even these distinctions must be used with care and some unresolved issues confronted, we shall see. The present discussion will only be able to provide an incomplete introduction to the complex agenda of issues and theses that can be described as follows.

The agenda:

- First, I will consider the remarkable persistence of the faulty quantitative-qualitative polarization and its surprising survival in Denzin and Lincoln's *Handbook of Qualitative Research*,[21] though this anthology's primary metatheoretical frame of reference is positivist versus interpretive methodologies.

- Second, I will trace the blindspots of Denzin and Lincoln's strategy to the ambiguities of the distinction between idiographic and nomothetic explanations and methodological strategies. As I will argue, this distinction is handled typically in a dichotomous way that obscures the variety of quasinomothetic or generalizing strategies found in social research.

- Third, I will sketch some of the key themes of what I have elsewhere termed a critical theory of methodology in order to reframe the preceding polarizations. The notion of what I have elsewhere termed *interpretive structuralism* will be used to identify the various ways in which efforts have been made to mediate between or transcend the idiographic-nomothetic polarization.

• Fourth, I will attempt to explore a set of distinctions that follow from a critical theory of methodology, that is, a differentiation of postpositivist empiricism; critical theory, and radical constructivism, especially in response to Egon Guba's formulations. In particular, this requires considering what can be called the "explanatory" moment of critical theory, a question that I will explore using the example of Daniel Liston's reconstruction of Claus Offe's account of selective mechanisms in state-capital relations.[22]

• Finally, I will argue against the tendency to reify this threefold classification, stressing the ultimate interdependence of these three strategies of inquiry, each of which suffers from internal tensions. In the context of educational research this argument forces the conclusion that critical pedagogy cannot be a self-sufficient political project; rather, it presupposes a theory of society—of social and cultural reproduction—and a critical theory of methodology that can serve as a unifying framework for much of the sociology of education.

## THE QUANTITATIVE-QUALITATIVE POLARIZATION: FROM METHOD TO METATHEORY

*Introduction*

The most useful starting point for understanding the social sciences is the differentiation between three distinctive types of theoretical discourse: *metatheory, empirical theory,* and *normative theory.* The implication of such distinctions is that "theory" is not a logically unified symbolic form; instead, it assumes different modalities with complex interrelations. Most fundamentally, metatheory is *theory about theory* and incorporates the classical philosophical questions suggested by logic, ontology, epistemology, methodology, and so forth. Normative theory performs a distinctive role in social theory because it is about value and value claims, including their criticism and advocacy. As a consequence, normative theory has a kind of quasi-empirical status that makes it distinctive from metatheory generally, as well as from empirical theory, that is, explanatory and interpretive analyses of concrete sociohistorical relations. Though the distinction between is and ought is fundamental and cannot be ignored, this should not allow ideologically glossing over the continuity between the two—there are contexts where is can imply ought—and the illusion of value-neutral concepts.

To make sense of the oppositions between quantitative and qualitative methods, or positivist and interpretive social science, we need to turn to *metatheory*, a topic largely excluded or dogmatically treated in traditional methods courses. The trouble with traditional discussions of methodology is twofold. On the one hand, methodology is equated with *methods as techniques*. Hence methodology is reduced to technical operations, for example, survey research, participant observation, and so on. Second, the problematic of explanation is reduced to a single, deductive form derived from the natural sciences, thus obscuring the significance of the actual variety of productive explanatory strategies in social research.[23]

As a consequence, the more general problematic of methodology is handled within a largely taken-for-granted conception of scientific knowledge, that is, a form of epistemology that is often labeled by critics as *"positivist."* The basic positivist argument here is that the sciences are logically unified in a way that can be identified by the *reconstructed logic* of its most advanced forms (e.g., physics). The simplistic quantitative-qualitative distinction derives in part from the dominance of this positivist model, which still reigns in many methods texts; but it is also reproduced in qualitative methods texts that define themselves in opposition to positivism.[24]

As American pragmatists and historians of science have long pointed out, however, analysis of the *logics-in-use* in research offers more insight into the nature and practice of science than idealized reconstructions.[25] From this perspective, it is clear that there are indeed two main types of social science with distinctive logics. The question then becomes that of finding a vocabulary for these different ways of constructing social scientific knowledge, that is, a more adequate metatheory than classical positivism or a theory of qualitative methodology based exclusively on *Verstehen* procedures, limited to interpretations of meaning. Whereas positivism reduces inquiry to the natural science model of a search for general laws, the purely interpretive approach (now identified as hermeneutics) limits research to uncritical "readings" of human experience.

## The Persistence of a False Dichotomy

Despite interminable challenges to the quantitative-qualitative distinction, it persists for various practical reasons and, in a sense, has been given a new lease on life with the advent of postmodernism in its guise as epistemological and methodological critique.[26] For that reason I make the problematic central to the problematic of methodology. In my *Critical Theory and Methodology* the more empirically oriented section of the book begins with a critique of the conventional methods discourse. On the one hand, it is argued that this contrast has been biased because structured in terms derived from the positivist tradition, thus marginalizing qualitative approaches as more or less defective because they fall short of the canonized "scientific" ideal.

On the other hand, this polarization also involves a false dichotomy that obscures more fundamental issues about the logics of research strategies. Such terminology is problematic for a simple, fundamental reason: so-called qualitative research does not preclude quantification, and quantitative analysis requires qualitative procedures. The mere presence of the quantitative is only an incidental feature of the contrast at stake. Qualitative research deprived of techniques of counting would be inconceivable.

Why does such problematic labeling then persist? Because it is a code word for two different strategies of theoretically constructing social facts.[27] So-called quantitative research is driven by statistical-causal modeling of variables (correlational analysis). In contrast, qualitative research is based on nonformalized accounts providing interpretive analyses of relations among structures and processes, whether at the symbolic (discourse analysis) or sociocultural levels (i.e., agency and structure relations).[28]

*The Case of Denzin and Lincoln's Handbook:*
*Old Wine in New Bottles?*

Denzin and Lincoln's recent *Handbook of Qualitative Research*[29] is a useful point of departure for assessing the current status of the quantitative-qualitative problematic in social research. As we will see, though this volume updates the issues in "postmodern" terms, and claims to provide an international perspective,[30] it remains in the grips of the same problematic polarizations and binary oppositions.[31]

> The word *qualitative* implies an emphasis on processes and meanings that are not rigorously examined, or measured (if measured at all), in terms of quantity, amount, intensity, or frequency. Qualitative researchers stress the socially constructed nature of reality, the intimate relationship between the researcher and what is studied, and the situational constraints that shape inquiry. Such researchers emphasize the value-laden nature of inquiry. They seek answers to questions that stress how social experience is created and given meaning. In contrast, quantitative studies emphasize the measurement and analysis of causal relationships between variables, not processes. Inquiry is purported to be within a value-free framework.[32]

But is should be stressed that in the Denzin and Lincoln volume there has been a shift of emphasis away from the quantitative-qualitative distinction as a way of framing these issues toward a contrast between *objectivist* and *subjectivist* approaches, or "positivist" and "interpretive" strategies. Despite the title "qualitative" research, the Denzin-Lincoln anthology is not organized around a simplistic quantitative-qualitative distinction; rather it works with a version of the positivist versus interpretivist (or constructivist) opposition. Yet Denzin and Lincoln's *Handbook* illustrates clearly the continuing if latent hold of the quantitative-qualitative distinction as a kind of deep-structure of social scientific discourse. Their formulation simply codifies our taken-for-granted understandings.

This shift of metatheoretical language reflects the increasing influence of continental metatheory. But this language deriving from the subject-object distinction poses as many problems as that of contrasting pure techniques as quantitative and qualitative. Again this descriptive contrast quickly hardens into a binary opposition between incommensurable categories defined by the classic between *idiographic* and *nomothetic* explanations:

> Qualitative researchers are committed to an emic, idiographic, case-based position, which directs their attention to the specifics of particular cases . . . whereas quantitative researchers, with their etic, nomothetic commitments . . . use mathematical models, statistical tables, and graphs, and often write about their research in impersonal, third-person prose.[33]

Let us pause for a moment to consider this use of the *nomothetic-idiographic distinction*, as this is a question I will pursue in more depth later on. As the *Penguin Dictionary of Sociology* reminds us: idiographic is "a term used to describe methods of study of individual, unique persons, events or things. It contrasts with nomothetic methods in which the object is to find general laws which subsume individual cases."[34] As another dictionary adds more explicitly, "an *idiographic* focus is on cultural and historical particulars, using methods such as ethnography and biography; while a *nomothetic* focus seeks to establish general laws following an explicitly natural-science model of knowledge."[35]

Most problematic for my purposes is the resulting characterization of qualitative research, the form of inquiry the authors seek to justify. The *first* problem is whether such research can be consistently "idiographic," at least without the loss of crucial *theoretical* questions. How are we to analyze the historical origins, organization, and transformations of particular cases without *generalizing* concepts? How can we recognize the peculiarities of a case without reference to other cases as part of a comparative methodology?

*Second*, though reference is made to the study of *"processes"* and *"meanings,"* there is considerable ambiguity about the implications of the study of "processes"; if they are not to be studied nomothetically in terms of "causal relationships between variables," *how are they to be conceptualized?* In other words, what are the logics (whether reconstructed or as a logic-in-use) of processual analysis? This seemingly central question then disappears; there is only one reference in an excellent index to the term under the heading of "processual evaluations."

Perhaps the omission of the logic of processual analysis just reflects a terminological accident. Such issues may be explored under other headings. But again one looks largely in vain and quickly becomes aware that *important bodies of nonpositivist qualitative research have been inexplicably marginalized by this definitional strategy*. The comprehensive, detailed index provides some clues with respect to omissions and suggest that, *despite occasional claims to the contrary, methodology has been sharply separated from social theory*.

The problematic of *comparison* is briefly noted as a possibility for case study analysis.[36] There is no entry for *society, power,* or *political economy*; one each for *institutions* and *social structure*; one for *social theory*; *ideology* is mentioned in passing in three articles; *hegemony* is mentioned largely in passing in six. Neither *functionalism* nor *macrosociology* are referenced; *structuralism* is mentioned several times in relation to the original linguistic model (hence exclusively as a technique for analyzing meanings), but is only discussed in depth once in relation to semiotics. *Critical theory* and *Marxist* are mentioned often, but mostly as catchwords for "paradigms" that are not discussed in depth aside from one chapter on "Rethinking Critical Theory and Qualitative Research,"[37] which would have been more accurately titled "Critical Theory and Ethnographic Research as Praxis" given the focus of the discussion. I will return to this essay momentarily.

*Why These Blindspots?*

A key question arises from these symptomatic omissions: Why these blindspots with respect to qualitative research? I think there are two key sources of confusion that shape Denzin and Lincoln's editorial project. *First*, they remain constrained within the deep structure of the objectivist-subjectivist polarization, which inhibits their ability to recognize mediating forms of theory construction. The result is that various perspectives outside this polarization cannot be effectively assessed from within it. All qualitative research gets reduced by default or omission to the logic of idiographic interpretation.

*Second*, this same polarization opens the way for a relatively uncritical standpoint theory of knowledge that resonates with postmodernist critiques but contributes to a fragmented conception of contemporary theorizing. Subjective knowledge (i.e., idiographic knowledge) is by definition derived from and limited by its social positioning but expresses the authentic voices of experience; positivist knowledge is positionless and formal, hence a universalistic illusion. Whereas positivist theory had the tendency of dismissing such personal knowledge as "subjectivistic," postmodernist standpoint theories romantically and uncritically valorize it as "indigenous" knowledge, though somewhat arbitrarily restricting it to the dominated or those on the margins.[38]

### The Inseparability of Methodology and Social Theory

What the Denzin anthology fails to do, despite its claims to the contrary, is to adequately link methodological questions to social theory. Though such possibilities are hinted at in some of the articles (e.g., in chapters on critical theory as well as historical methods; but especially Guba's discussion of paradigms, to which I will eventually turn), the editors largely work within a problematic objectivist-subjectivist framework that reinforces and reproduces the quantitative-qualitative polarization that already has long defined social research. As a consequence, qualitative research as a *methodological technique*—the interpretation of individual cases—is not differentiated from qualitative research as a *strategy of theory construction* oriented toward the historical-structural interpretation of the reproduction and transformation of social totalities.

## RETHINKING THE NOMOTHETIC VERSUS IDIOGRAPHIC DISTINCTION

### Windelband to Critical Theory

At this point I would like to digress a moment to reflect historically on a previously noted distinction that is often mentioned in passing, but rarely examined more closely, that is, the contrast between the nomothetic and idiographic. According to dominant interpretation of this distinction, the natural sciences are oriented to *Erklären* or explanation that takes the form of *nomothetic laws* (universal, ahistorical). On the other hand, the human sciences are limited to *Verstehen (hermeneutics)* and the ideographic interpretation of unique events and meanings.[39] Positivists, in contrast, follow John Stuart Mill and others in calling for a purely nomothetic account of society.

The key point to recognize is that there are *two nonpositivist stances* to take with respect to this distinction which originated in the work of the nineteenth-century German philosopher Wilhelm Windelband (1848–1915).[40] In one formulation, it leads to a fundamental divide between the natural and human sciences (*Naturwissenschaften* vs. the *Geisteswissenschaften*). The most well-known version is Wilhelm Dilthey's conception, which rejects nomothetic methods in the human sciences. This version has dominated interpretive and phenomenological research and continues to haunt the Denzin-Lincoln volume.[41] The second, known largely through the work of Max Weber, follows Heinrich Rickert in arguing that sociology could also selectively use nomothetic approaches. Most importantly, Weber sought to combine explanatory and interpretive techniques to provide both causal-adequacy and adequacy at the level of meaning.[42]

Bourdieu develops a complementary position based on a structuralist reinterpretation of this strategy, but one grounded in a theory of practice that incorporates a theory of action. As he puts it with respect to his *Homo Academicus*,

> One of the goals of the book is to show that *the opposition between the universal and the unique, between nomothetic analysis and idiographic description, is a false antinomy.* the relational and analogical mode of reasoning fostered by the concept of field enables us to grasp particularity within generality and generality within particularity, by making it possible to see the French case as a "particular case of the possible," as Bachelard (1949) says. Better, the unique historical properties of the French academic field—its high degree of centralization and institutional unification, its well-delimited barriers to entry—make it a highly propitious terrain for uncovering some of the universal laws that tendentially regulate the functioning of all fields.[43]

Aside from the problematic reference to "universal laws," I think this formulation effectively captures the essential features of a nonpositivist, interpretive structuralist perspective. Note that "laws" that tendentially regulate are not exactly "universal laws" in the strict nomothetic sense of covering-laws in hypothetico-deductive explanations. No, what is at stake here are typically structuralist notions of generative mechanisms that operate only historically and contextually as mediated by human agents. The shortcoming of most references to the nomothetic is that they implicitly restrict the conceptualization of generality to ahistorical, general laws; one of the most fundamental contributions of structuralism in social theory, on the other hand, is to provide a nonpositivist, historical account of social determination.[44]

*Critical Qualitative Research*

Now let us turn back to the implications of this interpretive structural-ist perspective as a way of approaching qualitative research's relation to social theory. By contrast, Denzin and Lincoln remain imprisoned within the logic of the Diltheyean (and later Husserlian) opposition between the nomothetic and idiographic. As a consequence, they find it difficult to focus on forms of qualitative research that go beyond this distinction. But there are several chapters in their anthology (e.g., the one on historical research by Tuchman[45]) that give some hints with respect to this hidden body of *marginalized qualitative research*. Most strategically, such issues are implicated in the critical theory article by Kincheloe and McLaren. Though focusing on critical ethnography ori-ented toward empowering the subjects studied, they begin with a list of assumptions of critical approaches which needs to be cited here:

> that all thought is fundamentally mediated by power relations that are social and historically constituted; that facts can never be isolated from the domain of values or removed from some form of ideological inscription; that the relationship between concept and object and between signifier and signified is never stable or fixed and is often mediated by the social relations of capitalist production and consump-tion; that language is central to the formation of subjectivity (con-sciousness and unconscious awareness); that certain groups in any soci-ety are privileged over others.[46]

I do not have any fundamental reservations with this statement as a general characterization. My point is only that the particular strategy they advocate *does not exhaust* the empirical tasks implied here. Most characteristic of their approach is the reduction of critical theory to the moment of practice without any indication of the complex explana-tory—and normative—problems that would have to be resolved *before* such knowledge is to inform transformative practice:

> Critical research can be best understood in the context of the empow-erment of individuals. Inquiry that aspires to the name *critical* must be connected to an attempt to confront the injustice of a particular soci-ety or sphere within the society.[47]

Two key issues are largely taken for granted in this formulation. *First*, the normative claim that the indentification of "injustice" can be authoritatively taken for granted, despite the increasingly chaotic babel identity and single-issue politics. Though this assumption is consistent with taking a standpoint within a social movement, it does not provide a frame of reference for mediating among standpoints. In other words, the dominant tendency in critical pedagogy is—despite much rhetoric to the contrary—to presume normative stances without pursuing the more complex strategy of a dialogical communicative ethics as suggested by Habermas and others.

And *second*, we are given no indication of how these power relations are to be studied qualitatively beyond an ethnography of the workplace; nor does the rest of the book provide much in the way of understanding how qualitative research is to deal conceptually and analytically with, say, concrete power relations and structures of domination. My argument is simply that it is difficult to talk about agency and emancipatory values without more explicit reference to agency-structure relations and the normative discourses that are to inform collective transformation. One of the central contributions of a critical theory of methodology is to more comprehensively frame the project of critical social research in relation to an integral theory of social and cultural reproduction.

## THE ALTERNATIVE OF A
## CRITICAL THEORY OF METHODOLOGY

### Introduction: Reframing the Question

As I have formulated it, a critical theory of methodology is not a unique feature of critical theory; more precisely, it is an adaptation of the new philosophy of social science and pragmatic (contextual) account of methodology that gives critical theory a central, if not exclusive place.[48] Its point of departure is an interrogation of the dualism of the subject-object dichotomy.[49] I will highlight the following key features as follows:

- Reconstructing the subjectivist-objectivist polarization through interpretive structuralism

- A pragmatic conception of the interdependence of reflexive and empirical methods, both viewed as internally differentiated and selected contextually

- A distinction between three moments of inquiry and explanation: actional, systemic, and mediational, and a resulting refusal to reify the distinctions between positivist, interpretive, and critical social sciences

### Reconstructing the Subjectivist-Objectivist Schema:
### Interpretive Structuralism

From the perspective of critical theory as qualitative research *the most fundamental dilemma of qualitative research is the problematic of ana-*

*lyzing social processes in terms of both structures and meanings.* In other words, the real question here is formulating a *nonpositivist* conception of objectivistic analysis.[50] The term interpretive structuralism attempts to link together the family resemblances between a variety of explanatory strategies that effectively analyze agency and structure.[51] Other terms can and have been used here: *hermeneutic* (Ricoeur) or *historicist structuralism* (Frankfurt tradition, Gramsci); *genetic structuralism* (Piaget, Bourdieu); *constructivist structuralism* (e.g., Bourdieu). In the context of the sociology of education, such strategies are evident in such diverse authors as: Margaret Archer, Bourdieu, Randall Collins, Raymond Murphy, and Michael Apple. I will return to this question in the next section where the explanatory moment of critical research is taken up.

### Reflexive versus Empirical Methods

Further, a critical theory of methodology challenges the postmodernist tendency to allow reflexivity to become an end in itself, rather than a means. Indeed, much reflexive argumentation comes to replace empirical analysis, at times implying that the very desire to represent reality is an illusion. In contrast, I have argued that such reflexive procedures are heuristic procedures central to the research process, hence complementary to traditional empirical methods. Further, a number of different forms of reflexivity can be identified and should be made a part of research training: analysis of the *logics-in-use* in research, as opposed to formal, reconstructed logic; *historicist* and *deconstructive* analyses of inquiry; *existential reflexivity* deriving from diverse standpoints; and the reflexivity implied by *normative theorizing* (including ideology critique).[52]

In place of the quantitative-qualitative distinction, it is more fruitful to conceptualize empirical research in terms of a distinction between *extensive and intensive research designs.* Whereas the former defines its objects of study in terms of statistical samples that are then analyzed through correlational analysis, the latter involves a wide variety of qualitative strategies that goes far beyond the more restrictive framework of the Denzin and Lincoln anthology.[53]

### Three Moments of Inquiry

Finally, an interpretive structuralist perspective differentiates between three interrelated modalities or moments of inquiry.[54] *Systemic inquiries* attempt to analyze the objective, structural properties of sociohistorical totalities; *actional accounts* interpret and explain the activities of agents and subjects as producers of and yet products of systemic relations; and *mediational analysis* attempts the illusive task of exploring moments of de-reification—the crises—where transformative potentials emerge, even if they are not successful in changing systemic relations. In this respect, a mediational perspective attempts to avoid the limitations of the macro-micro distinction that is embedded in a dualistic objectivist-subjectivist metatheory.

## THREE FORMS OF SOCIAL SCIENCE?

*Introduction*

On the basis of the refinements implied by a critical theory of methodology as just outlined, it becomes possible to consider again the distinction between three forms of social science: positivist, interpretive, and critical.[55] Instead of reifying these as three, distinct, autonomous, standalone paradigms, critical theory is grounded on the assumption of their interdependence. That interdependence has a general logical form, but it is even more importantly historically contingent.

The general logical form of critical theory as a mediation between analytical empirical and hermeneutic knowledge has been elaborated in Habermas's theory of knowledge interests and Ricoeur's complementary critical hermeneutics.[56] For sociology, this problematic has been most insightfully and influentially confronted in Habermas' social theory. His point of departure in reconstructing critical social theory is a refusal of the subjectivist-objectivist polarization, or what he termed in his early book *On the Logic of the Social Sciences* as the confrontation between "analytic" and "hermeneutic" approaches:

> Whereas the natural and cultural or hermeneutic sciences are capable of living in a mutually indifferent, albeit more hostile than peaceful, coexistence, the social sciences must bear the tension of divergent approaches under one roof, for in them the very practice of research compels reflection on the relationship between analytic and hermeneutic methodologies.[57]

The most fundamental insight of *Knowledge and Human Interests*[58] is that social knowledge ultimately requires a mediation between the reflexive subjects and their potential capacity to become aware of the causal structures that constrain and enable action and the production of knowledge. Whereas the *empirical-analytical interest* relates to our need for instrumental control of nature and society, the *hermeneutic-historical interest* corresponds to our need to interpret and make sense of different cultural forms and meaning systems. What this polarization obscures, however, is that empirical-analytical knowledge is crucial to the processes of enlightenment, especially in the transformation and critique of tradition.

Only with the third, the *critical-emancipatory interest*, does it become possible to understand the forms of reflexive knowledge that take shape when we are confronted with forms of analysis that make us aware of distorted communication, that is, the effects of asymmetrical power relations on past understandings of social forms. To use a term from Paul Ricoeur, it is precisely the *distanciation* produced by structural knowledge that allows us to reframe our self and collective understanding.[59] *What has remained ambiguous in these formulations, however, is the status of the quasinomothetic generalizations that inform such nonpositivist empirical analysis.*[60]

What is most fully distinctive about critical theory is not merely its interpretive structuralist methodological stance, but also the closely linked substantive claim about the nature of society in which it is embedded: the notion of a theory of society as a system of domination, that is, as a mode of producing and reproducing power relations as mediated by processes of coercion and consent.

## Paradigmatic Features of Critical Theory

More helpful than Denzin and Lincoln's introduction and conclusion is the effort by Guba and Lincoln to analyze "Competing Paradigms in Qualitative Research."[61] Four such paradigms are identified (*positivist, postpositivst, critical theory, constructivism*) and compared in terms of their central metatheoretical assumptions: ontology, epistemology, and methodology.[62] My concern here is primarily with the characterization of critical theory with which I generally concur:

> *Ontology: Historical realism.* A reality is assumed to be apprehendable that was once plastic, but that was, over time, shaped by a congeries of social, political, cultural, economic, ethnic, and gender factors, and then crystallized (reified) into a series of structures that are now (inappropriately) taken as "real," that is, natural and immutable. For all practical purposes the structures *are* "real," a virtual or historical reality.

> *Epistemology: Transactional and subjectivist.* The investigator and the investigated object are assumed to be interactively linked, with the values of the investigator (and of situated "others") inevitably influencing the inquiry. Findings are therefore *value-mediated*.

> *Methodology: Dialogic and dialectical.* The transactional nature of inquiry requires a dialogue between the investigator and the subjects of inquiry; that dialogue must be dialectical in nature to transform ignorance and misapprehensions (accepting historically mediated structures

as immutable) into more informed consciousness (seeing how the structures might be changed and comprehending actions required to effect change.[63]

Or later on critical theory's conception of knowledge:

Knowledge consists of a series of structural-historical insights that will be transformed as time passes. Transformations occur when ignorance and misapprehensions give way to more informed insights by means of a dialectical interaction.[64]

What is missing in Guba and Lincoln's account is a discussion of the *limitations* of such formulation as *reconstructed idealizations*. In reality, as a logic-in-use, even the production of critical knowledge is separated from the contexts in which it may take on transformative consequences. The communicative relations between knowledge creation and its many publics are historically diverse and continuously changing. For example, the current debates about the internet, the computer revolution and notions of an "information society" all point to novel contexts where knowledge and change interact.

It is quite misleading, therefore, to identify today critical theory exclusively with the classical model of the revolutionary proletariat coming to collective consciousness through the imbibing of revolutionary knowledge. Relaxing that model to address the diversity of the new social movements involves an important step in the right direction, but it still remains tied to a dangerously activist conception of knowledge that presumes in advance an understanding of how agents can respond to structural change. Critical theory cannot be identified exclusively with *participatory action research*, however effectively it may provide a rationale for it.

*The Explanatory Moment: Power Relations and Structural Analysis*

What is typically missing or at least glossed over in the Denzin-Lincoln anthology and most other characterizations of *qualitative methodology* is the status of structural accounts of power relations as found in political economy, state theories, organizational analysis, mass media analysis, the sociology of work, theories of hegemony, analyses of education and social change, and so on. Another way of putting this is that all such work is in important respects historical sociology concerned with the dialectic of power, agency, and structure. In the process, qualitative research ceases to become defined primarily as a tool kit of methodological techniques and becomes identified with the fundamental process of social theorizing.[65]

De facto, there has been a split in qualitative research that reflects this dilemma. The *Handbook* is devoted primarily to the *meaning-oriented forms of interpretive social inquiry*, whereas strategies more oriented toward *structural accounts of processes* are marginalized or rejected as involving a residual positivism (e.g., historical sociology, political economy, critical organization theory, much cultural sociology, etc.). What is consistently missing from the *Handbook of Qualitative Research* is attention to what is involved in analyzing those "*structural-historical insights that will be transformed as time passes*" (Guba and Lincoln's characterization of knowledge in critical theory). In this respect the tension between the purely *constructivist paradigm* (especially in its postmodernist reincarnations) becomes apparent, as well as some of critical theory's latent affinities with *postpositivist* approaches, at least in its concern with empirical evidence and causal hypotheses.[66]

It is in this context of justifying empirical claims that it is instructive to refer to Daniel Liston's discussion of the explanatory problems of Marxist theories of social reproduction in education. Though his analysis focuses primarily on models that suffer from a problematic functionalist correspondence assumption, his general strategy illuminates the claims that I have been making about the strategy of contemporary critical theory.[67] Not surprisingly, he uses the example of Claus Offe—an early collaborator with and influence upon Habermas—as the basis of an empirically justifiable account of state-school relations in capitalist society. I cannot summarize this complex argument here, which analyzes in detail problems of empirically identifying four levels of selective mechanisms: *structural, ideological, procedural,* and *repressive.*[68] The point I would like to stress is how Offe's strategy effectively illustrates the three moments of analysis that define critical theory, that is, systemic, actional, and mediational. To use Liston's terminology, the basis of an adequate explanatory strategy is a combination of what he calls a "mixed" functional claim (that only some "aspects of the selective curriculum persist because of the beneficial consequences for capitalism") and the "intentional claim" that selections are also "the direct outcomes of action that are unintentionally beneficial for capital." For example, "teachers may support tracking because of its positive effect for classroom order and not because tracking has beneficial consequences for capitalism."[69] In other words, this combination of a mixed functional explanation and an intentional analysis corresponds to relating actional and systemic moments of inquiry.[70] Finally, what I have referred to as mediational analysis takes the form of crisis analysis in Offe's strategy: "it is only when class conflict occurs that the implicit class options turn into empirical force, and it is only during these times of class conflict that the ruling class character of the state becomes evident. Offe's methodological route focuses on the eruption of class conflict, that is on times of crisis."[71] This example only illustrates one of the many possible forms of mediational analysis, but shares the essential feature of demonstrating the implications of the disruption of the smooth reproduction of agency-structure relations. This moment of analysis is the empirical foundation and focus of a critical theory of society, even though it cannot be ultimately separated from interpretive and structural analysis as a relatively autonomous research strategy.

## THE DANGERS OF REIFYING RESEARCH STRATEGIES

### Introduction: The Classic Standoff of Grand Narratives

Though the dichotomization of "positivist" versus "critical" social science is related to the quantitative-qualitative one, it is distinct in important ways. Above all, it is not a false dichotomy in the strong sense because this is a useful way of differentiating research strategies for many purposes. Furthermore, it is inevitably linked with a further distinction between positivist and interpretive research. The dilemma here is not that they are false or even inherently misleading distinctions; the problem is that they lend themselves to being reified and essentialized.

What is at stake here is what might be called the danger of the *chronic reification* of the otherwise useful distinction between three forms of social science: positivist, interpretive, and critical. Each of these terms is typically reified, essentialized, and superficialized in distinctive ways that obscures their interrelatedness, along with the contradictions within each of them. If I give critical theory a privileged place in this trio, it is because I think it provides the most powerful reflexivity for understanding these dilemmas. But it should be stressed that at the center of each strategy of inquiry lies a fundamental aporia or contradiction.

### Positivism: Value Free or Liberating?

A fundamental aporia or immanent dilemma of positivism is that it wants to be value-free and yet not abandon its commitment to human enlightenment. The famous Popper-Adorno controversy would not have been possible otherwise.[72] Empiricist research has rarely sought to be fully value-free; its primary aspiration has been to claim a certain "objectivity" that legitimates empirical findings. Indeed, this aspiration for objectivity derived in part from the self-conscious value orientation and political passion that has driven empirical research. Nowhere has this been more apparent than in educational research on social inequality and status attainment.[73]

*Critical Theory: Revolutionary or Unscientific?*

A fundamental aporia of critical theory is that it wants to be both revolutionary and scientific.[74] Most idealized reconstructions of critical theory gloss over the practical tensions between its "scientific" and "practical" claims. One of the key rationales of much activist oriented critical research is that it is "empowering." Yet paradoxically, the rise of the new right to power largely coincides with the explosion of "empowering" research. For the theory that would place its claim to truth, its proof in the pudding of revolutionary praxis, this is a sobering paradox.

On the other hand, this totalizing identification with praxis runs the risk of jeopardizing any empirical truth claims. Here the attack on positivism confronts two choices: either identification with some metaphysical metanarrative (the residual Hegelianism of the older Frankfurt School) or the offering of an alternative account of social scientific knowledge. The dilemma is that this latter, empirical question gets lost with the reification of critical theory as a normative theory of praxis, just as positivism's normative impulses get buried in the reifications of reconstructed logic.

*Constructivist Solipsism: The Paradoxes of Redneck Knowledge*

A fundamental aporia of radical constructivism is the paradox of what I have come to call "redneck knowledge." In the context of the polarization between grand paradigmatic explanatory narratives such as the preceding opposition between positivist and critical theory, it is rather too easy for radical constructivism to proclaim itself as the ultimate alternative, now recast as poststructuralist and postmodern. But here again the reifications of totalization raise their ugly head in the reductionism of a constructivist fallacy: social reality is nothing but arbitrary linguistic forms and every standpoint has its own truth. Above all radical constructivism founders on the limits of any uncritical valorization of everyday standpoints. The dilemmas here are typically resolved in two ways. On the one hand, the response is an unflinching relativism that grants equal validity to diverse standpoints, however personally uncomfortable the consequences.

On the other hand, the more typical tendency for progressive intellectuals is to grant the perspectives of the dominated and marginal as having some kind of intrinsic superiority derived, presumably, from their victimized status. The dilemma of this position becomes apparent when claims are voiced by groups who fall outside the "progressive" pantheon, as would be apparent in the paradox of what I sometimes describe as "redneck knowledge." With this term I refer to the structures of feeling and indigenous knowledge that define the experiences and forms of oppression linked to experiences of a white working class (both rural and urban). Here lie the ultimate origins of the *ressentiment* that has redefined American politics. Here is a passionate knowledge of the disadvantages of limited educational opportunity, of being laughed at for signs of a culture of poverty, and of being used as part of a divide and rule strategy of using ethnic conflict, that is, splitting whites and blacks, thus averting class-based mobilization. To simply label this as nothing but racist, right-wing ideology is to beg the question of a theory of ideology which cannot be generated from with a relativistic, radically constructivist perspective. The "Bubbas" of the world have united too.

However important it is to get such suppressed and previously ignored voices heard, this general imperative does not dispense with *the need of every standpoint to develop its own critical hermeneutics*, that is, forms of historical reflexivity that facilitate an internal process of critique and transformation. A crucial component of this process of self-critique is cross-standpoint communication and the development of mediating categories that can link all perspectives. My most fundamental suggestion is that contemporary *critical theory provides the most important questions for answering this challenge.*[75]

In short the reification of these three forms of research produces equally absurd conclusions. For positivists, social reality becomes *nothing but* verifiable propositions. For critical theorists, reality becomes *nothing but* the imperative of utopian transformation. For radical constructivists reality becomes *nothing but* arbitrary linguistic play. Only through fully relational and pragmatically contextual thinking can these essentializing paradoxes be avoided.


## CONCLUSION


My basic suggestion for critical theory as a research program in the context of education is twofold. *First*, each national and historical context, along with the increasing interplay between these as reflected in debates about globalization, must be specified with respect to the particular social formation, its political traditions, and the role of the social and human sciences within it. Within this context systemic, interpretive and mediational research all have a place in constructing an ever-changing understanding of concrete social totalities.

*Second*, within a specific tradition, it is necessary to identify the multiple sites of research practice, each of which defines distinctive priorities. Three of these may be taken as prominent in advanced, liberal democratic societies: the *relatively autonomous research* centers based primarily in universities; the forms of *policy-oriented research and social criticism* that define the debates within the media and the democratic public sphere; and the *participatory action research* that unifies theory and praxis in transformative social movements.

Though these metatheoretical reflections may be far from the everyday life struggles of East LA or Watts, I would hope that they could inform more self-consciously the research practices of those currently attempting to reveal the dynamics of agency, structure, and mediational crisis in urban educational settings. To do so requires the defense of contingently universal explanatory and normative principles. Social science may be a species of rhetoric, but its claim to knowledge—to persuade—is distinctively grounded in a world-historical story that cannot slide into postmodern "universal abandon" without abandoning its raison-d'être. In Andrew Ross's terms, *"In whose interests is it, exactly, to declare the abandonment of universals?"* [76] As he concludes, "To ask such a question is necessarily to survey the uneven effects of 'universal abandon' on our social and cultural landscapes. In asking that question, finally, we are obliged to fall back upon, not the faith, hope, and charity of History, but those resources at hand that can help a reconstructed agenda for our times, and a popular imagery of the future." [77]

My final point is simply that sociology as understood by a critical theory of methodology should have a place on this reconstructed agenda for our times; and that in grounding itself in the interpretive structuralist task of analyzing the universal in the particular *and* the particular in the universal, it mediates between the analytic and hermeneutic—between quasinomothetic generalizing and quasiideographic interpretive strategies, thus creating the formal *conditions of possibility of critical-emancipatory knowledge.*

## NOTES

My general approach has been influenced for some time by collaboration with Carlos A. Torres and David D. Brown, though the latter has not had a chance to read this essay. Also, more recently I have become aware of the affinity of my strategy with Charles Ragin's general approach to methodology. (See Charles C. Ragin, *The Comparative Method* (Berkeley: University of California Press, 1987) and Charles C. Ragin, *Constructing Social Research* (Thousand Oaks, Calif.: Pine Forge Press, 1994). Though not explicitly oriented to critical theory, his approach provides a wider context complementary to a critical theory of methodology. Aspects of the general argument developed here were initially formulated in a guest lecture on "Rethinking Qualitative Research: An Interpretive Structuralist Alternative" (30 November 1995) in a paper presented to the Critical Methodologies Lecture Series organized by Ragin at Northwestern University.

1. Robert Dreeben, "The Sociology of Education: Its Development in the United States," in *Research in Sociology of Education and Socialization*, ed. Aaron M. Palls (Greenwich, Conn.: JAI Press, 1994), p. 7.

2. The primary exception here is the work of Ivan Illich dating from the late 1960s; key aspects of his critique of education can be traced to his relationship to the Frankfurt tradition (Morrow and Carlos Alberto Torres, "Ivan Illich and the De-Schooling Thesis Twenty Years After," *New Education* 12:3–17).

3. E.g., Stanley Aronowitz and Henry A. Giroux, *Education under Siege: The Conservative, Liberal and Radical Debate over Schooling* (South Hadley, Mass.: Bergin & Garvey, 1985); Michael W. Apple, *Official Knowledge: Democratic Education in a Conservative Age* (New York and London: Routledge, 1993); Henry Giroux and Peter McLaren, eds., *Between Borders: Pedagogy and the Politics of Cultural Studies* (New York and London: Routledge, 1994); Wilfred Carr and Stephen Kemmis, *Becoming Critical: Education, Knowledge and Action Research* (London and Philadelphia: Falmer Press, 1986).

4. Henry Giroux, ed., *Postmodernism, Feminism, and Cultural Politics: Redrawing Educational Boundaries* (Albany: State University of New York Press, 1991); Aronowitz and Giroux, *Postmodern Education: Politics, Culture and Social Criticism* (Minneapolis: University of Minnesota Press, 1991).

5. From Donald E. Comstock, "A Method for Critical Research," in *Readings in the Philosophy of Social Science*, ed. Michael Martin and Lee C. McIntyre (Cambridge: MIT Press, 1994) to Joe L. Kincheloe and Peter L. McLaren, "Rethinking Critical Theory and Qualitative Research," in *Handbook of Qualitative Research*, ed. Norman K. Denzin and Yvonna S. Lincoln (Thousand Oaks, Calif.: Sage, 1994).

6. This strategy is parallel to but more comprehensive than Forester's notion of "the applied turn in contemporary critical theory," but shares a concern with "concrete analysis of structure and of contingently staged social action" (John Forester, ed., *Critical Theory and Public Life* [Cambridge: MIT Press, 1985], p. xiii; see also Raymond A. Morrow (with D. D. Brown), *Critical Theory and Methodology* [Newbury Park, Calif.: Sage, 1994], p. 24).

7. Morrow and Torres, *Social Theory and Education: A Critique of Theories of Social and Cultural Reproduction* (Albany: State University of New York Press, 1995).

8. Morrow, *Critical Theory and Methodology.*

9. For a perspective that introduces the problematic of critical theory and methodology in a manner parallel to the present discussion, see Thomas S. Popkewitz, "Whose Future? Whose Past? Notes on Critical Theory and Methodology," in *Paradigm Dialog*, ed. Egon G. Guba (Newbury Park, Calif.: Sage, 1990).

10. Three distinctive features of the Frankfurt tradition should be stressed here. First, that it consistently retains a concern with a historical structuralist approach to social knowledge. Despite its critique of positivism and the disciplinary division of labor, the Frankfurt tradition never abandoned the principle of the social sciences as empirically accountable strategies of knowledge construction. Second, that in its later disillusioned "dialectic of Enlightenment"

phase it never succumbed to a full-blown nihilism. As a consequence it is misleading to equate Adorno's later work with postmodernism. And third, that Habermas's work represents a sharp break with respect to social science methodology given his eventual attempt to reconcile critical theory and American pragmatism. It is in the spirit of this latter strategy that I approach the question of a critical theory of methodology. Paradoxically, as Dahms stresses, Habermas in certain respects "switched sides" by moving to a pragmatist consensus theory of truth that had been previously rejected by the older Frankfurt School as "positivist" (Hans-Joachim Dahms, *Positivismusstreit: Die Auseinandersetzungen der Frankfurter Schue mit dem logischen Positivismus, dem amerikanischen Pragmatismus und dem kritischen Rationalismus* [Frankfurt am Main: Suhrkamp, 1994], p. 403; see also Hans Joas, *Pragmatism and Social Theory* [Chicago and London: University of Chicago Press, 1993]).

11. Jerome Karabel and A. H. Halsey, eds., *Power and Ideology in Education* (New York: Oxford University Press, 1977).

12. Ibid., p. 1.

13. Ibid.

14. Ibid., pp. 26–28.

15. Freire is cited peripherally twice.

16. E.g., Henry Giroux, *Ideology, Culture, and the Process of Schooling* (Philadelphia: Temple University Press, 1981).

17. This, of course, is a contentious thesis that I will not pursue further here.

18. In this context, discussions oriented toward the relationship between critical theory and education had only just emerged (e.g., Dieter Misgeld, "Emancipation, Enlightenment, and Liberation: An Approach Toward Foundational Inquiry into Education," *Interchange* 6 (1975): 23–37). See also, Morrow and Torres, *Social Theory and Education: A Critique of Theories of Social and Cultural Reproduction* (Albany: State University of New York Press, 1995), p. 217ff.

19. Paul Willis's *Learning to Labor* (New York: Columbia University Press, 1981), a pioneering reference point for education and cultural studies, was first published in 1977, the same year as the Karabel and Halsey anthology. The question of the relationship between the Marxist tradition and education was still dominated by French structuralism and Bowles and Gintis's correspondence theory of educational reproduction (Samuel Bowles and Herbert Gintis, *Schooling in Capitalist America: Educational Reform and the Contradictions of Economic Life* (New York: Basic Books/Harper, 1977).

20. Karabel and Halsey, *Power and Ideology*, p. 59.

21. Norman K. Denzin and Yvonna S. Lincoln, eds., *Handbook of Qualitative Research* (Thousand Oaks, Calif.: Sage, 1994).

22. Daniel P. Liston, *Capitalist Schools: Explanation and Ethics in Radical Studies of Schooling* (New York and London: Routledge, 1988).

23. Daniel Little, *Varieties of Social Explanation: An Introduction to the Philosophy of Social Science* (Boulder, Colo.: Westview Press, 1991).

24. Nowadays, to be sure, there has been a partial toppling of positivist discourse under the heading of postmodernism, introducing new problems that

will not be the focus here. Suffice it to say that much postmodernism so undercuts the project of disciplinary knowledge that it risks total relativism.

25. Abraham Kaplan, *The Conduct of Inquiry: Methodology for Behavioral Science* (San Francisco: Chandler, 1964).

26. As opposed to postmodernism as a theory of genres and styles or a periodizing concept for social and cultural change (e.g., Krishnan Kumar, *From Post-Industrial to Post-Modern Society* [Oxford: Blackwell, 1995]).

27. What I think is less often noted is that much confusion stems from the lack of identity, or perhaps the largely *negative identity* of so-called "qualitative" approaches that are united primarily by their opposition to constructing social facts as statistically defined variables. One of the central goals of our book was to recast the relationship between interpretive and statistical-causal research, making the latter merely a heuristic method ultimately dependent on the primary of interpretive (hence qualitative) theory and research. More recently, however, alternative criteria have elaborated for qualitative research (e.g., Joseph A. Maxwell, "Understanding and Validity in Qualitative Research," *Harvard Educational Review* 62 [1992]: 279–300).

28. The dominance of the quantitative-statistical model in North America can be attributed to a number of historical factors (above all, the rhetorical appeal of natural scientific models for legitimating social science) that need not concern us here. But it should be recalled that the emergence of the sociology of education in the 1960s can be traced in part to its effective use of statistical methods in stratification, mobility and status attainment research (Robert Dreeben, "The Sociology of Education: Its Development in the United States," in *Research in Sociology of Education and Socialization*, ed. Aaron M. Palls [Greenwich, Conn.: JAI Press, 1994]).

29. Denzin and Lincoln, *Handbook*.

30. Though the dust jacket boasts of contributors from "three continents," the connection is exclusively through American/Commonwealth hegemony of the English language, rather than any authentic cross-cultural concerns. And despite the North American focus, one would never guess that French Quebec and Mexico have highly developed traditions of qualitative inquiry.

31. I will not discuss extensively what it does well, let alone convey the range, diversity, and vitality of the forms of research touched upon. Above all, it brings the problematic of a poststructuralist or postmodernist (the terms are used virtually interchangeably) questioning of representational realism and scientific authority are brought to the center of attention, along with the inevitable value-laden and subjective basis of all inquiry. Further, this is a multicultural text that reflects the rainbow of standpoints competing for the limelight of attention and is truly interdisciplinary in orientation.

32. Denzin and Lincoln, *Handbook*, p. 4.

33. Ibid., pp. 5–6.

34. Nicholas Abercrombie, Stephen Hill, and Bryan S. Turner, *The Penguin Dictionary of Sociology*, 2nd ed. (Harmondsworth, England: Penguin Books, 1988), p. 119.

35. David Jary and Juali Jary, *Collins Dictionary of Sociology* (Glasgow: Harper Collins, 1991), p. 297.

36. Robert E. Stake, "Case Studies," in *Handbook of Qualitative Research*, ed. Norman J. Denzin and Yvonna S. Lincoln (Thousand Oaks, Calif.: Sage, 1994), p. 242.

37. Kincheloe and McLaren, "Rethinking Critical Theory."

38. There are several consequence for their strategy of defining qualitative research. *First*, the consequences of Denzin and Lincoln's relativistic standpoint epistemology is evident in their attempts to classify theoretical strategies. Difference is always privileged over similarity. Five theoretical-methodological "paradigms and perspectives" in qualitative research are covered in the editors' introduction: constructivist, critical theory (often reduced to Marxist), feminisms, ethnic (racial), and cultural studies. This classification obscures the more fundamental features of these modes of inquiry. Obsessed by the search for difference, each is portrayed monadically, monologically, and with only occasional, half-hearted reference to problems of validity or comparable approaches. *Second*, the problematic of qualitative research is to a great extent reduced to ethnography and textuality. Another strategy of classification is based on more specifically methodological criteria that identify qualitative research with what is variously referred to as ethnographic, field or participant observation research, or more peripherally particular techniques of analyzing symbolic materials. Despite a chapter on historical research, the problematic does not enter into the overall structure of the book and remains marginal to virtually all of the individual chapters. *Third*, contemporary critical theory loses its specific identity as a strategy for overcoming the very dualisms around which Denzin and Lincoln organize their anthology. If we look at the five-phase model of the research process presented, it appears that critical theory gets implicitly subsumed in either "Marxist models" or "cultural studies models"; moreover, these are reduced to "theoretical paradigms and perspectives" whose conceptual and empirical relation to "research strategies" remains largely unclassified (except for critical theory and a specific form of postmodernist ethnography privileged by the authors of the chapter in question). The editors are more concerned with a triumphal evolutionary model of approaches culminating in celebrating the differences within the postmodern here and now, rather than clarifying the relationships among methodology, social theory, and practice (Denzin and Lincoln, *Handbook of Qualitative Research*).

39. For the contemporary philosophical implications of this problematic, see Karl-Otto Apel, *Understanding and Explanation: A Transcendental-Pragmatic Perspective*, trans. Georgie Warnke (Cambridge: MIT Press, 1984).

40. Space limitations preclude a more extended exploration of this problematic here, but see Guy Oakes, *Weber and Rickert* (Cambridge: MIT Press, 1988).

41. Though the basic stance of interpretive structuralism has been sketched above with reference to Weber and Bourdieu, it is useful to refer as well to contemporary manifestations of the polarization they are criticizing. In the social sciences this polarization has been associated with contrasts between qualitative and quantitative, phenomenological and behaviorist, antipositivist and positivist, and so on. In the humanities this contrast has been defined more in terms of existentialism versus structuralism. Though aspects of poststructuralism

could be associated with overcoming this dualism, much work so labeled in fact slips backs into subjectivist standpoint theory.

42. I would argue that such a conception is also implicit in the early Marx and that such an interpretive structuralist strategy is a pervasive feature of much classical sociology (Simmel, Mannheim), and more recent reformulations (Mills, Berger and Luckmann, Giddens, Bourdieu, etc.).

43. Pierre Bourdieu and Loïc J. D. Wacquant, *An Invitation to Reflexive Sociology* (Chicago and London: University of Chicago Press, 1992), p . 75.

44. The most rigorous formulation of this argument can be found in the work of Roy Bhaskar (e.g., Roy Bhaskar, *Scientific Realism and Human Emancipation* [London and New York: Verso, 1986]).

45. Gaye Tuchman, "Historical Social Science: Methodologies, Methods, and Meanings," in *Handbook of Qualitative Research*, ed. Norman J. Denzin and Yvonna S. Lincoln (Thousand Oaks, Calif.: Sage, 1994).

46. Kincheloe and McLaren, "Rethinking Critical Theory," pp. 139–40.

47. Ibid., p. 140.

48. E.g. James Bohman, *New Philosophy of Social Science* (Cambridge: MIT Press, 1991); Ragin, *Constructing Social Research*.

49. Though Denzin's roots in pragmatism should have alerted him to other possibilities, his linguistic and postmodernist turn has attenuated his relationship to pragmatism in the direction of a Rorty's postmodernist neopragmatism.

50. See the clear and cogent exposition of Hekman who contrasts Althusser's structuralist Marxism and Habermas critical theory as objective analyses, arguing that though Althusser succumbs to objectivism, Habermas "comes so close to achieving a synthesis of the subjective and objective" (Susan Hekman, *Max Weber, the Ideal Type, and Contemporary Social Theory* [Notre Dame: University of Notre Dame Press, 1983], p. 145). As she concludes, if social science is to have a cognitive status beyond the language of everyday life, it must "define a conception of social scientific analysis which begins with actors' conceptions of their actions yet grants social-scientific understanding an explanatory status vis-à-vis those concepts. . . . Weber's attempt to define a conception of objectivity which avoids the pitfalls of both positivism and subjectivism is highly relevant to contemporary discussions" (p. 152). While I agree with her contention that Weber's concept of ideal types provides an essential bridge for mediating between interpretive and structural analysis, she does not address the crucial importance of structuralist concepts as non-nomothetic forms of generalization, a theme of interpretive structuralism as developed here.

51. The specific term can and should be contextualized with respect to what it opposes, as well as within a family of similar notions. Interpretive structuralism should first be contrasted with *empiricist structuralism*, on the one hand, and *hyperstructuralism* of the type proposed by Lévi-Strauss for a structuralist anthropology or Althusser for a structuralist Marxism. Both of these later strategies largely eliminate the subject and history from social inquiry. Interpretive structuralism shares some elements with poststructuralism in its rejection of the limitations of classic structuralism. Empiricist structuralism, on the other hand, originates in a very different conception of empirical regularities

and their relationship to "effects" or the production of social phenomena. Empiricist structuralism corresponds to the standard positivist strategy of a search for causal laws that probabalistically determine social actions. In contrast, forms of structuralism influenced by linguistic models point to generative mechanisms that define the rules that constrain human action, but do not determine its specific outcomes any more than a grammar determines what we might say, as opposed to how we must speak whatever we will.

52. Morrow, *Critical Theory and Methodology*, p. 226ff.

53. For a more detailed sketch of intensive research designs, see ibid., 248ff. and Andrew Sayer, *Method in Social Science: A Realist Approach*, 2nd ed. (London and New York: Routledge, 1992).

54. Morrow, *Critical Theory and Methodology*, p. 221ff.

55. Though originating in critical theory, these distinctions have been increasingly employed in the philosophy of social science (e.g., David Braybrooke, *Philosophy of Social Science* [Englewood Cliffs, N.J.: Prentice Hall, 1987]) and sociological methods texts (e.g., W. Lawrence Neuman, *Social Research Methods: Qualitative and Quantitative Approaches* [Boston: Allyn and Bacon, 1991]).

56. Paul Ricoeur, *Hermeneutics and the Human Sciences*, trans. and ed. John B. Thompson (Cambridge: Cambridge University Press, 1981).

57. Jürgen Habermas, *On the Logic of the Social Sciences*, trans. Shierry Weber Nicholsen and Jerry A. Stark (Cambridge: MIT Press, 1988), p. 3.

58. Jürgen Habermas, *Knowledge and Human Interests*, trans. Jeremy J. Shapiro (Boston: Beacon, 1971).

59. Paul Ricoeur, *The Conflict of Interpretations*, ed. Don Ihde (Evanston, Ill.: Northwestern University Press, 1974).

60. Fay terms this form of knowledge quasi-causal, but this aspect of critical theory remains ambiguous (Brian Fay, *Social Theory and Political Practice* [London: George Allen & Unwin, 1975]). His objective clearly is to avoid identification with the presuppositions of nomothetic and covering law models of causality. As he later concludes, "ultimately the nature of social-scientific theory (with its herreronomic generalizations, limitations in scope and specificity, and restriction to a particular [sort of] cultural setting) is shaped by the essential historicity of the objects it seeks to explain" (Fay, "General Laws and Explaining Human Behavior," in *Readings in the Philosophy of Social Science*, ed. Michael Martin and Lee C. McIntyre [Cambridge: MIT Press, 1994 (1983)]). I have sought to link non-nomothetic generalizing strategies to various forms of historicist structuralism found generally in classical sociological theory. In his early writings Habermas relied rather too much on positivist definitions of the empirical-analytical interest and had not yet fully incorporated the structuralist principles that inform his later social theory.

61. It is unclear where Lincoln stands on these issues, having participated in both formulations. This present formulation appears to originate from Guba (Egon G. Guba, ed., *The Paradigm Dialog* [Newbury Park, Calif.: Sage, 1990]).

62. The term "postpositivist" here refers to a form of empiricism (largely Popperian) that is sensitive to the pitfalls and limitations of classical positivism.

63. Egon G. Guba and Yvonna S. Lincoln, "Competing Paradigms in Qual-

itative Research," in *Handbook of Qualitative Research*, ed. Norman J. Denzin and Yvonna S. Lincoln (Thousand Oaks, Calif.: Sage, 1994).

64. Ibid., p. 113.

65. From this perspective, quantitative methods perform a similar, complementary heuristic role. Though they have the advantage of formal precision and in some cases more decisive evidential "tests," they are fundamentally limited because extensive research designs are inevitably abstracted out of concrete, historical social relations. The resulting artificiality does not make such research meaningless or unimportant in constructing comprehensive social explanations and interpretations, but it does make it something less significant than the classic positivist idealization of the cover-law model of explanation.

66. There are two fundamental differences, however. Critical theory approaches are more radically *historicist* in that causal structures are not reified as "causal laws" but are integrated into historically specific case studies. For example, Stinchcombe's (1968) justifiably famous discussion of causal imageries in demographic, functionalist and historicist explanations remains tied to the positivist search for general laws to be decomposed in terms of causal variables. As a consequence, agency and historicity gets suppressed within formalized causal loops and chains that may serve a certain heuristic purpose, but do not literally map contingent, open systems. The rhetoric of formalization runs the risk of self-deception. (Arthur Stinchcombe, *Constructing Social Theories* [New York: Harcourt, Brace & World, 1968]).

67. For a good sample of more recent work illustrating such an integral approach to a critical sociology of education, see the international contributions in Heinz Sünker, Dieter Timmermann, and Fritz-Ulrich Kolbe, eds., 1994. *Bildung, Gesellschaft, sociale Ungleichheit: Internationale Beiträge zur Bildungssoziologie und Bildungstheorie* (Frankfurt am Main: Suhrkamp, 1994).

68. Liston, *Capitalist Schools*, p. 114ff.

69. Ibid., p. 107.

70. In the work of Habermas and others this problematic is often referred to in terms of the distinction between systemic and social integration (e.g., Nicos P. Mouzelis, *Back to Sociological Theory* [London: Macmillan, 1991]).

71. Liston, *Capitalist Schools*, p. 118.

72. Theodor W. Adorno et al., *The Positivist Dispute in German Sociology*, trans. Glyn Adey and David Frisby (London: Heinemann, 1976).

73. The real dilemma of empiricist research has always been elsewhere: connecting its piecemeal and middle range findings with a theory of society. The alliance between Merton and Parsons can be traced to this question, as well as that between later researchers such as Bowles and Gintis and Marxist theory. Again, educational research is instructive because it is here where the fruitful interplay between empiricism and social theory has often been apparent. Researchers concerned with status attainment and mobility analysis often see their work as contributing to a general theory of social and cultural reproduction. Partly as a consequence, it would be hard to find representatives of critical or Marxist theory in education who reject in toto quantitative approaches to social research.

74. Alvin Gouldner, *The Two Marxisms* (New York: Seabury, 1980).

75. Nicholas C. Burbules, *Dialogue in Teaching: Theory and Practice* (New York: Teachers College Press, 1993).

76. Andrew Ross, "Introduction," in *Universal Abandon? The Politics of Postmodernism*, ed. Andrew Ross (Minneapolis: University of Minnesota Press, 1989), p. xiv.

77. Ibid., p. xvii.

# CHAPTER 3

# Sociology of Education and Urban Education Policy

# Geoff Whitty

## INTRODUCTION

Some of you will know that the chair I hold in the University of London is named after the sociologist Karl Mannheim. Karl Mannheim himself was appointed to a chair of education at the Institute of Education in 1946, just a year before his tragically early death in January 1947. I recently trawled the institute archives for material about Karl Mannheim in preparation for a lecture to mark the fiftieth anniversary of his death.[1] In the wartime archives, I came across a paper by the then director of the institute, Sir Fred Clarke, in which he argued the case for appointing someone like Mannheim—and he clearly had Mannheim himself in mind—to a position at the institute as soon as the war was over. He said the case could be related to "the uneasy awareness, now so widespread and yet so ill-defined, that great changes in the social order and the inter-play of social forces are already in progress—and that educational theory and educational policy that take no account of these will be not only blind but positively harmful."[2]

Fifty years later, there is a similar sense that significant but ill-defined changes in the nature of the social order are in progress. Unless gatherings of sociologists here are very different from those in England at the moment, it will no doubt be a matter of some debate among us as to whether we are living in late capitalism, postmodernity, high modernity, post-traditionalism, or whatever. Yet, just as in the days of Mannheim, too much education policy and even a great deal of contemporary educational research—not least within my own institute—has lost sight of Clarke's important insight that education policy needs to be informed by a sensitivity to the nature of these changes. Meanwhile the education press is full of advertisements for posts in educational administration and management, and more particularly school effectiveness and school improvement, but there is not exactly a glut of positions in the sociology of education.

Like Clarke, I believe this neglect of our discipline can be positively harmful, not just to our own career chances but to education policy and practice. In my chapter, I want therefore to explore two main themes. First, the ways in which sociology might help us to make sense of contemporary education policy. And, second, the ways in which sociology might be positioned in relation to future developments in education policy and practice. In doing so, I will draw mainly on two areas of education policy that I have been studying in some detail over the past few years—school reform and the reformation of teaching as a profession. Most of this work has been carried out in urban settings and, like Grace, I would argue that the contradictions that characterize modern state education are at their sharpest within urban contexts and impact upon the lives of teachers and students there in particularly intense ways.[3]

## THEORETICAL INSIGHTS

To take the first question, what sociological accounts might, for instance, help us to make sense of the current trend in many parts of the world to restructure and deregulate state education systems? Central to these initiatives have been moves to disband centralized educational bureaucracies and create in their place devolved systems of schooling entailing significant degrees of institutional autonomy and a variety of forms of school-based management and administration. In many cases, these changes have been linked to an increased emphasis on parental choice and on competition between diversified and specialized forms of provision, thereby creating what we now call "quasi-markets " in educational services.[4]

Although such policies have received particular encouragement from New Right governments in Britain and the United States in the 1980s, and have subsequently been fostered by the International Monetary Fund and the World Bank in Latin America and Eastern Europe,[5] the political rhetoric of parties of the left has also begun to place increasing emphasis on diversity and choice in education. Even though these directions in education policy have not penetrated all countries,[6] and they have been mediated differently by the traditions of different nation states and different political parties, the similarity between the broad trends in many parts of the world suggests that education policy may be witnessing something sociologically significant—something perhaps rather more important than the passing political fashion of Thatcherism and the like.

Shilling argues correctly that too many analyses of education policy—and he includes some of my own work in his strictures—are characterized by a lack of theory and sociology.[7] So how far can contemporary social theory help us make sense of recent education policy? It is sometimes suggested that current shifts in the ways in which education is organized reflect broader changes in the nature of advanced industrial societies, characterized by some commentators as post-Fordism and by others as postmodernity.

Ball, for example, has claimed to see in new forms of schooling a move away from the "Fordist " school toward a "post-Fordist" one—the educational equivalent of flexible specialization driven by the imperatives of differentiated consumption replacing the old assembly-line world of mass production.[8] Kenway, though, regards the rapid rise of the market form in education as something much more significant than post-Fordism; she therefore terms it a "postmodern" phenomenon. In her own pessimistic version of postmodernity, "transnational corporations and their myriad subsidiaries . . . shape and reshape our individual and collective identities as we plug in . . . to their cultural and economic communications networks."[9] Her picture is one in which notions of "difference," far from being eradicated by the "globalization of culture," are assembled, displayed, celebrated, commodified, and exploited.[10] Such trends, she implies, can be detected in the current emphasis on both tradition and diversity in education policy.

In other accounts the rhetoric of "new times" seems to offer more positive images of choice and diversity, reflecting the needs of communities and interest groups brought into prominence as a result of complex contemporary patterns of political, economic, and cultural differentiation, which intersect the traditional class divisions upon which common systems of mass education were predicated. From this perspective, it is possible to contrast postmodernity to the oppressive uniformity of much modernist thinking—as "a form of liberation, in which the fragmentation and plurality of cultures and social groups allow a hundred flowers to bloom."[11]

It has been suggested that part of the appeal of the recent education reforms lies in their declared intention to encourage the growth of different types of schools, responsive to needs of particular communities and groups. Possibilities for community-based welfare, rather than bureaucratically controlled welfare, have sometimes been viewed positively particularly by women and minority ethnic groups. The concept of diversity seems to articulate with the ideas of radical pluralism and can seem more attractive than unidimensional notions of comprehensive schooling and, indeed, unidimensional notions of citizenship. Some aspects of the rhetoric of the new policies thus seem to connect to the aspirations of groups who have found little to identify with in the "grand narratives" associated with class-based politics. In this sense, the reforms might be viewed as a rejection of all totalizing narratives and their replacement by "a set of cultural projects united [only] by a self-proclaimed commitment to heterogeneity, fragmentation and difference."[12] In other words, support for schools run on a variety of principles may reflect a broader shift from the assumptions of modernity to those of postmodernity.

## EMPIRICAL GROUNDING

Suggestive as they are, however, it is perhaps too easy to get carried away by these contemporary versions of "correspondence theory." Michael Apple warns us to be wary of overstating the move into postmodernity and to avoid the danger of "substituting one grand narrative for another." He also points to the need to ground our understandings in the lives of teachers and students in schools, another important aspect of the sociological enterprise.[13] And, when we start to interrogate theory with research, we encounter various problems with these "new times" theses. Not only are they "notoriously vague,"[14] they also tend to exaggerate the extent to which we have moved to a new regime of accumulation. Insofar as recent changes in management practices represent an adjustment to the problems of Fordism rather than signifying an entirely new direction, neo-Fordism may be a more appropriate term than post-Fordism.[15]

Meanwhile, there is a growing body of empirical evidence that particularly the more optimistic readings of postmodernity are dangerously naive. Rather than benefiting the urban poor, as many of the advocates of quasi-market systems of public education claim,[16] the emphasis on parental choice and school autonomy in recent reforms seems to be further disadvantaging the disadvantaged. It is certainly increasing the differences between popular and less popular schools on a linear scale—reinforcing a vertical hierarchy of schooling types rather than producing the promised horizontal diversity. For most members of disadvantaged groups, as opposed to the few individuals who escape from schools at the bottom of the status hierarchy, the new arrangements seem to be just a more sophisticated and intensified way of reproducing traditional distinctions between different types of schools and between the people who attend them.[17]

Such evidence from a whole range of empirical studies suggests that to regard the current espousal of heterogeneity, pluralism, and local narratives as indicative of a new social order may be to mistake phenomenal forms for structural relations. Marxist critics of theories of postmodernism and postmodernity, such as Callinicos, who reassert the primacy of the class struggle, certainly take this view.[18] Even Harvey, who does recognize significant changes, suggests that postmodernist cultural forms and more flexible modes of capital accumulation may be shifts in surface appearance, rather than signs of the emergence of some entirely new postcapitalist or even postindustrial society.[19] At most, current reforms would seem to relate to a version of postmodernity that emphasizes "distinction" and "hierarchy" within a fragmented social order, rather than one that positively celebrates "difference" and "heterogeneity."[20] Thus, despite new forms of accumulation, together with some limited changes in patterns of social and cultural differentiation, the continuities seem as striking as the discontinuities.

## THE STATE, CIVIL SOCIETY, AND "AUTONOMOUS" SCHOOLS

Yet, if some of the flights of fancy of contemporary social theory focus too much on the rhetoric and not enough on the reality of education reform, other less ambitious theories in the field of political sociology can help us to dig beneath the rhetoric and identify something significant going on. Thus, even if current policies are new ways of dealing with old problems, there clearly have been changes in the state's mode of regulation. With the delegitimation of conventional political and bureaucratic control by democratically accountable public bodies, there are more and more quasi-autonomous institutions with devolved budgets competing for clients in the marketplace—a system of market accountability sometimes assisted by a series of directly appointed agencies, trusts, and regulators. Such quasi-autonomous institutions, state-funded but with considerable private and voluntary involvement in their operation, appear to make education less of a political issue. But sociologically, the new arrangements for managing education and other public services can be seen as new ways of resolving the problems of accumulation and legitimation facing the state in a situation where the traditional Keynesian "welfare state" is no longer viable.[21] They are, if you like, an attempt to "export the crisis."[22]

So, although the extent of any underlying social changes can easily be exaggerated by various "postist" forms of analysis, both the discourse and the contexts of political struggles in and around education have been significantly altered by recent reforms. Not only have changes in the nature of the state influenced the reforms in education, the reforms in education are themselves beginning to change the way we think about the role of the state and what we expect of it. Green has pointed to the way in which education has not only been an important part of state activity in modern societies, but also played a significant role in the process of state formation itself in the eighteenth and nineteenth centuries.[23] The current changes in education policy may similarly be linked to a redefinition of the nature of the state and a reworking of the relations between state and civil society.

The new education policies foster the idea that responsibility for education and welfare, beyond the minimum required for public safety, is to be defined as a matter for individuals and families. Not only is the scope of the state narrowed, but civil society becomes increasingly defined in market terms. Although one of the many origins of the concept of civil society was the attempt by late-eighteenth-century liberal economists to protect an autonomous economic sphere from the growing administrative power of the state, political radicals used it as a context for democratic debate and the fostering of active citizenship.[24] However, Meehan suggests that, by the mid-twentieth century in Britain and some other countries, the establishment of political democracy led to a view in many countries that state bureaucratic regulation itself might serve as "a tool to improve the collective life of society."[25] This reliance on the state led to a decline in the autonomy and vitality of civil society.

Now, however, civil society is being reconstituted. But, as many of the responsibilities adopted by the state during the postwar period begin to be devolved to a marketized version of civil society, consumer rights increasingly come to prevail over citizen rights. So some aspects of education have been "privatized" not so much in the strictly economic sense as in the sense of transferring them to the private sphere. Meanwhile, others have become a matter of state mandate rather than local democratic debate. This can be seen as part of that broader project to create a free economy and a strong state[26]—a minimalist state in most respects but a more powerful one in defining its parameters. As far as democratic citizenship is concerned, this seems to produce the worst of both worlds—reducing the opportunities for democratic debate and collective action about education within both the state and civil society.

Thus, despite the rhetoric about "rolling back" or "hollowing out" the state, in many countries certain aspects of state intervention have been maintained, indeed strengthened. This is particularly noticeable in Britain, but has also been noted, in differing degrees, in other contexts such as New Zealand and parts of Latin America.[27] This may appear to be less the case in the United States than elsewhere, though in a federal state one would need to consider the combined powers of state and federal governments in relation to local government, so that (for example) state-sponsored charter schools may strengthen the role of the state government and the individual institution at the expense of local school boards.

McKenzie claims that British governments have actually increased their claims to knowledge and authority over the education system while promoting a theoretical and superficial movement toward consumer sovereignty.[28] It is certainly the case that a great deal of recent education reform, notably the National Curriculum, was as much to do with transferring power from the local state to the central state as with giving autonomy to the schools. This suggests that it is not merely that the contemporary state has devolved responsibility to a remarketized civil society. In the British case at least, it has abdicated some responsibility for ensuring social justice by deregulating major aspects of education, but in increasing a limited number of state powers it has actually strengthened its capacity to foster particular interests while appearing to stand outside the frame. In this situation, the removal or marginalization of the influence of interest groups (such as local authorities and trade unions) between the state and the individual institution may not have empowered the poor but actually made them more vulnerable.[29]

There are similar issues at the institutional level, where it is often claimed that self-management empowers teachers. Yet a number of studies have shown classroom teachers to be less positive about the recent reforms than headteachers.[30] While heads usually say that local management has increased the involvement of teaching staff in decision-making, a study of the effects of self-management on industrial relations in British schools by Sinclair and colleagues suggests that the very logic of the reforms is that "headteachers are no longer partners in the process of educating pupils—they become allocators of resources within the school, managers who are driven to ensure that the activities of employees are appropriate to the needs of the business, and givers of rewards to those whose contribution to the business is most highly regarded." At the same time, teachers' work is intensified in the name of the interests of the school community. In this situation, the celebration of flexibility and claims of enhanced professionalism can easily become a cover for the exploitation of teachers and worsening conditions of service.[31]

As Blackmore points out in an Australian review of the evidence, the self-managing school retains "strong modernist tendencies for a top-down, executive mode of decision-making . . . [alongside its] 'weaker' post-modern claims to decentralize and encourage diversity, community ownership, local discretion, professional autonomy and flexible decision-making."[32] Even the more genuinely participatory forms of teacher involvement in decision-making can have unintended consequences. One report on Minnesota charter schools, for example, commented that "as much as teachers appreciated being board members and making administrative decisions, wearing two hats required a great deal of time and effort" from which they would eventually require some relief.[33]

Strategies of neighborhood empowerment also have their limitations, since communities are far from equally endowed with the material and cultural resources for self-management of their schools, as Gordon has demonstrated in the case of New Zealand.[34] In the case of the Chicago reforms, Lewis and Nakagawa claim that "even if the model is implemented well, a tall order in and of itself, the exogenous factors that lead to the failure of the minority poor in school . . . would seem to require more than a change in school governance can deliver."[35] Certainly, such strategies are unlikely to succeed in the absence of changes in the broader distributive policies adopted by the central state.

Such research calls into question the frequent assumption in current policy discourse that it is the poor and the teaching profession who have the most to gain from recent reforms. Yet much of this remains opaque to those who regard the autonomous schools spawned by the recent reforms as genuinely empowered. Not only neoliberal rhetoric, but also much of the school improvement literature, takes the discursive repositioning of schools as autonomous agencies at its face value rather than recognizing that the atomization of schooling too often merely allows advantaged schools to enhance their advantages.[36] For those schools ill-placed to capitalize on their market position, the devolution of responsibility can often merely lead to the devolution of blame. And, particularly for schools in the inner city, there is a danger that too much emphasis upon the power of individual school faculty to seek their own salvation may only result in further damage to the morale of an increasingly exploited workforce.

## IMPLICATIONS FOR POLICY

Sociologically informed studies of education policy can thus help to provide lenses that are at some variance with the taken-for-granted assumptions of much contemporary education policy.[37] We begin to move here into my second theme, which concerns the role of sociology in relation to future policies. Even if sociologists were able to agree on the epistemological status of our discipline, and that is unlikely, there would be a variety of ways in which sociology could be positioned in relation to other forms of practice. But, if few of us today believe that theorizing and charting changes in the social order and the interplay of social forces enables sociologists to provide solutions to urban educational problems in a direct or simplistic way, as Mannheim tended to assume in his later work,[38] does that mean that we should eschew engagement with policy altogether?

I would not want to argue, even if I once did, that there is some sort of imperative that requires all sociologists of education to forge explicit links with the world of policy and practice.[39] Nevertheless, many sociologists of education have, over the years, seen their work in these terms, particularly in relation to various forms of progressive policy and practice. Yet many sociologists of education seem somehow less engaged with social justice issues than they did, say, twenty years ago. Indeed, it is noticeable that, while sociologists of education seem to have become more isolated in the academy and increasingly disengaged from wider social movements, broader social theorists such as Giddens seem to be showing a greater willingness to address the political challenges posed by a changing social order.[40]

Of course, by no means have all sociologists of education abandoned engagement with the world of policy and practice. But some seem virtually to have abandoned their discipline, and more particularly its characteristically critical mode of engagement with the world of policy and practice, to engage more directly with technical issues of school effectiveness and school improvement.[41] Grace, who pioneered a sociological approach to urban education in Britain in the 1970s, has often dismissed the sort of "policy science" that typified American urban education in the 1970s on the grounds that it had become trapped within the assumptions of the particular policy context being studied.[42] Such work has laid itself open to the charge of "producing naive school-centered solutions with no sense of the structural, the political and the historical as constraints."[43] Much the same could be said of much of the work of the contemporary school improvement movement.

Grace's own alternative of "policy scholarship" maintains a sense of both theory and history that helps us to recognise the "bigger picture" and hints at the specific contribution that sociologists might make to our understanding of both the limits and possibilities of progressive policy and practice. Yet the term "policy scholarship" itself seems too detached to communicate the sort of relationship between critical theory and progressive practice that Grace, following Fay, envisages.[44] Whatever his own intentions, it could serve to reinforce that very disarticulation between the academy and the world outside that has led to a widening gulf between progressive educators and the communities they claim to serve—a gulf that is underscored by the juxtaposition of what, even after a period of retrenchment, is the relative affluence of the university with the devastation of the inner city.

This condition is, however, also a feature of other fields of professional and academic practice, including some in which the discourse seems unambiguously committed to an interventionist stance. Thus, it is not only sociology of education that, especially in Britain and the United States, has often become disarticulated from its object of study or engagement, so has education policy itself. Using Bourdieu's notion of social field, Ladwig argues that the field of education policy in the United States has developed a considerable degree of autonomy. He observes that the very fact that observations about the "failure" of education policy or its implications for particular groups pose no threat to the relatively autonomous field of education policy is indicative of the extent to which education policy as a field has become self-justifying and self-perpetuating.[45]

How, then, might sociologists who are dissatisfied with this condition not only re-engage with education policy but also help to re-engage education policy with the everyday experience of struggles in and around education while maintaining a critical stance? It would be comforting to think that we might rediscover what it means to be Gramscian organic intellectuals in the conditions of the late twentieth century. In this respect, neither the Mannheimian view of free-floating intellectuals or the Foucauldian concept of specific intellectuals is as appealing as the Gramscian one if we are concerned with the broad context of social injustice within which I have implied education is located. But what precisely this means in relation to new social movements is less clear than it was when, at least in the European context, there was a clearer notion of a labor movement with which to engage.[46]

## DEVELOPING NEW CONTEXTS OF ENGAGEMENT

In *Sociology and School Knowledge*, I suggested that "the practical implications of [sociological] work for . . . political and educational practice [are] as much concerned with the ways in which policy is made as with specific substantive policies."[47] One area where I would argue that sociologists may potentially have an important role is in advocacy—not so much of specific interests, but of the importance of identifying and bringing together those constituencies that have conventionally been excluded from education policy and decision-making either intentionally or, just as often, as an unintended consequence of decisions made with the best of intentions. If, as much of the initial research evidence suggests, recent reforms are encouraging advantaged schools and advantaged families to maximize their advantage, then it is particularly important that there is an arena in which equity issues can be considered collectively by the various stakeholders in public education.[48]

Yet I suggested earlier that social relations were becoming increasingly accommodated in the notion of the strong state and the free economy. If that is the case, then neither the state nor civil society is currently much of a context for active democratic citizenship through which social justice can be pursued. How then might the field of education policy be reconstituted, reinvigorated, and rearticulated with political and professional struggles over education? The reassertion of citizenship rights in education would seem to require the development of a new public sphere somehow between the state and a marketized civil society, in which new forms of collective association can be developed. Foucault pointed out that what he called new forms of association, such as trade unions and political parties, arose in the nineteenth century as a counterbalance to the prerogative of the state, and that they acted as the seedbed of new ideas.[49] We need to consider what might be the modern versions of these collectivist forms of association to counterbalance not only the prerogative of the state, but also the prerogative of the market.

However, given what has been dismantled by New Right governments, creating a new public sphere in which educational matters can even be debated—let alone determined—poses a considerable challenge. Part of the challenge must be to move away from atomized decision-making to the reassertion of collective responsibility for education without recreating the very bureaucratic systems whose shortcomings have helped to legitimate the current tendency to treat education as a private good rather than a public responsibility. We need to ask how we can use the positive aspects of choice and autonomy to facilitate community empowerment rather than exacerbating social differentiation. The left has done little yet to develop a concept of public education that looks significantly different from the state education so often criticized in the past for its role in reproducing and legitimating social inequalities.[50] And even if the social democratic era looks better in retrospect, and in comparison with current policies, than it did at the time, that does not remove the need to rethink what might be progressive policies for the next century.

Nevertheless, Apple argues that we should recognize that there are some aspects of past practice in schools that should be defended as gains of collective struggles by progressive forces over the years.[51] Certainly, our fascination with recent neoliberal reforms can blind us to the potential of other ways of struggling to achieve social justice. As Henig rightly says, "the sad irony of the current education-reform movement is that, through over-identification with school-choice proposals rooted in market-based ideas, the healthy impulse to consider radical reforms to address social problems may be channeled into initiatives that further erode the potential for collective deliberation and collective response."[52]

But if new approaches to collective decision-making are to be granted more legitimacy than previous ones, what new institutions might help to foster them—initially within a new public sphere in which ideas can be debated, but potentially as new forms of democratic governance themselves? It is clear that careful consideration will need to be given to the composition, nature, and powers of new institutional forms if they are to prove an appropriate way of reasserting democratic citizenship rights in education in the late twentieth century and beyond. They will certainly need to respond to critiques of conventional forms of political association in most modern societies. While market forms are part of a social text that helps to create new subject positions that undermine traditional forms of collectivism, those forms of collectivism themselves often failed to empower many members of society, including women and minority ethnic groups.

Paradoxically, current forms of democracy in England may be even less appropriate than those associated with directly elected school boards in the nineteenth century, which used "an advanced form of proportional representation [which] ensured that all the major political and religious groupings could be represented on the School Boards, so that positive policies at this level achieved a genuine consensus."[53] We now have to ask what are the appropriate constituencies through which to express community interests in the late twentieth century? What do we mean by communities? What forms of democracy can express their complexity? How do we develop a radical pluralist conception of citizenship that involves creating unity without denying specificity?[54] If appropriately constituted and given real resources and powers, Community Education Forums, which have been floated but not hitherto really implemented by Labour parties in England and New Zealand, might provide one way forward.

And what implications do such issues have for teachers? In calling on teachers to foster the emergence of hitherto "silenced voices," Keith argues that we need a new discourse that joins the themes of collaboration, care, commitment, and community to those of difference, equity, rights, dialogue, and a wider sense of community."[55] This suggests that, as well as gaining genuine involvement in policymaking at the institutional level, teachers need to become more accountable to constituencies that have tended to be ignored in the past.

Both state control and market forces imply a "low trust" relationship between society and its teachers.[56] Media characterizations of teacher unions often tend to encourage popular suspicion of teachers. Furthermore, the defense of the education service has too often been conducted within the assumptions of the "old " politics of education, which involved consultation between government, employers, and unions but excluded whole constituencies—notably parents and business—to whom the New Right has subsequently successfully appealed.[57] It is clear that even now not all groups have been granted a legitimate right to be involved in developing education policy. It is perhaps indicative of the paucity of thinking on this that some of the leftist teacher educators who, twenty years ago, were criticizing the elitism of the professions should now be among those suggesting that teachers should adopt the modes of self-regulation traditionally associated with the conservative professions of medicine and the law. Are state control, market forces, or professional self-governance the only models of accountability—or can we develop new models of teacher professionalism, based upon more participatory relationships with diverse communities?

In the Australian case, Knight and colleagues argue for what they call "democratic professionalism," which seeks to demystify professional work and facilitate broader participation in decision-making.[58] Why is it, I wonder, that the evidence that teachers and educationists are not always concerned principally with the welfare of their clients has been so successfully used by public choice theorists to justify neoliberal consumer-oriented reforms rather than to justify greater inclusivity in democratic decision-making in education? It is to the discussion of just this sort of issue that sociologists might usefully contribute. While sociologists of education clearly cannot claim a privileged role in such discussions, we may bring a distinctive one. Of course, this does not mean that our perspective will always be welcomed or that our role in relation to policy can ever be a straightforward one, as is clear from the experiences of sociologists working in education policy units in the new South Africa.[59]

## CONCLUSION

I have expressed some skepticism about the extent to which we are living under the postmodern condition, a skepticism that I have retained even when confronted with the reality of late-twentieth-century Los Angeles. But, whether or not those changes that are taking place in education do reflect fundamental changes in modes of accumulation and modes of social solidarity, signaled by terms such as post-Fordism and postmodernity, they do need to be confronted. At the level of rhetoric (though not reality), the recent reforms of the New Right have probably been more responsive than their critics usually concede to those limited, but nonetheless tangible, social and cultural shifts that have been taking place in modern societies. A straightforward return to the old order of things would be neither feasible nor sensible. Social democratic approaches to education that continue to favor the idea of a common school are faced with the need to respond to increasing specialization and social diversity. We have to remind ourselves that neoliberalism is but one response to this situation and one that effectively abandons the sort of social justice agenda implied by the call for papers of the conference at which this paper was initially presented.

But it seems clear that, if the only future for public education lies with the particular marketized forms that are currently fashionable, it will become increasingly difficult to articulate, let alone implement, such an agenda. Yet, while neoliberalism is increasingly regarded as part of the taken-for-granted world of education policy in many countries, it is but one possible response to current social conditions. If we are to avoid the atomization of educational decision-making, and associated tendencies toward fragmentation and polarization between schools and within schools, we need to create new contexts for determining appropriate institutional and curricular arrangements on behalf of the whole society. I have suggested that this will require new forms of association in the public sphere within which citizen rights in education policy—and indeed other areas of public policy—can be reasserted against current trends toward both a restricted version of the state and a marketized civil society. Otherwise education will become merely a private consumption good rather than a public issue.

In this context, I believe sociology of education still has a modest role to play in our understanding of the limits and possibilities of education policy in modern societies and in the future development of education as a public issue. In the 1940s, Mannheim argued that "no educational activity or research is adequate in the present stage of consciousness unless it is conceived in terms of a sociology of education."[60] Despite the hyperbolic character of this remark, I can see no case for going to the opposite extreme. Unlike Hammersley, I do not believe that we should be willing to accept the demise of our discipline on the grounds that what was once a distinctively sociological way of thinking about the world has somehow entered into the "commonsense" of other educators.[61] We have only to listen to the market advocates and the school improvement lobby to recognize that too often that is just not the case.

## NOTES

This is a revised version of a paper presented to the ISA Sociology of Education Section Mid-Term Conference on "Urban Education: Challenges for the Sociology of Education" at UCLA, 20–22 June 1996.

1. Geoff Whitty, *Social Theory and Educational Policy: The Legacy of Karl Mannheim* (London: Institute of Education, 1997).

2. "Post-War Facilities for the Study of Education: Some Notes by the Director on the Essential Professorships," attached to Report B of the Delegacy for the Institute of Education, 18 March 1943. Sir Fred Clarke Archive, Institute of Education, University of London.

3. G. Grace, ed., *Education and the City: Theory, History and Contemporary Practice* (London: Routledge, 1984).

4. J. Le Grand and W. Bartlett, *Quasi-Markets and Social Policy* (London: Macmillan, 1993).

5. Robert Arnove, "Neo-Liberal Education Policies in Latin America: Arguments in Favor and Against," paper delivered to the Comparative and International Education Society, Williamsburg, Va., 6–10 March 1996.

6. A. Green, "Postmodernism and State Education," *Journal of Education Policy* 9.1 (1994): 67–84.

7. C. Shilling, "The Demise of Sociology of Education in Britain?" *British Journal of Sociology of Education* 14.1 (1993): 105–12.

8. S. Ball, *Politics and Policy Making: Explorations in Policy Sociology* (London: Routledge, 1990).

9. J. Kenway, "Marketing Education in the Postmodern Age," *Journal of Education Policy* 8.1 (1993): 105–22.

10. K. Robins, "Tradition and Translation: National Culture in its Global Context," in *Enterprise and Heritage: Crosscurrents of National Culture*, ed. J. Corner and S. Harvey (London: Routledge, 1991).

11. K. Thompson, "Social Pluralism and Postmodernity," in *Modernity and its Futures*, ed. S. Hall, D. Held, and T. McGrew (Cambridge: Polity Press, 1992).

12. R. Boyne and A. Rattansi, eds., *Postmodernism and Society* (London: Macmillan, 1990).

13. Michael W. Apple, *Cultural Politics and Education* (Buckingham: Open University Press, 1996).

14. M. Hickox, "Situating Vocationalism," *British Journal of Sociology of Education* 16.2 (1995): 153–63.

15. J. Allen, "Post-industrialism and Post-Fordism," in *Modernity and its Futures*, ed. S. Hall, D. Held, and T. McGrew (Cambridge: Polity Press, 1992).

16. See, for example, Terry Moe, "The British Battle for Choice," in *Voices on Choice: The Education Reform Debate*, ed. K. L. Billingsley (San Francisco: Pacific Institute for Public Policy, 1994) and S. Pollard, *Schools, Selection and the Left* (London: Social Market Foundation, 1995).

17. See T. Smith and M. Noble, *Education Divides: Poverty and Schooling in the 1990s* (London: Child Poverty Action Group, 1995); Geoff Whitty, S. Power, and D. Halpin, *Devolution and Choice in Education: The School, the State and the Market* (Bristol, Pa.: Open University Press, 1988); H. Lauder, D. Hughes, S. Watson, I. Simiyu, R. Strathdee, and S. Waslander, *Trading in Futures: The Nature of Choice in Educational Markets in New Zealand*, Smithfield Project, Victoria University of Wellington, 1995; and S. Gerwitz, S. J. Ball, and R. Bowe, *Markets, Choice and Equity* (Buckingham: Open University Press, 1995).

18. A. Callincos, *Against Postmodernism: A Marxist Critique* (Cambridge: Polity Press, 1989).

19. D. Harvey, *The Condition of Postmodernity: An Enquiry into the Origins of Cultural Change* (Oxford: Basil Blackwell, 1989).

20. S. Lash, *Sociology of Postmodernism* (London: Routledge, 1990).

21. R. Dale, *The State and Education Policy* (Milton Keynes, UK: Open University, 1989).

22. M. Weiss, "New Guiding Principles in Education Policy: The Case of Germany," *Journal of Education Policy* 8.4 (1993): 307–20.

23. A. Green, *Education and State Formation* (London: Macmillan, 1990).

24. Michel Foucault, *Politics/Philosophy/Culture*, ed. L. D. Kritzman (New York: Routledge, 1988).

25. E. Meehan, *Civil Society*, Contribution to an ESRC/RSA seminar series on The State of Britain (Swindon, UK: Economic and Social Research Council, 1995).

26. A. Gamble, *The Free Economy and the Strong State* (London: Macmillan, 1988).

27. See, for example, Robert Arnove, "Neoliberal Education Policies in Latin America" and L. Gordon, "Controlling Education: Agency Theory and the Reformation of New Zealand Schools," *Educational Policy* 9.1 (1995): 55–74.

28. J. McKenzie, "Education as a Private Problem or a Public Issue? The Process of Excluding 'Education' from the 'Public Sphere,'" presented at the International Conference on the Public Sphere, Manchester, 8–10 January 1993.

29. It is interesting in this connection that, in an American book on school choice, K. B. Smith and K. J. Meier (*The Case against School Choice: Politics, Markets and Fools* [Armonk, N.Y.: M. E. Sharpe, 1995]) present data that suggest that neither local democratic control nor strong trade unions are necessarily associated with those large impersonal bureaucracies that are seen by neo-institutional theorists as the symbol of the failure of conventional mass education systems.

30. For example, R. Bowe, S. J. Ball, and A. Gold, *Reforming Education and Changing Schools* (London: Routledge, 1992); A. Bullock and H. Thomas, *The Impact of Local Management of Schools* (Birmingham: University of Birmingham, 1994); and R. Levacic, *The Local Management of Schools: Analysis and Practice* (Buckingham: Open University Press, 1995).

31. J. Sinclair, M. Ironside, and R. Seifert, "Classroom Struggle? Market Oriented Education Reforms and Their Impact on Teachers' Professional Autonomy, Labour Intensification and Resistance," presented to the International Labour Process Conference, 1 April 1993.

32. J. Blackmore, "Breaking out from a Masculinist Politics of Education," in *Gender and Changing Education Management*, ed. B. Limerick and B. Lingard (Rydalmere, Australia: Hodder Education, 1995), p. 45.

33. S. Urahn and D. Stewart, *Minnesota Charter Schools: A Research Report* (St. Paul, Minn.: Research Department, Minnesota House of Representatives, 1994).

34. L. Gordon, "'Rich' and 'Poor' Schools in Aotearoa," *New Zealand Journal of Educational Studies* 29.2 (1994): 113–25.

35. D. A. Lewis and K. Nakagawa, *Race and Educational Reform in the American Metropolis: A Study of School Decentralization* (Albany: State University of New York Press, 1995), p. 172.

36. See, for instance, L. Angus, "The Sociology of School Effectiveness," *British Journal of Sociology of Education* 14.3 (1993): 333–45 and R. Hatcher, "The Limitations of the New Social Democratic Agenda: Class, Equality, Agency," in *Education after the Conservatives*, ed. R. Hatcher and K. Jones (Stoke-on-Trent, UK: Trentham Books, 1996).

37. G. Whitty, *Sociology and School Knowledge: Curriculum Theory, Research and Politics* (London: Methuen, 1985).

38. K. Mannheim, *Freedom, Power and Democratic Planning* (London: Routledge and Kegan Paul, 1951).

39. Geoff Whitty, "Left Policy and Practice and the Sociology of Education," in *Schools, Teachers and Teaching*, ed. L. Barton and S. Walker (Lewes, UK: Falmer Press, 1982).

40. Anthony Giddens, *Beyond Left and Right: The Future of Radical Politics* (Cambridge: Polity Press, 1994).

41. D. Reynolds, P. Sammons, L. Stoll, M. Barber, and J. Hillman, "School Effectiveness and School Improvement in the United Kingdom," *School Effectiveness and School Improvement* 7.2 (1996): 133–58.

42. See G. Grace, ed., *Education and the City*, and G. Grace, "Welfare Labourism versus the New Right," *International Studies in the Sociology of Education* 1.1 (1991): 25–42.

43. G. Grace, *Education and the City*, p. xii.

44. B. Fay, *Social Theory and Political Practice* (London: Allen and Unwin, 1975).

45. J. Ladwig, "For Whom This Reform? Outlining Educational Policy as a Social Field," *British Journal of Sociology of Education* 15.3 (1994): 341–63.

46. I am grateful to Suart Hall for this observation.

47. Geoff Whitty, *Sociology and School Knowledge*, p. 82.

48. See, for example, Geoff Whitty, "Creating Quasi-Markets in Education: A Review of Recent Research on Parental Choice and School Autonomy in Three Countries," *Review of Research in Education* 22 (1997): 3–47, and Whitty et al., *Devolution and Choice in Education*.

49. Michel Foucault, *Politics/Philosophy/Culture*.

50. M. Young and G. Whitty, eds., *Society, State and Schooling* (Lewes, UK: Falmer Press, 1977).

51. Michael W. Apple, *Cultural Politics and Education*, p. 52.

52. J. R. Henig, *Rethinking School Choice: Limits of the Market Metaphor* (Princeton: Princeton University Press, 1994), p. 222.

53. B. Simon, *The State and Educational Change* (London: Lawrence and Wishart, 1994), p. 12.

54. Chantal Mouffe, ed., *Dimensions of Radical Democracy: Pluralism, Citizenship, Democracy* (London: Verso, 1992).

55. N. Z. Keith, "A Critical Perspective on Teacher Participation in Urban Schools," *Educational Administration Quarterly* 32.1 (1996): 70.

56. K. Sullivan, "The Impact of Education Reform on Teachers' Professional Ideologies," *New Zealand Journal of Educational Studies* 29.1 (1994): 3–20.

57. Michael W. Apple and Anita Oliver, "Becoming Right: Education and the Formation of Conservative Movements," in *Cultural Politics and Education*, ed. Michael W. Apple (Buckingham: Open University Press, 1996).

58. J. Knight, L. Bartlett, and E. McWilliam, eds., *Unfinished Business: Reshaping the Teacher Education Industry for the 1990s* (Rockhampton, Australia: University of Central Queensland, 1993).

59. J. Muller and N. Cloete, "Out of Eden: Modernity, Post-Apartheid and Intellectuals," *Theory, Culture and Society* 10 (1993): 155–72.

60. K. Mannheim and W. A. C. Stewart, *An Introduction to the Sociology of Education* (London: Routledge and Kegan Paul, 1962), p. 159.

61. M. Hammersley, "Post Mortem or Post Modern? Some Reflections on British Sociology of Education," *British Journal of Educational Studies* 44.4 (1996): 394–406.

# PART II

# Empirical Perspectives on Urban Education

CHAPTER 4

# Where Neoliberal Ideology Meets Social Context: A Comparative Analysis of U.S. Charter Schools and England's Grant-Maintained Schools

## Amy Stuart Wells

Since the early 1990s, various researchers and commentators have compared educational reforms taking place in the United States and Britain, pointing out cross-Atlantic similarities and differences.[1] Two reforms in particular—charter schools in the United States and grant-maintained schools (or GM schools) in England—have been compared, and much has been made of the impact that the British grant-maintained schools policy had on the early thinking of U.S. reformers interested in starting charter schools.[2]

At first blush, there are many parallels between the two types of schools: grant-maintained schools operate with greater autonomy than their Local Education Authority (LEA) while still receiving public funds via direct grants from the central government. They were instituted by the Education Reform Act of 1988 as part of the Thatcher government's effort to weaken the role of the LEAs by providing greater opportunity for schools to operate free of LEA oversight and thus, in theory, to become more directly responsive to the needs of parents and to increase diversity of provisions of schools. Conservatives believed that such a policy would infuse free-market competition into an otherwise complacent educational system.[3] By 1997 when the Labour Party came to power and began to curtail the expansion of the policy, there were 1,188 GM schools.

Charter school policies in the United States were also developed to provide publicly funded schools with greater autonomy from local and state educational bureaucracies, thus infusing choice and competition into the public system. The first charter school law was passed in 1991 in Minnesota, and since then, thirty-two additional states have passed charter school legislation. As of fall 1998, an estimated 1,100 charter schools were operating and an additional 160 were approved to open.

This chapter looks more closely at the relationship between charter and GM schools policies[4] and argues that there are differences between the two that relate to distinctions in the social and political contexts of the two countries. Furthermore, I argue that these distinctions should not be overlooked because they help to illustrate how the neoliberal ideology of market-based reforms that has driven educational policymaking across the globe over the last decade interacts with and becomes reinterpreted by national and local contexts that have their own histories and cultures.

According to Whitty, Power, and Halpin: "Educational reform is being conducted within contexts with different histories, different constitutional and administrative arrangements and different political complexions. . . . Within the range of political rationales, it is the neoliberal alternative which dominates, as does a particular emphasis on market-type mechanisms."[5]

Through such comparative work, we can better understand the true hegemonic power of neoliberal ideology and thus the possibility of hope for an alternative vision of educational reform.

## DEVOLUTION AND COMPETITION: THE SHARED POLITICAL PHILOSOPHY OF GRANT-MAINTAINED AND CHARTER SCHOOLS

Neoliberals advocate privatization of public institutions and services and increasing reliance on market forces, volunteerism, and individual demands to achieve social ends. The roots of this movement lie in classical political and economic liberalism in the eighteenth- and nineteenth-century laissez-faire sense, which "sees society as nothing more than a collection of atomistic individuals whose rational self-interested choices lead to optimal social efficiency."[6]

The rise of both the grant-maintained and charter school policies is due in large part to the political appeal of these neoliberal or free-market economic arguments to dismantle the welfare state, break up the public education monopoly, technically "free" schools from government bureaucracies and force them to compete for clients and thus state funds in the educational marketplace. This educational market theory, or the economic metaphor for school improvement has, for the last fifteen years, been the dominant ideology in both the United States and the United Kingdom and has fueled reforms that emphasize both devolution and competition.

Devolution, in theory, allows for placing more power and decision-making authority in the hands of parents and educators at the school sites; competition means breaking up the public school "monopoly" and forcing individual schools to compete with each other for pupils, public funds, and survival.[7]

Within this neoliberal framework, a competitive market system of education will maximize efficiency while assuring individual choice and freedom.[8] Thus, critics of neoliberalism and its privatization efforts note that it provides an ideological shift in which democracy is framed in terms of individualism, and education is framed in terms of consumerism. According to Kenway:

> markets require a shift in focus from the collective and the community to the individual, from public service to private service, and from other people to the self. Clearly, in promoting the marketization of education, policy makers seek to promote and tap into a cult of educational selfishness in the national interest. Educational democracy is redefined as consumer democracy in the educational supermarket.[9]

In a postmodern age in which global markets transcend and often dominate political nation states, the substitution of market forces for government-run services becomes a "natural" evolution. And thus, the educational system is increasingly reified, as social relationships between educators and families become material objects in the sphere of market exchange. Furthermore, the increasing reliance on market forces in providing educational services naturally lessens the impact of public policy in redistributing resources, such as educational opportunity, to those who most need it. According to Handler, "Privatization shifts power to those who can more readily exercise power in the market."[10]

Both charter schools and grant-maintained schools, with their autonomy from their local education authorities and state governments and their need to attract clients in order to stay in "business" fit this neoliberal paradigm, although, both also embody other reform ideologies and histories.

Members of the Thatcher and Major Conservative governments argued that competition between grant-maintained schools would not only lead to greater parental choice of schools, but also that the autonomy of these GM schools from their LEAs would enable them to be more directly responsive to parents' demands. This effort to simultaneously extend parental choice and foster a direct relationship between education's providers and consumers, it was argued, "will encourage healthy competition between schools in those LEAs directly affected and, as a result, lead to a gradual improvement in 'standards' throughout the educational system."[11]

Similarly, in the United States, charter schools have been seen as a new brand of specialized choice schools, designed to devolve educational governance by "freeing" schools of bureaucratic constraints and forcing schools to compete for parents and students in a more deregulated educational marketplace for their own survival.[12]

For instance, in a set of interviews conducted with policymakers in six states, my colleagues and I learned that neoliberal policymakers often connected charter schools philosophically to tuition voucher proposals, which would offer public money to students attending private schools. According to a gubernatorial aide in one state, charter schools and the voucher proposal together "link the continuing existence of a school to its ability to attract students and enroll students."[13]

Despite these common neoliberal political roots, both grant-maintained and charter schools were shaped by other political forces, including neoconservatives who sought more centralized control over curriculum, particularly in England, and so-called progressives and even radical liberals in the United States who have sought greater community control over schools for decades. Thus, in both countries, the simple theory of neoliberalism is redefined, rewritten, and resisted within these more complicated contexts. Still, neoliberalism's appeal lies in its call for individualism and consumerism—two prominent themes in both British and American society. These popular themes have allowed neoliberalism to define complex social issues in highly simplistic terms. And according to Apple: "One of the most crucial aspects of politics is the struggle to define social reality and interpret people's inchoate aspirations and needs."[14]

## NEOCONSERVATIVES AND ENGLAND'S NATIONAL CURRICULUM

From 1979 and 1997, when the Conservative Government was in power in Great Britain, the national agenda was dominated by the programs of the political "New Right," which incorporates two main political strands: neoliberalism, described above as the call to roll back the state and infuse market forces, and neoconservativism, or an emphasis on traditional and often nationalist and religious moral values. The neoconservative wing of the New Right represents a coalition of interests—

namely the religious right, fractions of disgruntled working- and middle-class whites, and cultural elitists—that see the salvation of Western society from its current decline embedded in "ideal forms of institutions" such as the patriarchal family and religion.[15]

The neoconservative/neoliberal strands within the politics of the New Right have led to what is referred to as "free market" and "strong state"—the seemingly contradictory efforts by the state to be rolled back and rolled forward simultaneously. The theory is guided by the notion that reforms should be non-interventionist and decentralized in some areas and highly decentralized in others.[16]

The free-market, strong state approach to educational governance is best portrayed in the Thatcher government's establishment of a highly centralized national curriculum and national assessment for England and Wales along with decentralization and deregulation via open enrollment plans, Local Management Schools (LMS), and grant-maintained schools. The central political argument of the New Right reform agenda as applied to education is that high-stakes competition within a system of centralized standards helps assure accountability because parents will compare schools based on their ability to teach students the national curriculum and therefore prepare them for national exams. The testing program is overseen by the National Schools Examinations and Assessment Council (SEAC) charged with devising and administering tests to all students age 7, 11, and 14.[17] These test scores are then published in the popular press.

At the same time, schools, especially the grant-maintained schools, are assumed to be "free" to figure out the best, most efficient way for them to deliver this curriculum and thus compete with other schools.

The government formed the National Curriculum Council (NCC) to oversee the design and implementation of the National Curriculum, which, not surprisingly, reflected traditional conservative values with much emphasis on traditional academic subjects and content.[18] As Hughes explains, while the New Right political groups were divided over the degree to which they thought a national curriculum was necessary, those who advocated such a curriculum saw it as "means of maintaining traditional standards and values."[19]

Another justification for the National Curriculum was that it would reduce variation between schools and thus between students' curricular experiences. This is an "equity argument" for centralized standards that is often heard in the United States as well.

Several researchers studying the impact of England's grant-maintained schools have concluded that the National Curriculum has interacted with neoliberal market ideology of choice and competition in some unpredictable ways. For instance, Halpin, Power, and Fitz[20] found that in part due to the National Curriculum, that far from "breaking the mold," grant-maintained schools (or opted-out schools as they are also called) seem to celebrate past visions of educational practice. This finding, they note, implies a trend toward "opting into the past." They argue that if GM schools, with their extra autonomy and resources, are unable to generate innovative practices, we need to consider from where alternative visions of state schools can be generated.

Similarly, Walford found that often parents and students see no difference between grant-maintained and other schools, except for the better facilities and attention to symbols of academic elitism.

> Indeed, one of the seeming paradoxes of government policy [GM schools] is that, although it claims to wish to increase diversity of provisions, its other policies act to greatly constrain the content of teaching that schools can offer. The imposition of the National Curriculum and regular inspection of all schools by the Office for Standards in Education (Ofsted) has ensured a greater uniformity in curriculum content and methods of teaching than even existed before.[21]

In fact, Whitty and Power write that rather than being academically innovative, some GM schools reverted to being overtly academically selective and only those schools that had clearly failed on traditional academic criteria in the past are likely to risk deviating significantly from the dominant definition of excellence in their curriculum offerings.[22]

Stearns argues that the standardization of the National Curriculum in England had not spurred the creation of academically superior schools overall, rather it led to a "pecking order" of schools, in which the least popular are the least able to improve and compete.[23]

Thus, the neoconservative push for a traditional national curriculum in England interacted with the neoliberal push to create a quasi-market of autonomous and competitive schools in a way that exacerbated the existing inequalities in the system as opposed to spurring all schools to improve.

## NEOCONSERVATIVES AND STANDARDS-BASED REFORM IN THE UNITED STATES

In the United States, the "New Right" political movement has slightly different connotations. As Giddens and others have pointed out, the term "New Right" has been used more to describe the socially conservative or religious right in the United States as opposed to a coalition of neoconservative and neoliberal forces. This is due in part to the fact that American conservatives have traditionally been fairly neoliberal or pro–capitalist, anti–welfare state.[24]

Furthermore, the term "neoliberal" has been more problematic, given the popular use of the word "liberal" in U.S. politics to describe supporters of the New Deal policies who subsequently favored the expansion of the welfare state and thus a more pro-active redistributive role of the government.[25] At the same time, many U.S. liberals have also been fairly libertarian when it comes to individual rights and freedoms.

The rise of the New Right in U.S. politics can be traced back to Goldwater, but seems to have coalesced around Reagan's vision of "New Federalism" or the shift of power from the national government to the state and ultimately the local level. The idea was to return greater control to local governments or individual schools and their constituents while getting "big government" out of their lives.[26] To the extent that this was appealing to both the socially conservative or neoconservatives and the pro-capitalist neoliberals, there was a convergence of "the right" in the 1980s and 90s that had seemed perhaps more fractured before.

In a similar vein, Edsall argues that Reagan's political popularity was due in large part to his ability to convince white working-class voters that the federal government's welfare state had gone too far in its efforts to redistribute wealth from "hard-working" taxpayers to the "undeserving" poor and to protect the rights of racial minorities, women and gays.[27] According to Carl, "Neoconservative rhetoric reserves special disdain for the 1960–era social movements, especially the counterculture, feminism, black power, and gay rights, in part because these movements threaten traditional conceptions of family and nation."[28]

Thus, Reagan's symbolic politics of "welfare queens" and useless bureaucrats fanned the flames of a deep resentment toward the federal government and a broader antigovernment rhetoric that is evident today in many political movements—from the call to end affirmative action to the bombing of the Oklahoma City federal building.

Antigovernment neoconservatives resent educational "regulations"—that is, legislation and court orders—that helped create educational bureaucracies at the federal, state, and local district level and thus a centralization of policymaking over the last thirty years. Many of these regulations and government mandates were designed to address the unequal access that certain students—that is, racial minorities, handicapped students, and non-English speakers—had to quality educational programs in more locally controlled schools.[29]

Carl also notes that both the United States and United Kingdom have long histories of marginalized groups—especially racial minorities and women—organizing within the state in order to redress grievances, with the schools being one of the most important sites for this organization. This historical perspective on the redistributive and regulatory role of the federal government is important to understanding the current political backlash against "big government" and the call for more parental choice and control.[30]

Harmer, a neoconservative who favors deregulated tuition voucher plans, argues that too much education funding is wasted on "narrowly focused categorical programs"—that is, Title 1, bilingual education, and special education—controlled by "administrators at the top of the top-heavy system." He adds that "These programs take money that should be spent on the academic basics."[31]

In addition to the antigovernment rhetoric of the New Right in the United States, there are aspects of this agenda that are reminiscent of the "free market-strong state" paradox of the United Kingdom. For instance, according to Jonathan, while the neoconservatives want less state intervention in most areas of their lives, they want the state to be sufficiently strong to maintain property relations and the current unequal distribution of wealth.[32] In education policy, as in the United Kingdom, the neoconservatives have in the past demanded that the state remain strong in the area of "standards" while at the same time getting out of the way of parents who want to choose schools for their children and have more say in how these schools are run and whose values are taught.

Carl argues that under Chubb and Moe's tuition voucher or "scholarship" plan in which students receive funding directly from the state, the authority of the state governments that would distribute and monitor the scholarships would be enhanced at the expense of district autonomy. "Bureaucracy disappears and reappears; New Right bureaucrats replace those officials who, to some extent, represent social groupings that struggled, often successfully, for more egalitarian educational policies."[33]

He adds that "the 'rolling back' of a generic state is not the issue. Rather, the New Right targeted for reorganization structures that had emerged in the New Deal and post–World War II accords . . . as a result, the state is reshaped in ways that eliminate venues where formerly dispossessed groups shared some power."[34]

## BIPARTISAN SYSTEMIC REFORM

Despite the strong connection between the New Right and deregulatory reforms, including but not limited to charter schools, the political landscape of the educational reform movement in the United States is more complicated, with many so-called liberals also supporting both devolution of governance systems and the creation of more centralized academic standards. Thus, the political support for centralized standards and decentralized governance structures for schools (the strong state–free market paradigm) would be bipartisan in nature and not just supported by those who fit politically into the New Right framework.

In the United States, the "free market" and "strong state" approach is described as "systemic reform"—a strategy that was largely popular on both sides of the political isle in the early 1990s. This reform effort included setting national goals, standards, and assessment measures while delegating implementation of reform to the states and their decentralized, autonomous districts and schools. On the state level, complementary systemic reforms were to take place, with state policymakers mandating standards, curriculum frameworks, and new student performance tests while calling for devolution of decision-making, school-based management, and greater parental choice.[35]

Ultimately, this systemic reform approach is embodied in the 1994 federal Goals 2000 legislation sponsored by the Clinton administration. This legislation originated in the Bush administration's policy proposal, called "America 2000." Interestingly, the Clinton administration did not dramatically alter Goals 2000 from its original form as it was drafted by the Bush administration. The main difference between the Bush and Clinton administrations regarding school reform is that President Bush favored taking the concepts of deregulation and competition to the extreme, arguing for privatization and voucher plans, whereas the Clinton administration stops short of such proposals, calling for greater parental choice and deregulation within the public sector—and thus providing federal support for charter schools.

Under this major piece of federal legislation, passed with bipartisan support in 1994 before the Congressional election, schools and districts are held accountable for students' performance by centralized, "world-class standards." Meanwhile, greater authority is decentralized to the local level, allowing educators, parents and students to decide how best to meet the standards. The legislation advocated the creation of charter schools and subsequent legislation supported by the administration provided federal funding for charter schools.

More specifically, Goals 2000 offers states funding to develop state curriculum frameworks and complementary assessment programs that would meet or surpass the rigor of the voluntary national standards in twelve subject-matter areas. Simultaneously, Goals 2000 called for states to grant greater autonomy and flexibility to schools as they implement the state frameworks.[36]

Yet when the federal legislation was first proposed, educators, researchers, and advocates argued that efforts to hold all schools accountable based on standards and student outcomes were being cast onto an uneven playing field in which some schools were less able to provide students with the "opportunities to learn" content reflected on the state tests.[37] The final legislation half-heartedly attempted to address these concerns by expanding the bill to include voluntary opportunity-to-learn standards to assess student access to educational resources and high-quality instruction.[38]

Thus, the concepts of national and state standards in the United States, unlike the National Curriculum in the United Kingdom, have enjoyed bipartisan support. In fact, after 1994, they have been more strongly supported by Democrats than Republicans.

The 1994 elections brought additional equity issues related to decentralization into clearer focus. Republican politicians, once the champions of educational standards, launched a political assault on the national standards movement. Robert Dole, 1996 presidential candidate and Senate majority leader, attacked the proposed history standards, calling them un-American: "The purpose of the national history standards seems not to be to teach our children certain facts about our history, but to denigrate America's story while sanitizing and glorifying other cultures."[39]

Overall, Congressional support for the national standards and systemic reform has dissipated, as is illustrated in the House of Representatives' 1995 legislative proposal to fold Goals 2000 and several other federal programs into one large block grant to the states while eliminating the opportunity-to-learn standards. Meanwhile, conservative groups lobbied Republican members of Congress to end federal involvement in standards setting of any kind.[40]

Conservatives have not, however, abandoned the goal of decentralization and deregulation of the educational system as they desert the standards movement. The same 1995 House proposal would allow states to use federal block grants for school choice programs that involve private schools, deregulated charter schools, and for-profit private management firms to run public schools.[41]

At the state level, the movement toward centralized standards has also encountered political roadblocks, particularly in California, where the implementation of standards-based systemic reform presaged the national movement by nearly a decade. In 1994, state funding was discontinued for the new state testing system, the California Learning Assessment System (CLAS), designed to test students on the content of the state curriculum frameworks. The demise of CLAS began with a political backlash by conservative religious groups over the content and morality of the test. Recent efforts to revise and reinstate CLAS have failed in the California Assembly.[42] Similar political protests have erupted in other states and districts implementing standards-based or outcomes-based reforms designed to hold schools accountable for student learning in an increasingly decentralized educational system.[43]

Still, in the state houses as in Congress, the backlash against standards has not lessened the enthusiasm for massive decentralization of decision-making and deregulation of the education system from government equity-based mandates or the infusion of market forces to foster greater competition between schools.

## THE SOCIAL AND POLITICAL CONTEXTS OF GRANT-MAINTAINED AND CHARTER SCHOOLS

Some of these U.K.-U.S. distinctions are related to major structural and cultural differences in the two countries' political and educational systems. For instance, the highly decentralized U.S. public educational system has nearly 16,000 school districts and the much smaller, more nationalized British system has about 120 Local Education Authorities.

### Centralized and Politicized Reform in England

Education in England and Wales was traditionally seen as a national system, locally administered through these LEAs, although the 1988 Reform Act and the National Curriculum "nationalized" the system to a much greater extent.[44] Public education in the United States, on the other hand, has always been considered a state and local concern. Children's guarantee of a free, public education is found in the state and not the federal constitution, and the federal government in the United States plays a rather minuscule role in funding public education—on average, only 6 percent of the total cost.

This structural and political difference means that in England, reforms of the central government can be mandated and quickly implemented in every educational authority, whereas in the United States, most major reforms are legislated by the state governments. Still, given the history of local control in U.S. education, even sweeping state reform efforts have limited impact on districts and schools.[45]

Related to these structural differences in the United States and England is the more direct political and ideological confrontation between the Conservative and Labour Parties in Britain. Although the Republican and Democratic Parties in the United States also battle—intensely at times—over specific legislation and educational reform efforts, these confrontations take place on various levels of educational policymaking—federal, state, and local—with local levels less clearly linked to specific party agendas.

Also, unlike the United States, where legislative process is generally meted out through a series of political compromises, the parliamentary system in Britain leads to policymaking that is more clearly identified with the party in power. Thus, the movement in Britain toward a more comprehensive secondary education for all children ages 5–16 during the decades following World War II, is clearly identified with the Labour (socialist) government's brief series of reigns in 1945–54, 1964–71, and 1974–79. The strict allocation of students to schools by the LEAs based on geographic location and school size was also part of the Labour Party's agenda, as the party fought against selectivity in the state-supported system and for greater "comprehensivisation," mixed ability groupings, social education, and the removal of inequality and discrimination in education.[46]

The more partisan bent to educational reform in Great Britain appears to have intensified when Thatcher came to power in 1979. Since that time, most of the education legislation passed by the central government is perceived a direct attack on the mostly Labour-controlled LEAs. For instance, the 1980 Education Act, which provided for open enrollment, gave parents the statutory right to request seats for their children in schools outside their designated attendance areas and empowered the Education Secretary to regulate the balance of planning and choice between LEAs and parents. The act also required LEAs to publish brochures describing their schools, including information on curriculum and policies concerning homework, uniforms, and school discipline, as well as exam results.[47]

This 1980 act along with the major, 1988 Education Reform Act are perceived by Labour Party leaders and leftist academics as the Thatcher government's measures to undermine the powers of the LEAs to organize education. In this way, these acts were also seen as conservative attacks on more "egalitarian" reforms that had been the trademark of the Labour Party's educational policy since 1944. The move then toward competition, decentralized, autonomous schools, greater parental choice, and a national curriculum against which individual child's progress can be measured ties in with the Conservative government's effort to increase streaming or tracking and the general thrust toward identifying and highlighting differences—a clear backlash against the prior Labour Party reforms.[48] According to Ball, "The path which the UK has hewn is far more radical in the undiluted application of ideologically driven policy."[49]

*Decentralized and Politicized Reform in the United States*

In the United States, similar attacks have been made on the so-called "educational establishment," which includes the teachers unions, school and district administrators, and anyone else associated with educational bureaucracy. But because of the legislative process in the United States these very groups continue to play an important role in the debates over education policy.

When educational change occurs in the United States, it often seems to take longer and is messier than in England, and specific reforms are often, but not always, less clearly identifiable with one of the main political parties. Charter schools in the United States are a good example of such a reform, because it is perceived by policymakers on both ends of the political spectrum as a compromise between maintaining a more regulated public education system and the annihilation of public schools through privatization schemes and voucher plans.[50] According to Pipho, the growth of the charter movement and more general support of efforts to reform education by using ideas from the consumer marketplace reflects "bipartisanship" in the United States.[51]

In fact, there has been ongoing, if uneven teacher union support for charter schools in the United States since their inception. For instance, in 1988 Budde wrote a report entitled *Education by Charter* in which he envisioned a group of teachers designing instructional programs.[52] Shortly afterward, the late Al Shanker, then-president of the American Federation of Teachers, presented an adaptation of Budde's vision to the National Press Club in Washington. The original discussions of the charter school concept in the United States then was directed by people who were most interested in eliminating regulations that prevent teachers from attempting more innovative practices.

Also, in the United States for the last thirty years liberal progressive and more radical reformers who are anti-authoritarian and anti-establishment, have argued for decentralization of state-run schools, greater parental choice, and nonselective, independent "alternative" schools. In urban areas, where large numbers of low-income students of color have been subjected to impoverished and politically bankrupt schools and poorly trained educators, activists have fought for greater community control of their schools.[53]

In more recent years, these advocates for urban school children have often sided with more economically conservative and libertarian reformers fighting for tuition voucher programs within a selective and highly competitive setting.[54] This "strange bedfellows" situation in the U.S. school choice debates has made party-specific politics on this issue more tentative, although conservative Republicans are more likely to favor deregulation and competitive private school choice whereas liberal Democrats generally are more supportive of public school choice plans.

Still, charter legislation in the United States is state legislation, not federal, which means that partisan politics and power struggles between state and local policymakers can play out in fifty different ways, depending on the political makeup of the statehouses and communities. In some states, such as Arizona, charter school reform, as most reform in that state, has been part of the conservative agenda. In other states, including Hawaii and Georgia, they are seen as more closely tied to the Democratic Party's vision of systemic reform.

The contrast between the United States and United Kingdom along these structural, political, and historical lines contributes significantly to differences between the grant-maintained schools in England and charter schools in the United States. These distinctions include the different roles that English LEAs versus U.S. local school districts play, the curricular focus of charters and GM schools and the amount of funding available for charter and GM schools.

Still, I argue that the power of an overarching neoliberal ideology is pushing charter school reform in the United States toward a more right-wing agenda, while in Britain, the election of the Labour Party in 1997 is pushing grant-maintained schools slightly in the opposite direction.

## THE ROLE OF THE LEAs AND LOCAL SCHOOL DISTRICTS

Efforts on the part of the Conservative government in Britain to strip the LEAs of political power and to eliminate them as organizing bodies for schools is evident in the design of the grant-maintained policy in both the 1988 and 1993 Education Reform Acts. Under the guidelines of the 1988 act, schools seeking grant-maintained status were to apply directly to the national Secretary of Education and if successful they received their funding from the central government and not through the LEAs.[55] Grant-maintained schools became accountable to the Department for Education, as the policy was designed to help these schools circumvent the bureaucracy of the LEAs.[56]

Also, under the original act, all grant-maintained schools were existing LEA schools that converted or opted out into GM status. (The 1993 act allowed groups of parents of independent sponsors to create GM schools.) Existing LEA schools that opted out were able to determine their own admissions policies, although they were required to retain LEA designated character in terms of size, selection criteria, religious basis, and age-range. Grant-maintained schools could, however, after a period of five years, apply to the central government to change their character.[57] This option to change the character of a grant-maintained school inhibited the LEAs' efforts to equalize access for all students who live within their regions and to reduce the level of "creaming" that some schools are able to accomplish.

Furthermore, because GM schools applied directly to the central government, schools facing closure or change of character by their LEA opted out as a way to overrule the local authorities and avoid closure. In fact, more than half of the comprehensive schools and one fourth of the grammar schools that achieved GM status in the first years of implementation had been identified for closure or redesignation by their LEAs.[58] When schools identified for closure or consolidation opted out or threatened to, the LEAs were unable to reorganize and try to balance enrollment at a time of falling secondary numbers and per pupil funding.[59]

In the United States, while charter school legislation is considered part of an overall agenda to decentralize and free schools from bureaucratic constraints, it is not usually perceived to be as much of a directed political attack on local school districts as the English grant-maintained reform. As mentioned earlier, in many states there has been bipartisan support for charter school legislation, and generally, state policymakers from both parties praise charter school reform as a way to help schools escape the burdensome regulations of both the state and local government.

This varies obviously from one state to the next, and with thirty-three different state charter school laws it is difficult to generalize. However, in most states, charters can be granted through the local school districts as well as other entities, such as the state board of education or a university. In California, for instance, the state with the second highest number of charter schools (156), virtually all charters are granted by local school districts. Thus, unlike England's grant-maintained schools that bypass the LEAs, many of the schools in the United States that apply for charter status do so through their local school districts.

By naming school districts as the sponsor or one of the sponsoring organizations for charter schools, state policymakers in the United States have allowed local school boards to maintain a degree of control over which schools are able to "opt out" of the public system and which are required to remain. Still, the more conservative and neoliberal supporters of charter schools in the United States favor charter school laws that allow for multiple charter granting agencies—either instead of or in addition to local school districts.[60]

Furthermore, when charters are granted through local school districts to existing public schools that apply to "convert" into charters, some of these schools remain highly dependent on their districts and do not break away to become fiscally independent. In fact, a study of charter schools in California found that only 27 percent of the charter schools in the state had financial autonomy—or full control over staff salaries and benefits and other budgetary expenses. About 85 percent of "start-up" charter schools were more financially autonomous, while only 15 percent of the "converted" charter schools—or those converted from public schools—were fiscally autonomous. About half of the 156 charter schools in the state are start-ups and half are conversion schools.[61]

Still, despite the relatively strong position that U.S. school boards find themselves in with regard to charter school legislation, they do in some ways feel threatened by these new laws and the burden placed upon them when they are caught between the demands of the new, "autonomous" charter schools for more flexibility and freedom and the demands of the state department of education that still holds the district accountable to the state education code. According to a school board member in Los Angeles, the state legislation sends mixed messages telling the school districts to let the charters go, but at the same time saying that the school's district is going to be held liable and responsible for how well they do.

> [The state says] let the charter schools operate without the restrictions of the state education code, without the restrictions of all the directives that come from the state department of education, but you [the district] are going to be responsible for them operating out of compliance with what the state code says ought to be standard for public schools.

In this way, the closer relationship between charter schools and their local school districts is more of a bane than a blessing. While the school districts maintain greater control over the charter proposal and granting process they also inherit the ambiguity of state legislation designed to deregulate individual schools while leaving their districts responsible *for* these schools and *to* their state education departments.

## THE CURRICULAR FOCUS OF
## CHARTERS AND GM SCHOOLS

The distinctions between England's grant-maintained and U.S. charter schools become even more clear in an examination of the stated reasons why schools want to opt out—for the flexibility to change curriculum and pedagogy or simply for flexibility to do as they please, whatever that may be. English schools, for instance, that decide to opt out of LEA control are not required to provide the Education Secretary with any reason for wanting to do so other than the desire to gain greater independence. GM schools are not required, therefore, to present a plan for teaching methods to be used, techniques to improve education at the schools or anything to do with curriculum.[62]

Obviously, the mandated National Curriculum greatly limits the degrees of freedom that grant-maintained schools have in devising innovative curricula and instruction. Grant-maintained schools, like all schools in England, are obligated to teach to the National Curriculum.[63] If the National Curriculum is not enough to dissuade schools from becoming overly innovative in the educational approach, the national testing and evaluation program, designed to assess student progress in learning the required curriculum, will.

Thus, in a competitive educational marketplace of deregulated schools fighting for survival, it is not in most schools' best interest to stray too far from the mandated curriculum. As I mentioned above, the ability to change their instructional program does not appear to be the central motivating factor behind opting out for the grant-maintained schools. Other factors, including becoming more selective, do seem to be important. There is evidence that schools are opting out to maintain the status quo—avoid closure or to fend off LEA efforts to change their current character—rather than to reform. This means that rather than extending parental choice by creating different schools, a grant-maintained school may simply preserve an existing choice.[64]

In the United States the many reasons why schools opt out and become charter schools do sometimes include the desire to create new educational programs. In fact, the charter proposal process in most states requires schools to spell out desired outcomes for students and the instructional strategies that will help the schools achieve those goals. Many states also ask charter school applicants to include a detailed plan including teaching and learning approaches as a key aspect of the charter proposal.[65]

Because the United States has no mandatory national curriculum, and few states have yet to implement state standards and matching assessment systems, individual schools have far more flexibility in what they teach and how it is taught. In fact, most of the states' charter school legislation explicitly states that the charter schools' central purpose should be to improve student learning outcomes through their focus on adopting innovative or different teaching methods.[66]

Some charter schools are innovative, blurring the institutional lines between schools and work or higher education. In Minnesota, a teamsters' local is working with a new vocational school and a utility company is helping to finance a year-round school requiring students to do community work. In California, about 15 percent of the charter schools in the state are home-schooling programs that provide support and guidance to parents who want to educate their children at home.

While all of this focus on curriculum and instruction sounds good in theory, the reality is that some charter schools are interested in serious reform while others are interested in continuing what they have been doing within the existing system and obtaining a charter for other reasons—for example, to establish stricter discipline standards, to maintain greater control over who gets in and who stays in the school, or to use their resources more flexibly. Other schools we studied were established to serve students of a particular racial/ethnic group and the curriculum was designed to reflect the history and culture of that group.[67]

It appears that charter schools in the United States have more flexibility to use their autonomy in different ways. And in states such as California that have not had a state assessment in place during the implementation of charter school reform, efforts to hold charter schools accountable to a single set of student outcomes have been futile.[68]

Thus, the range of possibilities of what charter schools can accomplish with their devolved status appears to be greater than what grant-maintained schools are able to do.

## THE AMOUNT OF FUNDING AVAILABLE FOR CHARTER AND GM SCHOOLS

Another striking difference between England's grant-maintained schools and U.S. charter schools is the substantial funding available to GM schools in Britain and the absence of public funds available for the U.S. charter schools. In part because of the partisan battles between the Conservative central government and the Labour-dominated LEAs for control of English education, grant-maintained schools are offered considerable financial inducement by the central government to take on that status. Former Prime Minister John Major stated that his government has made no secret of the fact that GM schools get preferential treatment in allocating grants for capital expenditure. The government clearly looks favorably on GM schools.[69]

Although the money available for GM schools in England has been cut back with the election of the Labour Government in 1997, at the peak of the reform, GM schools were eligible for two seed grants—known as transitional grants and special purpose grants—that could be used during the transitional period made immediately after grant approval.

Also, nonfinancial start up resources in the form of planning time for anywhere from a year to two months and outside consultation, mainly information, guidance, and advice to schools from the time of their approval for GM status were available to schools through the Grant-maintained Schools' Centre (GMSC). The center was established by the government and was supported during the 1993–94 school year by more than $1.35 million. GMSC ran professional development workshops and on topics such as adapting and setting up administrative and financial systems at the school site. It also promoted and encouraged grant-maintained schools by disseminating information about the opting-out process and, in an ongoing capacity, negotiating terms for various services and products on behalf of the schools. The center, in essence, took over many of the LEA responsibilities.[70]

In addition to the seed money available, all GM schools receive an annual allocation for capital structural repairs from the Department for Education. During the 1992–93 school year, each school received $18,000 plus an additional $36 per student. For major capital improvement programs, GM schools may bid for grants to finance the purchase of capital equipment and building work. For 1993–94, nearly $140 million was allocated for GM schools' capital development projects.[71]

In sharp contrast to all of funds available to GM schools in England, charter schools in the United States are generally poor. In California as well as most other states, charter schools are clearly "unfunded mandates"—educational decentralization without resources. While charter schools in California are technically funded on a per-pupil basis according to their school districts' averages, all of their funding is funneled through their local school districts. Thus, the exact amount that each school receives varies from one district to the next and even from one charter school to the next within a single district. Furthermore, new, start-up schools that are not already housed in a district-owned building must pay their rent out of their per-pupil operating budget. This means these schools are in reality receiving less public funding per pupil than the regular public schools.[72]

According to the former state senator who authored the California charter school legislation, "My bias is that if there is a will there is a way. I'm sounding very cliché [but] I really don't think resources is the primary obstacle to charters being established."

The education advisor to the governor was even more blunt: "If teachers and parents have the desire and the determination, they can do it without the special funds."

While there have been federal funds available—up to $100 million for 1999—these are generally dispersed through each state department of education and thus the size of the grants varies widely.

Yet perhaps the greatest danger of an unfunded state mandate to decentralize education is that some local school communities are in a better position to take advantage of them than others because they can muster the resources to fund unfunded mandates themselves, leading to inequities in who can and cannot participate. In this way, charter school legislation has led to increased privatization of public education as charter schools in more affluent communities scramble to raise private funds and write grant proposals to pay for their new programs.[73] This is how the highly educated, upper-middle-class leader of the parent council at one cluster of charter schools explained her group's fundraising efforts: "There is only one grant I've written so far that is going through the district and the others, we're going either through the booster clubs or the [parent council], which is becoming more and more just the financial arm of the charter schools."

The California charter school law allows for schools to raise private funds to pay for their public school programs. In fact, in the legislation, after the section that explicitly forbids private schools from applying for charters, the law clearly states: "This part shall not be construed to prohibit any private person or organization from providing funding or other assistance to the establishment or operation of a charter school."

Thus, while charter schools are completely free of state and district regulations related to instruction, they are also free of district regulations regarding private fundraising for public schools. With no additional government funding, each charter school is left to its own devices to find money to support new and innovative programs. The notion that some schools may be in a better position to do that than others—that is, some schools can draw upon the expertise of parents who are lawyers or the networks of parents who are executives in large corporations— did not seem to be of any great concern to most policymakers in Sacramento. But at the local level, advocacy groups and educators worry about the long-term implications of entrepreneurial charter schools in wealthy communities that are able to support exceptional programs through private funds while their counterparts in less affluent neighborhoods are left to survive on dwindling public resources.

## THE NEOLIBERAL HEGEMONY: SIMILARITIES BETWEEN THE UNITED KINGDOM AND UNITED STATES

According to Johnson, it is important to see the 1988 Education Reform Act in England as the product of many frustrations within the Conservative Party—"Aspirations were modified by external opposition and internal disagreement and by the need to take account of the past. The Act must not be read as a New Right blueprint or ideal. It is 'vouchers' which occupy this space in most of the writing. The Act is a more interesting and formidable thing: a transformative mechanism, a plan for transition in the long run."[74]

Similarly in the U.S. charter school–voucher plan connections are illustrated quite clearly in Mintron's study of the role of policy entrepreneurs in the development of charter school legislation. He reports that in Michigan, a coalition of voucher proponents strongly backs the charter school legislation as an "incremental" and "non threatening" way of introducing school choice–type innovations to the general public in hopes of building broader support for a constitutional amendment to allow vouchers. Thus, in Michigan, the charter school idea was seen as a useful measure for laying the groundwork for vouchers.[75]

As I mentioned above, the interviews that I conducted with colleagues reveal that state policy makers often view charter laws as laying the groundwork for voucher plans.[76] For instance, in Arizona, the governor's advisor for education noted that charter schools are helping people feel more comfortable with various options—"that it is okay to go to a school that's not part of the public system. [Charter schools] will begin to break down this attitude we have that we have to protect the public system at all costs or else our whole way of life is going to be crumbled."

An Arizona senator who likened public schools to prisons noted that charter schools offer the promise that new types of schools will evolve within an increasingly competitive environment. "As they [charter schools] move out into the future, I think what I'd see evolving is sort of a hybrid school that is supported both by the state and also might be able to . . . from an economist's standpoint, be able to, you know, in a sophisticated way, charge tuition."

Conceptually, legislators are linking charter schools and voucher plans, as is evident in the following quote from a California assemblyman: "when the charter school concept came along the Republicans right away said this is good . . . this is not a private school but it is the closest thing you are going to get to a private school and maintain public funding."

Thus, despite these vast differences in the social and political contexts of English grant-maintained and U.S. charter schools, research suggests that similar trends might have developed in both countries, or at least in England and certain states within the United States depending on the specifics of their legislation. For instance, in California, where charter schools are allowed to have admissions criteria and where charter schools are allowed to raise their own private funds, disturbing similarities between England and California can be seen even in this early stage of implementation.

The first similar trend appears to be that in both England and California the opting-out policies tend to have favored those who were politically empowered to begin with. Despite the rhetoric of charter school legislation as an act to empower the disempowered, the fact that no start up funds are available in California means that only those communities that are able to garner private and in-kind resources will survive.[77]

Furthermore, since the Labour government was elected in 1997, the extra funding for GM schools has been eliminated and the status of GM schools has been changed, through the 1998 School Standards and Framework Act, to "foundation schools," which receive grants from the government to operate. To the extent that the former GM schools have become highly dependent on their extra funding, those that have the connections may now turn to private donors to raise the extra funds.

The second emerging cross-Atlantic finding or trend is that greater competition between schools does not appear to benefit the losers of that competition. Despite political rhetoric about how competition will pull the bottom up by subjecting all schools to higher standards and putting them in a situation in which they must fight for their survival, in both England and California, evidence suggests that schools that lose in this competitive environment are not benefiting from this new deregulated system. For instance, in the UCLA study of charter schools, my colleagues and I found that the noncharter public schools were not spurred to action to dramatically improve because of the competition presented by the charter schools. Instead, due to overcrowding in many of the school districts we studied, these schools were not in a position to compete for students, and at the same time, they felt that the charter schools had an unfair advantage in this competition because they were able to establish admissions criteria and require parents and students to sign contracts.[78]

In England, the schools that did not opt out were left behind in LEAs that are less able to meet their needs because of the resources that had been drained off to pay for the more expensive GM schools. Furthermore, any increase in exam results for GM schools appeared to be the result of their increased selectivity rather than their success in improving student outcomes.[79]

And finally, evidence from both sides of the Atlantic suggests that GM and charter schools do increase choices for parents and students, but more importantly, they allow these schools to be more selective and thus to have more choices in terms of who they serve.[80]

These similarities between former GM schools and charter schools suggest that these reforms, both of which were inspired at least in part by neoliberal ideology, may be more successful in pushing the educational system toward privitization and increased stratification than they are at pushing the entire educational system toward "excellence."

## CONCLUSIONS

Although the neoliberal economic metaphor for educational improvement—that is, the notion that deregulation and competition will force positive reforms to take place—sounds powerful and convincing, there is virtually no empirical evidence to support its assertions in the real educational world. Emerging trends in the data being collected on both grant-maintained schools in England and on charter schools in the United States do not support the economic metaphor. Rather, in these two very different countries with their dissimilar political and social contexts, some of the same disturbing trends are emerging from reform efforts based on the idea that competition and deregulation will improve the educational experiences of all students.

Given this preliminary evidence, two things should occur: researchers should continue to study the impact of legislation predicated on this neoliberal ideology, with a particular focus on the three issues mentioned above. And second, policymakers and the general public need to think more carefully and critically about the usefulness of economic theory as a guiding principal to improving a fundamentally socialistic educational system in the United States and Britain.

As Whitty and Power point out, despite the negative impact of neoliberal educational policy, the left has done little yet to develop a concept of public education that looks significantly different. They write, "Even if the social democratic era looks better in retrospect, and in comparison with current policies, than it did at the time, that does not remove the need to rethink what might be progressive policies for the next century."[81]

## NOTES

1. Liz Bondi, "Choice and Diversity in School Education: Comparing Developments in the United Kingdom and USA," *Comparative Education* 27.2 (1991): 125–34; Tony Edwards and Geoff Whitty, "Parental Choice and Educational Reform in Britain and the United States," *British Journal of Educational Reform* 40.2 (May 1992): 101–17; and David Halpin and Barry Troyna, "Lessons in School Reform from Great Britain? The Politics of Education Policy Borrowing," paper presented at the annual meeting of the American Educational Research Association, New Orleans, La. (1994).

2. Priscilla Wohlstetter and Leslie Anderson, "What Can U.S. Charter Schools Learn from England's Grant-Maintained Schools?," *Phi Delta Kappan* 75.6 (February 1994): 486–91; Geoff Whitty, "Creating Quasi-Markets in Education: A Review of Recent Research on Parental Choice and School Autonomy in Three Countries," *Review of Research in Education* 22 (1997): 3–47; and Amy Stuart Wells, Cynthia Grutzik, Sibyll Carnochan, Julie Slayton, and Ash Vasudeva, "Underlying Policy Assumptions of Charter School Reform: The Multiple Meanings of a Movement," *Teachers College Record* 100.3 (Spring 1999): 513–35.

3. David Halpin, John Fitz, and Sally Power, "Local Education Authorities and the Grant-Maintained Schools Policy," *Educational Management and Administration* 19.4 (1991): 233–42.

4. This article will focus primarily on GM schools in England only because these are the schools most carefully studied by researchers. While Wales also has GM schools, educational reforms in Scotland and Northern Ireland are different and thus outside of the scope of this article.

5. Geoff Whitty, Sally Power, and David Halpin, *Devolution and Choice in Education* (Buckingham, UK: Open University Press, 1998), p. 35.

6. Richard Jonathan, "State Education Service or Prisoner's Dilemma: The 'Hidden Hand' as Source of Education Policy," *British Journal of Educational Studies* 38.2 (May 1990): 116–32, at 117–18.

7. John E. Chubb and Terry M. Moe, *Politics, Markets and America's Schools* (Washington, D.C.: Brookings Institution, 1990); David Hellawell, "Structural Changes in Education in England," *International Journal of Educational Reform* 1.4 (October 1992): 356–65; Whitty, "Creating Quasi-Markets in Education: A Review of Recent Research on Parental Choice and School Autonomy in Three Countries"; and Whitty, Power, and Halpin, *Devolution and Choice in Education*.

8. Anthony Giddens, *Beyond Left and Right: The Future of Radical Politics* (Stanford, Calif.: Stanford University Press, 1994).

9. Jane Kenway with Chris Bigum and Lindsay Fitzclarence, "Marketing Education in the Postmodern Age," *Journal of Education Policy* 8.2: 105–25, at 116.

10. Joel F. Handler, *Down from Bureaucracy: The Ambiguity of Privatization and Empowerment* (Princeton, N.J.: Princeton University Press, 1996), p. 9.

11. David Halpin and John Fitz, "Researching Grant-Maintained Schools," *Journal of Education Policy* 5.2 (1990): 167–80, at 167.

12. Chris Pipho, "Bipartisan Charter Schools," *Phi Delta Kappan* 75.2 (1993): 10–11.

13. Wells, Grutzik, Carnochan, Slayton, and Vasudeva, "Underlying Policy Assumptions of Charter School Reform."

14. Michael W. Apple, *Cultural Politics and Education* (New York: Teachers College Press, 1996), p. 22.

15. Jim Carl, "Parental Choice as National Policy in England and the United States," *Comparative Education Review* 38.3 (1994): 294–322.

16. Hellawell, "Structural Changes in Education in England," and Whitty, Power, and Halpin, *Devolution and Choice in Education*.

17. Hellawell, "Structural Changes in Education in England," p. 363.

18. Ibid.

19. Martin Hughes, "The National Curriculum in England and Wales: A Lesson in Externally Imposed Reform?" *Educational Administration Quarterly* 33.2 (April 1997): 183–97, at 185.

20. David Halpin, Sally Power, and John Fitz, "Opting into the Past? Grant Maintained School and the Reinvention of Tradition," in *Choice and Diversity in School: Perspectives and Prospects*, ed. R. Glatter, P. Woods, and C. Bagley (London: Routledge, 1996).

21. Geoffrey Walford, "Diversity, Choice, and Selection in England and Wales," *Educational Administration Quarterly* 33.2 (April 1997): 158–69, at 166.

22. Geoff Whitty and Sally Power, "Quasi-Markets and Curriculum Control: Making Sense of Recent Education Reform in England and Wales," *Educational Administration Quarterly* 33.2 (April 1997): 219–40, at 227.

23. Kathryn Stearns, *School Reform: Lessons from England* (Princeton, N.J.: The Carnegie Foundation for the Advancement of Teaching, 1996), p. 85.

24. Giddens, *Beyond Left and Right*.

25. Ibid.

26. Jeffrey Henig, *Rethinking School Choice: Limits of the Market Metaphor in Education* (Princeton, N.J.: Princeton University, 1994), p. 84.

27. Thomas B. Edsall (with Mary Edsall), *Chain Reaction: The Impact of Race, Rights, and Taxes on American Politics* (New York: Norton, 1991).

28. Carl, "Parental Choice as National Policy in England and the United States," p. 300.

29. Dan A. Lewis and Kathryn Nakagawa, *Race and Educational Reform in the American Metropolis: A Study of School Decentralization* (Albany: State University of New York Press, 1995); David N. Plank and William L. Boyd, "Antipolitics, Education, and Institutional Choice: The Flight from Democracy," *American Educational Research Journal* 31.2 (Summer 1994): 263–81.

30. Carl, "Parental Choice as National Policy in England and the United States."

31. David Harmer, *School Choice: Why You Need It—How You Get It* (Washington, D.C.: CATO Institute, 1994), p. 44.

32. Jonathan, "State Education Service or Prisoner's Dilemma."

33. Carl, "Parental Choice as National Policy in England and the United States," p. 303.

34. Ibid., p. 305.

35. Jennifer A. O'Day and Marshall S. Smith, "Systemic Reform and Educational Opportunity," in *Designing Coherent Education Policy*, ed. Susan H. Fuhrman (San Francisco: Jossey-Bass, 1993), pp. 250–312.

36. O'Day and Smith, "Systemic Reform and Educational Opportunity."

37. See, for example, Linda Darling-Hammond, *Standards of Practice for Learner-Centered Schools* (New York: National Center for Restructuring Schools and Teaching, Teachers College, Columbia University, 1992). And Jeannie Oakes, "Opportunity to Learn: Can Standards-Based Reform Be Equity-Based Reform?" Paper presented at "Effects of New Standards and Assessment on High Risk Students and Disadvantaged Schools," a Research Forum of New Standards Project (Cambridge: Harvard University, 1993).

38. Anne C. Lewis, "Winds of Change Are Blowing," *Phi Delta Kappan* 75.10 (1994): 740–41. And United States Department of Education. "The Goals 2000: Educate America Act: Making American Education Great Again" (Washington, D.C.: Author, 1994).

39. Mark Pitsch, Dole Decries History Standards for Dwelling on the Negative," *Education Week*, September 13, 1995), p. 1 (from downloaded story).

40. January 11, 1995, pp. 1 and 12. And K. Diegmueller, "Running Out of Steam: Special Report, Struggling for Standards," *Education Week*, April 12, 1995, pp. 4–8.

41. Mark Pitsch, "House Republicans Unveil Bill to Ax E.D., Create Block Grants," *Education Week*, May 31, 1995.

42. Drew Lindsay, "Panel Puts Brakes on Bill to Rebuild California Testing System," *Education Week*, September 13, 1995.

43. Diegmueller, "Running out of Steam."

44. Hughes, "The National Curriculum in England and Wales."

45. David Tyack. "'Restructuring' in Historical Perspective: Tinkering toward Utopia," *Teachers College Record* 92.2 (1990): 170–91.

46. Walford, "Diversity, Choice, and Selection in England and Wales," and Bill Inglis, "The Labour Party's Policy on Primary and Secondary Education 1979–89," *British Journal of Educational Studies* 39.1 (February 1991): 4–16.

47. See Andrew Stillman, "Legislating for Choice," in *The Education Reform Act 1988*, ed. Michael Flude and Merril Hammer (London: The Falmer Press, 1990), pp. 87–106.

48. Hellawell, "Structural Changes in Education in England.," p. 364.

49. Stephen J. Ball, "Education Markets, Choice and Social Class: The Market as a Class Strategy in the UK and USA," *British Journal of Sociology of Education* 14.1 (1993): 3–19, at 8.

50. Wells, Grutzik, Carnochan, Slayton, and Vasudeva, "Underlying Policy Assumptions of Charter School Reform."

51. Pipho, "Bipartisan Charter Schools," p. 102

52. Priscilla Wohlstetter and Lesley Anderson, "What Can U.S. Charter Schools Learn from England's Grant-Maintained Schools?" Paper presented at the Annual Meeting of the American Educational Research Association, San Francisco, 1992.

53. See Lewis and Nakagawa, *Race and Educational Reform in the American Metropolis*; Maurice R. Berube and Marilyn Gittell, *Confrontation at Ocean Hill-Brownsville: The New York School Strikes of 1968* (New York: Frederick A. Praeger, 1969).

54. Amy Stuart Wells, *Time to Choose: America at the Crossroads of School Choice Policy* (New York: Hill and Wang, 1993).

55. Hellawell, "Structural Changes in Education in England."

56. Halpin and Fitz, "Researching Grant-Maintained Schools."

57. Michael Flude and Merril Hammer, *The Education Reform Act, 1988* (London: The Falmer Press, 1990).

58. David Halpin, John Fitz, and Sally Power, "Local Education Authorities and the Grant-Maintained Schools Policy, *Educational Management and Administration* 19.4 (1991): 233–42.

59. Flude and Hammer, *The Education Reform Act, 1988.*

60. Center for Education Reform, www.edreform.com (1998).

61. SRI International, *Evaluation of Charter School Effectiveness* (Menlo Park, Calif.: Author, 1997).

62. Lori Mulholland and Mary Amsler, *The Search for Choice in Public Education: The Emergence of Charter Schools* (Tempe, Ariz.: The Morrison Institute of Public Policy, 1992), p. 14.

63. Wohlstetter and Anderson, "What Can U.S. Charter Schools Learn from England's Grant-Maintained Schools?"

64. Halpin, Power, and Fitz, "Opting into the Past."

65. Mulholland and Amsler, *The Search for Choice in Public Education*, p. 14.

66. Brunno V. Manno, Chester E. Finn, Louane A. Bierlein, and Greg Vanourek, "How Charter Schools are Different: Lessons and Implications from a National Study," *Phi Delta Kappan* (March 1998): 489–98. And Mulholland and Amsler, *The Search for Choice in Public Education*, p. 3.

67. UCLA Charter School Study, *Beyond the Rhetoric of Charter School Reform: A Study of Ten California School Districts* (Los Angeles: Author, 1998).

68. Ibid.

69. Hellawell, "Structural Changes in Education in England."

70. Wohlstetter and Anderson, "What Can U.S. Charter Schools Learn from England's Grant-Maintained Schools?," p. 488.

71. Ibid.

72. UCLA Charter School Study, *Beyond the Rhetoric of Charter School Reform: A Study of Ten California School Districts*.

73. Ibid

74. Richard Johnson, "Thatcherism and English Education: Breaking the Mold or Confirming the Patterns?" *History of Education* 18.2 (1989): 91–121, at 110.

75. Michael Mintron, "Policy Entrepreneurs and the Diffusion of Innovation," *American Journal of Political Science* 41 (1997): 738–70.

76. Wells, Grutzik, Carnochan, Slayton, and Vasudeva, "Underlying Policy Assumptions of Charter School Reform."

77. UCLA Charter School Study, *Beyond the Rhetoric of Charter School Reform: A Study of Ten California School Districts*.

78. Ibid.

79. Bob Doe, "Tory Competition Fails to Raise Standards," *The Times Educational Supplement* (9 January 1998).

80. Sharon Gewirtz, Stephen J. Ball, and Richard Bowe, *Markets, Choice and Equity in Education* (Buckingham, UK: Open University Press, 1995); UCLA Charter School Study, *Beyond the Rhetoric of Charter School Reform: A Study of Ten California School Districts*.

81. Whitty and Power, "Quasi-Markets and Curriculum Control: Making Sense of Recent Education Reform in England and Wales," p. 236.

CHAPTER 5

# Corporations and Classrooms: A Critical Examination of the Business Agenda for Urban School Reform

## Roslyn Arlin Mickelson

The campus of IBM's Palisades, New York Executive Conference Center was the site of the March 1996 Education Summit. Cosponsored by IBM, the National Governors' Association, and the Education Commission of the States, the two-day meeting was a response to IBM Chief Executive Officer Louis V. Gerstner Jr.'s exhortation to governors and business leaders to join ongoing efforts to restructure American public education. The summit highlighted the very public role of business leaders today in setting agendas for school reform and in commanding the attention of state educational decision-makers.

This chapter examines a local manifestation of the corporate role in educational restructuring. It is a case study of one community's experiences with a decade of intense business involvement in school reform. The community is Charlotte, North Carolina where national and local leaders of IBM and other firms participate intimately in the reform process. Using the city and its schools as a strategic case study, this chapter seeks to theorize more fully the corporate role in contemporary school reform. Its conceptual contributions lie in an explication of different kinds of business involvement and empirical illustrations of these. By approaching the corporate role in school reform from this perspective, the work mediates between abstractions of general social processes and microanalyses of conflicts within the educational system.[1]

The chapter provides an integrative analysis of corporate participation in educational policy formation and implementation in two distinct ways. First, it presents a typology of business involvement in school reform and the multiple motivations for these interventions. Next, it applies the typology in a concrete fashion to specific education policy initiatives in Charlotte. Rather than merely describing the reforms and key actors, the study analyzes various events and actions in terms of for whom and in whose interests local schools are being reformed. The case study serves as an example for examining and theorizing the contemporary corporate role in school reform more generally.

The chapter will focus primarily upon two reform initiatives sponsored by IBM, although related activities of other firms will be discussed as well. The first reform is ProjectFirst, a collaboration between IBM and the Charlotte-Mecklenburg Education Foundation (CMEF). ProjectFirst, staffed with Americorps volunteers, was designed to bring technology specialists into the district's nonmagnet middle schools. The second is a planned complex of four technology-rich schools adjacent to the Charlotte IBM facility. Originally called the Education Village, but renamed the Governors' Village following the bitter controversy that will be discussed in this chapter, this project was partially funded by a grant to the school district through IBM's Reinventing Education initiative. The third example describes the involvement of a prominent real estate developer in an educational policy decision that had broad implications for the wider school district. The relationship between corporations, their leaders and the Charlotte-Mecklenburg school system is instructive for understanding the larger ideological, political, and educational policy significance of corporate involvement in the school reform process. By tracing how various policies and reform initiatives were developed and contested, we gain insights into their meaning and theoretical significance, as well as the opportunities and dangers that accompany them.

## BACKGROUND

Since the early 1980s, business representatives across the United States have renewed their focus on public schools. How can we best understand the intimate involvement of firms and their leaders in educational reform? The answer most likely lies in the larger contemporary corporate environment that has been likened to turbulent, white water rapids. There are three critical features of this fierce environment: (1) intense globalization that demands both national and international competitiveness; (2) the growing, changing diversity of the modern workforce; and (3) the technological revolution that sets the stage for an information and communication-driven economy. Unable to control the course of macro economic trends like globalization or the advance of technology, corporate leaders appear to have turned their attention to elements of the broader social environment that may be more susceptible to their influence than the business cycle—for example, the public schools that prepare their domestic workforce. By focusing concern on the public schools, corporate leaders deflect attention from their own contributions to domestic and international productivity problems.

During the 1980s, business leaders' assignment to the flawed public school system of blame for the crisis in international competitiveness gained widespread acceptance among parents, school leaders, and policymakers. As this new definition of the situation facing the United States became standard, corporate actors intensified their involvement in the development and implementation of the solutions to the problems they helped to define. American corporate leaders attributed their reinvigorated involvement to the need to resolve the crisis in the U.S. educational system that, from their perspective, was responsible for the crisis in U.S. productivity and international competitiveness.[2]

The country's educational failings enumerated in *A Nation at Risk* reflected this perspective, as did former Secretary of Education Lauro Cavazos who observed in 1989 that the United States faced three deficits—the budget, trade, and education deficits—and that the first two would only be remedied after the last one was resolved.[3] The Reagan and Bush administrations embraced both market principles and the precept that privatization is the antidote to flawed, inefficient governmental bureaucracies. Encouraged by these administrations, the business critique of public education acquired even greater legitimacy. It also found systematic institutional strength through advocacy organizations like the Business Roundtable, the Conference Board, and chambers of commerce across the nation.[4] Furthermore, business leaders indirectly shaped the course and direction of school reform through their pivotal role in the first National Education Summit in 1989.[5]

In the 1990s, the U.S. economy regained its position as the most productive in the world. That return negated the argument that flawed public schools were responsible for lagging U.S. competitiveness in international markets. So corporate leaders adjusted their construction of the problems with public schools. Now they say that public schools are failing to prepare students for future information age jobs that will require advanced knowledge of technology.

There is perhaps no clearer expression of current corporate influence than the second nationwide education summit held during March 1996, at IBM's Executive Conference Center in Palisades, New York. It highlighted the very public role of business leaders today in setting agendas for school reform and in commanding the attention of state educational decision-makers.[6] Cosponsored by IBM, the National Governors' Association, and the Education Commission of the States, the two-day meeting was a response to IBM Chief Executive Officer Louis V. Gerstner Jr.'s exhortation to governors and business leaders to join ongoing efforts to restructure American public education. On March 26 and 27, 1996, forty-three governors, each joined by a CEO of his or her choice, met at IBM's Palisades conference center. The hosts were IBM's CEO, Louis V. Gerstner Jr. and Governor Tommy Thompson of Wisconsin. The summit was envisioned as a bipartisan effort, so Secretary of Education Richard Riley attended and President Clinton addressed the group on the second day of the conference. In addition to the governors and their honored corporate guests, thirty education experts were invited as resource people.

There are disagreements over the appropriateness, importance, motivation, and results of corporate involvement in school restructuring whether at summits or in school partnerships. However, there is no disagreement that that corporate financial and symbolic capital have stimulated programmatic innovation and technical support for local and national reform efforts. Some analysts and practitioners consider business leadership and involvement to be integral to reforming schools; others see corporate efforts as nothing more than feel-good gestures that do little systematically to reform public education. Other more critical observers contend that corporate philanthropy is a conscious venture into school reforms that will ultimately serve corporate long- and short-term interests more than improve public education. It is indisputable that business leaders have more than just a place at the table where restructuring is planned. Current reform efforts are intimately linked to the widely accepted corporate critique of the schools. Executives representing their corporations or acting as individual citizens are actively involved at local, state, and national levels in agenda-setting, formulation of reform designs, and the implementation of reforms.

Raymond Morrow and Carlos Alberto Torres observe that the key to a theory of educational reproduction lies in a theory of public policy that can analyze educational policy formation in specific empirical terms, thus mediating between abstractions of general social processes and microanalysis of conflicts within the educational system.[7] This chapter seeks to illuminate these general processes with a detailed case study of the corporate agenda for school reform in Charlotte, North Carolina. It introduces a comprehensive typology of corporate involvement in school reform. The typology distinguishes among types of corporate involvement and the multiple motivations that underlie business participation, and identifies the various consequences of that participation.

Using this typology we can examine the activities of corporate actors in Charlotte to see how business involvement and its consequences in Charlotte-Mecklenburg Schools (CMS) are emblematic of wider practices, political struggles, and contested policy processes and outcomes in communities across the nation.

## CORPORATIONS AND SCHOOL REFORM IN CHARLOTTE-MECKLENBURG, NORTH CAROLINA

*Recent History of Reform*

Charlotte, North Carolina, is a rapidly growing sunbelt city known for its landmark *Swann v. Charlotte-Mecklenburg Schools* decision wherein the Supreme Court upheld within-district busing as a remedy for segregated schooling.[8] Scholars and lay observers cite early and widespread business support for peaceful implementation of the plan as a crucial element in the creation of a communitywide consensus that desegregated education was good for the city. For almost twenty years, CMS served as a model for other systems of how to undertake the process of desegregation of public education using busing and other tools. The district remains under court order today, although much of the reform effort during the last decade has altered the manner in which the system desegregates its schools.[9] In the 1996–97 school year, the district had about 93,000 students who attend 130 schools scattered across a countywide district that covers 528 square miles. The student population was 52.5 percent white and 41 percent black. The remaining 6.5 percent of students were from Asian, Hispanic, and American Indian backgrounds.

This case study draws from a decade-long investigation of school reform in Charlotte-Mecklenburg. The data used in this chapter come from over 150 semistructured interviews conducted by the author with corporate and civic elites and educational policymakers in Charlotte and across the nation; interviews with educators and parents in Charlotte; field notes from observations of local task forces, community forums, and other public meetings about education; and official documents from business, government, and the schools. Direct quotations are attributed to an identified person, unless the individual specifically requested confidentiality. Initial drafts of this chapter were reviewed by local corporate executives, Americorps volunteers, citizen activists, and educators who were interviewed. Several activists and educators who were not interviewed also read earlier versions. All comments were considered in the subsequent revision of the chapter. The names of schools used in the chapter are pseudonyms.

Beginning in the late 1980s, Charlotte corporate leaders ceased to be the vocal, public champions of the school system that they had been for the previous fifteen years.[10] They began publicly to express their dismay over the city's scarcity of qualified entry-level workers, a problem for which they largely blamed the schools. Critics paid little attention to the contributions of rapid economic development and a low unemployment rate to the labor shortage during the last fifteen years. Instead, looking to the schools as both the source of and solution to their problems, corporate leaders began to shape the direction of reform with the explicit purpose of improving schools in order to enhance both the business climate and the future workforce.[11] Since the late 1980s, corporate involvement in CMS has been both formal (i.e., membership on task forces and the school board) and informal (i.e., creating political action committees that identify and fund school board candidates compatible with the business agenda).

About this time, the school system began reform in response to external pressure from corporate critics and dissatisfied parents many of whom were new to the district. Disappointed with initial efforts, in 1991 the school board hired a new superintendent, John Murphy. Shortly after arriving in Charlotte, Superintendent Murphy convened a panel of experts to advise him on systemic reform.[12] After he released the panel's report to the public, the superintendent launched a number of reform initiatives using the panel's recommendations to argue for their necessity and wisdom. Interestingly, Murphy's most controversial and sweeping reform—the end of mandatory busing for desegregation—was not a subject of the panel's deliberations. On March 31, 1992, the Charlotte-Mecklenburg school board voted to replace its historic countywide busing plan with a desegregation plan largely built around parental choice among magnet schools. Local corporate and civic leaders who found their corporate recruitment efforts hampered by the districtwide busing plan and the nascent nationwide reputation of the school system as mediocre supported this reform vigorously. Many middle-class parents from all racial backgrounds did as well.[13]

It is impossible to understand the push for reform in Charlotte without considering the spreading distaste for desegregated schooling among the business leaders and middle-class families who relocated to Charlotte since 1985. While improving the quality of the entry-level workforce was the formal goal of business leaders engaged in early reform efforts, ending busing for desegregation was at the heart of their informal agenda. This goal was not publicly articulated until the mid-1990s when it became more politically acceptable to support neighborhood schools. Despite these pressures, in 1997 the school district still formally maintained its commitment to becoming the nation's premier urban integrated school system. However, in each of the first four years since the adoption of the magnet desegregation plan, the district became modestly more segregated.[14] Overall levels of desegregation stabilized during the fifth year of the magnet plan, 1996–97, but levels of racial isolation intensified in a number of elementary schools in the central city and in prosperous white outlying suburban areas.

Until the last six months of his four and one half year tenure in CMS, Murphy enjoyed strong personal and organizational support from local business leaders. The relationship between the business community and the new superintendent was mutually supportive. For example, when the Chamber of Commerce was in the process of recruiting Transamerica Reinsurance for relocation to Charlotte, it dispatched Superintendent Murphy to the firm's headquarters. He assured employers that the local public schools were good and improving and that relocated employees purchasing homes in certain subdivisions could expect to attend nearby schools.

Two events are emblematic of business support for Murphy. In the summer of 1992, the chairman and CEO of First Union, one of the nation's largest banks and one of the most influential corporations in Charlotte, personally lobbied the school board on behalf of a substantial raise for Murphy, pacing the hallway outside the board room while personnel matters were discussed in executive session.[15] At the end of Murphy's first year as superintendent, an anonymous group of corporate leaders collected $30,000 as a bonus. The school board did not permit the donors to give him their gift; instead, the school board awarded him a smaller bonus.

Major corporate actors who have been critical of CMS's performance also have been highly supportive of reform efforts. Executives have served on numerous task forces, donated their facilities for educational functions, given money and equipment to the schools, and supported the creation of an educational foundation (the Charlotte Mecklenburg Education Foundation [CMEF]). CMEF's goals include raising community awareness of educational matters and supporting educational innovations with small grants they called venture capital. Executives have supported bond issues and lobbied the legislature on behalf of the public schools. Corporations have loaned executives to the schools and to CMEF; they have adopted schools, and their employees have volunteered in classrooms. To varying degrees, CMS's school leaders cultivate the support of corporate leaders, socialize with them, and consult with key individuals before launching important initiatives.[16] The executive president of the Charlotte Chamber of Commerce characterizes this as "an *aggressive* partnership with the school system [his emphasis]."[17]

IBM has been one of the most prominent and active forces in national and CMS school reform during the last decade. The prominent role of IBM's leaders makes the study of the nature of their involvement, their motivations, and examples of their activities in CMS useful for examining a number of general issues about corporate involvement in educational reform. IBM mid-level executives serve in a number of capacities on educational task forces and the executive in charge of the local facility was an active member of the Charlotte-Mecklenburg Education Foundation. The corporation's support of the local schools is most evident in two specific programs, ProjectFirst and the Education Village.

*ProjectFirst*

In the early 1990s, IBM funded a ProjectFirst (Fostering Instruction Through Service and Technology) program in Charlotte, Atlanta, and New York. IBM's formal purpose was to assist schools in bringing technology into classroom instruction. In Charlotte, the IBM grant paid for computer hardware in ten nonmagnet middle schools and a limited training program for the technology specialists who were to bring computer expertise to classroom teachers. Charlotte's ProjectFirst personnel were Americorps volunteers.[18] The Charlotte-Mecklenburg Education Foundation received one of the first Americorps grants awarded by the federal government. CMS placed the Americorps volunteers in ten nonmagnet middle schools as technology specialists. The expectation was that technology specialists would help teachers integrate technology into their instruction.

The choice of these particular nonmagnet middle school as ProjectFirst sites involved more than an empirical assessment of which schools had the greatest need. The superintendent's choice of nonmagnet middle schools was also a response to criticism that new magnet schools diverted district resources from older, inner city schools. Soon after the district replaced its mandatory desegregation plan with a voluntary one built around choice among magnet schools, it became apparent to many parents and other citizens that there were gross inequalities in resources available in magnets, newer schools, and older schools primarily in the urban core. They noted that the magnet strategy for reform left many schools in dire need of attention and additional resources. In the view of some critics, these inequities exacerbated existing race and class disparities in opportunities to learn.[19] People complained that the magnet program, rather than addressing educational inequality, was exacerbating it by draining funds that could be spent for all school. School district personnel explained that the magnet program was funded initially by federal desegregation monies, not local funding intended for all schools. However, critics insisted that in the future, magnet schools' special needs would likely create financial speed bumps when federal funding ended.

In his presentation to the August 1994 CMEF board meeting, the superintendent reported on his plans for improving technology in the schools. He mentioned a planned technology-rich educational complex (the formal announcement of the Educational Village was a few weeks away), and described ProjectFirst. In introducing ProjectFirst, he intimated that his choice of nonmagnet middle schools as ProjectFirst sites was strategic. First, ProjectFirst would bring technology specialists into schools desperately deficient in these tools. Second, it held the potential to mollify critics who charged that newly created magnet schools drained disproportionate shares of the district's resources and contributed to greater educational inequities.[20]

In fact, there was no way that ProjectFirst could balance the inequality of resources between magnet and nonmagnet middle schools. For example, in 1993 the science and technology magnet middle school, Sherwood, received $750,000 in resources. It was transformed from a highly segregated minority school into a racially integrated showcase magnet. A nonmagnet middle school, Westway, received an Americorps volunteer and several IBM computers. Westway and other nonmagnet ProjectFirst middle schools remained largely racially unbalanced and dilapidated. Furthermore, many of them could not use the ProjectFirst equipment effectively because of infrastructure problems like wiring inadequate to support computers and personnel problems like high teacher turnover and little teacher knowledge about computers and educational software.

CMEF staff touted IBM's ProjectFirst as an important, technology-based innovation that was making important contributions to staff development and students' learning in the nonmagnet middle schools where Americorps volunteers were placed. The validity of this claim remains unverified. The author's repeated requests to CMEF for program evaluation documents were ignored. However, a series of interviews with Americorps volunteers, teachers, and principals from these nonmagnet middle schools, revealed a picture of ProjectFirst's educational value at odds with CMEF's account.

The characterization of Americorps volunteers as technology specialists in the nonmagnet middle schools accurately described neither their qualifications nor what they were able to accomplish throughout most of the first year the project was in schools. Apparently, Americorps volunteers were not screened for either knowledge of computers or experience with educational technology. Consequently, volunteers had uneven technological backgrounds. Some had degrees in computer science, some had business backgrounds, but none had direct experience or any training in teaching computer technology or computer skills to others. Most volunteers anticipated that any gaps in their backgrounds, skills, and knowledge would be filled during their two weekend training sessions with IBM. However, midway through their first official training in the IBM's New York headquarters, the volunteers realized that they were not going to get from IBM any information or training about either computers or how to teach about computers. Instead of technology training, they were given a quick overview of schooling in America. Concerned, they formed a self-study group during that weekend.

> AUTHOR. Did they [IBM] give you technology training?
>
> AMERICORPS VOLUNTEER. No. If you were to talk to any of the ten [original Americorps volunteers], and ask them what was the biggest disappointment [of the IBM training] it would have been there was no training in technology. . . . They didn't talk about how to integrate technology into the curriculum. And there even was no basic stuff like, "Here's the latest technology that we have, here's how the technology works. This is what a hard drive is. This is some of the old technology that you're going to run into. You may know a lot about the latest Macs, but do you know what to do when you go to [your school]. You're going to see a whole bunch of old IBM PC's from 1984 and this is how to work with them." No, it was very disappointing. By Saturday night, when we realized there wasn't going to be anything, a group of us from New York and Charlotte got together and said, "let's just hold our own little training tonight." Two of the volunteers from New York sat down and went through the whole entire guts of a computer and told us about the Internet.

After the training sessions in New York, Americorps volunteers returned to Charlotte where they continued learning about technology on their own. During the first six months in their schools, Americorps volunteers were caught in a difficult situation: dedicated to public service and to improving public education, they were initially ill-equipped to do the very job for which they were placed in the schools. A number of them worked in fear that they would be asked a question by an educator before they had had the opportunity to learn about it on their own. During the first year, when asked a computer-related question by a teacher, one volunteer would say "Let me get back to you on this" and would then spend the next few days furiously researching the question. By the time the volunteer gained some clarity about the answer, the teacher's need for it had generally disappeared. ProjectFirst's Americorps volunteers were by-and-large unable to provide the technological support teachers needed for a very long time. Some were never able to do so.

The observations of a principal newly assigned to a troubled middle school midway through the period of the IBM grant underscored the dubious educational value of ProjectFirst.

I arrived at Crozier Middle School . . . and met with the Americorps volunteer to ascertain his responsibilities at the school. He had not been given "directions" from the previous principal who "did not believe in technology." There was little interest in technology by the previous principal and even less support and resources from CMS to provide needed hardware and upgrades to the [school] facility. The Americorps volunteer identified five computers purchased through the project, of which three computers were used by the administration. There was no accounting for these computers on school inventory lists.

The volunteer had limited skills and knowledge in technology and even less in instruction. Teachers expressed concerns that the volunteer was unable to assist or to train them. Consequently, the school computer teacher "trained" the volunteer. The volunteer spent a great deal of time "finding" someone who could help him relative to technical knowledge and curricular issues. Americorps volunteers served several schools, hence there was limited availability of the volunteer at my school. Finally, the placement of Americorps volunteers in nonmagnet needy schools wasn't equivalent to a band-aid; it was a cotton swab.

Overall, Americorps volunteers encountered widespread resistance to the use of computers among teachers and principals in many other ProjectFirst nonmagnet middle schools. This is in part because educators with knowledge, skills, and appreciation for computer technology tend to self-select themselves into schools with the best equipment. When the CMS magnet program began, the schools with technology themes drew technologically inclined educators from other schools across the district. Teaching staffs who remained in the ProjectFirst middle schools were therefore disproportionately computer illiterate or even computer phobic. Despite repeated opportunities for staff development during ProjectFirst's first year, most teachers in these schools resisted volunteers' efforts to teach them computer skills. Complicating matters, many of the ProjectFirst schools were older and physically unable to support the technology donated by IBM because their wiring was too antiquated to be updated.

The second year, most ProjectFirst Americorps volunteers were new, and the large turnover in the volunteers was matched by the teacher turnover in many of the ProjectFirst nonmagnet middle schools. Once teachers received training in technology, a significant number of them transferred to more desirable schools in the district. Consequently, much of what little ProjectFirst accomplished in the first year left the school with these teachers. A volunteer summed up this dilemma:

> What I see is that groundwork that you lay is not going to stay because at the nonmagnet schools there is such a high turnover rate, not only in teachers but also in principals—that they [Americorps volunteers]

can come in there and build a foundation, but then next year, it's going to change because you have new people coming in and you've got others leaving [to go to better schools].

This description of ProjectFirst raises doubts that IBM's grant to CMS had measurable positive effects on either teachers or students. Certainly ProjectFirst did not contribute to measurable, systemic reform in CMS. ProjectFirst suffered from (1) initial poor planning, (2) implementation in schools ill-equipped to support additional computers, (3) gross differences in Americorps volunteers' technical and instructional skills, (4) a lack of understanding of schools as organizations on the part of its project director (a young assistant at the Charlotte-Mecklenburg Education Foundation), (5) an overestimation of the power of technology to solve entrenched, complex educational problems, (6) little to no long-term staff development in ProjectFirst schools, and (7) staff instability. Examination of the project illustrates the more general proposition that, at a minimum, without teacher professional development in integrating technology into the curriculum, faculty stability, and a physical plant that can sustain modern technology, computers themselves cannot improve teaching and learning.

*The Charlotte-Mecklenburg Education Village*

Perhaps the most significant point about the example of the Education Village is that during the time the village was designed, the CMS school board in office—the entity with responsibility for policy decisions—was never formally presented the details of any plans. This fact became important in the political struggle that unfolded beginning in January 1996. The school board learned of the Education Village when, in fall 1994, IBM's Gerstner and Superintendent Murphy announced to the community the award of a $2,000,000 IBM grant to support an Education Village, the first of ten Reinventing Education grants awarded nationally by the corporation. IBM's Reinventing Education initiative is aimed at funding systemic reforms in public schools. In the program's first round of gifts, $2 million grants also were awarded to public schools in Philadelphia, Vermont, Chicago, Dallas, West Virginia, Broward County, Florida, San Francisco, San Jose, and Cincinnati.[21]

The village's plans were designed by Superintendent Murphy and Stanley Litow, IBM's Vice President of Corporate Community Relations. The village was designed as a four-school complex (two elementary, one middle, and one high school) to be built on 200 acres of land adjacent to the IBM facility in the University Research Park (URP). The land was purchased by CMS in 1993 for $6 million. The IBM site executive who participated in the negotiations described the

sale of the land to the district at $32,000 per acre as "a straight busi-
ness transaction of an IBM asset."[22] The construction of the actual
schools is financed by $82 million in public bonds approved narrowly
by citizens in the fall of 1995.

University Research Park is located in northern Mecklenburg
County close to the University of North Carolina, Charlotte. It is
designed to replicate the renowned Research Triangle Park associated
with Duke University, North Carolina State University, and University
of North Carolina, Chapel Hill. This area is a rapidly growing, prosperous section of Mecklenburg County (see figure 5.1). Its adjacent neighborhoods—largely affluent and white—tend toward bucolic suburbs,
rather than dense multiethnic urban neighborhoods. In addition to IBM,
Verbatim, and First Union National Bank, a number of other high-tech
and financial institutions have major installations there.

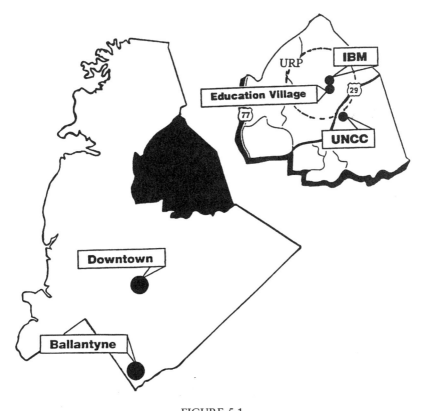

FIGURE 5.1
Charlotte-Mecklenburg School System with the
University Research Park Area and the Education Village in Relief

A defining feature of the Education Village was its designation as a workplace magnet. Parents of children who attend Education Village schools were to pledge to volunteer one hour per week in their children's school, and parents' employers were to be required to agree to this commitment of time. Classrooms were to have business mentors. When the four-school complex is completed, students were to learn in multi-age classrooms, were to experience a curriculum integrated from kindergarten through the twelfth grade, and were to use state-of-the-art technology. Parents were to be connected to the school with IBM's Wired for Learning educational software. Once admitted to a village school, children were to be able to attend one of its schools until they graduate from high school. Their siblings were to be permitted to attend as well.[23]

The development of Wired for Learning software utilizes over half of the IBM grant to CMS. In addition to software development, the grant supports a project manager, staff development, some network hardware, and computers in nearby libraries, the local science museum (Discovery Place), and the community center in the inner-city neighborhood. IBM retains the copyright for all software and intellectual property developed as part of the $2 million Reinventing Education grant awarded to the Charlotte schools.[24]

The Educational Village's original plans describe a partnership remarkably similar to the Downtown School, a workplace magnet in Winston-Salem, North Carolina. Gerstner, now the CEO and chairman of IBM, was the head of RJR Tobacco at the time the Downtown School was developed. The Downtown School was created with funding from the RJR Nabisco Foundation's Next Century Schools program in 1992.[25] The Downtown School's business partners are RJR Tobacco, RJR Tobacco International, and Planters LifeSavers. These firms give their employees, who are parents of students in the magnet, one hour of released time per week to volunteer in the schools "to tie learning to the business perspective."[26] Children who attend the school are selected by lottery. Sixty percent of the seats are allocated to children of full-time regular employees of the three business partners and 40 percent of seats are available to inner-city children who live in the immediate area.

The similarities between the Downtown School in Winston-Salem and the original plans for the Education Village are apparent. As outlined in a series of letters between Murphy and Litow, the Education Village was to be a partnership between IBM, other URP firms, and the school system. Murphy and Litow's original design allocated one third of the seats to children from University Research Park firms (of the URP's approximately 12,000 employees, about 4,000 worked for IBM at that time), one third from adjacent subdivisions, and one third for children who live in a specific inner-city neighborhood. In the original proposal for the Educational Village, Superintendent Murphy wrote:

> a number of seats will be reserved for children of employees who work in the immediate area (our private sector partners) [parentheses in the original].[27]

Seats for children of employees of URP firms and adjacent subdivisions were to be filled by lottery. The remaining third of the seats would be filled by inner-city children assigned to the schools in order to desegregate them.

In January 1996 a new CMS school board was seated. Its first task was to begin the search for a new superintendent (Murphy resigned effective the day the board took office); its second was to address pupil assignment for the coming 1996–97 school year. Because the district still operates under the terms of the 1971 *Swann* ruling, any pupil assignment decisions must take into account issues of racial balance. Although the school board had never voted to approve or accept the Education Village plans, the first of the four schools in the village was scheduled to open in fall 1996. Decisions about its attendance area were therefore part of the January discussion of pupil assignment. Members of the newly elected school board were very frustrated by the apparent *fait accompli* laid at their feet. They viewed the creation of the Education Village—especially the designation of who could attend it—as an usurpation of their statutory rights to make pupil assignment decisions. Moreover, when the details of the Education Village's original attendance formula became public knowledge, an intense controversy erupted, polarizing numerous sectors of the Charlotte-Mecklenburg community. The original attendance formula appeared to privilege employees of certain firms in the small geographic area of the URP (those referred to by Murphy as "our private sector partners"), while shutting out a majority of families who worked in other firms elsewhere in the school district. This was especially aggravating to county residents because they had just passed a large bond in part to support the building of these much-touted technology-rich magnet schools. Reacting to both the public outcry and their own anger over being bypassed in the planning, the school board canceled the Education Village's attendance plan crafted by IBM's Litow and the former superintendent.

The stakes were high: IBM and its URP neighbors were facing the loss of a plum amenity if the original plan were amended—a third of the prized 5,200 "workplace magnet" seats. Speaking confidentially, the CEO of a major employer in Charlotte described the Education Village as "a First Union[bank]-IBM-John Murphy deal." He elaborated:

Let me put it this way, . . . First Union had a tremendous desire to develop that area—tremendous desire to develop that area because they had already planned to come and build two million square feet [in URP]. And they wanted a place where their employees could be happy. They could encourage employees to get out of downtown and go north, and plus they had—they were doing some development on the rest of their land and so they had tremendous interest in that new development. And so education was a critical element of that. And so to get that done, they worked their magic. That is what corporations do. My understanding is . . . that they were investing in *their* amenity for *their* employees [italics added for emphasis].

From the point of view of the IBM and other URP corporate leaders, the school system had given its word and was now breaking it. Explanations from the new school board that previous oral agreements between IBM and the superintendent were not legally binding under North Carolina law only angered corporate actors. During a conference call following the board's revision of the Education Village design, a furious Litow insisted: "That's *not* how businesses operate." In Charlotte, URP leaders believed that school board revisions in the Educational Village plans amounted to "bureaucratic interference" with agreements previously concluded. The president of the URP association wrote in an editorial published in the *Charlotte Observer*:

> These companies [that donate money to schools] do not need to have their motives questioned. They do not need to be hassled. They do not need to be set straight by public officials. They need to be persuaded to offer even more support. Like me, people in other businesses are watching the Education Village situation unfold. If our school board can't understand the grant's purpose, won't honor agreements and can't act graciously, other companies will think twice before extending new offers of support.[28]

On the other side of this controversy were many other parents and employers in the countywide school district who were excluded from the lottery for seats by the original design because they neither worked in a URP firm nor lived in an adjacent subdivision. The public, which had just agreed to foot the bill for the four schools when they approved $82 million in bond money for the Education Village in November 1995, was outraged. Sentiments expressed at several open forums during school board meetings, in letters to the editor of the *Charlotte Observer,* and local talk radio programs indicated that citizens across the political spectrum and from all racial/ethnic backgrounds believed that provisions to allow only URP employees to apply for the Education Village workplace portion of the seat lottery amounted to an unfair advantage for IBM and other URP firms. A local conservative activist captured the resentment of many:

> So, at a cost of $2 million, they [IBM] bought a seat for the children of
> their employees at the newest, highest (sic) technology school in the
> county. To put their $2 million in perspective, consider that the total
> Education Village will cost in the neighborhood of $80 to $100 mil-
> lion. That means that IBM is putting up 2 to 2.5 percent of the total
> cost of the village to buy one-third of the seats there for the children of
> their employees—not a bad investment part.[29]

To set the public record straight, the recently elected chairperson
wrote an essay for the *Charlotte Observer* clarifying the school board's
position. She argued that, while the board welcomed corporate partners
and their resources, pupil assignment is the statutory responsibility of
the school board and not within the purview of superintendents or business leaders.

> I remember a call from a particular stay-at-home mom. This woman
> rightfully considers herself a working mother. She lives next door to
> someone who works in the URP and has children. Under the original
> proposal, the stay-at-home mom wouldn't be allowed to apply for a
> slot in the Village [lottery], but her neighbor's children could attend.
> The inequity of this situation was being repeated all over the
> county. . . . The political reality was fast becoming apparent. Our citi-
> zens didn't want a school that favored employees of a select group of
> businesses.[30]

On January 29, 1996, the school board exercised its statutory duty
and opened one third of the Education Village seats—the workplace
magnet portion—to all working families in the county with the proviso
that each family commit one hour weekly of parental time (or its equivalent over the course of the school year) to school involvement and that
employed parents obtain their employers' guarantee to cooperate. Reac-
tions from URP companies, particularly IBM, were swift and severe:
IBM froze its grant to CMS pending further negotiations.

A month of intense exchanges of letters and face-to-face meetings
between the school system representatives and IBM ended with an agreement that broadened the original workplace magnet theme so that it
included stay-at-home parents, too. The Village became a parental
involvement magnet. Eligibility to enter the lottery for the third of the
seats allocated to the magnet theme portion of the Village was expanded
to all families in the county. Parents of Governors' Village (the Education Village name was changed) students must sign a pledge to volunteer
in their child's school an average of one hour per week or the equivalent
over the course of the school year. Employed parents are required to
obtain a statement of support from their employer. The revised plan also
broadened the residential catchment area to include more suburbs in the
northeast portion of the county. The final agreement stipulated that :

IBM maintains the rights to any new products or intellectual property developed as result of the grant. The grant does not include future upgrades of the [yet-to-be-developed] software.[31]

IBM then released the $2 million in grant funds.

The head principal of the Governors' Village, Ann Clark, described how the grant was implemented: $500,000 was spent on training, a network server, and 240 IBM computers for community sites and teachers in the schools. The principal is given a budget and can allocate these funds for furniture, fixtures, equipment, and technology in classrooms. The remaining $1,000,000 of the grant went to the development of the software that will link homes to schools. Eventually Wired for Learning software will permit parents to have round-the-clock access to their child's classroom via their home computer. Families with an IBM computer that has at least a 486 processor and Windows95 software can readily access their child's record. In the first year of the grant, families with less powerful computers or no computers were be able to access their children's classrooms from community centers and libraries during the first year of the village's operation. Families with Macintosh home computers gained access to their child's school through the school's home page on the Internet.[32]

Reflecting on his colleagues' reaction to the Education Village imbroglio, the CEO of a Fortune 500 firm headquartered in Charlotte, speaking confidentially, confirmed that [URP] business leaders

> were very upset that the school board got involved, if you will, you know. It is business. It was business. It really was not an issue of quality education, it was an issue of developing University Research Park. And making that thing come to life. Making that new [area] in the north part of town come to life. [Corporate executives] were saying, "You want my money, play the game my way. We have a deal here. A deal has been struck and you're messing with this deal. How dare you undo our deal!" It [the school board's action] wasn't as much of a threat, as an affront [to corporate leaders]. . . . Bureaucrats got involved—the people who got involved, however, they were the people whose job it was to be there. And they [members of the school board] *had* been excluded.

Even after the settlement, the scent of corporate favoritism lingered over the community. A school board member, George Dunlap, expressed the concerns of many parents and citizens:

> What's to say some other company won't come into the area and want to buy into public education? What do you say to them? Do you say no? I don't think so.[33]

*Ballantyne*

Fears that the village's original arrangement sets a dangerous precedent whereby certain businesses, through their donations, could, in effect, "purchase" their own public schools were not idle speculation. In fact, what many believe was exactly such a scenario unfolded only a few months after the rancorous debate over the Education Village. In the late 1980s, the school system voted to take an option on land in a then-undeveloped part of the county that was donated by a politically-connected real estate developer. Unless schools were built on the donated parcels, they would revert back to their owner. When the Ballantyne neighborhood eventually developed in the 1990s, it emerged as an almost all-white enclave with average home prices of $500,000. The combination of the development's extremely expensive homes and its location in the most southerly corner of the county near the South Carolina state line made the prospects for desegregating the proposed schools exceedingly difficult (see figure 5.1).

In January 1995, the new school board confronted enormous pressure to exercise its option on the land from both the growing population in the Ballantyne area that required schooling, and from county and state officials because building schools on the donated parcels would obviate the need to use tax funds for the purpose of land acquisition. Faced with the need to obtain County Commissioners' approval to place a $400 million school bond measure on the November 1997 ballot, school board members feared the commissioners would refuse to approve the new bonds if the board turned down the "free" land. However, building schools on this land was tantamount to providing public schools for what would almost certainly become a segregated white, upper-income subdivision. This arrangement also violated the school board's own guideline for building new schools only in neighborhoods with 10 percent or greater minority populations. The donation of land for schools thus became a de facto school siting decision by a corporate actor.

Board members reluctantly accepted the Ballantyne land in spring, 1996. A condition of their acceptance, however, was that both elementary and middle schools would be magnets. Both would be constructed in such a manner as to minimize the likelihood that the schools would later revert to a neighborhood school (for example, a performing arts magnet would have space for theaters, recital halls, and recording studios that can only be used for these purposes). Eighteen months after the school board made the difficult and contentious decision to accept the land-for-schools deal, the ground had not yet been broken for construction. Ironically, there will be no school on the donated Ballantyne land designated for the elementary school; the seventeen-acre site was deemed unsuitable for a school because it is contaminated. It sits adjacent to a methane-producing landfill.[34] School system officials will likely build the elementary school on a second site originally designated for a middle school and a public park. The second site is slightly closer to the rest of the city and will be somewhat easier to desegregate by race and class.

## A TYPOLOGY OF CORPORATE INVOLVEMENT

The preceding section described several examples of business participation in reform efforts in Charlotte-Mecklenburg. To assist in theorizing these, table 5.1 presents a typology of corporate involvement in educational reform. The table identifies by type who the corporate actors are, what the nature of their involvement is, and their motivations, and it illustrates each type with examples. The first four types range from the activities of large philanthropic organizations to those of individual volunteers acting directly or indirectly in concert with the school officials who provide actual educational services. The fifth type specifies how corporate leaders can become state actors with regard to education. The sixth type reflects educational services purchased from a for-profit firm by state actors who themselves no longer provide the service. Because there is very little type I and VI activity in Charlotte, the case study focused primarily upon the activities and motivations of Charlotte corporate actors in types II, III, IV, and V.

- *Type I: Large Independent Foundations.* Large foundations can be considered corporate actors because their boards of directors are selected from the highest ranks of the corporate world. Foundations conceptualize and fund broad reform initiatives consistent with their worldview and political ideals. These initiatives often begin as support for a national task force or for empirical studies. Their empirical studies have been central to the nation's normative understanding of the condition of American schools. The Ford, Rockefeller, and Spencer Foundations are examples of this type.
- *Type II: Corporate Leaders.* They serve in largely symbolic roles on high-profile national task forces or use the respect and attention they command to advocate for systemic reforms. Corporate leaders at this level are able to commit their firm's resources. Combined with their corporation's material and financial support, their bully pulpit inspires national, state, and local reform efforts. The activities of IBM's Louis Gerstner and BellSouth's John Clendenin at the

Palisades summit illustrate this type of activity at the national level. IBM and Gerstner's involvement in Charlotte represents this type at the local level, as are the activities of the real estate developers involved in the Ballantyne land-for-schools deal.

- *Type III: Mid-level Corporate Actors.* They do much of the actual day-to-day labor on high profile task forces that design educational reforms at the state and local levels, but they rarely are able to commit their firm's resources to reform. Typically these mid-level executives have some experience with education (sometimes they are former educators), and they liaise with local and state school personnel as reforms are implemented. In some cases, they may served as executives-on-loan to a school system or an education foundation, or they may serve as the corporation's educational expert. A key actor in Charlotte's Education Village is IBM's Stanley S. Litow, Vice President of Corporate Community Relations. He is a former educator.[35]

- *Type IV: Corporate Employees, Hourly Wage Earners Working in Ongoing Reform Programs.* These men and women regularly volunteer as tutors or mentors in particular schools. They contribute thousands of hours in classrooms working directly with teachers, aides, and students in programs designed by their corporate leaders. They are guest speakers in classrooms, or they spend their weekends hard-wiring schools for the internet, or coaching student groups. Volunteers represent the majority of business people involved in the schools. Their dual status as parent and employee often underlies their attachment to particular schools.

- *Type V: Business Leaders as Educational Decision-Makers.* Individual men and women appointed or elected to positions in federal education bureaucracies, or state and local education authorities hold formal state power. Usually they are appointed to these positions or run for office because of their credentials as business people with a perspective quite different from professional educators. School boards are the most common forum in which business leaders exercise authority as educational decision-makers.

- *Type VI: For-profit Companies as Systemic Reform.* These firms sell their products (Channel One) or services (Education Alternatives, Inc. [EAI], the Edison Project) as systemic reform. They are not the same as vendors who sell specific services (drivers education instruction, maintenance, bus driving) or products (paper, sports equipment, computers, blackboards) to school systems. For example, the Edison Project is a prospective chain of for-profit private schools that markets its educational services as a cheaper, more efficient,

TABLE 5.1
Typology of Corporate Involvement in and Motivation for Educational Reform with Examples from Charlotte, NC

| Type | Nature of Involvement | Motivation | Examples in Charlotte* |
|---|---|---|---|
| TYPE I<br>Large, independent foundations | donations of millions through foundation grants | altruism; shape national debate; eleemosynary impulses; advance political goals | Carnegie, Pew, Ford, Lilly, Bush, Casey, Annenberg, MacArthur, Rockefeller, Spencer, Olin, Bradley, Johnson |
| TYPE II<br>Elite corporate heads, individual firms, business organizations | donations of corporate resources; service on boards; chairing task forces; bully pulpit in support of school reform | strategic self-interest; shape national and local debate; advance symbolic values | IBM's Gerstner; Bell South's Clendenin; CED, Business Roundtable Conference Board; Charlotte Chamber of Commerce: Charlotte-Mecklenburg Education Foundation |
| TYPE III<br>Mid-level executives, small business owners | service on task forces designing business/education collaborations; exec on loan to schools; corporate exec in charge of educational division in local firm | altruism; improve schools in one's nation or community; career advance; personal dedication to children and education | IBM's Litow; Susan Q. Corporate VP for Community Relations; John Q. Small Entrepreneur; Leslie Q. Regional Manager |

(continued on next page)

TABLE 5.1 (continued)

| Type | Nature of Involvement | Motivation | Examples in Charlotte* |
|---|---|---|---|
| TYPE IV Corporate employees, hourly wage earners working in ongoing reform program | volunteers in classrooms, tutors, mentors, guest speakers on company or own time | personal dedication to children and education; altruism; career advance | Americorps volunteers; Susan Q. and John Q. Public |
| TYPE V Corporate leader as state actor | elected or appointed status in federal bureaucracy | altruism; improve schools in one's nation or community; shape direction of reform consistent with ideology; advance corporate long-term interests | Xerox's David Kearns as Deputy Secretary of Education; Chicago School Finance Authority; corporate leader as school board member |
| TYPE VI For-profit firms as reform | for-profit schools; management, products, and school services for purchase | profit | Edison Project; EAI; Channel One; Vendors of educational products and services |

*There is very little evidence of type I and type VI activity in Charlotte.

and more effective educational delivery system than the public schools. It currently operates twenty-five public schools either in partnership with districts or with local charters. EAI sells its management services to school systems on much the same basis.

The third column in table 5.1 distinguishes among the varying forms of motivation underlying corporate involvement. Individuals or corporations may act for quite different reasons. And any involvement by corporate or individual actors may serve a number of purposes. To claim that mixed motivations exist is not meant to discount genuine eleemosynary impulses; altruism clearly stimulates much of what is done across the first four types of activities. Large foundations express their civic responsibility to the nation through their gifts. Business leaders and their firms express pride in and commitment to the larger social good of the communities in which they are located through their involvement and donations. Many business people, as human actors, care passionately about children and hold almost reverential personal values about the importance of education for individual and social betterment. Many individual actors across all five types of corporate involvement in reform approach their education work with missionary zeal and dedication. Service to children as tutors and mentors or to the school reform process (as members of task forces) is often personally satisfying and genuinely altruistic.

It is no secret, however, that business involvement in school reform, especially at the highest levels, springs as well from no small amount of long- and short-term strategic self-interest. Philanthropic ends are self-evident: schools do obtain human, material, and symbolic support from benefactors. Other motivations are much less obvious. For example, corporate actors' short-term strategic self-interests are served when improved school-to-work education transfers training costs from the private to the public sector or when better schools generate better appraisals of local infrastructures by mobile capital seeking an area for relocation.

Long-term strategic self-interest can be both ideological and material. For example, a long-term strategic interest is served when leaders shape the terms of the national debate over the putative educational crisis facing this nation. They influenced the social construction of the economic crisis of the last decade as largely the responsibility of the flawed public schools—a view essentially unchallenged until recently when the obvious economic recovery made it difficult to blame schools for a crisis that no longer existed. Now that the U.S. economy has regained its international competitiveness, corporations no longer hold public schools responsible for their international competitive standing. Firms now charge schools with failing to produce workers for future high-tech information-age jobs. Research suggests that the new charge of corporations may be as poorly focused as their earlier charge. For example, skill requirements for future jobs are expected to be highly variable and it is not at all clear if most high-tech information-age jobs will require highly skilled workers. Furthermore, evidence indicates no systematic shortage of appropriately skilled workers for contemporary jobs. Rather, employers are dissatisfied with the work ethic of their less skilled employees.[36] And technology cannot address that dissatisfaction.

There is one crucial negative latent consequence of corporations' continuing attribution to the public schools of responsibility for whatever they dislike in the attitudes and training of their workforce. If the derisive characterization of public schools as "ineffectual government schools" is accepted as conventional wisdom, it lays the foundation for widespread penetration of public education by the the private sector. In addition, it advances the neoliberal position that all that is public is suspect, while that which is private or market-driven is good.[37]

## COMPLEXITIES OF CORPORATE INVOLVEMENT

Table 5.1 presented a typology of corporate involvement in order to examine the full range of activities in which individuals and firms engage. ProjectFirst and the Education Village activities primarily fell within types II, III, and IV. It is useful to specify these types more fully in order to understand and theorize their contributions to systemic reforms in public education. The next section of this chapter will discuss the varieties of involvement that fall within each of the five types.

### Gifts from Independent Philanthropic Foundations

Without question, material support for reform from large independent philanthropic foundations has been critical both for stimulating reforms and in financing them across the nation. Without the material support of these foundations, it is unlikely that reform efforts would have gained broad-based constituencies or achieved the momentum they have since the 1980s. By definition, this form of involvement is unique to type I. Large independent philanthropic foundations have played a minor role in Charlotte reform efforts.

### Roundtables and Task Forces

Local, state, and national business roundtables or task forces raise questions, identify problems, and suggest (sometimes set) reform agendas.

Their public advocacy of school reform brings visibility and legitimacy to the needs of school systems, students, and their families. The Committee for Economic Development, the National Alliance of Business, the Business Roundtable, and the Conference Board are examples of prominent national organizations of this type. National task forces and roundtables provide crucial political and factual scaffolding for national and local reforms. Local task forces play a similar role in laying groundwork for reform at the school district level. An example is the Charlotte Chamber of Commerce's 1987–88 Task Force on Education and Jobs. This body's deliberations marked the critical moment when educational restructuring began in Charlotte. These activities fall within type II and Type III.

*Partnerships, Compacts, and Collaborations*

Local partnerships between a business and a specific school can take numerous forms. These typically involve adoption of a school or a school district; direct donations of funds, equipment, and other materials, and opportunities for employees to volunteer in schools as tutors or mentors. As of 1992, over 200,000 businesses in the United States had partnerships with over 40,000 elementary and secondary schools.[38] Currently, there are about 250 different business partnerships with some of Charlotte's approximately 130 schools. This number includes individual partnerships with specific schools or systemwide initiatives. These activities also fall within type II and type III.

*Education Foundations*

Education foundations are another form of corporate involvement in school reform. These organizations raise private money that is then given to fund specific innovative programs. The New American Schools Development Corporation's (NASDC) "break-the-mold" projects are examples of the reforms financed by such national-level foundations. Charlotte participated briefly in the Hudson Institute's Modern Red School House, one of NASDC's first eleven projects. Local educational foundations are nonprofit organizations that raise venture capital to support local innovations. Representatives of the most powerful businesses typically sit on their boards. Local education foundations such as the Charlotte-Mecklenburg Education Foundation serve a symbolic function as well in that the existence of these and their prestigious boards of directors lend legitimacy and status to local public education. They support various activities such as summer institutes for teachers, grants to teachers for innovative course development, or the purchase of equipment for specific schools. Increasingly, many have broadened their scope to focus upon governance issues. For example, a number of education foundations have become involved in nonpartisan civic actions in support of school board elections.[39] These activities fall within type II and type III.

### Business-Oriented Consultants

A national cadre of consultants with a neoliberal economic perspective and long-standing connections to corporate America participate in reforms efforts often as support personnel. Many are employed by conservative think tanks where they generate position papers that are then disseminated widely. They also serve as consultants to educational organizations where they help plan, design, and implement reforms. Their activities fall also within type II and type III.

Denis P. Doyle is an example of a business-oriented consultant. Through his writing and consulting, he serves as an intermediary between conservative ideology and corporate actors on the one hand and on the other, among educational practitioners around the country. Widely published in the business and education popular press, he works with school districts, business task forces, think tanks, and conservative foundations. He has co-authored two books about the necessity of corporate involvement and leadership in school restructuring. Doyle served as a consultant to the authors of the education chapter of the Heritage Foundation's congressional briefing book for new members,[40] and Doyle was one of several dozen experts who joined the governors and business leaders in Palisades, New York, in 1996.

In many important ways, school reforms initiated during the tenure of John Murphy were shaped by Doyle. He consulted extensively in Charlotte during the months before John Murphy became superintendent, and during the first few years of Murphy's tenure in CMS. (Between January 1991 and the end of 1995, he received compensation as a consultant to the Charlotte-Mecklenburg schools twenty-six times.[41]) Doyle helped to write the district's NASDC grant proposal (Charlotte-Mecklenburg Schools was one of the original districts participating in the Hudson Institute's Modern Red School House where Doyle was a research fellow), and he participated in the World Class Panel of educational experts convened by Superintendent Murphy to advise him on reform. Doyle developed the district's grant proposal to the RJR Foundation's Next Century Schools. At the time, Doyle was a member of the board of the RJR Foundation.[42] When in 1996 Murphy became a consultant to Chicago schools' CEO, Paul Vallas, Doyle collaborated again with Murphy.[43]

## Volunteers

This variety of involvement occurs in types II, III, and IV. Most volunteers come from the ranks of corporate workers, not leaders. They may be hourly blue-collar workers who regularly volunteer as tutors or mentors in particular schools or specialists who lecture students about their own jobs. Many times they are parents whose employers encourage them to work regularly with teachers, aides, and other students in their child's classrooms. In 1996, 3,300 employees from 250 companies volunteered 52,000 hours in CMS.[44] These type IV volunteers represent the majority of all business workers involved in the schools. Type III mid-level executives and small business owners who serve on task forces or work with local educational collaborations or partnerships are volunteers, too. Type II corporate leaders who serve on high profile national task forces or local foundations are also in some respects volunteers.

## Business Leaders as Educational Decision-Makers

Business leaders often serve as formal state actors in federal, state, and local educational bureaucracies. This form of involvement is unique to type V. The former CEO of Xerox, David Kearns, served as the Deputy Secretary of Education during the Bush administration. Thereafter, he took the helm of NASDC. Another example, the five-person Chicago School Finance Authority, composed of businessmen and attorneys, from 1979 to 1995 held statutory power to oversee school finances and approve all major budgetary decisions.[45] More often, corporate leaders serve on local school boards where they are able to have direct influence on educational reform. An extensive literature has documented the continued presence and influence of business leaders on school boards since George Counts[46] first demonstrated this in the early part of this century.

Business influence on school boards is informal as well. Bishop George Battle, the former chairman of CMS's board of education, illustrated this in remarks he made at a dinner honoring Bill Lee, the late chairman of Charlotte-based Duke Energy Corporation. Battle joked that, "Some of you thought I was chairman of the school board, while Bill Lee was probably the chair." Another member of the Charlotte school board commented that the downtown business interests "really sort of infiltrated the Board of Education so that we sometimes behave like a little Chamber of Commerce."[47]

Whether what is good for business is good for schools is both an empirical and ethical question. As is evident in Charlotte, business involvement both offers great opportunities and poses potential dangers for public education. The material, human, and symbolic resources brought to schools from corporations and their employees are consequential. A number of observers believe that without the support of the corporate sector, public schools and their reform would be stagnant or lost. At the same time, some aspects of the broader corporate reform agenda and its implementation bring a host of contradictions and questions about equity, fairness, accountability, and the wisdom of the reform trajectory implicit in certain policy choices. The blurry line between strategic self-interest and eleemosynary impulses makes it difficult to distinguish potential dangers from valuable opportunities. The following sections will attempt to make that distinction through an analysis of the actions, motivations, and consequences primarily of type II and type III corporate actors.

## OPPORTUNITIES PRESENTED BY BUSINESS INVOLVEMENT

### Resources

Corporate leaders have shared some of their firms' enormous material resources with large numbers of schools and entire districts. Philanthropy takes the form of individual gifts (like those of Walter Annenberg who gave millions to NASDC and to the Chicago public schools), or corporate gifts either as direct grants to schools or through business/education foundations. Donations of financial capital and land have provided needed resources to many schools and districts. So, too, have material donations like computers and the human capital made available to selected schools in the form of employee volunteers, tutors, pro bono technical assistance, and mentors who volunteer in schools on company time. Nevertheless, donated resources constitute a small portion of school budgets. Lewis C. Solmon, economist and one of the educational experts who attended IBM's 1996 National Education Summit, estimates only 6 percent of the total technology in the nation's schools has been donated by the private sector.[48] Some observers point to the financial speed bumps that lie ahead when current technology becomes outdated and school systems, having committed to a particular platform or software program, are required to upgrade. For example, future upgrades of Wired for Learning were specifically excluded from the finalized Reinventing Education grant to CMS.

### Symbolic Capital

The high profile of corporate leaders in local and national reform efforts raises the public's awareness of educational reform needs and helps to place education at the center of public discourse regarding the welfare of the nation, of states, and of local communities. In the case of urban districts surrounded by separate suburban systems to which many middle-class families escaped, business serves as a visible constituency in support of large urban public schools. Their advocacy in support of the public schools can fill the vacuum left by the flight of the middle class to the suburbs.

In certain large cities with corrupt and inefficient bureaucracies, business groups have at times aided school reformers by serving on task forces, conducting management and financial audits, and fighting long-established but educationally dubious practices that are entrenched either in administrative decisions and/or some union contracts. As Elizabeth L. Useem notes, often it is difficult for reformers to engage in struggles with teacher unions and educational bureaucracies but with business leaders as allies, reformers' chances of initiating reform are enhanced.[49] Useem's observation, however, says nothing about the direction, utility, equity, or value of a particular reform or set of reforms.

## Welfare of Children and Families

Corporate actors have placed on the reform table a host of broader issues pivotal to human learning and to successful school reform. In conjunction with renewed attention to public education, the related issues of early childhood education and the health and welfare of children and their families have become, by necessity, issues of legitimate public discourse. The Committee for Economic Development's (CED) widely disseminated reports illustrate how advocacy legitimates the need for public policy to attend to schools, students, and their families.[50] The Annie E. Casey and W. T. Grant foundation reports have been instrumental in identifying poverty and its attendant social dislocations as barriers to school success. Their reports brought widespread attention and support at the state levels for early childhood education, vaccination, and nutrition, and to parenting education as concomitant needs that must be addressed if schools are to be successfully reformed.

## Transition from School-to-Work

Business leaders' insistence that secondary schools must provide better prepared entry-level workers has resulted in renewed attention to the school-to-work transition for non-college-bound youth, an area many analysts describe as frequently slighted by educators.[51] Until recently, the post-graduation focus of secondary schools was on college preparation and neglected other avenues. Business complaints about the schools' failure to prepare the entry-level workforce have helped to push schools to reexamine, reinvigorate, and renew their school-to-work education programs. Today, there are cooperative efforts between local employers, local schools, and state departments of employment to build the pathways from school to work in many communities.

The Charlotte-Mecklenburg School system and a group of business leaders from small and medium firms have spent the last two years developing crucial linkages between the workplace and the schools. Their activities include a coordinating body named the School-to-Career Partnership; a planning task force for a prospective technical high school; the sponsorship of internships, apprenticeships, job-shadowing, and the mentoring of youngsters interested in certain careers; and several industry-specific training programs in certain schools (for example, one program trains Novell network administrators). The network of business actors, typically those characterized as type IV in table 5.1, serve as a broad base of support, information, and resources for CMS's efforts to enhance the programmatic offerings available to secondary students. For the youths who will not go directly to college, the results of the network's activities are designed to serve as the bridge from school to postsecondary work force participation.

*Support for Parental Involvement*

Corporations that encourage their employees to participate on company time in their children's schools provide an important opportunity for schools. Employees in these firms suffer fewer conflicts between their job, and their parental responsibilities when they must attend a parent-teacher conference or want to volunteer in their child's school. By establishing a formal mechanism whereby parents can participate in their children's schools, corporations support family involvement in education.

## DANGERS OF BUSINESS LEADERSHIP AND INVOLVEMENT

A problem for public schools is that while the possibilities of positive contributions by business are usually easy to see, any potential dangers they pose may not be visible until long after the contributions have been accepted uncritically. To complicate the matter more, corporate involvement in local reform can be at once an act both of altruism and of strategic self-interest. And that self-interest may, in the long run, harm the schools and the communities in which the reforms are located. It is important, then, to analyze why and when certain types of corporate involvement pose potential harm to public education.

*Data-Free Ideologues with a Bully Pulpit*

Some prominent business leaders and consultants do harm to public education when they make errors about American schools in their public pronouncements and writings. An example is IBM's Louis V. Gerstner Jr., lead author of *Reinventing Education: Entrepreneurship in America's Public Schools*. Gerstner's core argument is that public education, insulated from the discipline of the market, is a failure and that solutions lie in educational entrepreneurship of all kinds—choice among vouchers, magnets, charters, and other forms of privatization. To make the case, Gerstner uses anecdotes that describe schools or districts that have broken out of the strictures of government control and allowed market forces of some kind to flower. The book proclaims American public education "a wasteland."

A major problem with the book is that the evidence Gerstner and his coauthors use to make their case is frequently incorrect or taken out of context.[52] The book's errors regarding Charlotte reflect the often loose relationship among arguments and empirical data. For example, Gerstner and his coauthors wrote in 1994

> Charlotte-Mecklenburg school district was the first large district in the nation to fall under court order to integrate. Twenty-five years later the *Swann* decision has been lifted because Charlotte has successfully integrated.[53]

In fact, five years after the publication of Gerstner's book, the *Swann* decision has not been lifted. It was officially inactive until the original plaintiffs reopened the case on October 9, 1997. And the Charlotte-Mecklenburg school district's renown stems from its legacy as the first district to use mandatory busing to integrate its schools, not that it was the first large district under court order to desegregate. What is worse, the authors use their errors of omission and of fact to advance an argument that in marketization lies the answer to problems that plague American schools:

> What are the new terms that made it possible for the court to lift *Swann?* Schools of choice.[54]

Gerstner's conclusion that the implementation of choice in CMS made it possible for the federal court to lift *Swann*, therefore, rests on errors in his reporting of historical fact. However, his erroneous assertion is consistent with the reforms he advocates.

The book also ignores a host of respected scholarly publications and widely available reports that present the strengths and weaknesses of U.S. education, but also research that analyzes the institutional, organization, and cultural reasons for difficulties in achieving reform.[55] Gerstner and his colleagues do not engage the evidence or the debates that critically examine claims that market-based reforms are the silver bullet for all that ails the schools.[56] Gerstner's prominence as a national advocate of school reform who can mobilize governors and presidents to attend summits in his training facilities lends credibility to his arguments and thereby makes his errors in fact and inference that much more potentially harmful to public education.

### Romanticizing the Market

The influence of business leaders in defining the nature of the problems facing education and in shaping the terms of the debate over their solutions leads to a growing public acceptance of market principles as an appropriate mode for school reform. This influence is perhaps most evident in statements by the most ardent advocates of school choice. It is fair to ask what articles of faith market romantics bring to the reform table when they are employed by public school systems as reform consultants. For example, Denis P. Doyle, whose extensive consulting work in CMS was described earlier, lamented the absence of any discussion of school choice at the 1996 National Education Summit at the IBM facility in New York.

> The alternative to command and control, is a market, whether it is purely private, as many of us would like it to be, or regulated, a mix of public and private providers. Markets have two overwhelmingly important characteristics. First, they are exquisitely calibrated communication systems, letting willing buyers and sellers know what good or service is available at what price in what quantity and quality, and letting each know what the other would be like; second, as Schumpeter declared, they permit "creative destruction." Inefficient, corrupt, and ineffectual organizations disappear. That's what markets are all about. That is why in a market the consumer is sovereign. To create a system of high academic standards, and schools which are safe and disciplined, there must be choice among schools.[57]

Doyle's highly idealistic description of how markets operate only loosely relates to the actual workings of the commodities, health care, real estate, airline, or higher education markets. Despite what market-reform romantics assert are the powers of the market to cure the ills of public schools, a host of empirical studies of choice in education challenge such unqualified claims.[58]

The point here is not to enumerate the perils of privatization to public education. A vast literature on this subject already exists. The purpose of this discussion is to juxtapose the arguments made by market-romantics with their location in the larger vista of school reformers. Early in the current round of the privatization movement, prominent choice advocate Chester A. Finn Jr. admitted that claims that choice will bring about improved achievement "spring more from ratiocination and conviction than from airtight research." Eight years later, Finn urged conservatives to "look into our own blind spots" in order to accomplish more sound educational reform. Two among the eleven blind spots that he identified are that "private schools are doing fine if only more children could attend them" and that "vouchers will fix it."[59]

Jeffrey Henig argues that the market metaphor functions in two ways to make privatization more palatable. First, it bridges the gap between this radical way of providing education by linking it to familiar market arrangements in other spheres of life. Second, the market metaphor assists advocates in bridging the gap between evidence and their prescription. Lacking an empirical basis on which to support their claims, advocates assume school choice, magnets, and vouchers will act "like free markets."[60] Public discourse that romanticizes the market and understates its troubled track record in school reform sets the stage for educational entrepreneurs, like the Edison Project and Education Alternatives, Inc. (EAI), to step through the privatization door wedged open by local political skirmishes over school reform.

### Missing Evaluations of Business Interventions

Perhaps the most serious danger business interventions pose is that there are few if any systematic evaluations of these program. In the absence of evaluations of business partnerships, programs, and gifts, there is very little reliable evidence that these, in fact, lead to positive school outcomes for students. Timpane and McNeill label such partnerships feel-good associations that do not reform schools. In their estimation, with only modest exceptions, there has been no widespread impact of business involvement on educational outcomes.[61] Many partnerships and collaborations may well be diversions of valuable resources, opportunities, and participants' time. In such cases, the feel-good aspect of the interventions conveys the patina of genuine reform while it distracts people from effectively addressing the core problems facing their schools. ProjectFirst is a prime example of an unevaluated feel-good reform that, to at least a limited degree, diverted public attention from systemic reforms needed by CMS nonmagnet middle schools.

### Masking Business Contributions to Educational Problems

There is indeed heavy irony in the fact that the generous donations by corporations and their leaders of money, materials, and time to educational reforms often deflect attention from the far more serious damage they do to education through their actions to restructure the American economy. Firms contribute both directly and indirectly to educational problems by the way that they conduct their own business affairs—

extracting maximum profits from workers and communities. Since the recent economic expansion began, there has been a huge transfer of wealth from middle-class Americans to owners of capital assets. The owners of financial assets have been the overwhelming beneficiaries of the current economic expansion. At the same time, the wages of most working American families have stagnated. Furthermore, the spread between the pay of the typical worker and the chief executive has increased from 30–to-1 in the 1960s to more than 100–to-1 today. Often the actions of corporate leaders must negatively affect the families of precisely those students who are most at-risk for educational failure and whom they mean to benefit by their contributions to education.

Corporations indirectly contribute to educational problems when their policies undercut the economic health of entire communities or families. Certain demographic groups (poor racial and ethnic minorities) and geographic regions (inner cities, rural areas) continue to suffer from acute poverty despite the economic boom of the late 1990s. The outright disappearance of jobs paying livable wages in inner cities and rural areas has had profoundly negative consequences for families there. Children of the jobless poor and of IBM's downsized middle-class workers are at an increased risk for educational problems. For example, IBM world-wide employment stood at 241,000 in 1997, down from a high of 406,000 in 1985. Gerstner presided over the layoff of 60,000 workers beginning in 1993. In Charlotte, IBM has reduced its total workforce from a high of about 5,100 in the late 1980s, to 3200 by 1997.[62]

Business contributes to the economic problems facing communities and schools in other ways. Tax breaks that state and local governments often negotiate with corporations to induce them to remain in or relo-cate to a region often directly diminish for decades the tax bases that fund public education. Furthermore, such agreements often draw cor-porations and their employees to poorer regions where schools already suffer from inadequate funding. That influx of employees and their chil-dren increases the population of school-age children at the same time that the companies' negotiations limit the revenues necessary for the schools to provide for both new and continuing students. Critics of these agreements note that tax abatements distort the marketplace and shift the tax burdens unfairly to homeowners and consumers. Many of the corporate leaders who criticize schools for being inadequate also nego-tiate away their company's share of the community property taxes. In Westchester County, New York, state and local officials offered IBM tax incentives and a $75 million low-interest loan in 1995 after the firm con-sidered leaving its Armonk headquarters.[63]

State actors help deflect public scrutiny from corporate culpability for these problems when they effusively praise corporate philanthropy while uncritically accepting business assessments of the public schools as seriously flawed. The effects are the same whether they are the functional by-products of the reform process or are due to the conscious agency of business leaders and state actors. Educational decision-makers and other state actors who privilege firms and their leaders by giving them more than merely a place at the educational reform table often hinder the public's awareness of business contributions to educational problems.

*Threats to Public Accountability in Public Education*

Geoff Whitty argues that the practical implications of political and education practice are as much a matter of the ways in which policy is made as is the specific substantive policies.[64] In the case of the Education Village, by the time the reform initiative was announced, corporate actors had already shaped its terms. Because corporations are private entities, there is no legal imperative for public disclosure of their goals, processes, and resources. As corporate actors become more deeply involved in educational policy design and implementation, their *means* as well as policy ends must be scrutinized. For example, based on her analysis of corporatism in contemporary Chicago reform, Shipps concludes that the informal influence of parent and community groups is no match for the massive influence of business. In Chicago, there is no public debate to determine if business values and practices are appropriate for the schools; business actors have no accountability to the public. Once citizens in Charlotte scrutinized the proposed Education Village, they found that what appeared to be a tidy integration of work, school, and family was a reform initiative shaped to a considerable degree by the strategic interests of private corporations.

## DISCUSSION AND SUMMARY

The central points that emerge from the description and analysis of corporate involvement in Charlotte's school reform are summarized in table 5.2. The table is useful for theorizing the intersection of human agency with social structure with respect to corporate involvement in school reform. It delineates how corporate actors in certain structural locations are able to act in ways that offered limited benefits to CMS, while positioning their firm to realize future benefits of considerable potential value. The IBM reform initiatives and the Ballantyne gift to CMS illustrate how a single project may serve a number of purposes that simultaneously advance philanthropic, strategic self-interest, and symbolic ends. The examples also reveal how corporate involvement can have unanticipated negative consequences for the school system and the community at large.

## ProjectFirst

The philanthropic core of ProjectFirst is IBM's material support for Americorps volunteers working as technology specialists in CMS non-magnet middle schools. The funds provided badly needed computers for the schools and some training for the volunteers. But ProjectFirst also served the strategic self-interest of IBM. It helped the firm to garner a larger share of CMS's educational computing market. Symbolically, ProjectFirst promoted the image of IBM as a good corporate citizen and furthered the acceptance of the notion that in technology lies the solution to many educational problems.[65]

Were an objective evaluation done, it likely would show program outcomes were at best negligible and at worst, counterproductive. The program undercut a growing public demand for more equitable distribution of middle school resources across the district. In the instance of ProjectFirst, there was little public knowledge of and no debate over the program. Furthermore, by privileging technology as the key solution to poor quality middle schools, ProjectFirst partially derailed the attention of parents and educators from genuine, systemic reforms in the areas of curriculum, instruction, staff development, and infrastructural improvements—all desperately needed by ProjectFirst middle schools.

## The Education Village

By far the most far-reaching and important of the three examples analyzed in this chapter, IBM's role in the original design of the Education Village speaks directly to the central issues under investigation here. It illustrates how powerful corporate actors sought to use public schools for private ends. The entire episode demonstrates the necessity for citizens and democratically elected educational leaders to exercise oversight of school reform planning and implementation. The $2 million Reinventing Education funds offered the district a unique opportunity to develop a four-school complex, rich in technology and parental involvement. As a prototype, the successes of the village could be replicated across the district and the nation. Yet the grant cost the district dearly. The countywide struggle over access to the prized magnet school complex undermined community confidence in the fairness of the system's pupil assignment plan (in itself, a wound the district could ill-afford to suffer). It also generated rancor among citizens, parents, firms not included in the original plan, and the school board. This struggle

TABLE 5.2.
Conceptual Analysis of Corporate Involvement in Three Philanthropic Educational Reform Projects in Charlotte, NC

|  | Project First (as implemented) | Ballantyne (as designed) | Education Village (as designed) |
|---|---|---|---|
| Philanthropic activities | provides computers, media specialists' training for Americorps volunteers | donation of land to be used for elementary schools | $2 million grant for teacher, staff training software development & hardware, project and staff salaries |
| Strategic self-interest (short and long term) | advances use of technology in schools, increases IBM share in educational computer market | "private" public school in subdivision | R&D tax write-off for software development; software testing in real schools; diversion of public scrutiny from corporate restructuring's contribution to social, education problems |

(continued on next page)

TABLE 5.2 (continued)

| | Project First (as implemented) | Ballantyne (as designed) | Education Village (as designed) |
|---|---|---|---|
| Symbolic value | strategic placement mollifies magnet critics who believe magnets get more resources than nonmagnet schools; promotes good citizen image; legitimizes business role in educational reform | deal too good to forego, "saves" tax payers from purchasing expensive land; promotes good corporate citizen image | legitimizes use of technology in education; promotes good corporate citizen image; legitimizes business role in educational reform |
| Latent consequence | undercuts movement for equitable resources in all CMS schools; privileges some students in some schools; masks resource inequities between magnets and older, nonmagnet schools | contributes to resegregation of schools by race and social class; privileges wealthy subdivision parents; generates good will for developer who creates exclusive enclave that exacerbates racial and class isolation in public schools | undermines community confidence in fairness of pupil assignment; privileges some firms and neighborhoods; masks corporate layoff of engineers, managers, that contradicts "skill deficit" claims; masks relatively small material corporate contribution in relation to enormous potential returns |

unfolded just weeks after the new board was seated, at a time when it was important to build community support. In fact, the way the new board resolved the dispute garnered respect and trust from most of the community. The exception was the corporate leaders whose original design for the Education Village was revised. In the short run, however, IBM still enjoys tax and publicity benefits, the chance to develop and test an educational software program in a real school setting, and an increase in the local educational computer market. In the long run, it will earn profits from the software it developed in Charlotte. Perhaps the most crucial long-term benefit to IBM is the grant's advancement of Louis Gerstner's vision of educational technology's leading American schools into the high-tech, information-age twenty-first century. This was, of course, a pivotal goal of the Palisades summit.

*Ballantyne*

On its face, the gift of land to the school system appears to be an act of generosity that would benefit all citizens of the county whose taxes will not be used to acquire very expensive land for new schools. But if a school is built in the most southerly tip of the county, it will in a sense become what John Goodlad warned against—public schools used for private purposes.[66] Given the difficulty of racially integrating three elementary schools at least five miles closer to the center of the county than is the Ballantyne development, the school board abandoned its efforts in 1996 (board members refer to McCloud, McAndrews, and Montgomery elementary schools as the 3M problem). Only extraordinary efforts and long bus rides will permit the Ballantyne elementary school to be utilized by any children living outside the subdivision. By donating land, the developer in effect gained the amenity of a de facto private school for those who can spend an average of $500,000 on their homes. The donation exacerbated community tensions over both equity of resource allocations and sharing of the burden for racial balance across the district. Moreover, it set a precedent. Building upon the Ballantyne precedent of land-for-schools, a conservative politician who advocates neighborhood schools began to discuss with other developers the possibilities of setting aside land-for-schools in new subdivisions, some only one mile from the South Carolina border in areas that are nearly impossible to integrate.[67]

## CONCLUSION

It is possible to draw several general conclusions from this case study of corporate involvement in Charlotte school reform. First, it shows how political struggle and public contestation over the actions of corporate leaders, in some instances, can move the educational policy process and its outcomes away from serving a more narrow corporate agenda toward broader public goals. Second, this chapter demonstrates why we must neither universally praise corporate involvement in educational reform nor uniformly condemn it as pernicious. Many instances are quite helpful; others are rather benign; some are potentially ruinous to public education. Each corporate initiative, program, or donation plots along continua of philanthropic altruism and strategic self-interest; latent and manifest consequences; and dangers and benefits to communities, schools, individual and corporate actors. It is necessary to specify how and when each initiative offers opportunities and dangers for schools and communities. Third, the chapter shows that we cannot assume that every attempt by corporate actors to shape and implement educational policies and programs in ways that narrowly serve their strategic self-interest will be wholly successful. The three initiatives described in this chapter show how political contestation by citizen groups, individual parents, and elected members of the school board can undermine attempts to use public education for more narrow private ends.

## NOTES

1. An earlier version of this chapter was presented at the Urban Education Conference, Graduate School of Education and Information Science, University of California, Los Angeles, June 20–23, 1996. This research is supported by a grant to the author from the National Science Foundation (RED-9550763). Stephen Samuel Smith, Dorothy Shipps, Annelle Houk, and several confidential reviewers made helpful and incisive comments on earlier versions of this essay. Susan Masse and Damien Heath provided technical assistance in transcribing interviews; and Hillary Edwards, Anne Velasco, Angela Wadsworth, Debra Wakefield, and Matthew Walker assisted with research. Stella Nkomo provided valuable insight into the contemporary business climate.

2. David Kearns and Denis P. Doyle, *Winning the Brain Race: A Bold Plan to Make Our Schools Competitive* (San Francisco: ICS Press, 1988); Carol. A. Ray and Roslyn A. Mickelson, "Restructured Students for Restructured Work: The Economy, School Reform, and Noncollege-bound Youth," *Sociology of Education* 66 (1993): 1–23.

3. Lauro Cavazos, Address to Charlotte Conference on Parental Choice.(Charlotte, North Carolina, November 1989).

4. Kathryn L. Borman and K. Gallagher, "Business Involvement in School Reform: The Rise of the Business Roundtable," in *Politics of Education Yearbook*, ed. Catherine Marshall (London: Falmer, 1994).

5. S. R. Martin, "The 1989 Education Summit as a Defining Moment," in *Changing American Education. Recapturing the Past or Inventing the Future?*

ed. Kathryn Borman and Nancy P. Greenman (Albany: State University of New York Press, 1994).

6. The summit's formal purpose focused upon putative needs of corporations to assure a better skilled workforce for future high-tech information-age jobs. Prior to the summit, participants received a two-inch thick briefing book containing commissioned essays and other materials on standards, technology, and topics related to systemic school reform (1996 National Education Summit, Presummit Briefing Materials, Armonk, N.Y.: IBM Corporation, 1996). The topics in the pre-summit briefing book reflected this formal goal and the preferred means to this end. The informal agenda was clear as well. According to Denis P. Doyle, one of the resource persons,

> While the meeting's larger purpose was to reinvigorate the standards movement and highlight education technology, its real function was to solemnize the fact that the federal role in education is virtually at an end. (Denis P. Doyle, "A Personal Report from the Education Summit: What Does It Mean for Education Reform?" *The Heritage Lectures* [Washington, D.C.: The Heritage Foundation, 1996], p. 6)

7. Raymond Allan Morrow and Carlos Alberto Torres, *Social Theory and Education: A Critique of Theories of Social and Cultural Reproduction* (New York: State University of New York Press, 1995), pp. 343–44.

8. *Swann v. Charlotte-Mecklenburg Board of Education,* 402 U.S. 1 (1971).

9. Roslyn A. Mickelson and Carol A. Ray, "Fear of Falling from Grace: The Middle Class, Downward Mobility, and School Desegregation," *Research in Sociology of Education and Socialization* 10 (1994): 207–38. In the spring of 1999, CMS returned to court to defend its efforts to desegregate the school system. Sued by white plaintiffs who desire a return to neighborhood schools, and black plaintiffs who desire greater desegregation and equity, the school system's position is that while it has made progress since 1971, many schools remain segregated and unequal.

10. Ibid.; Roslyn A. Mickelson, Carol A. Ray, and Stephen Samuel Smith, "The Growth Machine and the Politics of Urban Educational Reform: The Case of Charlotte, North Carolina," in *Education in the Urban Context,* ed. Nelly Stromquist (New York: Praeger, 1994).

11. Carol A. Ray and Roslyn A. Mickelson, "Restructured Students for Restructured Work: The Economy, School Reform, and Noncollege-bound Youth," *Sociology of Education.* 66 (1993): 1–23; Carol A. Ray and Roslyn A. Mickelson, "Corporate Leaders, Resistant Youth, and School Reform in Sunbelt City: The Political Economy of Education," *Social Problems* 37 (1990): 178–90.

12. The group of experts, christened the World Class Panel by the superintendent, met three times between December 1991 and April 1992. In May 1992, the Chamber of Commerce sponsored a communitywide forum at the Charlotte Convention Center to present the findings of the panel. Members of the panel included Chester A. (Checker) Finn Jr., William Bennett, Denis P. Doyle, James Comer, M.D. (although he did not participate until the May 1992 public forum), Patricia A. Graham, Matina Horner, Donald Steward, and Ernest

Boyer. James Kelly was the moderator. The author observed at three of the four meetings, analyzed tapes of all three panel deliberations, and conducted in-depth interviews about the panel experience with six of the eight panel participants in the cities in that they lived. An analysis of the interviews, the proceedings of the panel, and related CMS documents revealed that the panel's deliberations and final report were largely generic and symbolic and had little to do specifically with reform in Charlotte. Nonetheless, for many of the reform initiatives he proposed, Superintendent Murphy invoked the imprimatur of the world-class panel to legitimize his actions. This was not true of his most controversial and far-reaching initiative: the recommendation to end mandatory busing and replace it with parental choice of magnet schools made independent of and prior to the panel's work. That reform was designed and enacted during the panel's deliberations, yet it was never a topic of discussion. Panelists occasionally referred to school choice in general, and all agreed with Patricia A. Graham's observation that with respect to school choice, "the devil is in the details."

13. Mickelson and Ray, "Fear of Falling."

14. Ibid.; Allison Marantz, "Desegregation at Risk: Threat and Reaffirmation in Charlotte," in *Dismantling Desegregation: The Quiet Reversal of Brown v. Board of Education*, ed. Gary Orfield, Susan E. Eaton, and the Harvard Project on School Desegregation (New York: The New Press, 1996); Roslyn Arlin Mickelson, "Expert Report to the U.S. District Court for the Western District of North Carolina in the Case of Capacchione v. Charlotte-Mecklenburg Schools et al.," December 1998.

15. Stephen Samuel Smith, "Hugh Governs? Regime and Educational Policy in Charlotte, North Carolina," *Journal of Urban Affairs* 19 (1997): 247–74.

16. Ibid.

17. Carroll Gray, Remarks to Technical High School Task Force (Charlotte, N.C., July 1997).

18. Americorps is President Clinton's volunteer service program. Volunteers work in their communities for two years. During their commitment they receive a minimal stipend but are entitled to grants for additional education once they complete their service.

19. Committee of 25, *Resource Subcommittee Report to the Board of Education* (Charlotte, N.C.: Charlotte-Mecklenburg Board of Education, April 1994); Committee of 25, *Pupil Assignment Subcommittee Report to the Board of Education* (Charlotte, N.C.: Charlotte-Mecklenburg Board of Education, July 1994).

20. John Murphy, Remarks to Charlotte-Mecklenburg Education Foundation board meeting (Charlotte, August 1994).

21. Stanley S. Litow, "IBM Introduces New Corporate Philanthropy Initiative; Charlotte Schools are First to Benefit," Press release (Armonk, N.Y.: IBM Corporation, September 14, 1994).

22. Herbert Watkins, Interview with the author, Charlotte, N.C., August 1995.

23. Litow, Letter to Superintendent John Murphy, September 12, 1994; Litow, Letter to Superintendent John Murphy, April 5, 1995; John Murphy, "The Charlotte-Mecklenburg Education Village: The Next Step in Reforming America's Schools" (Charlotte: Charlotte-Mecklenburg Schools, n.d.).

24. Litow, September 14, 1994.

25. RJR Nabisco's Next Century Schools program provided $32 million to forty-three schools nationwide (Gerstner). At the same time, RJR under Gerstner's stewardship, Camels became the most highly identified cigarette among children. The Joe Camel character helped RJR's share of the cigarette market rise from 1 to 32.8 percent, and this increase brought RJR an estimated $476 million in sales (see Derrick Jackson, "Louis Gerstner's Double Standards," *Rethinking Schools*, Summer 1996). The purpose of juxtaposing these two actions by one corporation is to illustrate how a firm can be motivated simultaneously by narrow self-interest (in this case, greater market share and greater profits) while it engages in what many consider to be child-centered philanthropy. Recent books by Alex Molnar (*Giving Kids the Business: The Commercialization of America's Schools* [Boulder, Colo.: Westview, 1996]) and Alfie Kohn (*Education, Inc.: Turning Learning into a Business* [Arlington Heights, Ill.: IRI Skylight Press, 1997]) describe and analyze these bipolar practices toward children among many other American corporations.

26. Winston-Salem/Forsyth County Schools, The Downtown School Information Sheet (1996).

27. Murphy, *The Charlotte-Mecklenburg Education Village*, p. 3

28. Seddon "Rusty" Goode Jr., "Don't Botch the Education Village," *Charlotte Observer*, February 29, 1996, p. A10.

29. Joe Miller, "Grants Are Not Free as IBM Has Shown the BOE," *Conservative Views: NC Free Society Foundation* 3 (1996): 1.

30. Susan Burgess, "IBM and the Education Village: Setting the Record Straight," *Charlotte Observer*, February 22, 1996, p. A7.

31. Stanley Litow, Letter to Acting Superintendent Dennis Williams, March 13, 1996.

32. Ann Clark, Interview with the author, Charlotte, North Carolina, June 3, 1997.

33. John Minter, "IBM Grant Not Worth as Much as Taxpayers Put," *Charlotte Post*, January 30, 1996: p.1A.

34. "The Famed Ballantyne School Could be a Dump," *The Leader*, October 31, 1997, p. 5. This is not the first time that this developer sought to donate land in the hopes of future profits. In the early 1990s, Sears Roebuck and Company announced its intentions to move from Chicago to the Sunbelt. The developer offered to sell the corporation land for its new headquarters for $1.00 (the land later became part of the Ballantyne development). Sears Roebuck negotiated a more satisfactory fiscal agreement with Cook County and, instead, moved from its famed tower to the Chicago suburbs. Rumors circulated that the loss of Sears was due, in large part, to the poor quality of Charlotte's schools. Many observers in Charlotte believe that the loss of Sears inspired the downtown business elite to ratchet up their pressure on CMS to improve.

35. Clark. Litow declined to answer a written request for an interview.

36. Roslyn. A. Mickelson,"The Need to Build Bridges from School to Work . . . and Much, Much More." *Advances in Educational Policy* 3 (1997): 158–89; National Center on Education and the Economy, *America's Choice: High Skills or Low Wages!* (Rochester, N.Y.: NCEE, 1990); National Center on

Educational Quality of the Workforce, *Educational Quality of the Workforce: National Employer Survey* (Philadelphia: University of Pennsylvania, 1995); Ruy Teixeira and Larry Mishel, "Whose Skill Shortage—Workers or Management?" *Issues in Science and Technology*, Summer 1993, 69–74.

37. Philip Wexler, *Social Analysis of Education* (Boston: Routledge and Kegan Paul, 1987).

38. National Association of Partners in Education, *Handbook of Education Partners* (Alexandria, Va.: National Association of Partners in Education, 1995).

39. See Elizabeth. L. Useem, and R. C. Neild, "A Place at the Table: The Changing Role of Urban Public Education Funds," paper presented at the meetings of the American Educational Research Association, New Orleans, April 1994. At times, however, an educational foundation's actions challenge this characterization of nonpartisan civic-mindedness. For example, at its August 1994 board meeting, the Charlotte-Mecklenburg Educational Foundation (CMEF) announced that one of its 1995 projects would be the identification of appropriate candidates to run for the next school board election when, for the first time, six of the nine seats on the board were to be selected by district rather than at-large.

A school board member explained why corporate elites felt this initiative was necessary. She described the fear the anticipated switch from at-large to school board election by district had engendered among the corporate elites:

> Well, now districts are scaring the Chamber of Commerce to death. And they are already really actively working on getting, recruiting their own candidates in the districts. And talk about throwing money at them, I think that you will see that a lot. . . . [The Chamber ] is scared they are going to get a group of people out of the districts that they cannot control. (Quoted in Stephen Samuel Smith, "Education, Race, and Regime Change in Charlotte-Mecklenburg," paper presented at the annual meeting of the Urban Affairs Association, New York, March 1996)

40. Allison Tucker and W. F. Lauber, "Chapter 6. Education," *Briefing Book for Newly Elected Members of Congress* (Washington, D.C.: Heritage Foundation, 1994).

41. Charlotte-Mecklenburg Schools, *Financial Ledger, Accounts Payable* (Charlotte, N.C.: Charlotte-Mecklenburg Schools, 1991–95). Doyle was paid a little under $77,000 in expenses and consulting fees during this period.

42. Denis P. Doyle, Personal interview with the author, (Charlotte, N.C., March 1993); Denis P. Doyle, Personal interview with the author (Washington, D.C., June 1993).

43. Dorothy Shipps, personal communication, January 1999.

44. Neil Mara, "Schools Weigh Business Impact," *Charlotte Observer*, March 10, 1996), p. 1B.

45. Shipps, "The Invisible Hand: Big Business and Chicago School Reform," *Teachers College Record* 99 (1997): 73–116.

46. George Counts, *Social Composition of School Boards: A Study in the Social Control of Education* (Chicago: University of Chicago Press, 1927).

47. Peter Sola, "The Corporate Community on the Ideal-Business School Alliance: A Historical and Ethical Critique," in *The New Servants of Power*, ed C. M. Shea, E. Kahane, and P. Sola (New York: Praeger, 1990); "Insider," *Charlotte Observer*, (September 29, 1997), p. 14D.

48. Lewis C. Solmon, Interview with the author, Santa Monica, Calif., June 1996.

49. Thanks to Elizabeth L. Useem for this bringing this and many other insight to my attention.

50. Committee for Economic Development, *The Unfinished Agenda: A New Vision for Child Development and Education* (New York: CED, 1991); Committee for Economic Development, *Children in Need. Investment Strategies for the Educationally Disadvantaged* (New York: CED, 1987); Committee for Economic Development, *Investing in Our Children: Business and the Public Schools* (New York: CED, 1985).

51. Ivan Charner, "School to Work Opportunities: Prospects and Challenges," in *Implementing Educational Reform: Sociological Perspectives on Educational Policy* ed. Peter Cookson, Kathryn Borman, Alan Sadovnik, and Joan Spade (Norwood, N.J.: Ablex, 1996); Gary Orfield and Faith G. Paul, *High Hopes, Long Odds: A Major Report on Hoosier Teens and the American Dream* (Indianapolis, Ind.: Indiana Youth Institute, 1994).

52. In his article,"The Right's Data-Proof Ideologues," *Education Week*, January 25, 1995, p. 42, Gerald Bracey uses the moniker "data-proof ideologues" to characterize those who dismiss evidence contrary to their positions and continue to advance in their public speeches and writings the claim that American education is stagnant and ineffectual. Several of the data-proof ideologues were consultants to the authors of the Heritage Foundation's 1994 Briefing Book for new members of Congress (Tucker and Lauber). The briefing book's gross inaccuracies in fact and interpretation of educational matters prompted the Department of Education to prepare a document that rebuts each point (see U.S. Department of Education, *Setting the Record Straight: Responding to Key Factual Errors and Assertions in the Heritage Foundations' Brief for Congress*, Office of the Undersecretary, Washington, D.C.: U.S. Department of Education, 1994). This rebuttal was then sent to all new members of Congress.

53. Gerstner et al., *Reinventing Education*, p. 45.

54. Gerstner et al., *Reinventing Education*. For a detailed discussion of Gerstner et al.'s numerous errors in fact and interpretation, see Roslyn Arlin Mickelson, "Opportunity and Danger: Understanding Business Involvement in School Reform," in Borman, Spade, and Cookson.

55. See David C. Berliner and Bruce Biddle, *The Manufactured Crisis*. (Reading, Mass.: Addison-Wesley, 1995); Bracey; Larry Cuban, "The Great School Scam," *Education Week*, June 15, 1994, p. 44; Lawrence C. Stedman, "The Achievement Crisis is Real: A Review of *The Manufactured Crisis. Educational Policy Analysis Archives* 4.1 (1996), http://seamonkey.ed.asu.edu/

56. Peter Cookson, *School Choice. The Struggle for the Soul of American Education*. (New Haven: Yale University Press, 1994); Jay Greene, Paul E. Peterson, and Jiangtao Du, "Effectiveness of School Choice: The Milwaukee Experiment," paper presented at the Annual Meeting of the American Educa-

tional Research Association, Chicago, April 1997; Jeffrey Henig, *Rethinking School Choice. Limits of the Market Metaphor* (Princeton: Princeton University Press, 1994); Edith Rasell and Richard Rothstein, *School Choice. Examining the Evidence* (Washington, D.C.: Economic Policy Institute, 1993); John Witte, A. Bailey, and C. Thorn, *Fifth Year Report. Milwaukee Parental Choice Program,* Robert LaFollette School of Public Policy (Madison: University of Wisconsin, 1996); Geoffrey Walford, "Educational Choice and Equity in Great Britain," *Educational Policy* 6 (1992): 123–38.; Douglas Willms and Frank Echols, "The Scottish Experience of Parental Choice of Schools," paper presented at "Choice: What Role in American Education?" (Washington, D.C.: Economic Policy Institute, 1992).

57. Doyle, *A Personal Report,* p. 9.

58. See note 56; Alexander W. Astin, "Educational 'Choice': Its Appeal May Be Illusory," *Sociology of Education* 65 (1992): 255–60.

59. Chester A. Finn Jr., "The Choice Backlash," *The National Review,* November 10, 1989, pp. 30–32; Finn, "Blind Spots on the Right," *The National Review,* September 25, 1995, 68–69.

60. Jeffrey Henig, *Rethinking School Choice: Limits of the Market Metaphor* (Princeton: Princeton University Press, 1994).

61. Michael Timpane and L. M. McNeill, *Business Impact on Education and Child Development Reform* (New York: Committee for Economic Development, 1991), p. 32.

62. David Boraks, "IBM Trims Workforce," *Charlotte Observer,* October 18, 1997, p. 1D; Harry Greyard, "IBM Cuts New for Charlotte," *Charlotte Observer,* July 11, 1987, p. 10A; Greyard, "IBM's Charlotte Facility May Shrink," *Charlotte Observer,* August 8, 1992, p. 1D; Douglas Massey and Mary Denton, *American Apartheid: Segregation and the Making of the Underclass* (Cambridge: Harvard University Press, 1993); Louis Uchitelle, "1995 Was Good for Companies and Better for a Lot of CEOs" *New York Times,* March 29, 1996; William Julius Wilson, *When Work Disappears* (New York: Alfred A. Knopf, 1996).

63. Kerry A. White and Robert C. Johnston, "Schools' Taxes Bartered Away to Garner Jobs," *Education Week,* March 12, 1997, p. 1f.

64. Geoff Whitty, *Sociology and School Knowledge: Curriculum Theory, Research, and Politics* (London: Methuen, 1985), p. 82.

65. See Larry Cuban, "High-Tech Schools and Low-Tech Teaching," *Education Week,* May 21, 1997, p. 38.; Douglas D. Noble, "Selling the Schools a Bill of Goods: The Marketing of Computer-Based Education," in *Education, Inc.,* ed. Kohn and Todd Oppenheimer, "The Computer Delusion" *The Atlantic Monthly,* June 1997, pp. 45–65, for trenchant critiques of both the underlying conceptualization of the role of technology in education and current practices that implement it.

66. John Goodlad, "Making Democracy Safe for Education," *Education Week,* July 9, 1997, p. 56.

67. John Deem, "Okay, So Now Who Controls School Siting?" *The Leader,* November 7, 1997, pp. 4–5.

CHAPTER 6

# A Comparative Analysis of Existing Secondary School Discipline Policies: Implications for Improving Practice and School Safety

Pamela Fenning, James D. Wilczynski, and Marianela Parraga

Violence is increasingly a concern in schools and surrounding communities. While some researchers explain that schools remain relatively safe places in comparison to other environments, safer even than their own homes,[1] the fact still remains that an increasing number of students are reporting, witnessing, or being exposed to acts of violence within school halls and in surrounding communities. Statistics indicate that between 43 percent and 55 percent of inner-city adolescent males have witnessed a robbery, assault, or shooting. Ten percent of adolescent inner-city females have been raped, while up to 16 percent have been threatened with rape.[2] Furthermore, increasing numbers of students are bringing weapons to school. According to the U.S. Centers for Disease Control, it was estimated that 5 percent of students brought a gun to school at least once a month.[3] Since many students report that they bring weapons to school for protection, one may wonder if these numbers will increase now that some states have passed concealed weapons laws in which adults may carry concealed weapons in public.

Violence and the threat of violence dramatically impact the school routine and the learning of youth in urban communities. A case example in Chicago involves a school for youth with emotional disorders. The administrative personnel have changed the school hours to allow the students to leave the building earlier than the usual Chicago Public School dismissal time. This decision was made because of continual victimization of these youth as they boarded their buses at the end of the day. Many students also fear for their own safety while at school. Just as a poor child who is perpetually hungry may not learn well in school, one will expect a child who is fearful of being injured or killed to also have difficulty learning. For instance, 80,000 children stay home from school at least one day a month due to fear of being hurt at school.[4] The U.S. Department of Education reinforces that even being forced to cope with the constant risk of violence interferes with learning. At times, violence impacts our youth to such an extent and in so many ways that students' education is completely halted.

To address issues of violence and related urban issues, educators have taken a number of theoretical approaches. Recent classroom management approaches, such as responsive classroom management, have focused on teaching children responsibility within a specific context.[5] General guidelines and standards guide classroom activity versus enforcement of specific rules. The focus within the classroom management approach is to develop students' internal control through acceptance of logical consequences for behavior.

Attention has been given to the presentation of curriculum in the creation of an accepting learning environment for all students. Cooperative learning is effective in promoting student discovery in learning, social skills, and positive classroom behavior.[6] Proactive classroom management, which focuses on teacher skills that prevent or de-escalate behavioral difficulties, has documented success in creating a supportive learning environment and reduction of behavior problems.[7]

Ancillary schoolwide interventions, involving peer mediation and conflict resolution, focus specifically on reduction of violence.[8] Schools have also begun to adopt violence prevention curricula, which tend to involve problem solving and role-playing alternatives to aggression.[9]

But the previously described interventions fail to consider the larger social context in which violence and school discipline issues emanate. Poverty and social marginalization are factors that contribute to the proliferation of violence.[10] Few researchers have examined the multiplicity of larger societal variables that impact the display of aggressive behavior in school settings. An extensive review of the literature related to the causes of aggression in school settings and the efficacy of programs to address school violence was completed by Tolan and Guerra.[11] The authors cited a variety of cultural and social factors that increase the risk of aggression and violence. These cultural and social factors include socioeconomic status, peer influences, family resources, and coping skills.[12] School culture and the social context in which schools operate may actually be contributing to violence seen in schools. Schools attempt to exert a great deal of control in managing behavior. When these school expectations and the social context of the school are not consistent with the social norms of the student, problem behaviors may emerge.[13] Individual student behavior is not in isolation, but within the context of each specific school.[14] Punitive behaviors of teachers, in addition to discipline policies themselves, may contribute to the proliferation of violence seen in schools.[15] For example, harsh verbal abuse and, in some states, corporal punishment, contribute to an abuse of power between teacher and student. This, in turn, contributes to the establishment of a negative social context in which students are expected to function.

Without considering the social context and sociological variables that promote aggression, teachers and school administrators have relied on reactionary interventions as an attempt to achieve immediate reductions in violence. For example, metal detectors and in-house police have been placed in all Chicago secondary public schools. Many school districts across the nation boast of a "zero tolerance policy" in which violent students are removed from public schools and are placed in an alternative private school setting. Another common, but controversial, strategy is to conduct searches of students if they are suspected of possessing drugs or weapons.[16]

Many schools are attempting to adopt "get tough" approaches and are becoming more punitive in their efforts to illustrate how they do not tolerate violence. Effective efforts, however, address the specific problems children have within a larger social context and do not solely focus on a specific violation.[17] Hyman and colleagues explain that there are few simple solutions and "the best solution must take into account the total ecology of the school situation."[18]

Schools can address violence and problem areas effectively by implementing good discipline policies. There is a body of literature suggesting that effective discipline policies possess many similar features. The most basic feature is that discipline policies must clearly state what behaviors are violations and what consequences will result if violations do occur.[19] Therefore, an effective policy does not leave any room for inconsistent messages regarding acceptance or nonacceptance of behavior and subjective application of consequences. Each violation, however, may have different circumstances surrounding it, and would necessitate some latitude in applying the policy. This is because each specific school has larger community needs, and the behavior must be placed within the social ecology in which it operates. Students would be treated equitably, but not necessarily in the same manner for every circumstance. For instance, if a policy simply indicates that stealing will result in a two-day suspension, it would seem illogical to give the same consequence to a student who has committed his or her first offense and another student who has committed his or her fifth offense. These situations are plausible scenarios and should be handled differently, with a consideration of the specific needs of the student within the school community. In order to adequately address the multitude of scenarios in schools, a range of possible consequences for each offense is provided so that the disciplinarian can consider specific mitigating circumstances of an incident.[20] The range of consequences is clearly specified and an explanation of why there is a range should be provided. Again, this procedure must be implemented with sensitivity to the social context in which the student is operating.

Another major factor believed to relate to effective discipline policies is the degree to which they are consistently and fairly enforced.[21] If teachers attempt to make examples out of some students while allowing others to break rules, students will quickly learn that the discipline policy is a farce and the important lesson to learn is which teachers or staff allow which infractions.

Rubel and Blauvelt also believe it is important for a policy to delineate between violations of school rules and violations of state laws.[22] Students also need to be aware of when outside authorities, such as police, will be contacted. For instance, if two students are fighting, a criteria for police involvement versus internal handling of the incident needs to be specified. In some schools, police are called only if a weapon is involved. However, what constitutes a weapon is unclear as a gun, knife, lock, book, or any object used with an intent to injure could potentially be defined as a weapon. These issues need to be explicitly clarified within the policy. Some states also require a school to report certain incidents to law enforcement authorities.[23] Consequently, not only do students need to be aware, but staff must know when to refer the incident to authorities outside the school.

Discipline policies tend to be more effective when the school is sure that students have read and understand the policy.[24] In some schools, students are required to read the policy or handbook and pass a test measuring their understanding of the rules and consequences.[25] If a student fails, he or she receives additional instruction and is later retested. While the emphasis thus far has been placed on the students, teachers and staff also need to be fully aware of the policy so that they can consistently enforce the rules and apply consequences fairly.[26]

Effective policies generally reflect the values of the community and can be adapted to meet the specific needs of the school. This aspect suggests that very large school districts need to be flexible and, possibly, individualized policies need to be developed for each school building. Some schools within large cities like Chicago, for example, have had success in forming a "discipline committee" consisting of school staff, parents, and students who develop the policy and determine the proper consequences.[27] However, according to a national survey, school principals feel that they and the district personnel are most responsible for developing discipline policies. Only 18 percent of principals said teachers should share responsibility in setting the policy.[28] The principals were not even asked if members of the community should be involved in developing the discipline policies. This is counter to consideration of these behaviors within the social context in which they are expressed.

While prior research has reviewed discipline policies in terms of what makes a general policy effective, there are several neglected areas in light of recent educational trends concerning violence prevention and intervention. The degree to which discipline policies vary in relation to the setting of service (e.g., urban versus suburban and public versus private) and in terms of the student population serviced (students referred for emotional or behavioral problems versus students in general education settings) has not been examined. We believe it is imperative to examine such policies within a cultural context and to individualize the policy for the diverse needs of the student population. We need to focus on clear communication among school personnel, students, and families in our establishment of standards for school behavior and subsequent development of formal policies. This is particularly pressing as a major component of our attempt to grapple with complex, larger social issues related to violence and in our mission to create a safe environment for all within public schools. These issues must be considered in the development of discipline policies which are not a means of control, but address the deeper sociological issues that contribute to school violence.

## METHODOLOGY

As an attempt to begin addressing these larger questions regarding the content of discipline policies across settings, we chose seven discipline policies in a variety of secondary school settings. We engaged in the technique of purposive sampling. This technique involves choosing subjects because of known parameters of interest.[29] We were interested in obtaining discipline policies from schools that had a range of socioeconomic levels, specialized services, and economic support (public versus private). Our settings included large city public schools, a public school bordering the city, a large private city school with a religious affiliation, a large private high socioeconomic status (SES) suburban school with a religious affiliation, a public high SES suburban school, a private school for students with emotional and behavior disorders and a public school for adjudicated students.

In the city, all public secondary schools utilized a uniform discipline code. This policy is established for use across the variety of neighborhoods and settings. However, there is a qualification to school personnel that modifications can be made for the individual school site, with the understanding that any changes should not replace the uniform guidelines.

The developed school policies also followed basic regulations established by the Illinois School Code and the Illinois Criminal Code. The Illinois Criminal Code applies most directly to mandated reports of illegal activities of students to the Bureau of Safety and Security. However, the policies varied in terms of their interpretations of the legal guidelines.

The qualitative data-reduction technique of grounded theory was utilized in the development of a coding system. In this approach, the data drives the development of the categories, which are collapsed as common themes emerge.[30] Advantages of this approach are the generation of hypotheses for the variables of interest. A weakness of this approach is the lack of experimental control, and related threats to internal validity.

Two female psychologists, one Ph.D. and one M.Ed. level, created and utilized the coding system, based on their analysis of the content of the existing discipline policies. Their backgrounds are in applied psychology, including learning theory, assessment and evaluation of school-aged children and adolescents. They have experience across all school settings examined in the current study. The purpose of the coding system was to examine behaviors and the range of consequences referenced by each specific school discipline policy.

Specifically, behaviors related to violence or a negative school climate were examined within the school policy. Behaviors such as truancy, tardiness, and proper dress were not examined. The coding system was continually altered to encompass the extensive range of behaviors specified in the various policies. Initially, broad categories were created and were expanded to include specific subcategories, enabling a more detailed analysis of frequently addressed behaviors across all policies.

When the behaviors were coded, each specific instance of a behavior was tallied as a separate frequency. For example, if using slanderous verbalizations was mentioned more than once within the policy, it was coded each time it occurred. A decision was made regarding whether the behavior met the criteria for one of the larger categories or a specific subcategory. In this example, slanderous verbalizations could be classified under the broad categories of harassment and academic disturbance. Depending on the situation and content, one would make a decision regarding which classification to follow. In this case, whether the focus of the behavior was on an individual student/staff or the larger school context would determine which code was chosen. If the statement within the policy closely matched the defining features of a category/subcategory, it was classified as such, and did not have to match the prose in the code verbatim. During the coding process, the examiners discussed behaviors that could not clearly be categorized, and made a joint decision after deliberation.

The minimum and the maximum consequences for each behavior were coded if they were identifiable within the policy. Some behaviors within the discipline policies did not have a stated consequence, and this was indicated within our coding system. In addition, some behaviors listed only one consequence. If this occurred, the stated consequence was coded without an indicated range.

## RESULTS

### Findings across All Policies

We examined all discipline policies in terms of the relative importance given to each of the discipline categories. The percentage of total attention that each category obtained in relation to the overall percentage is displayed in table 6.1 for all school settings. Our main finding was that every school policy, with the exception of one, focused mainly on student misconduct relating to possession, distribution or use of prohibited objects on school grounds. Prohibited objects were defined either as being illegal by a state or federal mandate, or deemed unacceptable by school authorities. Schools tended to be specific and elaborate regarding the type of object(s) that were prohibited. The subcategories included narcotics, alcohol, tobacco, destructive devices, electronic devices, and weapons. This generally increased the number of codes within this category, yielding a higher percentage in relation to the overall policy.

However, an examination of physical aggression indicated that this broad category received much less attention, with the exception of one school. This relative lack of attention is evidenced in both the relatively lower resulting percentages of attention to physical aggression in relation to the overall categories, and with regard to the lack of specificity to defining features. Physical aggression was defined only in terms of whether or not it resulted in a physical injury, or involved individuals or groups. There was virtually no attention to sexual assault, and only one policy mentioned molestation or rape.

Apart from the dominant category of possession, distribution and use of prohibited objects, there was a general trend across all policies for relatively higher levels of attention to the categories of academic distur-

### TABLE 6.1
Percentage of Attention in Discipline Policies
for Behavioral Categories: All Schools

| | Public, Urban | Urban Detention Center | Private, Urban, Religious Affiliation | Public, Suburban High SES | Private, Suburban with Religious Affiliation High SES | Private School for Children with Emotional and Behavioral Disorders | Public School on Border of City, Low SES |
|---|---|---|---|---|---|---|---|
| Possession/distribution of prohibited objects or substances | 32 | 27 | 53 | 63 | 45 | 26 | 22 |
| Academic disturbance | 19 | 18 | 11 | 10 | 5 | 19 | 22 |
| Physical aggression | 12 | 15 | 5 | 3 | 3 | 3 | 11 |
| Theft | 10 | 4 | 16 | 3 | 0 | 6 | 4 |
| Insubordination | 10 | 6 | 5 | 3 | 3 | 3 | 4 |

(continued on next page)

TABLE 6.1 (continued)

| | Public, Urban | Urban Detention Center | Private, Urban, Religious Affiliation | Public, Suburban High SES | Private, Suburban with Religious Affiliation High SES | Private School for Children with Emotional and Behavioral Disorders | Public School on Border of City, Low SES |
|---|---|---|---|---|---|---|---|
| Academic dishonesty | 7 | 7 | 0 | 3 | 11 | 0 | 0 |
| Harassment | 6 | 8 | 0 | 6 | 21 | 23 | 11 |
| Group offenses | 2 | 4 | 5 | 3 | 2 | 0 | 7 |
| Disruptive bus behavior | 2 | 0 | 5 | 0 | 2 | 4 | 0 |
| Display of affection/ physical conduct | 0 | 1 | 0 | 0 | 0 | 6 | 0 |
| School damage/ destruction | 0 | 10 | 0 | 6 | 8 | 10 | 19 |

bance, harassment, and school property destruction. While each school tended to emphasize one of these categories more than another, based on the specific mission of the school, these categories emerged as the next major area of school policy focus.

In terms of consequences and alternatives to traditional discipline procedures, none of the policies that were reviewed formally stated the need for student participation.

*Comparisons among Specific School Settings*

A comparison was made between the various school policies in terms of the emphasis placed on specific categories, subcategories of behavior, and consequences. The policies presenting the most significant differences will be emphasized within the chapter.

*Variations among Public Urban versus*
*Public Suburban in High SES Settings*

In comparing a high SES suburban public school with the uniform policy for the city public schools, as depicted in table 6.2, we found a much greater focus by the suburban school (63 percent) toward the discipline categories of possession, distribution, and use of objects than the city policy (32 percent).

TABLE 6.2
Percentage of Attention in Discipline Policies for Behavioral Categories:
Public Urban vs. Public Suburban in High SES Setting

|  | Public, Urban | Public, Suburban High SES |
|---|---|---|
| Possession/distribution of prohibited objects or substances | 32 | 63 |
| Academic disturbance | 19 | 10 |
| Physical aggression | 12 | 3 |
| Theft | 10 | 3 |
| Insubordination | 10 | 3 |
| Academic dishonesty | 7 | 3 |
| Harassment | 6 | 6 |
| Group offenses | 2 | 3 |
| Disruptive bus behavior | 2 | 0 |
| Display of affection/ physical conduct | 0 | 0 |
| School damage/destruction | 0 | 6 |

With regard to physical aggression, more attention was given to this area by the city policy code (12 percent). However, these two settings varied in terms of the consequences given for these behaviors. In the city policy, the minimum consequence was a teacher, resource person, and administrator conference, while the suburban policy chose suspension as its minimal consequence for physical aggression. The maximum consequence for physical aggression was expulsion for both policies.

The policies also varied significantly in terms of other stated consequences for behavior. The suburban policy outlined an alternative to traditional consequences for alcohol consumption and use, identifying a specific program of service to students, and the option to obtain an approved outside counselor of student/parent choice. The city policy mentioned the mandate for free and appropriate counseling services as students' rights, but did not identify a specific program or procedure for obtaining services.

Related to consequences, a specified procedure for students with grievances and perceptions of unfair treatment was outlined in the suburban policy, while the city policy mentioned the necessity of due process rights without a delineated procedure.

*Variations among Public Urban versus*
*Private Urban with Religious Affiliation*

While there were no major differences in the relative emphasis of categories and subcategories of behavior, we found some differences for the consequences. Please see table 6.3. In the public urban (city) policy, a range of consequences were stated with every behavior. However, in the private urban policy, possible consequences were listed, but not in association with any specific behavior. In general, there was much discretion given to the private school administrators regarding the application of consequences and grounds for removal of the students.

*Variations among Public Suburban in High SES versus*
*Private School for Students with Behavior/Emotional Disorders*

The private school that was examined, as can be seen from table 6.4, placed more of an emphasis on behaviors involving harassment than the public suburban school. There was a notable difference regarding the consequences given for behaviors such as physical aggression and threats of physical aggression. In the private school, consequences were unique to the setting and involved time-out from the school activity, and problem-solving, although suspension was listed as a potential consequence. Within the public school, consequences focused more on traditional procedures, and emphasized in-school suspension, out-of-school suspension, and expulsion.

TABLE 6.3
Percentage of Attention in Discipline Policies for Behavioral Categories:
Public Urban vs. Private Urban with Religious Affiliation

| | Public, Urban | Private, Urban, Religious Affiliation |
|---|---|---|
| Possession/distribution of prohibited objects or substances | 32 | 53 |
| Academic disturbance | 19 | 11 |
| Physical aggression | 12 | 5 |
| Theft | 10 | 16 |
| Insubordination | 10 | 5 |
| Academic dishonesty | 7 | 0 |
| Harassment | 6 | 0 |
| Group offenses | 2 | 5 |
| Disruptive bus behavior | 2 | 5 |
| Display of affection/ physical conduct | 0 | 0 |
| School damage/destruction | 0 | 0 |

TABLE 6.4
Percentage of Attention in Discipline Policies for Behavioral Categories:
Public Suburban in High SES Setting vs. Private School
for Students with Behavioral/Emotional Disorders

| | Public, Suburban High SES | Private School for Children with Emotional and Behavioral Disorders |
|---|---|---|
| Possession/distribution of prohibited objects or substances | 63 | 26 |
| Academic disturbance | 10 | 19 |
| Physical aggression | 3 | 3 |
| Theft | 3 | 6 |
| Insubordination | 3 | 3 |
| Academic dishonesty | 3 | 0 |
| Harassment | 6 | 23 |
| Group offenses | 3 | 0 |
| Disruptive bus behavior | 0 | 4 |
| Display of affection/ physical conduct | 0 | 6 |
| School damage/destruction | 6 | 10 |

Another remarkable difference concerned the use of counseling as a consequence. Within the private school, counseling was specified, but not in relation to any one specific behavior. In the public school, counseling was tied to a specific behavior of concern, such as alcohol or narcotics abuse.

### Public Urban versus Urban Detention Center School

There were no general differences between the policies in terms of relative attention to major categories of behavior, as can be seen in table 6.5. However, one slight difference was the mention of security issues and related behaviors within the urban detention policy (e.g., walking down the hall, and having an adult escort at all times).

### Public Urban versus Public Suburban Border School

The comparative analysis of these two policies is demonstrated in table 6.6, and reveals no major differences in terms of the relative importance given to specific categories of behavior. However, the secondary school bordering the city had a broader range of consequences, which varied in severity as well as mention of appeal for most behaviors. The city policy did not discuss levels of appeal.

TABLE 6.5
Percentage of Attention in Discipline Policies for Behavioral Categories:
Public Urban vs. Urban Detention Center

|  | *Public, Urban* | *Urban Detention Center* |
|---|---|---|
| Possession/distribution of prohibited objects or substances | 32 | 27 |
| Academic disturbance | 19 | 18 |
| Physical aggression | 12 | 15 |
| Theft | 10 | 4 |
| Insubordination | 10 | 6 |
| Academic dishonesty | 7 | 7 |
| Harassment | 6 | 8 |
| Group offenses | 2 | 4 |
| Disruptive bus behavior | 2 | 0 |
| Display of affection/ physical conduct | 0 | 1 |
| School damage/destruction | 0 | 10 |

TABLE 6.6
Percentage of Attention in Discipline Policies for Behavioral Categories:
Public Urban vs. Public School on Border of City

|  | Public, Urban | Public School on Border of City, Low SES |
|---|---|---|
| Possession/distribution of prohibited objects or substances | 32 | 22 |
| Academic disturbance | 19 | 22 |
| Physical aggression | 12 | 11 |
| Theft | 10 | 4 |
| Insubordination | 10 | 4 |
| Academic dishonesty | 7 | 0 |
| Harassment | 6 | 11 |
| Group offenses | 2 | 7 |
| Disruptive bus behavior | 2 | 0 |
| Display of affection/ physical conduct | 0 | 0 |
| School damage/destruction | 0 | 19 |

## DISCUSSION

The main finding regarding the emphasis given by all schools to the categories of possession, distribution, and use of prohibited objects, and the relatively less attention focused on physical aggression is somewhat surprising, in light of recent regional and national movements calling for school prevention and intervention efforts in the area of violent behaviors.

Suarez emphasizes the need for discipline policies to have clear and established guidelines for behavior and consistent application of consequences across incidents.[31] Given our knowledge of the relatively vague descriptions of physical aggression across all policies examined, it would seem appropriate that clearer definitions of physical aggression need to be established. The definition of physical aggression needs to be understood within the context of the school. This would assist in the consistent and fair application of the policy to all individuals, including those who experience social marginalization. The greater attention to the distribution, possession, and use of prohibited objects, such as weapons and narcotics, is encouraging in that these issues relate to violence. However, the actual issue of violent actions is not directly addressed.

The discipline policies address, to some degree, external methods of control and intervention when misbehavior occurs. However, this focus could be greatly expanded by attending to other interventions that are also associated with problematic behaviors within the classroom. These approaches are based on teacher behaviors that influence the expression of positive and negative social behaviors, and include the responsive classroom management model,[32] curricular modifications, and proactive classroom management.[33] These approaches consider the need to develop teacher competencies in addressing behavior. These interventions go beyond considering the student's behavior in isolation, but address the role of the teacher in discipline issues.[34]

Another significant finding involves the absence of any written content in the policies regarding violence prevention and intervention activities within the schools. Indeed, the Goals 2000 program, which has mandated violence prevention and intervention efforts, has not forged its way into formal written and established policies governing the behavior of students in school settings. While many schools are beginning to assume an active approach in the provision of these services, written communication about them within the discipline policy has not occurred. From a sociocultural and organizational perspective, this lack of attention may provide some evidence that these programs have not been formally sanctioned within the school institution, or integrated into the daily functioning of the school. Possibly, these programs do not follow traditional school norms, which tend to focus on punitive, reactionary means of control to the exclusion of flexibility in meeting the student's individualized broader social needs.

A third conclusion concerns the relatively few alternatives offered to traditional discipline practices across all school settings. Basically, formal counseling options were mentioned only in a specialized school focusing on children with emotional and behavior disorders. This intervention was also a component of the discipline policy within a bordering city school, and a high SES suburban school. In the higher-income setting, a well-defined program is offered within the school to students at no cost, and students have the added option of obtaining a school-approved outside counselor at parent expense. Unfortunately, while counseling services were mentioned as an option for students in the city schools, a procedure for obtaining them was not specified. It would seem important that accessible services be provided for students in the city environment, as they may or may not have the personal resources or referral information to obtain them. This finding would be consistent with economic issues that impinge on a student's behavioral functioning within the school setting.

Qualitative observations within specific policies revealed several areas for further study. It is important to note that sexual assault was seldom addressed within the policies, and was scarcely coded in our current system. Only one policy mentioned rape or molestation within the school setting, and police involvement was not clearly indicated as a consequence. The need to consider acts of sexual exploitation as aggression would seem to be important as part of the teaching strategy of a discipline policy.

Another qualitative observation concerned the relatively few schools that explicitly involved parents, students, support personnel, and community leaders in the development of the policies. Schools that did involve community members through a committee or advisory board tended to encourage active participation in all phases of the policy, ranging from its inception to grievances brought forth by students. This collaboration is beneficial in bridging the gap between community, social, and family factors, and the need for schools to operate in a safe, supportive environment. In the city public school codes, one uniform policy was the main blueprint for conduct across all participating secondary schools, decreasing the possibility of involvement from those in the surrounding neighborhood. These observations would match a national study, indicating that school administrators feel primarily responsible for the establishment of discipline policies.[35]

## IMPLICATIONS

The primary implication of this study is the recommendation that discipline policymakers integrate the larger body of literature focused on student development of internal control and responsibility versus solely relying on external control. Further, attention to proactive classroom management and related teacher behaviors needs to be considered in the implementation of discipline policies and procedures. It is imperative that discipline policies be considered within the larger social context in which schools operate if they are to have any chance for success. Schools must consider themselves as part of the larger social context and community in which they operate, and cannot continue to function as isolated entities.

A second implication involves the need for increased involvement of parents, community members and support staff in the development and implementation of discipline policies within a culturally appropriate context. The discipline policies need to consider the norms of the neighborhood and community regarding appropriate behavior. Currently, the uniform discipline policy that was evaluated within the city public schools is applied across a range of school settings, without regard to socioeconomic status, size of school, age of school, ethnic composition of students and faculty, and a range of other demographic variables. Although modifications are allowed, schools are required to follow the basic tenets of the uniform policy, which may or may not fit the needs and concerns of the specific neighborhood. While principals tend to feel ultimately responsible for discipline within their schools, it is imperative that parents are provided an opportunity to participate in the initial development, implementation, modification and evaluation of discipline policies within their children's schools. This is essential if students' behavior is to be viewed within an ecological context. Possibly, a regional committee could be developed with representation from parents, students, school personnel, related agency members, and community residents. The charge of this committee would be the development of general guidelines that would serve as a framework for each individual school district to adopt and modify as needed. The general guidelines would serve as a benchmark for developing specific competencies to be achieved by students at various levels. However, the guidelines would be flexible enough to be adapted to the specific needs of the diverse population within each school district.

An additional outcome of this study is that school policies need to include more specific and comprehensive definitions of physical and related aggression. Specifically, attention to types of aggression, such as sexual and physical assault need to be attended to in the consideration of discipline policies. It is imperative that policymakers agree on what is meant by violence or violent acts. Otherwise, students will not learn consistent expectations for nonviolent behavior, and will have no opportunity to internalize these guidelines.

An additional implication relates to the lack of consistency between policies in relation to alternative interventions, such as counseling, and related alternatives to traditional disciplinary measures. Policy makers, particularly within urban environments, need to make efforts at developing mental health interventions for youth. These interventions must consider the range of sociological variables rarely addressed within the literature.

## LIMITATIONS OF THE STUDY AND IMPLICATIONS FOR FUTURE RESEARCH

The limitations of the current study involve the small sample number of discipline policies that were used in the analysis. This limits the generalization of the study to other school districts, and the findings could be related to specific parameters and irrelevant characteristics of the discipline policies that were chosen. However, the study represents an initial attempt to examine the content of discipline policies, with a consideration of variables rarely studied in the school violence literature. These sociological variables include socioeconomic status, school resources, and specialized services.

Another limitation concerns the reliability and validity of the coding system. While initially useful for pilot studies and the development of specific hypotheses, the current system should be replicated with a larger sample size, and continually validated for the purpose of examining discipline policies across a wider range of settings. Future work should conduct inferential statistical analyses of the data to expand the findings of the current study.

The current study was an initial attempt at examining larger social and community variables in which students exist. Future research should empirically evaluate the degree to which the social context, and larger community influence the development and implementation of discipline policies. A major hypothesis developed in the current study indicates that discipline policies must vary by community to be effective. A follow-up study of greater depth in examining this issue would be an important area for future research.

Implications for practice and policy development suggest the need for empirical evaluation of multi-dimensional programs which address the social and familial context in which discipline concerns arise. The involvement of parents and community members in the development and implementation of discipline policies needs to be a focus of further study.

## NOTES

1. I. A. Hyman et al., *Policy and Practice in School Discipline: Past, Present and Future*. Paper presented at Safe Schools, Safe Students: A Collaborative Approach to Achieving Safe, Disciplined and Drug-Free Schools Conducive to Learning Conference, Washington, D.C., October 1994.

2. R. Gladstein et al., "A Comparison of Inner-City and Upper-Middle-Class Youths' Exposure to Violence," *Journal of Adolescent Health* 13.4 (1992): 275–80.

3. W. Landen, "Violence and Our Schools: What Can We Do?" *Updating School Board Policies* 23 (1992): 1–5.

4. Ibid.

5. J. A. Queen, B. B. Blackwelder, and L. P. Mallen, *Responsible Classroom Management for Teachers and Students* (Upper Saddle River, N.J.: Merrill, 1997), pp. 18–35.

6. R. E. Slavin, *Educational Psychology: Theory and Practice* (Needham Heights, Mass.: Allyn and Bacon, 1997), pp. 266–303; C. R. Greenwood, J. J. Carta, and R. V. Hall, "The Use of Peer Tutoring Strategies in Classroom Man-

agement and Educational Instruction," *School Psychology Review* 17 (July 1988): 258–75.

7. M. Gettinger, "Methods of Proactive Classroom Management," *School Psychology Review* 17 (July 1988): 243–57.

8. G. S. Heller, "Changing the School to Reduce Student Violence: What Works?" *NASSP Bulletin* 80 (1996): 1–10; D. W. Johnson and R. T. Johnson, "Reducing School Violence through Conflict Resolution Training," *NASSP Bulletin* 80 (1996): 11–18; K. E. Powell, L. Muir-McClain, and L. Halasyamani, "A Review of Selected School-Based Conflict Resolution and Peer Mediation Projects," *Journal of School Health* 65 (1995): 426–31.

9. D. Prothrow-Stith, *Violence Prevention Curriculum for Adolescents* (Newton, Mass.: Education Development Center, 1987); R. Pesce, personal communication, August 19, 1996.

10. C. Burnett, "School Violence in an Impoverished South African Community," *Child Abuse and Neglect* 22 (1998): 789–95; P. Bourgois, "Confronting Anthropology, Education, and Inner-City Apartheid," *American Anthropologist* 98 (June 1996): 249–58.

11. P. H. Tolan and N. G. Guerra, *What Works in Reducing Adolescent Violence: An Empirical Review of the Field* (Boulder, Colo.: Center for the Study and Prevention of Violence, Institute for Behavioral Sciences, University of Colorado, Boulder, 1994).

12. P. C. Kratcoski, "Perspectives on Intrafamily Violence," *Human Relations* 37 (1984): 443–54; S. K. Steinmetz, "The Violent Family," in *Violence in the Home: Interdisciplinary Perspectives*, ed. M. Lystad (New York: Brunner/Mazel, 1986), pp. 51–70; M. A. Strauss and R. J. Gelles, "Societal Changes in Family Violence from 1975 to 1985 as Revealed by Two National Surveys," *Journal of Marriage and Family* 48 (1986): 465–79.

13. J. A. Baker, "Are We Missing the Forest for the Trees? Considering the Social Context of School Violence," *Journal of School Psychology* 36 (1998): 29–44.

14. I. A. Hyman and D. C. Perone, "Introduction to the Special Theme Section on School Violence: The Ecology of School Violence," *Journal of School Psychology* 36 (1998): 3–5.

15. I. A. Hyman and D. C. Perone, "The Other Side of School Violence: Educator Policies and Practices That May Contribute to Student Misbehavior," *Journal of School Psychology* 36 (1998): 7–27.

16. T. M. Suarez, *Creating Safe Environments for Learning in North Carolina's Public Schools* (Chapel Hill, N.C.: North Carolina Educational Policy Research Center, ERIC Document ED 373 406, 1992).

17. Ibid.

18. Hyman and Perone, "Introduction to the Special Theme Section," p. 3.

19. R. Linquanti and B. Berliner, *Rebuilding Schools as Safe Havens: A Typology for Selecting and Integrating Violence Prevention Strategies* (Portland, Or.: Western Regional Center for Drug Free Schools and Communities, ERIC Document ED 376 600, 1994).

20. Suarez, *Creating Safe Environments*.

21. R. J. Rubel, and P. D. Blauvelt, "How Safe Are Your Schools?" *Amer-*

*ican School Board Journal* 181 (1994): 28–31; U.S. Department of Education, *Safe, Disciplined, Drug-Free Schools: A Background Paper for the Goals 2000: Educate America Satellite Town Meeting, July 20, 1993* (Washington, D.C.: Department of Education, ERIC Document ED 366 103, 1993).

22. Rubel and Blauvelt, "How Safe Are Your Schools?"

23. Suarez, *Creating Safe Environments*.

24. Ibid.

25. U.S. Department of Education, *Safe, Disciplined, Drug-Free Schools*.

26. Rubel and Blauvelt, "How Safe Are Your Schools?"

27. U.S. Department of Education, *Safe, Disciplined, Drug-Free Schools*.

28. U.S. Department of Education. *Who Runs the Schools? The Principal's View* (Online). Available: http//www.ed.gov/pubs/OR/ResearchRpts/prinview. html (September 1, 1996).

29. F. N. Kerlinger, *Foundations of Behavioral Research* (New York, New York: CBS College Publishing, 1986), pp. 120.

30. B. G. Glaser, *Grounded Theory* (Mill Valley, Calif.: Sociology Press, 1995).

31. Suarez, *Creating Safe Environments*.

32. Queen, Blackwelder, and Mallen, *Responsible Classroom Management*.

33. Gettinger, "Methods of Proactive Classroom Management."

34. Hyman and Perone, "Introduction to the Special Theme Section."

35. U.S. Department of Education, *Who Runs the Schools?*

CHAPTER 7

# Modeling of the Effects of Changing Demography on Student Learning: Applications Designed to Change School District Practices

Anthony Gary Dworkin,
Laurence A. Toenjes, Margaret K. Purser,
and Ayman Sheikh-Hussin

In 1968, the U.S. Congress amended the Title XI Higher Education Act of 1965 to create the Urban Community Service Program, which called for universities to provide expertise to enable cities to address their urban problems, particularly in the field of education. The 1968 program was initiated to attempt to redress some inequalities that had led to several years of urban revolts in minority communities. However, the legislation was passed without appropriation by Congress and signed by then President Lyndon Johnson. In 1986, the legislation was up for renewal and was again passed without funding by Congress and the Reagan administration. Finally, in 1992, out of concerns for urban revolts occasioned by the Rodney King beating in Los Angeles and worries over a reelection bid, President Bush encouraged funding of the program. Congress passed the enabling legislation and grant applications were accepted in May 1992.

Our Urban Community Service project called for us to assist school districts in the metropolitan area to improve their forecasting of the changing demography of their student bodies and to develop models to explain the impact of that changing demography on student learning.[1] With the completion of the project, our center remains committed to

195

working with the districts beyond the funding period and has established research relations with several districts to continue our work. The congressional elections of 1994 and subsequent federal budget impasses have resulted in the effective termination of the Urban Community Service Program. Allocations have been made only to complete projects that were approved during the 1995 fiscal year. Consequently, the U.S. Department of Education solicited nonfederal strategies to continue the services created by the program. We offer our approach as an example of how social science and sociology in particular can maintain a research/service relationship with urban school districts in the absence of continued federal funding. While there are a plethora of available models for the conduct of urban education, we have found this one to be successful for us and for the school districts with which we work. In the course of this chapter, we shall describe the forecasting project and findings, as well as our activities that have led to an ongoing relationship with school districts. In so doing, we can specify some of the elements that work in redefining one role of sociology of education in urban school districts. The chapter is divided into three parts: (1) the development of a forecasting model and summary of findings; (2) the creation, testing, and summarized findings of our student learning outcomes model; and (3) the establishment of a set of ongoing deliverables to districts to retain a working research relationship with urban schools. This final element resembles an urban education equivalent of the "agricultural experiment station" model. This third element further raises issues of role ambiguity and conflict associated with the multiple expectations of school districts, the academic community and our standards for research, and the needs of assorted stakeholders in the public schools, including the students and their parents.

## BACKGROUND OF THE FORECASTING MODEL

### The Need for Better Forecasting

It is estimated that in the United States, by the year 2000, more than four fifths of all first-time workers entering the labor market will be women, minority group members, or persons with limited facility in English.[2] To date, the public schools have met with limited success in promoting the needed reforms to insure that the new labor force will be able to maintain the effort to keep the United States economically competitive. Concerns over the products of the public schools generated the 1983 report of the President's Commission on Excellence in Education known as *A Nation at Risk*[3] and more than three hundred task force reports since then.[4]

Conditions in Houston, Texas, are no different. Houston is the fourth largest city in the United States and its metropolitan area ranks fifth. The Houston area, even more than many other large urban communities, is at a crossroads in its thinking about development, growth, and service provision, especially in the area of public education. Houston has a history of being the epitome of a "free-enterprise city" under a laissez-faire government. Oilmen, bankers, and developers controlled Houston's future, as they controlled its past. Money flowed freely and public sector agencies often had fiscal surpluses at the end of the year. Growth was so rapid that public agencies, including public schools, had no time to respond adequately, much less to plan for change. During the 1980s, however, the rapid decline in oil prices coupled with the severe overbuilding of retail, office, and residential space led Houston into the worst economic recession seen by a major city since the Great Depression following the 1929 stock market crash. Despite the recession of the mid-1980s, however, Texas, California, and Florida are expected to absorb over 50 percent of the nation's total population growth.[5] As a result of sustained population growth coupled with economic decline in the 1980s, both public and private sectors began rethinking the need for accurate accounts of existing economic and demographic conditions, accurate predictions of Houston's general future and the future of individual neighborhoods, and solid objective rationales for implementing programs to respond to and direct emerging trends.

### Trends in Houston and Harris County

The Houston Primary Metropolitan Statistical Area (PMSA) is comprised of some 5,400 square miles (8,775 sq. km.) or nearly one half the area of Belgium, of which 1,775 square miles (2,863 sq. km.) are in Harris County. Harris County, of which Houston is the principal city, grew from 1.741 million people in 1970 to 2.818 million in 1990 or an increase of nearly 62 percent over the two decades. Harris County changed from 30 percent minority in 1970 to 47 percent minority in 1990. Houston, which includes 35 percent of the public school children in the county and one third of Harris County's land, is the largest city in the nation without zoning or a comprehensive plan. In the past, when school districts in the metropolitan area have attempted to estimate future student populations, they have relied upon relatively simple cohort survival models, or have surveyed the parents of current students to determine whether there are other children at home who might be attending school in the future. These surveys have not been tied to community-based data and do not enumerate community dynamics, the major driver of changing enrollment patterns. In addition, using enrollment patterns in lower grades to predict enrollment in middle and higher grades is effective only when the neighborhoods within the school attendance zones are stable and homogeneous. In Houston, not only are families becoming more diverse and more mobile, the vast number of immigrant (from Latin America and Asia) and in-migrant (U.S.-born from other states) students precludes use of the previous enrollment patterns to predict future ones.

Houston area school districts experienced dramatic and often unforeseen changes in enrollment and composition during the 1980s, with no apparent end in sight. Three area districts grew by over 80 percent between 1980 and 1990, with another six increasing in student enrollment by more than 40 percent. Two districts lost more than 20 percent of their student body during the same time period due to a redistribution of the population. Every suburban district but one decreased in the percentage of Anglo or white students, with seven losing more than 20 percentage points in Anglo enrollment. Black enrollment increased significantly in two districts (increasing between 5,000 to 7,500 students), but decreased by nearly 14,000 in the Houston Independent School District, as the middle-class African American population migrated from the inner city to the suburbs. Asian and Hispanic enrollment has increased across all district lines, with the exception of one district that is overwhelmingly black and has experienced an overall decline in enrollments. In addition to changes in the minority student populations, school districts have been facing alarming increases in the numbers of underserved populations—those school-aged children who are not enrolled in school at all—as well as increases in the percentages of children enrolled in private schools or who are home schooled. The consequence is that by 1990, the enrollment rate among children between the ages of 6 and 17 was well under 95 percent, a decline from 1980.

To illustrate the nature of changing ethnic characteristics in Houston area schools, we turn to a middle school on the western edge of the Houston Independent School District. The attendance zone for this school is a group of neighborhoods which were built in the 1960s and contain some small apartment complexes that were traditionally family-oriented housing for Anglos and Hispanics; more than ten thousand apartment units that were previously adult only and predominantly Anglo; and several large middle-income, Anglo neighborhoods of single-family homes. In the 1974–75 school year, the student body was 86 percent Anglo, 8 percent Hispanic, 4 percent black, and 2 percent Asian. By the 1981–82 school year, the neighborhoods had become desegregated, but only a few had opened family sections by 1982. The ethnic distribution of the students was 52 percent Anglo, 18 percent Hispanic, 17 percent black, and 13 percent Asian. By 1990, the U.S. Supreme Court had outlawed adult-only complexes, the real estate market plummeted, and the multifamily complexes in this school's attendance zone were virtually 100 percent minority—mostly Hispanic. The student body was 12 percent Anglo, 70 percent Hispanic, 14 percent black, and 4 percent Asian. With the majority of the students being Hispanic, and of that 70 percent, a majority being new immigrants from Central America, the middle school was faced with an unanticipated educational crisis. While middle schools in stable communities can look to the enrollment patterns of the feeder elementary schools to forecast enrollments, schools that have a large percentage of students who were not previously served in Houston, in the United States, or at all during their elementary school years must employ other methods for anticipating change.

*Changing Demographics Lead to Changing Programs*

School reform efforts are driven by population dynamics operating in schools, neighborhoods, and communities. Urban and increasingly suburban communities are characterized by greater degrees of diversity and heterogeneity, which, in turn, change demands upon the public schools.[6] As housing stocks change and as birth rates among populations are modified, the schools become recipients of children with needs that differ from those of earlier cohorts. Borman and Spring report that schools are affected by some twenty-eight different demographic variables that display four factor patterns.[7] Changes in housing mix and housing condition, changes in neighborhood makeup, changes in employment patterns in and around the neighborhoods, and changes in the quality of schools or the emergence of alternative school options each affect the likely composition of the student bodies of school districts, as well as, obviously, individual campuses.

In practice then, transformations of neighborhoods through the aging of the housing stock or other ecological patterns are likely to lead to shifts in the social makeup of the neighborhood and the magnitude of needs and resources that individuals attending schools from the neighborhood are likely to bring with them to school. Changing student bodies with different needs make obsolete some educational programs, while calling forth programs not previously implemented. Administrative and teaching styles, course offerings, the scheduling of school events, length of school day and year, and the extent to which the schools can depend upon parental support and involvement are all modified by changing school demographics, which are driven in part by changing neighborhood demography. The demographic shifts and changed organizational structures, along with changes in programmatic offerings are likely to affect patterns of interaction among teachers, students, and the parents of the students. They will also affect the extent to which schools can depend upon traditional curricular formats to produce desired student learning outcomes. Finally, student self-esteem, retention rates, and student dropout behavior are likely to be affected by the goodness of fit of programs and personnel as they mesh with organizations and population dynamics.

Thus, a transition from single-family, middle-class housing in which the majority of the residents are white and are in intact families—the image around which the schools of the 1950s were built—to multifamily housing in which the residents are ethnically diverse and in which there are a substantial proportion of single-parent families reflects a major distributive or demographic change that will have profound organizational consequences for schools and that will also affect interpersonal relationships in schools. It is not our intent to suggest that changing demography and changing diversity are negative factors. Rather, the difficulties itemized arise when school districts fail to anticipate change and continue outmoded practices, policies, and procedures. Below is only a partial list of the school factors affected by changing demography and about which school districts must focus efforts for changes in administrative and teaching practices.

Organizational consequences for schools include:

1. Increased population density will affect the ability of existing buildings to house increased student body size, which will affect:
   a. The need for new classrooms;
   b. The need for new campuses;
   c. The employment and deployment of additional teaching and support staff;
   d. The need to obtain waivers from the state on the classroom enrollment limits enforced in Texas law.

2. Changes in the student body mix and the ethnic and socioeconomic status of the families served by the school will affect:
   a. The extent to which extended day programs are needed for latch key children;
   b. The level of intergroup relations training needed by the instructional staff;
   c. The amount of resources needed to be spent on free and reduced lunches;
   d. The deployment and employment of bilingual and special education teachers;
   e. The need to apply for Chapter I funding;

   f. The proportion of time spent by instructional and administrative staff on remediation;

   g. The level of community relations efforts needed to be made by the principal;

   h. The degree to which the school can rely upon parental support for PTO or PTA activities;

   i. The extent to which the schools can expect the parents to support them in maintenance of discipline at home and in insuring that the students do their homework;

   j. The content of instruction and the extent to which traditional teaching methods can be used.

3. Failure of the school to adjust to the changing demographic makeup of the student body may lead to:

   a. Unanticipated negative changes in student academic performances;

   b. Increased student dropout rates;

   c. Diminished student attendance;

   d. Difficulties in getting parents to participate in their children's education and to be supportive of their children's teachers;

   e. Diminished student self-esteem;

   f. Increased student reliance upon gang activities as a source of esteem enhancement and identification;

   g. Increased levels of school-based violence, vandalism, and threats against school personnel.

4. Declines in student performance and parental support for the schools may lead to:

   a. Greater difficulties in passing tax increases and floating school bonds;

   b. Greater migration of middle income families to the suburbs and increased enrollment in private schools;

   c. More difficulty in attracting and retaining qualified teachers in urban schools.

5. Increased student problems, diminished support for schools, and increased suspicion about the capacity of schools to meet needs may lead to:

   a. Increased administrator stress and depersonalization of students and staff;

   b. Higher rates of teacher burnout and diminished morale;

   c. Increased teacher absenteeism;

   d. Greater reliance upon substitute teachers and the attendant effect upon student achievement;

e. Higher turnover rates among teachers as well as higher rates of entrapment of certain groups of teachers (those who hate their jobs but have no salable skills to permit them to leave teaching);

f. More litigation against school districts by teachers.

In turn, school districts that fail to address demographic changes that challenge current policies, programs, and practices are likely to experience lowered student achievement and diminished public confidence in public schools; in turn the negative consequences will have a cumulative, circular effect.[8] Clearly, then, it is in the best interest of school districts to engage in short-, intermediate-, and long-range planning for changes in neighborhoods that are likely to affect schools. The future of public education, the labor force needs of the coming century, and the continued societal well-being depend upon school systems that adequately address the dual demands of equality of educational opportunity and academic excellence for all of their children.

The benefits of changing demography and the progressive response to that change are manifold. The changes in demographic characteristics of student bodies can result in greater student diversity, rather than new forms of segregation. This diversity can offer what Leon Warshay once described as "the breadth of perspective" to all that experience that diversity.[9] Expanded perspectives enhance adaptation skills in a more global society. Thus, all benefit when students, teachers, administrators, and educational stakeholders come to draw upon the plethora of distinct insights that diversity can offer.

Generally speaking, a large district such as Los Angeles, California, which developed the Los Angeles Unified School District Forecasting Model, have begun to monitor Census data.[10] The Houston Independent School District is in the process of beginning to use census data to establish attendance area boundaries. However, most small school districts, including those adjoining large cities, have access to no such tools for forecasting student body changes. Further, most of the forecasting models project only one or two years into the future.[11] Further, when the models are built upon census data (as was the case with the Los Angeles County Planning Council), they are not updated between decennial censuses. Thus, the models become increasingly inaccurate over time. Models are needed that are subject to updating and validity checks.

The traditional forecasting by school districts relies upon variants of the cohort-survival model, which has been associated with as much as ten percent error over three years.[12] Shaw describes the usual format for the cohort survival approach as generally used as a short-range (1–7) years forecasting tool and is based on the calculation of a series of survival rates that indicate the fraction of students in one grade in a given year who "survive" to the next grade the next year. The survival ratios encompass all of the individual factors influencing enrollments, such as death, in-migration, out-migration, retention, annexation, housing changes, and employment changes. Enrollments in the initial grade, most typically kindergarten, are calculated independently on the basis of past birth data.[13]

The University of Houston (through cooperation between the Center for Public Policy [CPP] housed in the College of Social Sciences and the Texas Center for University School Partnerships then housed in the Office of the University President and now part of the College of Education) and Harris County Department of Education have been creating a set of viable forecasting equations and models that will assist local school districts in their planning efforts and will allow for replication in other urban areas in the nation. The process involves the mapping of Census data to attendance zones for the schools within each of the participating districts, followed by the matching of student-level data (according to home address) and block- and block group–level statistics from the Census. Forecasting occurred initially using a "shift-share" model, which is simply the tracking of the shifting shares in population that each sub-area has been of the region and moving that trend forward in time. It takes into account saturation of sub-areas and the reallocation of growth when the sub-areas reach maximum potential. The Census data are then augmented by more current data provided by the Houston-Galveston Area Council and the local utility companies and finally a small area model is built, using twelve equations driven by ten local and national exogenous variables. This aspect of the forecasting was completed by the Center for Public Policy of the University of Houston, a coprincipal investigative partner in the project.

The collaborative effort has been directing services to school districts in Harris County by providing:

• Detailed 1990 Census data by school district, census tract, and census block group

• Biennial estimates of population by age and ethnicity by school district and census tract

• Biennial estimates of land use and land value by district and census tract

• Biennial estimates of employment by Standard Industrial Classification and employee location

- Forecasts for 5-, 10-, 20-year horizons of population and school age population by school district and census tract
- Forecasts for five-year horizon of population by age and ethnicity by school district
- Models for translating current and predictive data into quantifiable forecasts of school-aged children by student status, socioeconomic status (SES), and program needs

*Forecasts for Schools in the Houston Metropolitan Area*

The 1990 Census for the school-aged population reported that 536,512 children between the ages of 6 and 17 lived in the atteidance boundaries of the twenty-five school districts in the study area, with 180,494 living in the central city district's attendance boundary. Since some portion of children under six and some portion of those over seventeen attend school, these figures are conservative. The forecast model developed under the aegis of the grant indicated that by 1995, the population of potential students between the ages of six and seventeen years old living in the attendance boundaries of all districts would grow to nearly 567,000, while the central district would expand to almost 181,000. This metropolitan area figure could be incremented by a portion of the 329,000 children under the age of six estimated to be living in the attendance boundaries of the twenty-five school districts by 1995, while the central school district figure could be increased a portion of the nearly 116,000 children under age six forecast for its attendance zone. By the year 2000, the forecast for six to seventeen year olds is almost 625,000 for all of the districts and 181,000 for the central district, and by the year 2030, the forecasts estimate that over 772,000 children between the ages of six and seventeen will live in the boundaries of the sum of the districts and 173,000 will live in the central district. Again, the 2030 estimates can be incremented by some portion of the children under six in the districts; those figures being over 370,000 across the twenty-five districts and 111,000 in the central district. The purpose for restricting the forecasts to ages six to seventeen was that this population had the highest probability of actually being in school. School participation is voluntary for children under six, and graduation, retention, GED programs, and dropout behaviors make figures for those over seventeen more unstable. Actual enrollments of all ages in the twenty-five districts, as reported by the Texas Education Agency (AEIS reports for 1990 and 1995) amounted to over 574,000 in 1990 and 623,000 in 1995.

The figures that were forecasted for the period between 1990 and 2030 summarize the following trends: growth in the central school district will initially increase slowly through the early years of the new century and then decline; growth in the eastern suburbs will be small, with some districts experiencing slight declines over the time period before regaining their population; growth in the northern and western suburbs will be substantial. The growth in the west and north is occasioned by the availability of land, the relocation of jobs to those areas, and the continued decline of the central business district. The limited growth to the east is a function of limitations on available land and the status of the petrochemical industry. The engines that will drive the total population and ethnic makeup of the region over the ensuing decades is foremost a dramatic increase in the Hispanic population both from natural increases and internal and external immigration, and to a considerably lesser degree, some continued white and Asian American flight, primarily from the central school district and those districts immediately contiguous to it. Beginning in the 1970s, the central urban district changed from predominantly one with a white plurality and a small Hispanic population, to one in which Hispanics currently represent half of the total student body, and whites represent less than 12 percent.

## STUDENT LEARNING OUTCOMES MODEL

Estimates of changes in student demography are by themselves important to school districts, as administrators need to establish plans for new campuses, teacher hiring, and programs to meet the needs of students from diverse backgrounds. However, changing demography also has ramifications for test performance and the state-mandated accountability standards to which districts are subjected. Dramatic shifts in student bodies can result in schools that were seen as exemplary at one time period becoming low performing at another. Not only are there financial rewards offered to districts and campuses that have high standardized test scores, there are the possibilities of severe costs, including the loss of accreditation, wholesale firing of staff, and the failure of school bond elections that accrue from continued low student performance. The Texas Education Agency is mandated by the legislature annually to report the passage rates on the Texas Assessment of Academic Skills (TAAS) of all districts and to indicate which districts are exemplary or recognized (both high-performing categories), which are acceptable, and which are low performing. In turn, districts are required to make public the TAAS passage rates of students disaggregated by campus, grade level, and ethnicity. TAAS passage rates within districts frequently appear on the front page of local newspapers, fueling the debate over public confidence in public education. A significant aspect of our work with schools has been to develop models of the factors that affect student learning in each district. Not only do the models estimate the effect of student, campus, and community factors on student achievement, they also provide indications of the potential impact on TAAS performance of future demographic mixes in the districts as estimated by the forecasts. We have used a common core of variables to account for aggregate TAAS performance in reading and mathematics among students in the districts in the metropolitan area, and then have run separate versions of the models on data on individual districts and campuses.

Our general models reflect those adopted by researchers since the release of *The Equality of Educational Opportunity* by Coleman and his associates[14] and are further informed by a myriad of studies that have attempted to isolate factors associated with effective educational practices and student learning. Early studies isolated blocks of student, peer, neighborhood, campus, and teacher effects that are influential in explaining the academic performances of students.[15] More recent work has suggested additional blocks of variables that we found useful in our model.[16]

Common among many of the contemporary models are blocks of variables representing factors that a student brings to the school setting, demographic factors associated with the school itself, peer group factors associated with classmates of the individual student, teacher factors that are experienced by all students in the classroom, as well as neighborhood and even school district effects. Increasingly common is the use of hierarchical analyses to understand the complexity of the different levels of effects on student learning. Early work tended to aggregate campus and teacher demographics to all students, as if all students experienced the mean or median characteristics of teachers or schools identically (such as the percentage of teachers with M.A. degrees or the per capita funding at the school or the district).

The widely used *High School and Beyond* and the *National Educational Longitudinal Survey* have provided researchers with many of the attitudinal effects, but such data sets are national random samples and do not permit the modeling of the classroom experience.[17] By contrast, our longitudinal data consist of all information contained in the permanent record cards and test score tapes; such records do not contain attitudinal information. Our task was then to model some of the effects, without losing significant blocks of data.

The data we used to assess student performance include extensive demographic information on every student in the participating districts for up to four years (1990–91 through 1993–94) and five years in two districts (1994–95 data also included) and TAAS scores and related information on all students tested between 1990 and 1995. Since the 1992–93 TAAS administration, annual test score data are available on one half of all enrolled students. Grades three through eight and ten are routinely tested, while in years prior to 1992–93, selected grades were tested. The population sizes varied from roughly 3,000 students in the smallest district to 202,000 students in the largest. The total database consisted of 506,000 students.

In our reports to school districts, we attempted to capture some of the relevant variables useful in explaining standardized test performances of students in the Houston metropolitan area. Data limitations often necessitated that we utilize surrogate measures for some of the constructs identified in national studies. This was particularly the case when reference group effects, usually measured in other studies in terms of peer attitudes, were included in analyses of data contained in student records. In the reports, we presented a test of a general model, gleaned from our review of current research and based on a demonstration using a less circumscribed data set that includes both student and teacher information collected by the Texas Center for University School Partnerships (TCUSP) in 1992. Finally, we presented a test of the model to each district, using their own data. The intent of the presentation strategy was to permit school district personnel to see what analyses were possible given data resident in the district.

## TAAS Scores as the Dependent Variable

Because of its salience to school districts, the dependent variables in our student learning outcome model are the student's performances in mathematics and reading on the state-mandated achievement test. Under pressure from the Texas State Legislature, the Texas Education Agency commissioned National Computer Systems and its subcontractors, the Psychological Corporation and Measurement Incorporated, to develop a criterion-referenced test intended to assess both the problem-solving and critical-thinking skills of the children of Texas public schools in reading, mathematics, and writing. The test, known as the Texas Assessment of Academic Skills (TAAS), was intended to deviate from the previous state practice of testing only minimal or basic skills. Implementation of testing began in October 1990. Beginning in 1994, an attempt was made to develop a vertical scale score system for the TAAS, thereby permitting direct comparison of student progress, year by year. The attempt was abandoned and replaced by a metric known as the Texas Learning Index (TLI), which, like a z-score, gives the relative standing of students, year by year, compared with others. TLI scores have a theoretical maximum of 100, but the empirical maximum at some grade level tests may have maximum scores as low as 91. Further, the content of earlier TAAS tests was not equivalent to later ones. Thus, a passing score on earlier tests was 1500, with a range from around 500 to somewhat over 2200, depending upon year and grade level, while a passing score in later years was 70. The content of the tests also changed. As a result, we often present longitudinal data on TAAS in terms of z-scores.

*Selected Empirical Generalizations from the Student Learning Outcome Model*

1. The amount of variance explained by the campus and student structural variables and peer variables differed by districts. In some districts, the over-all model could account for more than 50 percent of the total variance, while in others it could account for only ten percent. Factors such as tracking, exemptions from testing of some LEP (Limited English Proficiency) populations, the magnitude of the special education population, and intergenerational stability of minority populations seemed to account for many of the differentials. Districts that have had stable populations and those where the class structure is flattened and where ethnicity and social class are not highly correlated tended to have lower $R^2$ values than districts that have experienced dynamic population shifts and substantial inequality. Consequently, variances are smaller and hence, less variance could be captured.

2. In most districts, African American children consistently score lower than other children even with the introduction of controls for poverty and other factors. This may be a function of the limitations with the measure of poverty and the persistence of racism in a Southern city. There is a notable exception: in one predominantly African American district with the highest poverty rate in the county, African American student passage rates among students in the lower grades outstrip other high poverty districts and nearly equal that of some relatively affluent, predominantly white districts. This district, once with the lowest test scores and placed in receivership by the state, hired a dynamic superintendent who replaced all the principals and many of the teachers, supplanting them with talented people from all over the state.

3. Some of the smaller, working-class districts, especially those in the eastern part of the county, where the "urban cowboy" stereotype prevails, produce generally lower and more homogeneous test scores. After controlling for LEP status, Hispanic test scores equal those of Anglo students. In these eastern districts parents and even grandparents attended the same schools as their children do, and all expect to continue the family traditions of working in blue-collar jobs in the petrochemical industry. Graduation rates are high in

these districts, as the oil companies require a high school diploma for employment, but parents do not aspire to have their children attend college or attain above-average test performances. Nevertheless, in these districts, African American students had lower TAAS scores than either the Hispanic or Anglo children by as much as one full standard deviation.

4. Asian American academic advantages, even in math, are not uniform across the districts. In districts that have recently experienced a substantial influx of Asian American students who are recent immigrants, Asian Americans are associated with lower performances than other groups.

5. Stability of enrollment (attending the same school until graduation) and family (not being shifted from parent to grandparent each year, for example) universally raises achievement, even if family stability consists of remaining in a single-parent family. We have urged districts to work with social service agencies to encourage parents not to change residences frequently and not to shift children from parent to parent or parent to grandparent if possible. School districts are also working with owners of large apartment complexes to change from offering free rent for the first month to offering free rent for the last month.[18]

6. Poverty and being older than one's classmates generally lower achievement, but in some districts this effect washes out because of enrichment programs directed toward the economically disadvantaged and because of strategies designed not to stigmatize children who are older than their classmates.

7. Students in higher grades perform less well than those in lower grades, reflecting the impact of more recent innovations that have been applied earlier rather than later in a student's career. Additionally, as school districts take more seriously the accountability mandates, they teach more to the test, a test that now more accurately measures the critical skills established by the state. Additionally, early intervention clearly is more effective than intervention in later grades.

8. In a related fashion, test scores have been rising since the implementation of the accountability system, but some of this can be explained by the tendency for some districts to exempt more students from having their tests scored and counted. While exemptions are permitted for LEP and special education students, some districts test fewer of their students than others. Exemption rates sometimes exceed 70 percent of all students in a grade.

9. Gain scores for LEP and special education students and some minorities have been greater than for non-LEP, non-special education, and majorities. This pattern tends to be more common in the suburban districts, especially the smaller suburban districts, than in the large central district. It may reflect the ability of such districts to integrate such students into the campus community because of the smaller scale of such districts and the higher probability that teachers, students, and parents live in the same communities and have established a "functional community."[19] Alternatively, it may reflect the overall lower performance of all students in these small suburban districts.

10. In more working-class districts, girls and boys do not differ in reading performance, but boys perform better in math than girls. In many more middle-class districts, girls perform better in reading than do boys and perform equally to boys in math, at least through the fifth grade.

11. By aggregating the achievement scores for classmates in the same grade and campus, we were able to create a surrogate measure of peer effects. We further created same race peer influence by aggregating only the test scores of classmates of the same race as the individual student. This measure proved to be very interesting. For third graders, the scores of all classmates better predicted individual test performance, but beginning with fourth grade for African American students, the better predictor of individual performance was African American peers. Hispanic peers were a better predictor for Hispanic students from the fifth grade onward, while the whole class remained the better predictor for Anglo and Asian American students across all grades. The results are suggestive of the findings of Ogbu and Mickelson regarding the "cultural myths" about the value of schooling.[20] They may well be passed on from classmate to classmate, especially within ethnic groups.

*Poverty, Campus Demography, and Achievement:*
*A Cross-District Comparison*

Presented in table 7.1 are the 1993–94 year TAAS results aggregated across fourteen districts in the Houston area expressed as Texas Learning Index (TLI) scores. Poverty for the children was defined as participation in the free or reduced lunch program, while poverty level for campuses was the percentage of students on a campus participating in the free or reduced lunch program. The analysis links the TAAS performances of individual children with the poverty rate on the campus attended by those children. Unfortunately, reliance upon the free lunch

TABLE 7.1

Elementary School TAAS Performance in TLI Mean Scores by
Poverty Level of Child and Campus for Urban and Suburban Districts

| | | *Urban Districts* | | *Suburban Districts* | |
|---|---|---|---|---|---|
| | | *TAAS* | | *TAAS* | |
| *Child* | *Campus* | *Math* | *Reading* | *Math* | *Reading* |
| Subsidized | High Poverty | 63.9 | 72.8 | 50.3 | 55.2 |
| lunch | Med. Poverty | 62.5 | 70.2 | 57.7 | 64.4 |
| | Low Poverty | 66.9 | 74.8 | 60.0 | 66.9 |
| No | High Poverty | 65.3 | 70.9 | 65.3 | 72.2 |
| subsidized | Med. Poverty | 66.8 | 74.8 | 68.5 | 76.3 |
| lunch | Low Poverty | 75.7 | 83.2 | 77.5 | 84.1 |

measure does not permit us to distinguish between children from relatively low-income families, but whose income is just enough above the poverty line not to qualify for the lunch supplement, and children from much more affluent families. Both would be coded as not on free or reduced lunch. As there is a substantial fall-off in participation in the program after elementary school, only data on elementary school children are presented. The urban district was the central city district, while the suburban districts included all others. The analysis is based upon the scores of nearly 195,000 students who took the TAAS. The aggregated poverty levels of the campuses were trichotomies in which high-poverty schools had two thirds or more of their students on free or reduced lunch, medium-poverty schools had less than two thirds and more than one third of their students on free or reduced lunch, and low-poverty schools had one third or fewer of their students on free or reduced lunch. The cutting points of the trichotomy were chosen to permit both sufficient numbers in each cell while considering the relatively high levels of poverty extant in many school districts.

Table 7.1 displays mean TLI scores in math and reading for the students whose tests were scored (many of the nonscored tests were from students with LEP exemptions and students with significant levels of retardation). To explore the nature of the interaction, the data were analyzed for simple main effects using successive one-way analyses of variance. Scheffe tests revealed that any difference of one or more TLI points was statistically significant. Passing a section of the TAAS test requires a score of 70 TLI points or higher. Thus, in math, the mean score for children on free or reduced lunch was a failing grade in high-, medium-, and low-poverty schools in both types of districts, and a failing grade for children not in poverty for all schools but the low-poverty campuses in both the urban and suburban districts. Children, regardless of their lunch subsidy status, performed better in reading than in math. Higher reading than math scores characterizes TAAS performance throughout the state. The mean scores in reading for all combinations of students and schools in the urban district is a passing grade, but a failing grade for children in poverty in the suburban districts.

With one exception, that being the reading scores in high-poverty urban schools, children in poverty scored lower than those not in poverty at each kind of campus. This exception could be a function of the amount of teachers' time allocated to a child not in poverty in an overwhelmingly low-income school. In addition, in reading in the urban district, children in poverty in the high-poverty urban campuses performed as well (no statistically significant difference) as children not in poverty in the medium-poverty school. There were also no differences in reading in the urban district between children not in poverty in the medium-poverty campuses and children in poverty in the low-poverty campuses.

Children in poverty performed better on the reading and math tests in each type of school poverty level in the urban district than in the suburban districts. On the other hand, children not in poverty performed better in the suburban districts than the urban district, with the exception that there were no differences in math scores between children not in poverty in the high-poverty urban and suburban campuses.

There are several possible explanations for the overall advantage of the urban district over the suburban districts in the teaching of children in poverty. Many of the children in poverty in all of the districts are minority group members. The urban district has vastly greater numbers of minority teachers who can serve as role models than do any of the suburban districts. In addition, the suburban districts have only recently had substantial numbers of children in poverty in their schools. This rapidly changing demography was one of the motivations for school districts to participate in the University of Houston's Urban Community Service project. The suburbs have had less of a history of teaching low-income children who bring to school few educational resources from home than has the urban district. Teaching children who bring few resources to school requires different kinds of teaching skills, many of which have not been expected of suburban teachers. Gary Orfield once commented on the difficulties that many middle-class teachers experienced when they began teaching low-income minority children after the implementation of desegregation plans:

I met many white teachers who said that they didn't realize that they didn't know how to teach because they were teaching in a very pleasant middle-class professional neighborhood. All the kids came in and all the kids went out and went to college, and they all got C's. Then when they had children who came from a more troubled background who needed to be taught, they found that they didn't know how.[21]

Until the influx of minority and low-income children to their districts, many of the suburban schools were able to ignore the small pockets of suburban poverty. The children on free or reduced lunch did not need to excel for suburban districts to show high aggregate passage rates on the tests. By contrast, for decades the urban district has had to educate large numbers of minority children, many of whom live in poverty. Two suburban districts that most resembled the urban district's student body also resembled the urban district's TAAS performance for children in poverty (see table 7.2). One is a predominantly African American district with the highest percentage of children on free or reduced lunch in the metropolitan area (66.4 percent compared to the urban district that has 57.7 percent). The second suburban district has the third highest percentage of children on subsidized lunch (54.7 percent) and has a higher percentage of minority teachers than any suburban district other than the predominantly African American district, and nearly as high a percentage as the urban district. All three districts have had a long history of teaching children in poverty and have had to rely upon the academic performance of the poor to satisfy their accountability mandates.

TABLE 7.2
Elementary School TAAS Performance in TLI Mean Scores by Poverty Level of Child and Campus for Urban, Diverse, and Other Suburban Districts

| | | *Urban District* | | *Diverse Suburban Districts* | | *Other Suburban Districts* | |
| | | TAAS | | TAAS | | TAAS | |
| *Child* | *Campus* | Math | Reading | Math | Reading | Math | Reading |
| Subsidized lunch | High Poverty | 63.9 | 72.8 | 69.8 | 75.7 | 44.0 | 48.6 |
| | Med. Poverty | 62.5 | 70.2 | 65.1 | 72.8 | 52.9 | 58.8 |
| | Low Poverty | 66.9 | 74.8 | 72.7 | 79.2 | 58.8 | 65.8 |
| No subsidized lunch | High Poverty | 65.3 | 70.9 | 72.7 | 79.1 | 62.0 | 69.1 |
| | Med. Poverty | 66.8 | 74.8 | 70.5 | 78.8 | 67.2 | 74.7 |
| | Low Poverty | 75.7 | 83.2 | 78.2 | 85.7 | 72.1 | 79.8 |

Finally, many of the children in poverty also have little stability in their lives. We have been told that some of the schools that have a predominant number of children in poverty on their campuses and also have high TAAS scores rely upon greater amounts of structured instruction, which serves as a kind of anchor for these children. Structured instruction and set routines add predictability and regularity to the lives of the children, many of whom are shuffled from relative to relative. Suburban districts are used to working with children who have much more stability in their lives (even the divorce and abandonment rates in the suburbs are a fraction of those in the inner city) and who can thrive in the absence of structured instruction.

Table 7.2 represents a disaggregation of the data presented in table 7.1. The suburban districts with high percentages of children on subsidized lunches, a relatively long history of teaching children in poverty, and a high percentage of minority faculty are separated out from the other suburban districts. The table lends support to the previous contention that the urban district's advantages stem from experience with children in poverty and a high percentage of minority faculty. As evident in table 7.2, the urban district even more substantially outperforms those suburban districts with few minority faculty and a limited history of working with children in poverty in reading and math among children in poverty. In fact, the children not in poverty in the low poverty schools even outperform their suburban counterparts. By contrast, the suburban districts with a history of teaching children in poverty outperform the urban district and greatly outperform the other suburban districts. Even children not in poverty do better in these suburban districts than comparable children do in the other suburbs. Perhaps the reduced organizational scale and complexity that allows for the quick adoption of innovations, conjoined with a history of working with a diverse student body result in academic benefits for all.

The findings presented in tables 7.1 and 7.2 have implications for the issues of school choice and voucher plans discussed in Texas. If children living in poverty perform less well in most suburban school districts than in the urban district, and the reasons are associated with the inability of many suburban schools to meet the needs of these children, voucher plans that send inner-city children to the suburbs may actually lower the test performances of the children. These findings are tentative and will require further analysis.

ONGOING ROLES IN SOCIOLOGY OF
EDUCATION BEYOND FEDERAL FUNDING:
A RESEARCH SHOP FOR SMALLER DISTRICTS

In an effort to support our continued research interests, fund our students, and serve the research needs of some of the districts in our

Urban Community Service Program, we have become an off-site research department for smaller school districts. These smaller districts in the metropolitan area do not have the operating budgets to hire a full-time research staff, often costing $30,000 to $50,000 per year plus fringe benefits per staff member. Districts have often relied upon the regional educational service centers operated by the state education agency. However, district employees often complain that the state agency is either unresponsive to their needs or is overworked to the extent that they cannot address the district's research issues. A few districts have banded together to form a collaborative, but by its very nature the collaborative can address only issues held in common by the participating districts. With increased state and corporate demands for school accountability, especially as it relies almost exclusively on the TAAS, districts are in greater need for quantitative research on student learning. TCUSP has signed research contracts with several districts to serve as their research departments. A standard package includes the use of our student learning outcome model to explain achievement results, the assessment of nonschool factors, such as neighborhood demographics and community resources to predict passage rates on the test and to isolate policies, practices, and programs that may affect TAAS passage, and the presentation of the findings to the school board, the superintendent, community and corporate groups, and to appear at press conferences for the districts. Itemized below are a few of the additional services we have provided for the districts. These represent aspects of our "urban extension," or "off-site research department" model.

*Determining District Capture Rates*

The availability of updated Census data linked to school attendance boundaries allows us to compare the number of school-aged children living in an attendance zone with school data (from the aggregated PEIMS [Public Education Information Management System] database maintained by the Texas Education Agency) to determine what percentage of the school-aged population was being captured by the districts. Since the Census information and those data supplied by the National Center for Educational Statistics also had information on public and private school enrollments, as well as numbers of children of school age not enrolled in schools, districts could then assess how effective they had been in attracting children of school age to their campuses. In general, districts captured 70 to 80 percent of the eligible students, although low-performing districts tended to capture a much smaller percentage of Anglo American and Asian American school-aged children who lived in the attendance zones. Likewise, as the percentage of African American and

Hispanic students in a district increased, the capture rate for Anglo and Asian Americans diminished, even in districts where test scores were comparable to those districts with smaller minority populations. Such discrepancies in capture rates reflect prejudice and stereotyping about the "educational costs" of sending one's children to districts with high minority populations. The largest urban district captured 94.6 percent of the Hispanic students, 94.6 percent of the African American students, 85.0 percent of the Asian American students, and 63.3 percent of the white (Anglo) students living within the attendance zone boundaries. Further inspection revealed that in the largest district approximately 4 percent of those not in school, but of school age, were in neither public nor private schools. Some districts have viewed these results as a challenge to locate and enroll students not currently in any school by targeting neighborhoods where student undercounts were highest. It must be recognized that there the student enrollment data used in the analysis lag behind the Census data by six months, as the 1990 Census enumeration was conducted in April and the PEIMS count was in October. This introduces some marginal amount of error in the estimation of the "capture rate."

*Parental Educational Resources*

Another analysis incorporated the Census data on percentages of adults without any college education as one of a group of predictors of student achievement. A few of the districts in the eastern part of the county are in communities where generation after generation of adults have worked in the local petrochemical plants as blue-collar workers. While income levels are high enough to produce smaller than average percentages of children on lunch subsidies, test scores are generally not commensurate with income or even property tax revenues generated. Parents often did not strongly urge their children to consider going to college, except to obtain technical training at a community college, as they and their parents had not attended college. They assumed that the children would graduate from high school and enter the same petrochemical jobs that they had. Unfortunately, many forecasts suggest that many of these jobs will disappear in the next century, seriously handicapping the children in the labor market of the twenty-first century. Students were not taking advanced courses and gifted and talented children were not enrolling in the accelerated programs. Our analyses have permitted school district personnel to explain the lower than expected test performance to petrochemical executives, while identifying strategies to increase advanced course taking and college applications in these districts. The districts are going to work with the employers to convince parents of the educational needs of the future labor force. The expectation is that test scores will eventually rise as the curriculum becomes more challenging and as more students have college goals. While the model building using school and Census data has the potential of providing school districts with an "out" to explain away low student performance, we have viewed our role as not merely to explain results, but to isolate practices that may attenuate achievement.

*Interdistrict Comparisons on TAAS Passage Rates*

We have established regression lines for TAAS passage, locating campuses within districts that are performing above, at, or below expectation given the rates of poverty on the campus. Error bands are computed to locate similarly performing campuses. Next, the rate of exemption from having a test scored is determined. This permits districts to compare their passage rate, that is, poverty levels with similar districts, and to discern whether some districts are taking advantage of the regulations that allow the exemption of some LEP and special education students. Districts that test all students tend to appear to perform below expectation, while districts that selectively exempt potential low scorers who fit the established categories tend to perform above expectation. Further analysis has revealed which of the exempted students actually would have performed well enough to pass the test, thereby permitting districts to reclassify children and end the labeling of such children as LEP or special education students.

*Locating Underserved Populations*

The socioeconomic status of children in school districts is most commonly measured by free or reduced lunch status. Annually, districts send out applications for lunch subsidies to parents and when verified, the children become eligible for benefits beyond meals, including Title I activities, compensatory education resources, and the like. However, because free lunch status is often stigmatizing to middle and high school students, there is a substantial fall off in participation beyond the elementary grades. For example, in the largest school district in our study (student body size is 202,000), over 70 percent of the elementary school students were in the free/reduced lunch count, but fewer than 40 percent of the middle and high school students were so registered. In many of the smaller districts, the free lunch count for high school juniors and seniors fell to less than 22 percent of the participation rate among first and second graders. The consequence is that there exists a severe underestimation of poverty rates in higher grades in schools, especially as there is considerable reason to expect that poverty is fairly uniform within a family. Not only does the undercount affect statistical modeling of the impact of poverty on student learning and diminish the opportunities for low-income students to eat during the school day; it also reduces the state compensatory educational funding for the school districts. Under the Texas school finance system, property-poor districts receive up $800 per child per year in funding for resources for disadvantaged children on the lunch subsidy roll, while property-rich districts avoid up to $1,000 per child per year in state recapture payments for each child on the roll (Texas Education Agency). These monies are separate from the lunch subsidy per se, but their funding formula is driven by the lunch subsidy count. It is not actually necessary for students to receive the subsidized lunches for a district to receive the state compensatory education funds, which can then be used to hire additional staff, purchase computers for the classrooms, augment the campus library, or meet any other educational purpose.

We utilize our data on every child enrolled in the districts to locate children whose siblings are on the free/reduced lunch count. Matching students by address alone has increased the estimated free/reduced lunch count by about 8.6 percent per district, or by as many as 10,100 students in the largest district and by 150 to 2,200 students in most of the other districts. A more refined technique that we have identified as "Operation Child Find," has been conducted for districts that have agreed to contact each parent and certify the children using the current year's data matches students on combinations of same surname, same address, and same telephone number. Triple matches (same surname, address, and phone number) provide almost certain additions to the count. Double matches provide somewhat lower probabilities of success in adding to the count. That is, matches by surname and phone number may involve a mismatch by address because of differences in the spelling of the address or data entry errors; matches by surname and address may involve a mismatch by phone number because one child used a parent's work phone, while another used a parent's home phone; and matches by address and phone number may involve a mismatch by surname because the children had different fathers. Other factors which may reduce the chance of compensatory funding might include the possibility that the previously unidentified child has already dropped out of school, has moved to another district, no longer is in the custody of a low-income parent, or lives with a parent who refuses to grant the district permission to certify the child. As such, rarely will the technique add more than one quarter of the identified children to the free/reduced lunch count for the district, and thus, districts are likely to receive between 10 and 30 percent of the compensatory education funding from the state. Nevertheless, to date this has brought in over $1 million to a group of smaller districts.

More accurate free lunch counts also improve the explanatory power of that variable in accounting for student achievement. The zero-order effect of free/reduced lunch status as determined from the school district data has been $b = -.210$ (*s.e.* $= .030$, $t = -7.06$). By contrast, reclassifying the siblings of children on free/reduced lunch status has increased the effect size of poverty on student achievement to $b = -.310$ (*s.e.* $= .037$, $t = -8.20$). With the very large data sets, the increment in $b$ is statistically significant.

An additional component of our work with the free/reduced lunch count has been to advise districts on ways of increasing eligible student participation in the subsidized lunch program. Older students are frequently afraid that participation in the program will lead to teasing by classmates. To reduce the stigma of lunch subsidies we have urged school districts to eliminate separate lines for free or reduced lunch students, issue all students meal cards that bear no indication that the meals have been subsidized or purchased by parents, and eliminate the practice in middle and high schools of having teachers ask students to come forward and request lunch subsidy application forms during class. One district has installed a computer-activated debit card system so that all students and even teachers use an identical card. Only key administrators know whether the individual or the subsidy pays the funding of the card's balance.

Another underserved population that can be located using our database are LEP students who are not enrolled in programs. In many urban areas, up to 10 percent of the LEP students are not in bilingual or ESL programs and have not received waivers to be placed in regular programs. They simply get lost in the system. As we have data on every student in the school districts, we can locate such students and notify the districts. Districts then initiate the paperwork to determine the preferences of the children's parents and then assign students to programs. The slippage in assignment of LEP children is a serious problem, one in which the parents of the children, many of whom are immigrants and are themselves non-English speakers, have little voice in the schools. There are few advocates for either the children or the parents and too often the schools appear not to care. In part this is because the schools are overwhelmed by the numbers; in part, it is because immigrants and minorities often have much less political and social capital; and finally, it is because surveys conducted by the school districts repeatedly reveal that Hispanic parents, especially those who are relatively recent immigrants, are most likely to report that the schools are doing an excellent job in teaching their children. Reductions in Title VII funding are likely to mean that even more LEP students will get lost in the system. It has become one of our assumed responsibilities to goad school districts by reporting the slippage.

CONCLUSIONS, CONCERNS, AND RECOMMENDATIONS

The Urban Community Service Program was developed to enable universities to assist public agencies, including public schools, to create plausible responses to the plethora of problems present in urban areas. As the program ends, many of the funded projects are seeking strategies to continue their work, as well as continue the funding of their staffs. During the course of the project we developed a forecasting model for urban schools, projecting enrollment characteristics through the year 2030. The urban district utilized the forecasts to determine siting of new campuses that would have been funded by a $390 million school bond election (unfortunately, the voters defeated the bond election). Other districts are using the forecasts to plan for the substantial demographic change they are experiencing, especially large increases in minority and low-income students and students with limited proficiency in English. To understand the impact of the changing demography on state-mandated accountability standards, we developed a student learning outcome model, containing the variables usually associated with sociological research on student achievement.

Since the end of federal funding, we have adopted the role of research department for many of the smaller school districts. Work with small districts has its pitfalls. Often the districts have been infrequent consumers of research. They may not know how to phrase researchable questions, or they expect us to tell them what questions they need to raise, or they may raise questions that can not be answered with existing data, but do not want to fund the collection of new data. However, as district administrators become more familiar with the benefits of research into their students' performances, some districts develop limitless interest in asking questions, but no awareness of how much data analysis costs. It is advisable to develop a research contract that specifies what can be done for a given quantity of funds. A research contract that specifies what is to be delivered, when, and for how much is a necessary protection of the research shop. Additional services then become defined as needing additional compensation. Finally, the transition from research funded by the federal project and the research contracted by the school districts is sometimes a difficult one to negotiate. Small districts may not have budgeted for the research services and sometimes will attempt to redefine the research as merely part of the federal project. One district administrator pointed out that he had no funds to pay for the contracted services and had assumed that we were not really going to charge him for the services. It is an ongoing problem, although some districts later allocated funds for the research services in their future budgets.

The student learning outcomes model that we developed, with its inclusion of neighborhood and parental resource factors, has the potential of creating new dilemmas, including those associated with split loyalties. Specifically, below the surface are always issues of "whose side are you on?" Nonschool factors permit school districts to shift the onus of blame for low achievement from themselves to their communities, students, and the parents of their students. While schools have often explained poor achievement by looking to parental involvement and student commitment, we offer the potential of hard data to support their claims. When faced with corporate stakeholders who ask why the students of their district have low passage rates on the TAAS, despite relatively high property tax rates in a district, school boards and superintendents appreciate a model that incorporates nonschool variables that have substantial explanatory power.

In fact, three variables describing communities that have significant effect sizes on the percentage of students in a district that pass the TAAS include the percentage of children on free or reduced lunch ($b = -.44$), percentage of female parents with no college experience ($b = -.60$), and percentage of male parents with college degrees ($b = .68$). Thus, for each increment of a percentage point in the poverty rate of children, there is a drop of almost a half of a percentage point in the passage rate of the TAAS; while each increment in the percentage of female parents without college lowers the passage rate by sixth tenths of a percent; and each increment in the percentage of male parents with college degrees raises the percentage rate of TAAS passage by over two thirds of a point.

While these community resource effects do account for a significant amount of the variance in student achievement, they enable schools to report to taxpayers, state governmental bodies, and the business community that they can only do a limited amount with the resources and students they have.

The desire for school districts to shift blame is understandable. Elsewhere, we have written about the hierarchy of distrust that has become more pervasive since the recent waves of school reform.[22] The public has reported decreasing confidence in public education, as exemplified by two decades of Phi Delta Kappan polls conducted by the Gallup Organization (See any of the Phi Delta Kappan "Annual Gallup Polls"). States have enacted school reform legislation in terms of new curricular standards, competency testing of teachers, more stringent graduation standards, and heightened demands for public school accountability. In Texas, as in many other states, the new accountability systems gave decision-makers access to information on how well schools were doing in serving their students. The accountability system further had built-in rewards and punishments, making it imperative to school administrators that their children perform well on standardized tests, not drop out, and graduate within a prescribed period. Competency testing of teachers begun in the 1980s resulted in the removal of teaching certificates and forced resignations of several thousand teachers, many from minority groups.[23] Districts in which student performances on the standardized tests have been consistently low have been taken over by the state education agency, had their superintendents and boards removed, and campuses where students consistently failed the standardized tests have been reorganized into charter schools or have experienced the wholesale termination of faculty and principals.

Later waves of school reform and restructuring included state-mandated site-based management plans and decentralized decision-making, which often resulted in vesting much more power in the hands of principals, while simultaneously holding them more directly responsible for the test score performances of their children. Since the state education agency authorized exemptions of some categories of LEP and special education students, principals had the means to determine which students took the test, and hence, how well their campuses performed. Not uncommon was the practice in some schools and districts of exempting a majority of the students in a grade from taking the TAAS (one of the participating districts was subject to a TEA investigation because of excessive numbers of exemptions). It was understandably the case that those children exempted either had been low scorers on the previous year's exam, or were expected to perform poorly on the exam that was to be administered. Decentralization of decision-making meant that central district offices were frequently unaware why test scores on some campuses rose dramatically from year to year. The use of our database provided districts with insights into campus practices.

Blame shifting is rampant. In our research relationship with the districts we have attempted to focus upon programs and practices that could nevertheless facilitate student learning, even in the presence of the community demographics. That is, we sometimes function as an external gadfly, reminding the smaller districts of resources available to them that could enhance student learning and some of their practices that have tended to diminish outcomes. Additionally, we have employed a rule that we will never willingly help a school district get around the state accountability criteria. Rather, we often explore with district administrators changes in practices that might help to raise student achievement in order to meet the state's accountability standards. It is important to recognize that the ultimate beneficiary of the research endeavor ought to be the children in the schools.

An example of our gadfly role occurred in the districts in the eastern part of the county. Low rates of parental college attendance significantly accounted for the lower than expected TAAS performances of the students. The districts also had lower than expected participation rates of their students in gifted and talented programs and in advanced courses in high school. The superintendent noted that the parents do not expect their children to go to college and seem satisfied with the education their children get. These districts are linked to the petrochemical industry and the children expect to follow their parents and grandparents into blue-collar jobs in the communities. We pointed out the forecasted downturn in employment in high-paying blue-collar jobs and expectation that good jobs, even in the petrochemical industry will require college degrees and even graduate training. We then urged the superintendent to speak to the petrochemical stakeholders to offer to inform their employees of the need for their children to go to college.

This chapter began with the promise that we would address three issues relevant to urban education. First, the use of forecasting models for school districts that are experiencing rapid demographic change, and this clearly typifies most districts in metropolitan areas, is essential. Without the ability to anticipate new populations school districts are likely to continue to offer programs and curricula that increasingly fail to address the needs of their students. Simple cohort survival models, as are used by many urban districts, are inadequate, as they utilize recent student populations to predict future ones. If new populations are entering neighborhoods as a result of changing housing characteristics and political and economic forces in the region or the nation, then data based upon neighborhood dynamics will be more useful than school-based information. While the school districts in metropolitan Houston could not anticipate future civil wars and monetary crises in Latin America and Asia, they could take into consideration the state of housing stocks, and transportation systems, and should be attentive to recent changes in neighborhood compositions. Each of the school districts in which we work now concerns themselves with more accurate and more frequent forecasts.

Second, we offered a student learning outcomes model that revealed numerous unexpected results. The sociological and educational literature is replete with national studies that aggregate data across school districts and do not capture entire districts, campuses, and classrooms. Our work does not suffer in that sense; yet, there is sufficient interdistrict diversity that common structural variables applied across different parts of the metropolitan area have substantially different effect sizes. Knowing the ethnicity, the level of poverty, or the family constellation of students in different districts in the county will not assure one of capturing similar amounts of variance. The effect sizes of these structural variables are greater for new residents than for children whose parents and grandparents attended the same schools.

Most interesting and potentially most disturbing are the differing effects of poverty status on student achievement among children in urban and suburban districts. The issue appears to be whether the district considers the teaching of children in poverty as its prime mandate. The data suggest strongly that urban schools and those suburban districts with large numbers of minority faculty and an extensive history of serving low-income students should not be abandoned to the more affluent suburbs, especially by low-income parents hoping to use vouchers to purchase a quality education for their children. Nevertheless, all suburbs are experiencing the influx of a more diverse student body, including children from more economically disadvantaged backgrounds. It is vital that those suburbs view the academic success of all of their students as central to their mandate. There is a great need for increased ethnic diversity among the teaching populations in the suburbs and there is much that the suburbs can learn from the urban districts. Quite simply, the suburbs will not remain bastions of privilege.

Finally, we recommend our "outsourced" research department approach as a strategy for academic researchers. We have recently had our contracts with our districts renewed. Districts find that sociologists can offer structural explanations for the dynamics that affect their campuses and welcome our efforts to explain how TAAS works in their districts. We are not always bearers of good news. While some in academia believe that school districts will not want to work with researchers who find that programs are not working or that district performances are significantly below the regression lines, the reality is that most superintendents want accurate information and not glowing myths. Eventually, the myths are shattered by the dynamics of demographic change.

## NOTES

1. The research presented in this chapter was supported in part by a U.S. Department of Education, Urban Community Service grant (P252A20004–94).

2. K. Geiger, *The Cost of Excellence* (Washington, D.C.: National Education Agency, 1992).

3. National Commission on Excellence in Education, *A Nation at Risk: The Imperative for Educational Reform* (Washington, D.C.: U.S. Government Printing Office, 1983).

4. M. Haberman, "Urban Schools and the Problems They Face," in *A Framework for Educational Excellence*, ed. The Greater Houston Partnership (Houston, Tex., 1990), pp. E1–3.

5. J. Waldrop, "2010," *American Demographics* 11 (1989): 53–55.

6. K. M. Borman and J. H. Spring, *Schools in Central Cities: Structure and Process* (New York: Longmann, 1984); W. J. Wilson, *The Truly Disadvantaged: The Inner City, the Underclass, and Public Policy* (Chicago: University of

Chicago Press, 1987); and M. D. LeCompte and A. G. Dworkin, *Giving Up On School: Student Dropouts and Teacher Burnouts.* (Newbury Park, Calif.: Corwin/Sage, 1991).

7. Borman and Spring, *Schools in Central Cities.*

8. A. G. Dworkin, *Teacher Burnout in the Public Schools: Structural Causes and Consequences for Children* (Albany: State University of New York Press, 1987).

9. L. Warshay, " Breadth of Perspective," in *Human Behavior and Social Process,* ed. A. Rose (Boston: Houghton Mifflin Company, 1962), pp. 148–76.

10. T. Hart and L. Lumsen, *Demographic Analysis: Using Today's Data to Plan for Tomorrow's Schools* (Portland: Oregon School Study Council, 1990).

11. Ibid.

12. See, e.g., R. C. Shaw, "Enrollment Forecasting: What Methods Work Best? *NASSP Bulletin* 68 (1984): 52–58, and W. B. Strong and R. R. Schulz. "Models for Projecting School Enrollment," *Educational Evaluation and Policy Analysis* 3 (1981): 75–81.

13. Shaw, "Enrollment Forecasting," pp. 52–58.

14. J. S. Coleman, E. Q. Campbell, C. J. Hobson, J. McPartland, A. M. Mood, F. D. Weinfeld, and R. L. York, *The Equality of Educational Opportunity* (Washington, D.C.: U.S. Government Printing Office, 1966).

15. See, e.g., S. S. Bowles and H. M. Levin, "More on Multicollinearity and the Effectiveness of Schools," *Journal of Human Resources* 3 (1968): 393–400; M. T. Katzman, *The Political Economy of Urban Schools* (Cambridge: Harvard University Press, 1971); E. A. Hanuschek, *Education and Race* (Lexington, Mass.: Lexington Books, 1972); C. Jencks, Smith M., H. Acland, M. J. Bane, D. Cohen, H. Gintis, B. Heyns, and S. Michelson, *Inequality: A Reassessment of the Effects of Family and Schooling in America* (New York: Basic Books, 1972); and R. J. Murnane, *The Impact of School Resources on the Learning of Inner City Children* (Cambridge, Mass.: Ballinger, 1975).

16. See, e.g., more recent work by Dworkin, *Teacher Burnout*; LeCompte and Dworkin, *Giving Up On School*; and national studies by J. S. Coleman, T. Hoffer, and S. Kilgore, *High School Achievement* (New York: Basic Books, 1982); G. Cohen and R. A. Lotan, "Can Classrooms Learn?" *Sociology of Education* 62 (1989): 75–94; J. S. Coleman and T. Hoffer, *Public and Private High Schools: The Impact of Communities* (Basic Books: New York, 1987); D. R. Entwisle and L. A. Hayduk, "Lasting Effects of Elementary School," *Sociology of Education* 61 (1988): 147–59; Gamoran, "The Stratification of High School Learning Opportunities," *Sociology of Education* 60 (1987): 135–55; C. L. Garner and S. W. Raudenbush, "Neighborhood Effects on Educational Attainment: A Multilevel Analysis," *Sociology of Education* 64 (1991): 251–62; M. T. Hallinan and R. A. Williams, "Students' Characteristics and the Peer-Influence Process," *Sociology of Education* 63 (1990): 122–32; V. E. Lee and A. S. Bryk, "Curriculum Tracking as Mediating the Social Distribution of High School Achievement," *Sociology of Education* 61 (1988): 78–94; V. E. Lee and A. S. Bryk, "A Multilevel Model of the Social Distribution of High School Achievement," *Sociology of Education* 62 (1989): 172–92; J. D. Willms, *Monitoring School Performance: A Guide for Educators* (Washington, D.C.: The Falmer

Press, 1992); V. E. Lee and J. B. Smith, "Effects of School Restructuring on the Achievement and Engagement of Middle-Grade Students," *Sociology of Education* 6 (1993): 164–87; and K. Namboodri, R. G. Corwin, and L. E. Dorsten "Analyzing Distributions in School Effects Research: An Empirical Illustration," *Sociology of Education* 66 (1993): 278–94.

17. See especially, Coleman, Hoffer, and Kilgore, *High School Achievement*; and Lee and Bryk, "Curriculum Tracking."

18. Greater Houston Partnership, eds., *A Framework for Educational Excellence* (Houston, Tex., 1990).

19. Coleman and Hoffer, *Public and Private High Schools*.

20. J. U. Ogbu, "Minority Status and Schooling in Plural Societies," *Comparative Education Review* 27 (1983): 168–90; and R. A. Mickelson, "The Attitude-Achievement Paradox among Black Adolescents," *Sociology of Education* 63 (1990): 44–61.

21. G. Orfield, "Examining the Desegregation Process," *Integrated Education* 13 (1975): 127–30.

22. Dworkin, *Teacher Burnout*; LeCompte and Dworkin, *Giving Up On School*; and A. G. Dworkin. "Coping with Reform: The Intermix of Teacher Morale, Teacher Burnout and Teacher Accountability," in *The International Handbook of Teachers and Teaching*, ed. B. J. Biddle, T. L. Good, and I. F. Goodson, (Dordrecht, The Netherlands: Kluwer Academic Publishers, 1997).

23. Texas Education Agency, "Performance on the Texas Examination of Current Administrators and Teachers: March 1986 Administration," Austin, Texas, mimeograph.

CHAPTER 8

# Gangsta Pedagogy
# and Ghettocentricity:
# The Hip-Hop Nation as
# Counterpublic Sphere

## Peter McLaren

Race is the modality in which class is lived.
—Eric Lott, "Cornel West in the Hour of Chaos"

I was beautiful; after all, my skin was as rich and as dark as wet, brown mud, a complexion that any and every pale white girl would pray for. . . . My butt sat high in the air and my hips obviously gave birth to Creation.
—Sister Souljah, *No Disrespect*

Black athletes . . . white agents
Black preacher . . . white Jesus
Black entertainers . . . white lawyers
Black Monday . . . white Christmas
—Chuck D, "White Heaven . . . Black Hell"

When Harvard scholar Henry Louis Gates Jr. defended the imagery and lyrics of 2 Live Crew at their highly publicized 1990 trial, claiming that the group's album, *As Nasty as They Wanna Be,* was not obscene on the grounds that the lyrics and imagery were derived from the venerable African American tradition of "signifying" and "playing the dozens," no doubt many critics were thinking that the controversy over rap would probably go the way of the debates over rock 'n' roll in the 1950s: it would generally "fade away." At the time of the trial it was difficult to imagine not only the public furor over rap music—gangsta rap in particular—but also the extent to which Washington would develop its anti-rap campaign, signaling a "moral panic" destined to become one of the lightning rods in the 1996 presidential campaign and a flashpoint in the current debate over race relations. As former Secretary of Education and Drug Czar William J. Bennett joins forces with C. DeLores Tucker, the conservative activist with the National Political Caucus of Black Women, to publicly denounce gangsta rap as a seductive, immoral force, presidential candidates, Bob Dole, Phil Gramm, and Pat Buchanan have decided not only to join in the condemnation of Time Warner (which up to the time of this writing owns interests in a number of rap record labels) but also to launch a frontal assault on Hollywood's entertainment industry and all those liberals who were likely to defend affirmative action, government assistance programs for nondocumented workers, or gay-rights initiatives.

Despite the fact that the Geto Boys' lead rapper, Bushwick Bill, recently thanked Dole for $300,000 worth of publicity,[1] the attacks have had a considerable negative effect on the rap industry, prompting Time Warner to fire record executive Doug Morris and to be reportedly (as of this writing) negotiating its way out of a $100 million share in Interscope Records, distributor of Snoop Doggy Dogg, Dr. Dre, and Tupac Shakur.[2]

Gangsta rappers follow a long line of musicians denounced by the moral custodians of U.S. culture as prime instigators of juvenile delinquency—a list that includes, among others, Frank Sinatra, Elvis, the Beatles, the Sex Pistols, Metallica, and Prince. Members of my generation, puzzling over the 2 Live Crew trial or reflecting on the earlier public debates surrounding the subliminal messages purportedly inserted into songs by Judas Priest and Ozzy Osborne, are perhaps reminded of earlier controversies that accompanied the Rolling Stones' hit "Satisfaction," or the two-and-a-half-year analysis by J. Edgar Hoover's G-men of the Kingsmen's 1963 hit, "Louie, Louie."[3] The investigation by FBI sound technicians and cryptographers of this pop chant (which merely recounts a lovesick sailor's return to his Jamaican sweetheart) seems ironic now, given the fact that the teen anthem has since appeared as the backdrop of numerous films, charity telethons, and wine cooler ads.[4] The debate over gangsta rap has captured the public imagination at a time when the nation is vigorously reevaluating public policies surrounding affirmative action and urban reform. This has given gangsta rap an urgency and public visibility far greater than earlier debates over rock 'n' roll and morality. Sister Souljah had been criticized by President Clinton and others for inciting violence against white people when in fact she had told a journalist only that she could understand why some black people might want to kill white people: "In the mind of a gang member, why not kill white people? In other words, if you've been neglected by the social and economic order of America, and you've become casual about killing, you would have no hesitancy about killing somebody white."[5] In providing a sociological insight she was roundly condemned—unfairly—as a hate-mongerer. Rapper Chuck D maintains that rappers themselves don't necessarily feel violent toward whites. Rappers are contemporary urban messengers from God: "It's not me, or Ice Cube, or Sister Souljah's feelings—we're just the messengers, and how you gonna kill the messenger? The best thing about rap is it's a last-minute warning, the final call . . . a last plea for help on the countdown to Armageddon."[6] Chuck D sees rap as the 'hood's equivalent of CNN.

As I complete some final editing to this essay, which takes the form of an interrogative excursion into the subject of gangsta rap, the *Los Angeles Times* reports that rap singer Dasean Cooper (J-Dee), a member of Da Lench Mob, was recently sentenced to twenty-nine years to life for the 1993 murder of his girlfriend's male roommate at a party in Inglewood.[7] Terry (T-Bone) Gray, another member of Da Lench Mob, has also been charged with murdering one individual—and wounding another—at a Los Angeles bowling alley. Da Lench Mob's 1992 single, "Who You Gonna Shoots Wit Dat," was cited in the Cooper case by the prosecuting attorney in an attempt to paint murders by rap artists as "life imitating art." Criminal charges have recently been filed against Snoop Doggy Dogg (who is awaiting trial for allegedly driving the get-away car during a murder) and Tupac Amaru Shakur, San Francisco Bay Area rapper and former member of the Digital Underground (arrested for sexually assaulting a nineteen-year-old woman whom he and his friends had held captive in a hotel room). The widow of slain Texas police officer Bill Davidson has sued Tupac for allegedly inciting a nineteen-year-old car thief, Ronald Ray Howard, to murder Davidson with a nine-millimeter pistol. After listening to the mantra-like lyrics of Shakur's song "Crooked Ass Nigga," from his album *2Pacalypse Now,* which describes a drug dealer on a rampage with a nine-millimeter pistol and contains a reference to "droppin' the cop," Howard claims that he "snapped" and shot Davidson as a result of being instructed by the lyrics. Dan Quayle cashed in on the media attention by visiting Davidson's grieving daughter and announcing that Tupac's music 'has no place in our society." These events have induced the breach birth of the gangsta rap media elite and have added to hip-hop's hype as hard-edged urban drama muscled onto a compact disc. (As the original printing of this chapter went into production, Tupac lay dead of gunshot wounds that he received in Las Vegas after attending the Mike Tyson–Bruce Seldon boxing match. He was shot while driving in a car with Death Row

Records co-founder and president, Marion "Suge" Knight.) Although he bragged defiantly about the tough life in the 'hood, and had "Thug Life" and an AK-47 assault weapon tattooed across his abdomen, his Grammy-nominated 1995 hit single, "Dear Mama," was a tender ballad written for his mother. Tupac's mother, Afeni Shakur, was a member of the Black Panther Party and was pregnant with Tupac while she was serving time in a New York prison for allegedly plotting to blow up department stores and police stations. He sang: "Even as a crack fiend always was a black queen." The name Tupac Amaru comes from a sixteenth-century Incan chief whose name means "shining serpent." Tupac Amaru was the last Incan leader to be defeated by the Spanish. He was executed in 1572. The Tupac Amaru Revolutionary Movement led by Nestor Cerpa Cartolini is currently holding hundreds of international diplomats hostage in the Japanese embassy in Lima, Peru. Tupac's posthumous *The Don Killuminati: The 7 Day Theory* is expected to replace the Beatles' *Anthology 3* as the nation's best-selling album.

Eazy-E's recent death from AIDS (Eazy-E was a former member of NWA, a financial contributor to the Republican Party and the head of Ruthless Records, the first significant rapper-owned record label) has left the hip-hop nation stunned. Early this April, the Los Angeles Police Department joined with FBI agents in Operation Sunrise, sweeping through a thirty-block area of South Central Los Angeles, arresting gang members of the Eight-Tray Gangster Crips, a gang that came into public prominence during the 1992 uprising with its involvement in the attack on truck driver Reginald O. Denny and other motorists at the intersection of Florence and Normandie. East LA Chicanos are still recovering from the news of the slaying of Selena, superstar of Tejano music and heroine of Molinatown's Chicano barrio in Corpus Christi. Among gangsta rappers, the mood of the city felt all too familiar.

By late October, when jury selection in the murder trial of Snoop Doggy Dogg, his bodyguard, and his friend began in Los Angeles, defense attorneys (including Johnnie L. Cochran Jr.) were preparing to "play the LAPD card" in their attack on police evidence tampering. In the post-Simpson era, the lawyers representing Snoop Doggy Dogg (a.k.a. Calvin Broadus, former member of the Long Beach Insane Crips) and his associates stand a good chance of landing further blows to the credibility and integrity of the police. A few months earlier Snoop Doggy Dogg was praised by President Bill Clinton and Ice-T for writing a letter to sixty gang sets in Los Angeles and honoring their efforts to "keep the peace." As Snoop Doggy Dogg's words of thanks were sounded at a celebration at the International House of Blues in West Los Angeles, sets from the Imperial Courts, Jordan Downs, and Nickerson Gardens housing projects in Watts sat down with the Fruit Town Pirus of Compton and sets from Long Beach, the Pueblo Bishops 5 Duce Mid-City Gangsters, the 5 Duce BCG, the Santana Block Crips, the V-13s and Shoreline Crips of Venice, and the Parkside Manor Circle City Pirus of Los Angeles. When, at this afternoon gala, a Crip, a Blood, and a Latino gang member cut a cake in unison, gangsta rappers had symbolically joined forces with Bill Clinton's four-member Color Guard, present at the ceremonies as a sign of "respect."

For someone who grew up listening to Robert Johnson's Delta Blues, who used to frequent the Colonial Tavern on Toronto's Yonge Street to hear musician friends jam with Muddy Waters, who idolized Lightning Hopkins, and who wanted to play the blues harp like Little Walter, rap music was not a natural transition for me. Ska, rock-steady, and reggae helped to broaden my musical sensibilities, but, even so, rap was a taste that was difficult to acquire at first. In recent years I have grown to greatly appreciate gangsta rap as an oppositional political practice, but despite its possibilities for articulating an oppositional performative politics, gangsta rap remains, in some senses, a problematic cultural practice. In this article I am generally referring to *gangsta rap* and do not wish to conflate this term with those of *rap* or *hip-hop*. When I speak generally about rap music as a form of black cultural address, without specifically calling it gangsta rap, I am emphasizing rap music's situatedness within hip-hop culture, its criticism of the dominant white culture's racial and economic discrimination, and the contradictory urban expressions of African American economic and racial marginality. Here I share Tricia Rose's perspective that rap "is a black idiom that prioritizes black culture and that articulates the problem of black urban life."[8] I am referring to rap artists as cultural workers engaged to a large extent in "the everyday struggles of working-class blacks and the urban poor."[9] Jeffrey Louis Decker refers to such cultural workers as "hip hop nationalists" who function in the manner suggested by Gramsci's description of organic intellectuals.[10]

With what some rap critics might call its numbing psychorealism; its fixing of "in-your-face" rhymes to social meltdown and bass rhythms to urban disaster; its commodification of black rage through high-volume and low-frequency sound; its production of sexualizing fugues for an imploding Generation X; its ability to provoke a white hellification of black youth with "attitude"; its seventh sons in blue or red bandanas and ten-dollar gold tooth caps "droppin science" and warning their homeboys against "tell-lie-vision," the "lie-bury," and public school "head-decay-tion"; its dance culture of the Handglide, Flow, Headspin, King Tut, Windmill, Tick, Float, Wave, and freestyle; its production of affective economies of white panic around a generalized fear of a black planet; its sneering, tongue-flicking contempt of public space; its visceral intensity and corporal immediacy; its snarling, subterranean resistance; its eschatological showdown of "us" against "them"; its "edutainers" down with the brothas in the street; its misogynist braggadocio; its pimp-inspired subjectivity; its urban war zone counternarratives; its home-brewed polymerized anarchism; its virulent autobiographical hype; its Five Percenters flashing their ciphers, 7s, and crescent moon and star within a large sun, praising "Father Allah"; its irreverent first-person narratives powered by gats and urban souljahs high on malt liquor; its rhythmic macho boastfests by brothas in Carhartt jackets; and its dissentious themes and high-pitched contempt for the white petit bourgeoisie and the yuppie heirs of the overclass who can afford to sidestep the frenetic dizziness of reality, gangsta rap has occasioned much public debate over the last few years. Gangsta rap is merely the latest incarnation of the rap music industry in general.

Tricia Rose notes that rap music was "discovered" by the music industry, the print media, the fashion industry, and the film industry during the five years after music entrepreneur Sylvia Robinson released "Rapper's Delight" in 1979.[11] Rose further declares that rap music needs to be situated within Afro-diasporic traditions and cultural formations of the English- and Spanish-speaking Caribbean and in the context of specific historical musical junctions such as urban blues, be-bop, and rock 'n' roll. Further, rap needs to be considered in light of such factors as the creation of the postindustrial city and the larger social movement of hip-hop. For instance, rap music can be traced to, among other cultural and social elements, the hip-hop nationalism of the 1960s, such as the Black Panthers, Malcolm X, gender politics; New York City's political context of the 1970s; postindustrial shifts in economic conditions, including access to housing, the formation of new communication networks; blaxploitation films such as Melvin Van Peebles's *Sweet Sweetback's Baadasssss Song;* deindustrialization; the relocation of people of color from different parts of New York City into the South Bronx; city planning and projects such as the Title I Clearance program; the system of crews or posses as means for alternative youth identities: disco music and the cross-fertilization among rapping, break dancing, and graffiti writing.[12]

In the 1980s we started to see rap music emerging in other urban ghettos in major cities such as Houston's fifth ward, Miami's Overtown, Boston's Roxbury, and South Central, Watts, and Compton, in Los Angeles. The Los Angeles rappers have spawned a specific rap style that, Rose notes, must be seen in the context of narratives specific to poor, young, black, male subjects in Los Angeles. Rose writes that Los Angeles rappers "defined the gangsta rap style."[13] and "spawned other regionally specific hardcore rappers such as New Jersey's Naughty by

Nature, Bronx-based Tim Dog, Onyx, and Redman, and a new group of female gangsta rappers, such as Boss (two black women from Detroit), New York–based Puerto Rican rapper Hurricane Gloria, and Nikki D."[14] When examining the roots of rap, or rap's inflection into gangsta rap genres, we need to examine the conjunctural specificity of many factors, including those listed above.

White and black listeners alike are drawn to this surly form of urban apostasy, fashionable deviancy, and stylized outlawry, whose message and transgressive status dig pretty close to the eschatological roots of holy war. Gangsta rap has been accused by some middle-class whites as well as some black professionals of fomenting the anger, racial hatred, and lawlessness that led to the LA uprising of 1992. Of course, in tandem with such dispatches from the bourgeoisie was a studied ignorance about the irreversible structural unemployment faced by many blacks in the inner city, the dismantling of social services, and the progressive hardening of racial lines.

The LA media have not been known for their celebration of rap as a musical genre since the heyday of its Compton rappers: MC Ren, Dr. Dre, Yella, Ice Cube, and Eazy-E (who left groups such as The CIA and World Class Wreckin Cru in order to work collaboratively as NWA— Niggas With Attitude—from 1987 to 1992). Instead, the media have preferred to demonize and hellify the genre that these young Angelenos from Watts, Compton, and South Central—"the nihilistic school of Los Angeles–centered gangsta rappers"—helped to create.[15] Following their more politicized hard-core and hard-beat counterparts in New York (such as Run-DMC and KRS-1) on the East Coast (such as Notorious B.I.G.), in the footsteps of New York's Grandmaster Flash and the Furious Five, and fellow Angelenos Gil Scott-Heron, the Watts Prophets, and the Last Poets (a group of black nationalist lyricists), LA rap artists provided the space for the development of a new form of social criticism. This form of social criticism was apotheosized in Ice Cube's *The Predator,* which offered a potent commentary on the LA uprising of 1992. The cultural power and promise of rap resided in its powerful dramatization of white racism. In "We Had to Tear This Motherfucker Up" Ice Cube (a.k.a. O'Shea Jackson) sentences former LAPD officers Stacey Koon, Laurence Powell, and Timothy Wind to death for the beating of Rodney King.

Like their New York counterpart, Afrika Bambaataa, former member of the Black Spades street gang and founder of the hip-hop community, Zulu Nation (made up of African American, Puerto Rican, Afro-Caribbean, and Euro-American youths and based on the Zulu military system), LA rappers Ice-T, Tone Loc, Ice Cube, and Eazy-E were also former gangbangers. Many of these rappers were products of the eco-

nomic and cultural upheavals that had assaulted and displaced numerous multiethnic urban communities; their futures were bound up in the
dimming job market by inner-city trade vocational schooling. For
instance, hip-hop originator DJ Kool Herc (whose original rap style was
influenced by prison "toasting") attended Alfred E. Smith auto
mechanic trade school; Grandmaster Flash studied electronic repair
work at Samuel Gompers vocational high school; and Salt 'n' Pepa both
worked as telemarketing representatives at Sears and were intent at one
time on nursing school.[16] These working-class black youths were able to
escape the uncertain futures constructed for them in an era of deindustrialization. They are some of the lucky few to succeed as part of a financially lucrative musical phenomenon. However, it is a phenomenon
often accused of fomenting racial panics and urban youth criminality.
Just ask Charlton Heston and Oliver North.

Emerging in the 1970s from the epicenters of hip-hop culture—the
blue-collar housing units of America's postindustrial cities—rap music
developed among relocated black and Puerto Rican male youths of the
South Bronx who celebrated break dancing, graffiti, B-Boy, and wild
style fashions.[17] Puerto Rican rap has incorporated inflections from
salsa, variations of which are drawn from *Santéria* rhythms, as is the
case of the music of Tito Puente (himself a priest of *Santéria).*

Some of the major strands of hip-hop culture (in which rap, style,
and politics become mutually informing inflections) can be traced from
the jive talkers of the be-bop era to the reggae-based sounds of Jamaican
DJ Kool Herc in the West Bronx in 1973 and Jah Rico in north London
around 1976. Hip-hop youth in the Bronx and London sympathized
with the economic and social struggles of young people in Jamaica and
Soweto, wore dreadlocks ("Funki Dreds") with shaved back and sides
created by Jazzy B and Aitch for the Soul II Soul crew, or combined the
Philly Cut or skiffle with shaved diagonal lines, bleaching, or perms.[18]
Shifts in clothes displayed a taxonomy of funky sartorial motifs, from
Teenybopper to Home Boy to hard-rocker to Afrocentric; and from
Hustler to Superfly to Daisy Age to Cosmic (via Rifat Ozbek). With
styles eventually shifting to athletic and leisure wear, Home Boys and
Fly Girls started sporting sweatshirts, cropped shorts, "pin-tucked"
baggy jeans, baseball caps, chunky gold chains, Dukie Ropes, and
leather pendants.[19] Then came the "hoodies" and the "triple fat" goose-
down jackets.

Influenced by the music of Curtis Mayfield, the funk of James
Brown, be-bop, and rhythmic jazz, rap is an impressive amalgam of
complex musical formations. Some ethnomusicologists consider such
formations to be extensions of African expressive forms such as "playing the dozens" and "signifying" as well as the praise songs of the

African storyteller, or *griot*.[20] In saying this, however, I am reminded of Tricia Rose's important admonition that hip-hop not be reduced to its African musical origins as oral traditions.[21] Hip-hop needs to be understood, argues Rose, as a "secondary orality" bound up in an electronically mediated reality that is conjuncturally embedded in relations of power and politics. Rose further notes that "rap musicians are not the only musicians to push on the limits of high-tech inventions. Yet the decisions they have made and the directions their creative impulses have taken echo Afro-diasporic musical priorities. Rap production resonates with Black cultural priorities in the age of digital reproduction."[22]

Tricia Rose's discussion of mass-produced repetition undercuts perspectives by Adorno, Attali, and Jameson by arguing that repetition in rap is not always connected to the commodity system of late capitalism in the same way as other musical forms. She argues that repetition in mass-cultural formations can also serve as a form of collective resistance.[23]

The operational or performative logics of gangsta rap vary but what is constant is what Lawrence Grossberg calls "affective agency"—its ability to articulate "mattering maps" in which agency is defined as brushing up against the prison of everyday life.[24] Michael Dyson describes the emergence of rap within a context that emphasizes its situatedness as a cultural form of resistance. According to Dyson,

> Rap music grew from its origins in New York's inner city over a decade ago as a musical outlet to creative cultural energies and to contest the invisibility of the ghetto in mainstream American society. Rap remythologized New York's status as the spiritual center of black America, boldly asserting appropriation and splicing (not originality) as the artistic strategies by which the styles and sensibilities of black ghetto youth would gain popular influence. Rap developed as a relatively independent expression of black male artistic rebellion against the black bourgeois *Weltanschauung,* tapping instead into the cultural virtues and vices of the so-called underclass, romanticizing the ghetto as the fecund root of cultural identity and authenticity, the Rorschach of legitimate masculinity and racial unity.[25]

Tricia Rose describes hip-hop culture, from which rap and eventually gangsta rap evolved, in a more global context:

> Hip hop is an Afro-diasporic cultural form which attempts to negotiate the experiences of marginalization, brutally truncated opportunity and oppression within the cultural imperatives of African-American and Caribbean history, identity and community. It is the tension between the cultural fractures produced by postindustrial oppression and the binding ties of Black cultural expressivity that sets the critical frame for the development of hip hop.[26]

Rap's beginnings as highly politicized and powerfully eclectic music can be seen in such songs as "Rapper's Delight" by the Sugarhill Gang in 1979, Brother D's (Daryl Asmaa Nubyah) "We Gonna Make the Black Nation Rise," recorded in 1980, and Afrika Bambaataa and Soul Sonic Force's 1982 recording of "Planet Rock." According to Dick Hebdige, Bambaataa "has been known to cut from salsa to Beethoven's Fifth Symphony to Yellow Magic Orchestra to calypso through Kraftwerk via video game sound effects and the theme from *The Munsters* television series back to his base in James Brown."[27] Bambaataa—who ran a sound system at the Bronx River Community Center—would also mix the theme from the *Pink Panther* with bits and pieces of songs from the Monkees, the Beatles, and the Rolling Stones.[28]

Poison Clan, AMG, Hi-C, Nu Niggaz on the Block, Compton Cartel, 2nd II None, Mob Style, and Compton's Most Wanted did not emerge in a social vacuum. When former LAPD Chief of Police Darryl Gates proclaimed that "we may be finding that in some Blacks when [the chokehold] is applied the veins or arteries do not open up as fast as they do on normal people," he was reflecting the sentiments of the white dominant culture of law enforcement in Los Angeles.[29] Not only was he demonizing African Americans as biologically subnormal, he was adding to the criminalization of black youth in general, corralling connotations of black masculinity into the operative lexicon of unimpeachable white common sense. The LAPD term describing "African Americans in the vicinity" as "Gorillas in the Mist" provoked Da Lench Mob to title their album *Guerrillas in tha Midst*. Some cultural critics were beginning to view rap artists as agents of revolutionary consciousness. When Operation HAMMER sent Chief Gates and his minions into the streets of South Central to pick up "suspicious looking" black youth, harass them, and build up the data base of the LAPD's task force, gangsta rappers were portraying the practice of law enforcement as a form of racial and class warfare.

After the release of NWA's 1988 debut album, *Straight Outta Compton,* white audiences were treated to urban nightmares of white throats being slit in midscream. NWA's hit crossover recording, "Efil4zaggin"—"niggaz 4 life" spelled backward—was the first hardcore rap collection to reach number one on the pop charts. Then "Cop Killer" hit the airwaves, with Ice-T's hard, pounding, and pimpified lyrics smashing through listeners' ribs like a brass-knuckled fist, tagging a "don't fuck with me" on their hearts with an aerosol can of his digitized blood. The media went ballistic in condemnation of this new transgressive musical form known as "gangsta rap," which was even propelling white audiences into adopting black inflection and "ghetto" identification. Ice-T became buoyant after President Clinton publicly criticized "Cop Killer" and sixty congressmen signed a letter condemning the song: "Very few people have their names said by the president, especially in anger. It makes me feel good, like I haven't been just standing on a street corner yelling with nobody listening all the time. . . . It lets you know how small this country is."[30]

Ice Cube's 1990 hit "Endangered Species," from the album *Amerikkka's Most Wanted,* captures the attitude that many gangsta rap lyrics reflect with respect to law enforcement agencies:

> Every cop killer ignored
> They just send another nigger to the morgue
> A point scored.
> They could give a fuck about us
> They'd rather find us with guns and white powder
> Now kill ten of one to get the job correct.
> To serve, protect and break a nigga's neck.

This was heavy stuff in a society too preoccupied with consolidating its hegemony through frontal assaults on the welfare state and labor coalitions to concern itself with a bunch of "lowlifes" singing about their crime-ridden hoods. Latino rap didn't really become popular until 1990, during a groundswell of public panic surrounding the growing Latino population in the United States and amidst the reactionary tactics of the English Only Movement. Mellow Man Ace went gold with *Mentirosa,* and Kid Frost's (a.k.a. Arturo Molina) Chicanismo-inspired debut album, *Hispanic Causing Panic,* became the rap anthem of La Raza.[31] Chicano rapper ALT (a.k.a. Al Trivette) fuses insights of barrio life in El Monte and Rosemead into African American rap in albums *ALT* and *Stone Cold World.*

The amazing thing about the disjunctive barrage of ghetto moments known as rap was that it sold, turning inner-city homeys such as Mixmaster Spade into deities in gold chains, hawking their rap wares on the very mean streets that they rapped about. Since those early days, gangsta rap has even gone platinum with Dre's *The Chronic* and Snoop's *Doggystyle.*

In the eyes of many ghetto youth, society is going under and gangsta rappers and hepcats from the barrios are the new prophets, sounding their nationalist warnings over a Roland TR 808 drum synthesizer as the world about them swirls into the urban vortex, like DeNiro's ex-convict character in *Cape Fear,* whose savaged and tattooed body writhes while his soul speaks in tongues as both sink beneath the foaming waters.

Death Row Records, run by Andre (Dr. Dre) Young and Marion "Suge" Knight, is the nation's most profitable producer of gangsta rap, grossing a total of $90 million from tape, CD, and merchandise sales in 1993 and 1994.[32] Affiliated with media giant Time Warner, this West-wood-based firm boasts a corporate logo of a hooded man in an electric chair. Death Row Records has not escaped the controversies surrounding its stars' involvement in criminal violence. At a party for its out-of-town retailers and promoters held hours after Snoop Doggy Dogg (Calvin Broadus) took top honors at the Soul Train Music Awards, a fan was brutally stomped to death. Young is currently serving a five-month term in Pasadena City jail for parole violation. (In 1992 he was convicted of breaking another rap producer's jaw and hitting a New Orleans police officer in a hotel brawl.) A year earlier he was convicted of slamming a TV talk-show host into a wall at a Hollywood club. Knight was also convicted of assault with a deadly weapon. According to Dre, "America loves violence. America is obsessed with murder. I think murder sells a lot more than sex. They say sex sells. I think murder sells."[33] However, Death Row Records publicly denounces gang violence, and the firm has donated $500,000 to a South Central antigang program.

Russell Simmons, CEO of Def Jam Recordings (the largest African American–owned company in the record business) defends rap as a way to reach kids in Beverly Hills:

> And the most important thing is this. It's very, very important that there be communication between kids that would generally not talk to each other. Your kids may not be bad, but it's pretty sure they know some who are. Your kids are surrounded by those kids. So maybe some kid in Beverly Hills listens to rap and gets a better idea of what some kids in Crenshaw are thinking. And as that kid in Beverly Hills grows up and goes to college, maybe he'll keep a little bit of that in his consciousness, and maybe even grow up to do something about it.[34]

Simmons's justification for rap and gangsta rap as the contemporary hope for shaping the consciousness of rich white kids in Beverly Hills certainly overestimates rap's potential for political resistance and social transformation through the mobilization of Generation X. Yet it vastly underestimates the power of capitalist hegemony to produce, promote, and protect the vested interests of dominant culture in Western society, and what it takes to construct counterhegemonic social practices.

Shortly after the 1992 LA Intifada, pop singer Michelle Shocked and freelance writer Bart Bull mounted a powerful (if not profoundly misguided) denunciation of gangsta rap in an issue of *Billboard*. Claiming it to be a contemporary recoding of a turn-of-the-century white racist stereotype, a racist revival of the minstrel tradition as embodied in the nineteenth-century "coon song," they proclaimed that the "chicken-thieving, razor-toting 'coon' of the 1890s is the drug-dealing, Uzi-toting 'nigga' of today."[35] Ice Cube is criticized by Shocked and Bull as a "greed artist" who, through albums such as *The Predator,* is profiting from the conditions that produce the underclass through his production of a "Zip Coon Toon Town" version of Los Angeles, "a coon song fantasyland." This perspective is echoed by New York essayist and music critic Stanley Crouch, who calls gangsta rap "the selling of coon images" and who compares record executives who produce gangsta rap to "high tech slave traders."[36] Crouch condemns gangsta rap for portraying black people as wild savages and as badges of black authenticity, as the "real" voices from the hood. Taking issue with Crouch's position, the Geto Boys' lead rapper, Bushwick Bill (whose physical status as a one-eyed midget has not been lost on rap's media critics) describes rap as an "opera to people in the ghetto."[37] Rock critic Dave Marsh argues that the attack on rap is directed at new access to the mainstream media by America's underclass. He condemns the anti-rap campaign by William Bennett and C. DeLores Tucker as 90s-style McCarthyism. Former *Wall Street Journal* writer and critic Martha Bayles blames the offensive lyrics in much of today's music not on African American music but on the avant-garde European art school thinking that she calls "perverse modernism."[38]

In Mexico border towns like Tijuana, *narcocorrido* ballads (historically derived from the narrative style of Nahuatl epic poetry and Andalusian romantic verse from the sixteenth century) tell stories of drug dealers who prevail in the face of the authorities. Narcocorrido balladeers have provoked the wrath of anti-drug spokespeople such as Marta Rocha de Diaz, president of Housewives of Playas de Tijuana. The public debate is similar to that surrounding gangsta rap. Los Tucanes sing narcocorridos about smugglers who take heroin, cocaine, and marijuana across the border into the United States. The popularity of Los Tucanes and Los Tigres del Norte has provoked critics to condemn narcocorridos for mimicking U.S.-style gangsta rap.

David Troop's *Rap Attack: African Jive to New York Hip Hop,* Houston Baker's *Black Studies: Rap and the Academy,* and Tricia Rose's brilliant *Black Noise: Rap Music and Black Culture in Contemporary America*[39] are just a few of the burgeoning scholarly commentaries on rap that offer a much more congenial account of rap's potential for developing forms of counterhegemonic resistance than the account of gangsta rap that is offered by Shocked and Bull. For these critics, it is important to understand how and why the terms governing the popular responses to rap have come into being and how they have, to a large extent, become naturalized. Accordingly, these writers maintain the need to see hip-hop in a much broader context: as a global cultural practice that is articulated through the tropes and sensibilities of the African diaspora and the history of Afro-America, and that creates a "diasporic interchange" and "diasporic intimacy" among struggling black peoples the world over who are fighting racism and capitalist exploitation.[40] As Nick De Genova emphasizes, "rather than as an expression of social pathology, gangster rap's imaginative empowerment of a nihilistic and ruthless way of life can be better understood as a potentially oppositional consciousness—albeit born of desperation, or even despair."[41] Common subjective understandings of alienation among oppressed groups are articulated through rap; as a cultural force it is integral in providing black urban youth with both an expression of race and with codes of solidarity. As De Genova puts it, "gangsta rap can be found to transcend the mere reflection of urban mayhem and enter into musical debate with these realities, without sinking into didacticism or flattening their complexity."[42] Rap needs to be understood not so much for its musical poaching through "sampling" as for the way that it is premised on what Tricia Rose calls "transformations and hybrids"—developing "a style that nobody can deal with." She writes that

> transformations and hybrids reflect the initial spirit of rap and hip hop as an experimental and collective space where contemporary issues and ancestral forces are worked through simultaneously. Hybrids in rap's subject matter, not unlike its use of musical collage and the influx of new, regional and ethnic styles, have not yet displaced the three points of stylistic continuity to which I referred earlier: approaches to flow, ruptures in line and layering can still be found in the vast majority of rap's lyrical and music construction. The same is true of the critiques of the postindustrial urban America context and the cultural and social conditions which it has produced. Today, the South Bronx and South Central Los Angeles are poorer and more economically marginalized than they were ten years ago.[43]

Strutting apocalyptically across the urban landscape, today's gangsta rappers have, for some listeners, become the new black superheroes invested with dangerous, ambiguous, uncontrolled, and uncontrollable powers, the force of nature bound up with self-conscious and grandiose marginality. You don't fuck with these brothers and sisters and live to tell about it. Shocked and Bull's dismissive appraisal of gangsta rap as a message primarily mediated by whites eager to be titillated by the thrilling despair within aggrieved black urban communities in the form of "bad nigga" narratives and hyperbolic masculinism underscores their view that the production and performativity of rap is directly at the expense of the structurally subordinated black subject. But is gangsta rap really "an exaggerated defiance feigned for commercial purposes," signifying steroids for sculpting rage, or perhaps a "mock nihilism that parallels the ambiguous accommodationism displayed in subversive forms of minstrelsy"[44] or, to borrow a phrase that Charles Pierce used in another context, a "phony menace that is little more than Tomming with your hat turned backward"?[45]

Some gangsta songs, for instance, promote a stereotypical (re)framing that depicts the gangsta rapper as both sociopath and criminal. Stereotypes are recast and refigured so that the negative connotations (of laziness, violence, etc.) become positive attributes of strength, of power, and of resistance to white domination. While the mock nihilism in gangsta rap "is an inherently resistive element," it has also "been a key element in its commercial exploitation."[46] While Angela Davis has decried the sexism of rap, she comments, somewhat reluctantly, on the power evoked by the image of the black man—as gun-toting revolutionary—that is offered up to the public by gangsta rap: "Many of the rappers call upon a market-mediated historical memory of the black movement of the sixties and seventies. The image of an armed Black man is considered the 'essence' of revolutionary commitment today. As dismayed as I may feel about this simplistic, phallocentric image, I remember my own responses to romanticized images of brothers (and sometimes sisters) with guns."[47]

Bell hooks argues that much of the sexism and misogyny that riddles rap songs is based on an assertive patriarchal paradigm of competitive masculinity and its emphasis on physical prowess. Decker presents Sister Souljah's role as a member of Public Enemy between 1990 and 1992 as deflecting gender-based criticism away from Public Enemy and constructing "an alibi for the stereotypical hypermasculinity of black men"[48] through her exclusive emphasis on racial politics and her allegiance to a hip-hop nationalism that tends to objectify the black woman as a sign of "Mother Africa."[49] However, black female rappers have done much to present affirming images of black women outside the binary couplet of good girl/bad girl that dominates the patriarchal culture of gangsta rap. For instance, Queen Latifah (Dana Owens) has challenged racist white America's view of black women as "welfare queens" and unwed mothers as well as challenged the view of some black nationalists that women accept roles subordinate to men. For Latifah, women are not the "bitches" signified by some male rap artists. According to Steven Gregory,[50] the welfare mother (defended by Queen Latifah and other female rappers)

> is a privileged site, where the brutalities of racism, patriarchy, and post-Fordist economic restructuring are mystified and, indeed, eroticized as the reproductive pathologies of black poverty. It is precisely this displacement of a politics of real bodies for a biopolitics of patriarchal desire that renders the iconography of the welfare mother and

the inner city serviceable to a wide spectrum of cultural and political projects, ranging from the misogynist beats of gangsta rappers, to the more sober, but no less phallocentric, politics of welfare reform. What these projects share, whether as an appeal for a more "paternalistic" state authority . . . the aggressive policing of "group home turnstiles" or the selective re-tooling of black masculinity à la *Boyz 'N the Hood*, is the conviction that patriarchy is the bedrock of nation-building.[51]

Queen Latifah refuses the role given to the black woman within hip-hop nationalism—that of Isis—which merely symbolizes the imperialist glories of Egypt and the African empire. Latifah's Afrocentric expression is remarkable, not only because it is devoid of the concomitant sexism of nationalism but because it challenges the masculine logic of the idea of nation as well.[52]

Rose believes that it is hypocritical of black middle-class critics of rap lyrics not to launch the same level of moral criticism at black urban poverty as well as sexism and racism. She asserts that

the problem is: one, that technology brings these vernacular practices, the practices most vulnerable to middle-class outrage, into spaces where they might never have been heard twenty-five years ago; and two, rappers are vulnerable, highly visible cultural workers, which leaves them open to increased sanctions. But sexism, at the level of the toast and the boast, is only a subset of structurally sanctioned sexism. In that way, all manner of cultural practices and discourses that do not challenge the structures upon which these ideas are based wind up confirming them. Why, then, is the concern over rap lyrics so incredibly intense, particularly from Black middle-class guardians? Why not the same level of moral outrage over the life options that Black folks face in this country? It seems to me we need a censorship committee against poverty, sexism, and racism.[53]

Few cultural formations exist within popular culture that are stronger and more potent politically than gangsta rap. According to Kristal Brent Zook, "To say that rap is no more than a sad by-product of oppression is to take an explanatory, defensive stance when, in actuality, rap is a fundamental component of what may be the strongest political and cultural offensive gesture among African Americans today."[54] Rap is a powerful offensive medium in the way that it raises havoc with white middle-class complicity in and complacency with institutionalized racism; its dialogic pulsions disarticulate white supremacist governing narratives; it ruptures consensual images of blacks whom middle-class whites wish would "know their place." As De Genova argues,

for its white listeners, gangster rap truly reconstitutes "the tyranny of the real"—both by musically and lyrically reconfiguring the real

tyranny of the ghetto-space of death and destruction, and by recon-
firming, *through* these phantasms of the "other," the sanitized comfort
(and privilege) that comes with the tyrannical tedium of suburban,
middle-class reality. It is here that we can discern a shared "culture of
terror," a musical conjunction of the terror lived in Black ghettoes, and
the enchanting terror *dreamed* in white suburbia.[55]

Rap unmakes feelings of security and safety in middle-class homes and
neighborhoods. It indexes areas of concrete rage and generalized despair
that are normally hidden from the official view of American democracy.
De Genova powerfully captures this reality when he argues that gangster
rap evokes

a bilateral "culture of terror" in a dislocated "space of death": hegemonic (racist) fantasies about stereotypical "Blackness" and the self-
destructive ("savage") violence of the urban ghetto-space, are conjoined with the nihilistic, lawless (oppositional) terror-heroism of
proud, unapologetic self-styled "niggers"—Niggas With Attitude, Geto
Boys, Compton's Most Wanted, et al.—who fulfill the prophesy and
the promise of systemic violence and orchestrated destruction. Thus,
gangster rap serves up white America's most cherished gun-slinging
mythologies (heroic American dreams) in the form of its worst and
blackest nightmares, while it empowers Black imaginations to negate
the existential terror of ghetto life (and death) by sheer force of the
will.[56]

Following Kobena Mercer, George Lipsitz notes that rap is not a
radical form in itself but has to be understood as a function of culture.
He remarks that "culture functions as a social force to the degree that it
gets instantiated in social life and connected to the political aspirations
and activities of groups. It is here that hip hop holds its greatest significance and its greatest challenge to interpreters."[57]

Bell hooks lucidly illustrates that the context out of which rap has
emerged is intertwined with the public stories of black male lives and the
history of the pain suffered by black men in a racist society. She is worth
quoting at length:

Rap music provides a public voice for young black men who are usually silenced and overlooked. It emerged in the streets—outside the
confines of a domesticity shaped and informed by poverty, outside
enclosed spaces where . . . [black bodies] . . . had to be contained and
controlled. . . . The public story of black male lives narrated by rap
speaks directly to and against white racist domination, but only indirectly hints at the enormity of black male pain. Constructing the black
male body as site of pleasure and power, rap and the dances associated
with it suggest vibrancy, intensity, and an unsurpassed joy in living. It
may very well be that living on the edge, so close to the possibility of

being "exterminated" (which is how many young black males feel) heightens one's ability to risk and make one's pleasure more intense. It is this charge, generated by the tension between pleasure and danger, death and desire, that Foucault evokes when he speaks of that *complete total pleasure* that is related to death. Though Foucault is speaking as an individual, his words resonate in a culture affected by anhedonia—the inability to feel pleasure. In the United States, where our senses are daily assaulted and bombarded to such an extent that an emotional numbness sets in, it may take being "on the edge" for individuals to feel intensely. Hence the overall tendency in the culture is to see young black men as both dangerous and desirable.[58]

The most politically astute rappers take the racist and sexist stereotypes of black males and recontextualize them so that within popular culture, criminalized and hypersexualized black youths now become fearless rebels "standing up" heroically to the white man's exploitation. This fusion of heroism and criminality, of pleasure and pain, occurs without denying the endemic effects of institutionalized racism, patriarchal structures, heterosexist relations, and class exploitation. De Genova captures this point when he notes that "gangster rap exposes the multivalence and equivocation of racial essentialism: it evokes all of the conflicted meanings and opposed values which congeal simultaneously around a shared set of socially charged signifiers that comprise a single racial nomenclature."[59] Matthew Grant argues that gangsta rap results from the relationship between the criminalized underclass and the overclass reaching a point "where they can mutually benefit from the destabilization of the middle-class majority."[60] According to Grant, what makes gangsta rap so attractive to the middle-class white consumer is not its attempt to develop a revolutionary consciousness among its listeners, but rather the actively transgressive character of its assaults on middle-class taboos against violence. Gangsta rap provides white consumers who yearn to be part of the hip-hop nation with shocking images in which "the norms of bourgeois liberality are violated in an orgy of paradoxically subaltern elitism."[61] Through the politics of voyeurism, white youth can become the menacing urban *baaadman*.

Far from being a dispiriting successor to rhythm and blues, gangsta rap occupies a formidable yet not unproblematic space of resistance to racial oppression. A more productive account of gangsta rap, Grant argues, would examine its "celebration of insanity based as a singularly gendered obsession"—what he calls "the insane investment of the real."[62] Grant writes that

> the fantasy of losing it, of stepping over the limit of reason and civility, of surrendering oneself to the intoxication and ecstasy of violence uninhibited by the strictures of reason, is an important component of

male subjectivity (which herein seems to cross boundaries established by class or skin color). Madness, among men, is something that must be endured or overcome (unless one is completely overwhelmed and obliterated by it). The flip side of this adventurist relation to the insane is the wholesale projection of insanity onto women as one legitimation of their exclusion from certain segments of the social order.[63]

Maintaining that the criticism leveled at rappers—that they wildly sensationalize urban life—is wrongly dependent upon holding rappers to the same ineluctable standards that inform the genre of social realism. Grant offers a spirited defense of gangsta rap, noting that the

> insanity that speaks through the voice of rap music is not simply a brand of psychic exoticism: it is the mental state produced by the process of racist oppression to which these bodies are subjected. The radical decentering of the subject, either through the use of drugs or through the use of semiautomatic weapons (and what could be more decentering than "a hole in your fuckin' head"?), which finds its expression in rap, a decentering celebrated by poststructuralists and postmodernists everywhere, results from an intensely decentering material configuration of the real. The insane distortions of gangsta rap actually make their representations realistic. It's just a psychorealism thing.[64]

Representation, as Grant points out, is not just about adducing an accurate or realistic depiction of an event from many possible interpretations. It also speaks to forms of political advocacy that, in the case of gangsta rap, deal primarily with the Kafkaesque and carceral universe of the black urban male. (There are also "hard-core" female rappers such as Manhole, a Latina from LA, and Boss, a classically trained African American musician who did not grow up in the hood but raps about it as if she did.)

Echoing the music of Dr. Dre and Snoop Doggy Dogg, Grant remarks that prison has become the educational alternative for black men: "the generalized form of social space for the underclass." Moreover, he argues that "hard-core" gangsta rap constitutes a political program that he describes as an urban guerrilla movement. As a social force, however, gangsta rap overwhelmingly fails in its attempt to organize effectively, since, according to Grant, it has at its disposal only an "anarchofascist politics of drug dealership and gang-bangerism."[65] After all, NWA's drug dealing was decidedly "precapitalist" and, Grant maintains, no match for "the internationally organized capitalist bloc with its huge armies, advanced armaments, and high-tech domestic security systems."[66] Despite its failure to bring forth the hegemonic articulations that would make Gramsci proud, gangsta rap does present what I would call a contingent or provisional utopian longing—a trace, within a tapestry of violent imagery, of what is needed to bring about social justice. Grant puts it this way: "Gangsta rap, in spite of its contradictions, in spite of what is retrograde in it (like its often vicious sexism and homophobia), at least contains elements that give us a glimpse of what a radically oppositional culture could look like."[67] De Genova echoes a similar sentiment when he remarks that "rap music flourishes in the contradictory interstices of hegemonic appropriation and a fairly self-conscious and articulate politics of oppositional maneuvering."[68]

I locate gangsta rap as an "oppositional practice" in the sense that Michel de Certeau uses the term. While de Certeau is referring to the actions of the Amerindians, I believe his ideas are applicable to many contemporary groups—for example, African Americans—who find themselves exploited and oppressed. According to de Certeau,

> even when they were subjected, indeed even when they accepted, their subjection . . . often used the laws, practices, and representations that were imposed on them by force or by fascination to ends other than those of their conquerors; they made something else out of them; they subverted them from within—not by rejecting them or by transforming them (though that occurred as well), but by many different ways of using them in the service of rules, customs, or convictions foreign to the colonization which they could not escape. They metaphorized the dominant order; they made it function in another register.[69]

For instance, Shocked and Bull's criticism of rap overlooks rap's oppositional possibilities. It overlooks the fact that, among other things, gangsta rap has conflated the image of the "real nigga" and the "bad nigger" of black urban folklore. However, this distinction is admittedly unclear at times and, as Tommy Lott himself notes, the mass media's politicizing of the "bad nigger" idiom has led to a "troublesome conflation" of the "heroic badman" of folklore and the "bad nigga" of rap.[70]

The politics of resistance in gangsta rap needs to be located within the globalization of capital, the international circuit of debt and consumption, the deindustrialization, deskilling, and de-unionization of work in the expanding service sector. For instance, while it points to the structural instability of capitalist America and the production of urban rage, and while it wages political war against the white sentinels of the status quo, it remains ideologically aligned with capitalist interests, glorifying crass materialism and celebrating conspicuous consumption. As such, rap as a form of resistance can be conflictually located along a series of semantic axes; it varies, in other words, from song to song, from artist to artist, and from listener to listener, depending upon the performative moments that are meant to be signified. In other words, gangsta rap does not constitute a master trope of urban criticism, an urtext of cultural resistance but is read differently by different groups. Oppressed minorities are more likely to resonate with rap for its political critique, while middle-class white groups are more likely to be drawn to rap for its aestheticization of transgression. De Genova makes an important point when he claims that "what emerges in gangster rap, like the figure of Bigger Thomas, is 'a snarl of many realities.' Gangster rap would seem to provide a very different kind of 'therapy' for those who live its nihilism, than the shock treatment it provides for those who live in mortal terror of it."[71] Tommy Lott notes, for instance, that "with the commercializing of gangsta rap we can no longer speak in a totalizing manner of rap music. Instead, this designation must be reserved for specific rap tunes."[72]

I believe that it is instructive to locate rap as a challenge to the bourgeois political and racialized structures that discursively articulate what counts as the quintessential American experience. Elsewhere I have argued that the cultural logic of late capitalism has reinscribed the moral order within the United States around the practice of consumption and the secular redemption of acquiring wealth.[73] The structural unconscious of American popular culture (the term *structural* is meant to draw attention to the fact that the social structure is folded into individual and collective forms of subjectivity that operate through the language of myth) has been occupied by the figure of the serial killer as the last frontiersperson, the last autonomous subject, the last "true" American who can act.

America—Europe's other—has often been considered the promised land.[74] But when all the old myths based on America as the promised land are demythologized, when the Protestant millenarianist project to recreate Zion in the streets of Los Angeles end in the Intifada of 1992, then the quintessential apocalyptic moment becomes the act of random murder. America is exporting this myth through film *(Love and a .45, Natural Born Killers, Pulp Fiction),* music, and other cultural formations.

The gangsta rapper serves in this context to remind white audiences that utopia is lost, that the end of history has arrived (but not in the way Francis Fukuyama predicted), that the logic of white utopia is premised upon white supremacy and exploitative social relations, and that whites have mistakenly pledged their loyalty to the Beast. Gangsta rap reveals the white millenarianist project of democracy to be grounded upon a will to sameness, a desire to drive out people of color from the mythic frontier of the promised land. In this sense, gangsta rap transforms the "brothas" into avenging angels who call upon whites to redeem themselves or face the wrath of God—a God who will send forth not locusts or floods but angry black urban dwellers taking to the streets.

Just as the black subject has always operated as a metaphor for chaos and instability, the Los Angeles uprising of 1992 literalized this metaphor as one of physical terror. In a world where history has already been purchased by the wealthy, the losers have no choice but to steal some of history back again. The agents of leadership will not be the good Rodney Kings on television but the "bad niggaz" in the streets.

Before we can answer the question of whether hip-hop culture itself is preventing gangsta rap from evolving into a social movement, we need to gain a deeper understanding of the semantic orbit surrounding the politics of difference in gangsta rap. Do we accept, for instance, the resistive elements of gangsta rap only in the context of the production of aesthetic pleasure, rather than the promotion of a political agenda only because acts of resistance can be defused as well as diffused into a politics of the sublime? Has the commercialization of gangsta rap imploded into the political such that these two characteristics are indistinguishable? Does the conflation of gangsta rap's commodification and political project effectively cancel both rather than dialectically reinitiate a productive political tension around a project of social justice and a praxis of liberation? Does rap's repackaging of oppositional codes along aesthetic lines merely reduce gangsta rap to a more marketable form of cultural capital that can be traded within existing capitalist frameworks of power and privilege? Can the same questions be raised about hip-hop movies such as *Krush Groove, A Thin Line between Love and Hate, Set It Off,* and *Booty Call?*

De Genova argues that gangsta rap does escape the nihilistic aestheticism of which it has been accused by linking such aestheticism with the politics of the street:

> Gangster rap, even more than other types of hip hop, raises the free-for-all aesthetic far above and beyond the music's formal level: gangster rap celebrates a free-for-all in the streets. Here it becomes possible to imagine the transcendence of a merely aesthetic nihilism which can be contained by commodification to imagine an articulation of this highly public nihilist aesthetic with the street, the place where the sideshow can become the main event.[75]

The street or neighborhood, it should be pointed out, becomes a liminal site: "The symbol of 'the ghetto' in gangster rap becomes its fire-brand of 'authenticity.' The ghetto comes to be valorized not only as a 'space of death' (and destruction) but also as a space of survival and transcendence; not merely a 'heart of darkness,' it is also the heart of 'Blackness.'"[76]

Gangsta rap is concerned with the articulation of experiences of oppression that find their essential character among disenfranchised urban black and Latino populations. Rap helps to communicate symbols and meanings and articulates intersubjectively the lived experience of social actors. The ontological status of the gangsta rapper resides in the function of the commodity of blackness, but a certain quality of blackness that is identified through the expressive codes of the rapper is the "inner turmoil" of the oppressed black subject of history. Here, blackness (or Latino-ness) marks out a heritage of pain and suffering and points to the willingness and ability of oppressed groups to fight against injustice "by any means necessary." Gangsta rap songs are able to demonstrate how popular white constructions of black men and women ultimately seek to instantiate control over people of color in order to contain them culturally as well as physically. Rap exposes the hidden and hardened fissures and faultlines of democratic social life, revealing the underpinnings of social justice to be little more than a convenient cultural fiction.

Much of the hard-core political gangsta rap provides a type of hallucinatory snapshot of everyday life on America's mean streets—a video canvas of Fortress USA—that evinces fearful images of black rage and destruction, images that typically endure in gangsta rap videos but unfortunately do little to transform the social and material relations that produce them. Violence in gangsta rap has become an Adamic ritual that creates a world of order through disorder that performatively constitutes both the gangsta himself or herself and the object of their violence. In other words, the founding language of the gangsta is violence. It is within this rationality that the image of the gangsta circulates like a political sign within an imagined community of oppressed and resisting subjects. Invading the space of other gang bangers or that of dominant groups in binary-coded struggles (black vs. white, male vs. female, cops vs. black community) helps to stabilize the subjectivity of the gangsta rapper and to contingently anchor identity through a negative interjection of the Other, a negation of whatever threatens it: bitches, rival gangs, the police, and so on. The paramount hegemonic voice that gangsta rappers struggle against—and this is true for its eastern Caribbean and East London counterparts—is law and order. Gangsta rappers challenge the hegemonic modes of thought that are embedded in formal conventions—educational, legal, sexual, and others.

It is important to understand that while gangsta rap suffers from problems of misogyny and nihilism and while the capitalist culture industry amplifies the aesthetic dimension of rap at the expense of its political pronouncements, rap also produces important forms of nationalistic thought that work to nurture forms of coalition building and community. For instance, Zook notes that both the form and content of rap express black autonomy, self-determination, and cultural pride. But what is perhaps most fascinating is not only the way that rap confirms a sense of imagined, metaphorical community, but rather, the fact that this fantasy of "home" is simultaneously constructed materially through the very modes of production, marketing, and the critical discourses which surround it. In other words, just as [Benedict] Anderson argues that literary forms such as the newspaper and the novel made European nationalisms possible, I would say that the forms of television, music videos, film, literary works, and the networks involved in producing these forms are also nurturing a heightened sense of racial collectivity, group solidarity, and even political responsibility—all of which are important elements of nationalist thought.[77]

Gangsta rappers assume a contradictory attitude to black nationalism. On the one hand, they identify with the liberation struggles in Africa, yet on the other hand, they are wary of focusing too much attention on Africa and Afrocentrism for fear of deflecting concern from the serious problems in America's inner cities. According to Robin D. G. Kelley, rappers "contend that the nationalists' focus on Africa—both past and present—obscures the daily battles poor Black folk have to wage in contemporary America."[78]

While it does little to offer a project of transformation, gangsta rap manages, by bursting through the representational space of whiteness and by advancing political solidarity in the form of an imagined community of struggle, to depict what Grant describes as the "proprietary position that whites occupied during the days of slavery (and *mutatis mutandis* still enjoy today)."[79] Whites who are most threatened by gangsta rap's aggressive and adversarial masculinity attempt to consolidate their opposition in a white woman/black beast symbolic order mythologized in white supremacist discourses that have lately been discursively reinforced by prominent politicians such as Newt Gingrich, Jesse Helms, Pat Buchanan, and Pete Wilson. It is possible, too, that white consumers of gangsta rap are drawn to a self-consciously exaggerated display of sexuality, much the same way that rhythm and blues artists captured white audiences in the fifties. As Medovoi notes,

> Of course, sexuality had long been a principal theme of rhythm and blues, but the youthful white audience now took an interest in exaggerating and redirecting its sexual themes symbolically across the race line. Chapple and Garofalo quote R&B artist John Otis recalling: "We found that we moved the white audiences more by caricaturing the music, you know, overdoing the shit—falling on your back with the saxophone, kicking your legs up. And if we did too much of that for a black audience they'd tell us—'Enough of that shit—play some music!'"[80]

While hard-core rap artists such as Snoop Doggy Dogg, Da Lench Mob, Ice Cube, Eazy-E, Niggas with Attitude, and Naughty by Nature unquestionably create politically motivated music, the politics can often be traced to a black nationalist focus. A key issue emerges here. It has to do with the fact that the aesthetic power of the music creates a pleasure among listeners that may even be against the values of the progressive listeners. Tommy Lott reports on a similar issue when he notes that the rap group Public Enemy (which often expresses black nationalist imperatives) is the favorite rap group in some racist white communities such as South Boston.

The controversial rap single "Fuck Rodney King" by former Geto Boy Willie D., makes the powerful claim that during the LA uprising of 1992, "Rodney King so willingly took the moral low ground and turned himself into an establishment ad for social harmony" through his plaintive plea, "Can we all get along?"[81]

> Fuck Rodney King, and his ass.
> When I see the motherfucker I'm a blast
> Boom in his head, boom boom in his back
> Just like that
> Cause I'm tired of the [ ] niggers
> Sayin' increase the peace
> And let the violence cease
> When the Black man built this country
> But can't get his for the prejudiced honkey . . .
> But when it's time for the revolution
> I'm a click click click, fuck this rap shit
> Cause money ain't shit but grief
> If ya ain't got no peace
> Gotta come on with it
> Get down for my little Willies
> So they can come up strong and live long
> And not be scared to get it on![82]

Rather than identifying the song as an example of black nihilism—the image typically conjured by the lyrics—Lott suggests that it constitutes an incisive political critique. In Lott's view, Willie D.'s song "demands the autonomy and agency wards of the state lack."[83] Willie D.'s rap demands the type of political change that would make the violence he calls for unnecessary.

Tommy Lott's analysis of the term *nigga* is instructive. He claims, rightly in my view, that gangsta rap has creatively reworked and recoded in a socially transgressive and politically retaliatory manner the social meaning of the term in ways that distinguish it from the taboo term used by white racists and from the often self-hating inflections of the term expressed by black professionals.[84] Not only is the racist meaning of the term *nigga* recoded by the gangsta rappers but its ambiguity now shifts, depending on the contexts of its enunciation and reception. When gangsta rappers revise the spelling of the racist version of the word *nigger* to the vernacular *nigga* they are using it as a defiant idiom of a resistive mode of African American cultural expression which distinguishes it from the way that, for instance, white racists in Alabama might employ the term. Further, Lott notes that the vernacular *nigga* permits a form of class consciousness among the black urban "underclass" or lumpen proletariat in the sense that it distinguishes black urban working-class youth from those middle-class black professionals who feel denigrated whenever the term is used. According to Robin D.G. Kelley,

> Nigga speaks to a collective identity shaped by class consciousness, the character of inner-city space, police repression, poverty, and the constant threat of intraracial violence. . . . In other words, Nigga is not merely *another* word for black. Products of the postindustrial ghetto, the characters in gangsta rap constantly remind listeners that they are still second-class citizens—"Niggaz"—whose collective experiences suggest that nothing has changed *for them* as opposed to the black middle class. In fact, Nigga is frequently employed to distinguish urban black working class males from the black bourgeoisie and African Americans in positions of institutional authority. Their point is simple: the experiences of young black men in the inner city are not universal to all black people, and, in fact, they recognize that some African Americans play a role in perpetuating their oppression. To be a "real nigga" is to be a product of the ghetto. By linking identity to the "hood" instead of simply skin color, gangsta rappers implicitly acknowledge the limitations of racial politics, including black middle-class reformism as well as black nationalism.[85]

Within the sociohistorical conjuncture of current U.S. urban centers, the gangsta has become a sign of immanence, an alteration of signification between *nigger* and *nigga* relayed to infinity. Through its cultural fusions, intercultural encounters, and expressive articulations, we are invited by gangsta rap to visit spaces we have never lived physically, nor would ever wish to—spaces that function significantly in the manufacturing of identity. George Lipsitz remarks that "music not only shapes and reflects dominant and subordinate social and cultural relations, but . . . music making and other forms of popular culture serve as a specific site for the creation of collective identity."[86] Rap artists continue to move within Henri Lefevbre's "theatrical or dramatized space" by creating a new legacy of insurgency and struggle, one that menaces the prestige hierarchies of white supremacy, that constructs critical aperçus about human dignity and suffering, and that sets itself in opposition to melioristic reform and on the side of revolutionary transformation. As such, it serves as a "social force."[87] Yet I wish to underscore that it cannot be celebrated as a form of oppositional consciousness by uncritically attributing political consciousness to rap artists merely because of their social location as urban "underdog" musicians. Nor can we, as Lipsitz maintains, after Kobena Mercer, argue that music is in itself politically transgressive. Rather, music becomes a "social force" only "to the degree that it gets instantiated in social life and activities of groups."[88] The political inflections of music need to be understood in terms of their cultural, historical, and geopolitical specificity. Lipsitz further argues that the expansion of transnational capital does not, prima facie, sound the death knell of political resistance but rather that "the reach and scope of transnational capital" can make indigenous musical forms more powerful as forms of resistance.

Gangsta rap is essentially a diasporic cultural politics and positions itself as such against cultural displacement and capitalist exploitation. For this reason we can't unproblematically articulate white rappers ("wiggers" or "white niggers") into the rap resistance movement. Cultural borrowings by white rappers are not necessarily problematic but can be seen as troublesome when consideration is given to the way gangsta rap is cognitively mapped by white rappers: the cultural circuits along which such borrowings travel and how these borrowings become fused to dominant Euro-American "universal" meanings, knowledge claims, and social conventions addressed to "the other." Imitation *of* the other doesn't necessarily mean identification *with* the other, yet at the same time it doesn't necessarily exclude such an identification. The Beastie Boys and House of Pain are examples of white rappers with some crossover appeal to black audiences. However, Lipsitz warns that "powerful institutions attach prestige hierarchies to artistic expressions in such a way as to funnel reward and critical attention to Euro-American appropriators, and because ethnocentric presumptions about the universality of Western notions of art obscure the cultural and political contexts that give meaning to many artifacts from traditional cultures that are celebrated as pure form in the West."[89] While there is, to be sure, a depoliticizing aspect to commodification, this contradiction is also a primary condition of gangsta rap's political enablement. Following bell hooks, Grant underscores the fact that because consumers could ignore the political message or information disseminated throughout the music that it also implies the contrary: consumers could pay attention to precisely that element.[90] Gangsta rap creatively exploits the contradictions brought on by commodification to construct a guerrilla warfare of the airwaves—a war waged through what I have called elsewhere the media's "perpetual pedagogy."[91] Grant speaks to this issue when he writes that

> we could thus conceive of a diffuse war of resistance and liberation being waged against the forces of white supremacy with rap music serving as its communication system. . . . Rap music, as the objectified representative of the gangsta, invades the white world and steals white kids. . . . Ice-T also understands his intervention, his invasion, pedagogically. He teaches white kids about racism and power. In addition, he maintains that this music supplies the white youth with an alternative vocabulary in which to articulate their rebellion against the parental authority structure.[92]

At its best, gangsta rap urges the creation of cooperatives of resistance, zones of freedom, where strategies and tactics of liberation can emerge, where the opposite of local struggles does not collapse into some abstract universalized call for emancipation in the form of a master narrative that brings premature closure to the meaning of freedom, where the opposite of local struggles brings to mind not the master trope of the universal but rather the concept of reciprocal relations at the level of the social. This alternative points to the idea of peoples' collective struggle to advance a project of hope lived in the subjunctive mode of "as if" yet grounded in the concreteness of everyday life. It is within the dialectical relationship between local and more broad, collective struggles that gangsta rap accelerates the anger and rage that is the very condition of its existence. Unlike more mainstream musical forms such as heavy metal or rock, which tend to displace issues dealing with relations of power between black and white populations onto quarantined spaces, and which often elide conflicting and contradictory relations premised upon racialized and differential relations of power and privilege, gangsta rap troubles the certainty and unsettles the complacency of existing power arrangements between blacks and whites. I would argue that the multicultural nihilistic hedonism that Newt Gingrich's authoritarian populist millenarianism hates with such a frenzied passion is really one of the few sources of oppositional popular discourses remaining in a nation morally flattened by the weight of the New Right's rhetorical cant that demonizes, hellifies, and zombifies African Americans, Latinos, the poor, and the disenfranchised.

Yet in saying this there is evidence that gangsta rap is running its course within the circuits of capitalist commodification. In a recent issue of *The Los Angeles Reader,* Steve Appleford[93] writes that "another album cover with a gun thrust in your face is as shocking and dangerous now as Madonna without clothes."[94] He cites M. C. Ren as saying that "we wanted to put Compton on the map, so we rapped about what went on in Compton. . . . But now it's like everybody's talking the same shit, people talking about shit we did years ago, you understand? You've got to advance, man. . . . Everybody right now is just stuck."[95] Ren remarks that "you got all these fools coming out now, they think all you got to do is just cuss, talk about weed, low ridin', shit like that, and you can get a record deal, you know what I'm saying? Rap is fucked up, man. It started a few years ago when somebody realized this shit is making money."[96]

According to Appleford, Ice-T now rejects the gangsta label, preferring to describe his music as "reality rap." When gangsta rap restricts itself to the politics of the ghetto, white viewers see it as a threat that is constrained to certain areas of life that they can avoid at the everyday level. When you have easy access to the "black threat" for entertainment purposes, it becomes more familiar and therefore less intimidating. On the other hand, ghettocentricity is a constant reminder to white viewers that they themselves are white. Whiteness—that absent presence that outlines the cultural capital required for favored citizenship status—becomes, in this instance, less invisible to whites themselves. The less invisible that whiteness becomes, the less it serves as a tacit marker against which otherness is defined.

There have been some recent alternative movements within rap, such as G-funk and rap/be-bop fusion. For instance, R&B artists such as Me'Shell Ndegéocello are experimenting with aspects of hip-hop and soul. Recently in the *LA Weekly,* Donnell Alexander[97] surveyed some alternative rap, arguing that while hard-core gangsta rap (Big Mike, M. C. Eiht, Jeru, Treach) is now mainstream, alternative rap groups such as Digable Planets, Spearhead, Justin Warfield, the Broun Fellinis, and Michael "Basehead" Ivey haven't been able to develop much of a following outside of white college students. And there is the question of the powerful forces of commodification from the marketplace. Is rap's restricted code of black solidarity against oppression being elaborated for financial gain by the white-dominated culture industry? Is it being diffused into an aesthetic style that can be danced to or played because of its growing availability as a cultural code?[98] Is it being depotentiated because it is being wrenched away from the cultural contexts that made it meaningful?

The politics of commodification and appropriation that have been confronting gangsta rap artists in the face of the hypermobility of capital is reminiscent of the phenomena occurring with salsa and *rockero* in the context of Puerto Rico. For instance, Javier Santiago-Lucerna[99] discusses how artists like Ruben Blades and Willie Colon, whose earlier musical productions resonated with a progressive politics, have been absorbed into the politics of the marketplace. According to Santiago-Lucerna, salsa music and the cultural *comarrona* have been transformed into spaces constituted with the cynical sign of consumer culture. In fact, the music being produced in the local rock scene and among local punk bands is currently far more hard-edged politically than salsa, *nueva trova,* and *musica campesina,* as the bands Whisker Biscuit, Kampo Viej, Descojon Urbano, La Experiencia de Tonito Cabanillas, and Sin Remedio can attest. For instance, in "Urban Fuckup," Descojon-Urbano sings:

> Oye es que me da gusto
> Cada vez que cogen a un politico corrupto
> Que cabroneria, que barbaridad
> el pobre se jode y el rico tiene mas
>
> [It gives me so much pleasure
> every time they catch a corrupted politician
> What shit, what an atrocity
> the poor are fucked, while the rich have more][100]

The issue of political domestication and product commodification is on the surface somewhat different in the case of gangsta rap because oppositional political rap is now mainstream. Therefore, it is hard to see what other kinds of music might soon replace rap's hard-edge political critique. Perhaps forms of rap will develop that are not coded in the image of the hypersexualized gangbanger and that begin to address issues of economic exploitation, misogyny, and homophobia.

Critics of gangsta rap need to take seriously Rosemary Hennessy's[101] suggestion that "in postmodern consumer culture the commodity is a central means by which desire is organized."[102] In other words, listeners of gangsta rap affectively invest in the music and video productions. The music produces certain structures of feeling, particular economies of affectivity. But the logic of the commodity conceals certain invisible social relations that need to be considered. The commodity, argues Hennessy, after Marx, is not material in the physical sense alone but rather in the sense that "it is socially produced through human labor and the extraction of surplus value in exchange."[103] Commodity fetishism refers to the "illusion that value resides in objects rather than in the social relations between individuals and objects."[104] In other words, commodity fetishism "entails the misrecognition of a structural effect as an immediate property of one of its elements, as if this property belonged to it outside of its relation to other elements."[105]

Gangsta rap as a commercial product needs to be understood not simply in terms of the way it transgressively signifies social life but in terms of the exploitation of human labor and the way in which the social relations of production and consumption organize everyday human life: in short, in terms of its commodity fetishism. De Genova notes that

> commodified rap music was able to proliferate through the virtual pillage of an ever-expanding universe of already-existing commodified music—instantiating the semblance of something like a parodic auto-cannibalization of the commodity form. The very essence of hip-hop music, as a musical genre which begins with the unabashed appropriation of pre-recorded, mass-produced, commodified music, demonstrates that "public culture" is inevitably and unassailably "public-access culture"—a free-for-all.[106]

Gangsta rap's relation to the corporate marketplace, its potential for expropriation, and its reproduction of ideologies historically necessary to commodity exchange—such as patriarchal ones—is an important issue that needs to be addressed. In other words, gangsta rap needs to be viewed not merely as an ideological formation, cultural signifier, or performative spectacle, but also as the product of historical and social relations. Gangsta rap needs to be seen not only in discursive terms but rather in terms of the materiality of discourse. By materiality of discourse I refer to "the ways culture constructs subjectivities, reproduces power relations, and foments resistance" insofar as these relations and practices are "shaped by social totalities like capitalism, patriarchy, and imperialism as they manifest differently across social formations and within specific historical conjunctures."[107] This is not to say, however, that gangsta rap at the level of the oppositional spectacle is not an important popular counterdiscourse.

Thomas Cushman's important work on understanding the diffusion of revolutionary musical codes raises some important questions about rap (which, unfortunately, exceed the scope of this essay). These questions demand an analysis of the social evolution of gangsta rap as a musical style as it is situated within the world capitalist system. This suggests examining gangsta rap as a restricted code (condensed, context-specific cluster of symbols and meanings) that articulates the existential experience of subordinate groups of African Americans and Puerto Ricans and their everyday dissent. It also means tracing rap's diffusion into an elaborated code (context-free, universal) across time and space into new social contexts and analyzing how its original, organic, revolutionary expression as a means of addressing race and class exploitation has been diffused.[108] For instance, what is to prevent gangsta rap from becoming, in Cushman's terms, a casualty of "a highly developed, world-wide culture industry that operates precisely by scanning the world environment for disturbances, selectively amplifying and altering certain aspects of those disturbances and re-presenting them to large audiences who receive them as entertainment commodities"?[109]

Gangsta rap creates identity through a racial system of intelligibility that produces binary distinctions between blacks and whites, an us-against-them discursive matrix. As a performative signification anchored in the context of the urban ghetto, it constitutes part of the regulatory practices of the dominant culture while at the same time resisting and critiquing this culture.

Diane Fuss, following Frantz Fanon, argues that under conditions of colonialism, blacks are "forced to occupy, in a white racial phantasm, the static ontological space of the timeless 'primitive.'"[110] In this "imaginary relation of fractured specularity," blacks are denied by the white Imperial Subject, the alterity or otherness necessary to achieve subjectivity. Interpellated and fixed into a static objecthood, blacks become neither an "I" nor a "not-I," becoming instead a degraded and devalorized signifier, a fragmented object, a form of pure exteriority.

The transcendental signifier "white," according to Fuss, is never a "not-black," but rather operates from its own self-proclaimed transparency, as a marker that floats imperially over the category of race, operating "as its own Other" and independent from the sign "black" for its symbolic constitution. In terms of the colonial-imperial register of self-other relations, which, as Fuss notes, operates in psychoanalysis and existentialism on the Hegelian principle of negation and incorporation in which the other is assimilated into the self—the white subject can be white without any relation to the black subject because the sign "white" exempts itself from a dialogical logic of negativity. But the black subject must be black in relation to the white subject.

For instance, whereas white rap singer Vanilla Ice was once referred to as "the Elvis of rap," the black singer Al B. Sure was referred to as "the Black Elvis." Lionett cites remarks made by Patricia Williams, who points out the parodic nature of these labels: "Elvis, the white black man of a generation ago, reborn in a black man imitating Elvis." Lionett adds that Elvis is "reborn in Vanilla Ice, a white man imitating the black rapper imitating Elvis: a dizzying thought." The point here is that in the depiction of each rap artist, the major point of reference is white culture.[111]

Imperialist acts of assimilation and incorporation are located at the level of the unconscious. The gangsta is simultaneously a mimicry of subversion and subjugation. Drawing on Homi Bhabha's notion that colonial mimicry possesses the possibility of resisting and subverting dominant systems of representation (through the possibility of mimicry slipping into mockery) as well as subtending them, I want to argue that when it ironizes the role of the incorporated black subject, gangsta rap (at least in its video incarnations) undermines the image of the impotent black subject, de-transcendentalizing it and rendering it unstable.[112] However, when the gangsta rapper undertakes a "parodic hyperbolization" (to borrow Fuss's term) of the subjugated black man—in the figure of the gangsta with a gun—but does not connect it to a larger political project of liberation, this may rupture the image of the subjugated black subject but fail to unsettle the exploitative relations connected to white supremacist patriarchal capitalism. By not connecting its subversion to a larger politics of possibility, gangsta rap runs the risk of ironizing its own act of subversion and parodying its own performance of dissent in such an I-don't-give-a-fuck fashion that, rather than erode dominant social relations of exploitation and subjugation, it may actually reinforce them.

The social realism that accompanies much of the gangsta rap of Ice Cube, Ice-T, and others is situated within a larger political agenda and sets the context for portraying the role of the rapper (qua oppositional cultural forms) as a "truth sayer" and noble revolutionary subject fighting the injustices of the white-controlled megastate. It also builds the ground for a more sustained critique of racist and capitalist social relations.

But in some of the rap videos of, say, Sir Mix-A-Lot or 2 Live Crew, unrealistic portrayals occur of the dissenting black male subject, depicting him as living in ostentatious luxury, surrounded by black and white women massaging their breasts on his car window ("put 'em on the glass") or swaying their G-stringed buttocks in his welcoming face. In this instance, there is a tendency to recuperate a reversionary politics, because the lifestyle of the black hepcat dissenter appears to be exaggerated to the point of parody. Such a parodic representation of the successful black consumer (where women are presented as thong-clad commodities to be plucked from swimming pools) tends to defray and to occlude a larger politics of liberation outside of commodity culture. In this case, the landscape of rap is defoliated in terms of race, class, and gender issues, while dissent is defused into issues of who has the most "babes who got back." In another sense, however, it's also possible to look at 2 Live Crew's videos in a different light. It's possible to overlook the sexism and the hyperbolizing of the black male-as-womanizer by focusing on the consumer trappings of the black rapper—swimming pools, fancy cars, beautiful houses, and available sex. Acquiring these "trappings" becomes a form of resistance because they are not available to the average white or black subject. The problem here is rap's apparent legitimation of capitalist social relations of consumption. Do rappers—including gangsta rappers—just want to make the pleasures of patriarchal capitalism available to all black males?

Can gangsta rap move beyond Benjamin's shock effects, its decontextualization as an effect of its mechanical reproducibility, beyond the space of its own commercial structures, beyond its ideological prohibitions, its structures of expectation, its demarcations of despair—all of which create a locus of signifying phantasms and perverse forms of the "other," which, in turn, collaborate with neoliberal approaches to politics that ultimately wrest away rap's oppositional potency? To create a praxis of both opposition and possibility, gangsta rap needs to undertake the construction of new identities that are refractory to commodification. It must continue to perturb society, to shape culture on a deeper level. Hip-hop culture must provide spaces of resistance and transgression, without succumbing to political incoherence. Only in this way will it be able to prevent its revolutionary potential from being articulated to the terms of the official culture of consumption that defuses adversarial codes into the cultural logic of the aesthetic.

Despite the always-present threat of commodification, gangsta rap still poses a serious challenge to the formation of new identities of resistance and social transformation. The new identities surrounding various articulations of gangsta rap hold both unforeseen promises and potential dangers. As Lipsitz remarks, "to think of identities as interchangeable or infinitely open does violence to the historical and social constraints imposed on us by structures of exploitation and privilege. But to posit innate and immobile identities for ourselves and others confuses history with nature, and denies the possibility of change."[113]

The challenge that confronts gangsta rap in particular and hip-hop culture in general is the extent to which it contributes to the defamiliarization of the Western sovereign subject, the Euro-American imperial subject, and the extent to which it can become self-conscious of the relations of power and privilege that create the context for and overdetermine its cultural exchanges. This means, as I have argued above, linking a politics of semiotic subversion to a critique of the material social relations of exploitation that have been largely responsible for the problems faced by people of color in the United States.

Manning Marable speaks to a new articulation of the concept of blackness that is defined not in racial or ethnic/cultural terms but as a political category that speaks to new forms of political mobilization:

> We must find new room in our identity as people of color to include all other oppressed national minorities—Chicanos, Peurto Ricans, Asian/Pacific Americans, and other people of African descent. We must find the common ground we share with oppressed people who are not national minorities—working-class people, the physically challenged, the homeless, the unemployed, and those Americans who suffer discrimination because they are lesbian or gay. I believe that a new mul-

ticultural America is possible, that a renaissance of Black militancy will occur in concert with new levels of activism from the constituencies mentioned above. But it is possible only if we have the courage to challenge and to overturn our own historical assumptions about race, power, and ourselves. Only then will we find the new directions necessary to challenge the system, to "fight the power," with an approach toward political culture that can truly liberate all of us.[114]

In its most politically enabling formations, gangsta rap is able to create a space of resistance in which black identity is not dependent upon whiteness to complete it. It escapes colonial mimesis through a series of cultural relays that keeps identity fluid and shifting. The particular liberatory values that are affirmed in gangsta rap need, however, to co-reside with other resonant values rooted in the contingency and radical historicity of oppressed groups throughout the globe. For white folks this means not simply a *tolerance of* difference but rather a critical *engagement with* difference on a global scale.

The recent death of Tupac Shakur provides a bitter lesson about the best and worst of gangsta rap. Tupac's reputation as one of the most hard-core of the gangsta rappers and his obsession with living the "authenticity" of the streets as a "real nigga" eventually rebounded against him as he brought together his own brand of what Mike Dyson calls "thuggery and thanatopsis."[115] Dyson remarks that "the Real Niggas are trapped by their own contradictory couplings of authenticity and violence. Tupac's death is the most recent, and perhaps most painful, evidence of that truth."[116] Dyson further notes that Tupac's own project constituted "a sad retreat from a much more complex, compelling vision of black life that gangsta rap and hard-core hip-hop, at its best, helped outline."[117] In his art of "celeterrogation" (what Dyson calls "the deft combination of celebration and interrogation") Tupac embodied the best and the worst of gangsta rap. Dyson eloquently comments:

> by joining verbal vigor to rage—about material misery and racial hostility, about the avalanche of unheard suffering that suffocates black lives before they wake, walk or will their own survival—hard-core rappers proved that theirs was a redemptive vulgarity. At their best, they showed that the real vulgarity was the absurd way too many black folk perish on the vine of fruitless promises of neighborhood restoration, of racial rehabilitation. The hard-core hip-hopper proved that the real vulgarity was the vicious anonymity and punishing silence of poor black life, with which they broke faith every time they seized a mike to bring poetry to pain. . . . But, in the end, despite all his considerable gifts, Tupac helped pioneer a more dangerous, even more destructive, trend in hard-core hip-hop that, ironically, draws from the oral energy of the orthodox black culture from which he sought thuggish refuge.

Tupac yearned to live the life he rapped about in his songs. That golden ideal was the motive behind gospel passions in black culture to close the gap between preaching and practice, between what one said and what one did.[118]

As long as African Americans and other historically marginalized social groups are perceived by whites to be artificial constructions—in effect, artificial white people—who exist largely to be economically exploited or else reinvented and rewarded by whites in the sphere of leisure culture for their own entertainment, then it is unlikely that democracy will ever be achievable. As long as the rules by which society functions continue to be defined by the white majority, and the interpretation of such rules continues to be controlled by a dominant capitalist elite, then the concept of equality is nothing but a hollow term. As long as the liberal pluralistic society in which we all participate is controlled a priori by our failure to address the problem of material exploitation, then gangsta rap will operate out of necessity as a serious critique of U.S. cultural life. As long as the politically unifying cultural understanding that pluralists posit as the framework for democratic social life continues to read narratives such as gangsta rap as necessarily threatening to social harmony, then success in our society will always be racially determined.

Equal access to shared symbols of nationhood do not spell democracy for any group when such symbols are discouraged from being interrogated, reanimated, and transformed. More importantly, equal access to the material necessities of human survival and dignity must be made a fundamental prerequisite for democracy. Anything less than this makes a mockery of the ideal of social justice. In this context, the "brothas" and "sistahs" of gangsta rap are demanding that democracy live up to its promises. They challenge—by any means necessary—democracy to rearticulate its mission in view of the current urban nightmare in which the melting pot itself has melted in a postpluralist firestorm. How must we rethink identity when the container can no longer contain, when the ladle dissolves in the mixture, when the signifier ceases to signify?

If British sociologists Scott Lash and John Urry are correct in asserting that "we are not so much thrown into communities, but decide which communities—from youth subcultures to new social movements—we shall throw ourselves into," then what sort of aesthetic (hermeneutic) reflexivity is required in the case of gangsta rap?[119] What is at issue when the ideographic mode of gangsta-ing is counterposed to conduct regulated by the abstract norm-governed social structure of the state? Is this a question of what Lash and Urry call "race-baiting neotribes" or the beginning of "new communitarian social movements"? What happens when the wild zones of information flows and networks of the so-called underclass enter into a marriage with the new informational bourgeoisie?

In an era in which the subject is located as ambivalent and grounded in lost referents and instabilities within signifying chains, gangsta rap draws needed attention to the importance, not only of disidentifying with the cultural obvious but also of recognizing that the difference rendered most invisible in the production of postmodern cultural representations is the difference between rich and poor. We are viscerally reminded by gangsta rappers that cultural identities and practices remain tied to capital's drive to accumulate profits through the appropriation of labor that relies historically on forms of racism, patriarchy, and imperialism.[120]

## EPILOGUE

The casket carrying the body of Notorious B.I.G. (Christopher Wallace, a.k.a. Biggie Smalls) rests in a hearse winding its way past 226 St. James Place in the rapper's old Brooklyn neighborhood toward the Frank E. Campbell Funeral Chapel in Manhattan's Upper East Side. Two black Cadillacs filled with flowers—the letters B.I.G. are spelled out in brilliant red carnations—are spotted driving through Bedford-Stuyvesant. At the open casket service, fans stricken with grief catch a glimpse of Junior M.A.F.I.A., Flavor Flav, Dr. Dre, Spinderella, and Sister Souljah. For the postmodern theorist, there is a whole lot of signifying going on. For the people lined up outside the funeral home—who don't have the consolation of the sociology seminar room—the issue is not one of semiotics but of survival. It is not an event that calls for interpretation. It is an event that calls for a commitment to struggle.

## NOTES

This chapter comprises approximately forty-two pages from *Revolutionary Multiculturalism: Pedagogies of Dissent for the New Millennium*, ed. Peter McLaren. Copyright 1997 by Westview Press. Reprinted here with the generous permission of Westview Press.

Special thanks to Carlos Tejeda. Ash Vasudeva, Warren Crinchlow, Makeba Jones, Karl Bruce Knapper, Michelle Knight, Mike Seltzer, and Nicole Baker for their helpful suggestions.

1. Jesse Katz, "Rap Furor: New Evil or Old Story," *Los Angeles Times,* August 5, 1995, pp. 1, 18, 19; Steve Proffitt, "Russell Simmons: Defending the Art of Communication Known as Rap," *Los Angeles Times,* August 27, 1995, p. M3.

2. Time Warner Inc. has formally abandoned its $115 million stake in Interscope Records, blaming the split on contractual provisions that prevented the company from monitoring the content of Interscope's gangsta rappers such as Dr. Dre and Snoop Doggy Dogg. Bob Dole claimed responsibility for this development claiming he "shamed" Time Warner into dropping their gangsta rappers ("Time Warner to Abandon Gangsta Rap," *Los Angeles Times*, September 28, 1995, pp. 1, 13).

3. Katz, "Rap Furor." Richard Berry's original hit in 1955, "Louie Louie," was Afro-Calypsonian yet was influenced by the Rhythm Rockers, a Chicano-Filipino band from Orange County, California. Band members had introduced Berry to René Touset's "Loca cha cha," which provided Berry with the model for "Louie Louie." See George Lipsitz, "The Bands of Tomorrow Are Here Today: The Proud, Progressive and Postmodern Sounds of Las Tres and Goddess 13," in *Musical Aesthetics and Multiculturalism*, ed. Steven Loza (Los Angeles: University of California, Department of Ethnomusicology and Systematic Musicology, 1994), pp. 139–47. "Louie Louie" has been recorded by more than three hundred artists, for example, Ike and Tina Turner, the Kinks, the Beach Boys, Tom Petty and the Heartbreakers, Frank Zappa, Iggy Pop, and even the Rice University Marching Owl Band. A resident of South Central Los Angeles, Berry contributed vocals to the Robins' "Riot in Cell Block No. 9" and Etta James's "Roll with Me Henry (the Wallflower)."

4. Ibid.

5. Cited in Douglas Rushkoff, *Media Virus* (New York: Ballantine Books, 1996), p. 163.

6. Ibid.

7. John L. Mitchell, "Third Trial Ruled out in Slaying by Officer," *Los Angeles Times*, February 4, 1995, pp. B1, B8. See also Rosalind Muhammad, "LA Gangs Honored in Keeping the Peace," *Final Call* 14.21 (Aug. 16, 1995): 4, 10.

8. Tricia Rose, *Black Noise: Rap Music and Black Culture in Contemporary America* (Hanover, N.H.: Wesleyan University Press, 1994), p. 4.

9. Jeffrey Louis Decker, "The State of Rap: The Time and Place of Hip Hop Nationalism," in *Microphone Friends: Youth Music, Youth Culture*, ed. Andrew Ross and Tricia Rose (New York: Routledge, 1994), p. 101.

10. Ibid.

11. Rose, *Black Noise*.

12. Ibid.

13. Ibid., p. 59.

14. Ibid.

15. Tommy Lott, "Black Vernacular Representation and Cultural Malpractice," in *Multiculturalism: A Critical Reader*, ed. David Theo Goldberg (Cambridge, Mass.: Basil Blackwell, 1994), p. 246.

16. Tricia Rose, "A Style Nobody Can Deal With: Politics, Style, and the Postindustrial City in Hip Hop," in *Microphone Friends*, ed. Ross and Rose, pp. 71–88.

17. George Lipsitz, *Dangerous Crossroads: Popular Music, Postmodernism, and the Poetics of Place* (London: Verso, 1994).

18. Carol Tulloch, "Rebel without a Pause: Black Street Style and Black Designers," in *Chic Thrills: A Fashion Reader*, ed. Juliet Ash and Elizabeth Wilson (Berkeley: University of California Press, 1993), pp. 84–98.

19. Ibid.

20. Kristal Brent Zook, "Reconstruction of Nationalist Thought in Black Music and Culture," in *Rockin' the Boat: Mass Music, and Mass Movement*, ed. Rebee Garofalo (Boston: South End Press, 1992), p. 257.

"Playing the dozens" and "signifying" are variations of African American linguistic practices or traditions that can be characterized as ritualized verbal contests or wars of words. The "dozens" are confrontations of wit, intellect, and repartee played out in lingual games of one-upmanship that are distinguished by lexical originality and creativity, mental dexterity, and verbal innovation and agility in the effective deployment of clever and sarcastic insults or put-downs. A continuation of a rich African diasporic oral tradition that has been distilled through the lens of the African American experience, playing the dozens and signifying are the ultimate expression of brains over brawn—spoken word show-downs that have transformed and elevated a marginalized community's collective humor, anger, joy, and pain in the face of adversity into a game of survival, a ritualized form of entertainment, and a highly valued and respected sociocultural art form. See James Percelay, Monteria Ivey, and Stephan Dweck, eds., *SNAPS* (New York: Quill/William Morrow, 1994), pp. 8–9, 16–23, 27–35, 161–67.

21. Rose, *Black Noise*.

22. Tricia Rose, "Give Me a (Break) Beat! Sampling and Repetition in Rap Production," in *Culture on the Brink: Ideologies of Technology*, ed. Gretchen Bender and Timothy Druckrey (Seattle, Wash.: Bay Press, 1994), p. 251.

23. Rose, *Black Noise*, p. 4.

24. Lawrence Grossberg, "Is Anybody Listening? Does Anybody Care? On 'The State of Rock,'" in *Microphone Friends*, ed. Ross and Rose, pp. 41–58.

25. Michael Dyson, "The Politics of Black Masculinity and the Ghetto in Black Film," in *The Subversive Imagination: Artists, Society, and Social Responsibility*, ed. Carol Becker (London: Routledge, 1994), pp. 159–60.

26. Rose, "A Style Nobody Can Deal With," p. 71.

27. Dick Hebdige, *Cut 'n' Mix* (London: Comedia, 1987).

28. Ibid.

29. Robin D. G. Kelley, *Race Rebels: Culture, Politics, and the Black Working Class* (New York: Free Press, 1994), p. 184.

30. Cited in Rushkoff, *Media Virus*, p. 164.

31. Juan Flores, "Puerto Rican and Proud, Boyee! Rap, Roots, and Amnesia," in *Microphone Friends*, ed. Ross and Rose.

32. Jack Cheevers, Chuck Philips, and Frank B. Williams, "Violence Tops the Charts," *Los Angeles Times*, April 3, 1995, pp. 1–18.

33. Ibid., p. 18. Young and Knight have since broken up their partnership. With a record eight criminal convictions (mostly for assault and weapons charges), Marion "Suge" Knight is currently serving time in a Chino prison while awaiting a Superior Court hearing. In 1995 he entered no-contest pleas to two accounts of assault that involved the beating of two rappers in a Hollywood

recording studio. Under a plea bargain he was given a suspended nine-year prison term and five years probation. Since it was discovered that Knight had cut a record deal with the original prosecutor's eighteen-year-old daughter and had lived in the prosecutor's Malibu Colony house through the summer of 1996, the prosecutor was dropped from the case. At the MGM Hotel in Los Vegas, just hours before Tupac Shakur was fatally wounded in a car driven by Knight, a surveillance videotape showed Knight and several Death Row employees attacking a Crips gang member. This led to the revoking of Knight's parole. Death Row Records is currently under investigation by the Federal Bureau of Investigation, the Internal Revenue Service, the Bureau of Alcohol, Tobacco and Firearms and the Drug Enforcement Administration for funding crimes by the Mob Piru set of the Bloods street gang, for allegedly engaging in business deals with "drug kingpins" Michael Harris and Ricardo Crockett, and for dealing with entrepreneurs linked to organized crime factions that included New York Mafia figures Joseph Colombo Jr. and Alphonse "the Whale" Mellolla (Chuck Philips and Alan Abrahamson, "U.S. Probes Death Row Record Label's Money Trail," *Los Angeles Times*, December 29, 1996, pp. A1, A34, A35).

34. Proffitt, "Russell Simmons," p. M3.

35. Matthew T. Grant, "Of Gangstas and Guerrillas: Distance Lends Enchantment," *Appendx* 2 (1994): 44.

36. Katz, "Rap Furor," p. 18

37. Ibid.

38. Ibid.

39. David Troop, *Rap Attack: African Jive to New York Hip Hop* (London: Pluto Press, 1984); Houston Baker, *Black Studies: Rap and the Academy* (Chicago: University of Chicago Press, 1993); Rose, *Black Noise*.

40. Lipsitz, *Dangerous Crossroads*.

41. Nick De Genova, "Gangster Rap and Nihilism in Black America: Some Questions of Life and Death," *Social Text* 13.2 (1995): 113.

42. Ibid., p. 114.

43. Rose, "A Style Nobody Can Deal With," p. 83.

44. Tommy Lott, "Black Vernacular Representation," p. 247.

45. Charles P. Pierce, "Sunshine Is Back!" *Los Angeles Times Magazine*, April 23, 1995, pp. 12–15, 35, 36.

46. Tommy Lott, "Black Vernacular Representation," p. 246.

47. Angela Davis, "Discussion," in *Black Popular Culture*, ed. Gina Dent (Seattle, Wash.: Bay Press, 1992), p. 327.

48. Decker, "State of Rap," p. 109.

49. Ibid., p. 110.

50. Steven Gregory, "Race and Racism: A Symposium," *Social Text* 13.1 (1995): 16–21.

51. Ibid., p. 20.

52. Decker, "State of Rap," p. 116.

53. Tricia Rose, "Black Texts/Black Contexts," in *Black Popular Culture*, ed. Dent, p. 226.

54. Zook, "Nationalist Thought," p. 256.

55. De Genova, "Gangsta Rap and Nihilism," p. 111.

56. Ibid., p. 107.

57. Lipsitz, *Dangerous Crossroads*, p. 38.

58. bell hooks, *Black Looks: Race and Representation* (Boston: South End Press, 1992), pp. 35–36; emphasis in original.

59. De Genova, "Gangsta Rap and Nihilism," p. 107.

60. Grant, "Gangstas and Guerrillas," p. 45.

61. Ibid. See also the important work of Stephen Haymes, *Race, Culture, and the City: A Pedagogy for Black Urban Struggle* (Albany: State University of New York Press, 1995).

62. Grant, "Gangstas and Guerrillas," p. 47.

63. Ibid.

64. Ibid.

65. Ibid., p. 51.

66. Ibid.

67. Ibid.

68. De Genova, "Gangsta Rap and Nihilism," p. 105.

69. Michel de Certeau, *The Practice of Everyday Life* (Berkeley: University of California Press, 1984), pp. 31–32.

70. Tommy Lott, "Black Vernacular Representation," p. 249.

71. De Genova, "Gangsta Rap and Nihilism," p. 116.

72. Tommy Lott, "Black Vernacular Representation," p. 246.

73. Peter McLaren, *Critical Pedagogy and Predatory Culture* (London: Routledge, 1995).

74. Jon Stratton, "The Beast of the Apocalypse: The Post-Colonial Experience of the United States," *New Formations* 21 (Winter 1993): 35–63.

75. De Genova, "Gangsta Rap and Nihilism," p. 106.

76. Ibid., p. 119.

77. Zook, "Nationalist Thought," p. 263.

78. Kelley, *Race Rebels*, p. 212.

79. Grant, "Gangstas and Guerrillas," p. 52.

80. Leerom Medovoi, "Mapping the Rebel Image: Postmodernism and the Masculinist Politics of Rock in the U.S.A.," *Cultural Critique* 20 (Winter 1991–92): 165.

81. Eric Lott, "Cornel West in the Hour of Chaos: Culture and Politics in *Race Matters*," *Social Text* 12.3 (1994): 41.

82. Ibid., pp. 41, 43.

83. Ibid., p. 42.

84. Tommy Lott, "Black Vernacular Representation," p. 246.

85. Kelley, *Race Rebels*, p. 210; emphasis in original. Kelley also points out that the term *nigger* made a "comeback" at the height of the Black Power movement of the 1960s when a distinction was made between *nigger* and *negro*—the latter signified a sellout or a brainwashed black person.

86. Lipsitz, *Dangerous Crossroads*, p. 127.

87. Ibid., p. 89.

88. Ibid., p. 90.

89. Ibid., p. 58.

90. Grant, "Gangstas and Guerrillas," p. 40.

91. McLaren, *Critical Pedagogy.*

92. Grant, "Gangstas and Guerrillas," p. 41.

93. Steve Appleford, "The Rise and Fall of Gangsta Rap," *Los Angeles Reader,* March 3, 1995, pp. 8–11, 56.

94. Ibid., p. 9.

95. Ibid.

96. Ibid., p. 11.

97. Donnell Alexander, "Closed Border: The Hip-Hop Nation Deports Alternative Rap. Michael Ivey's B.Y.O.B.," *LA Weekly* 17.17 (March 24–30, 1995): 39–40.

98. Thomas Cushman, "Rich Rastas and Communist Rockers: A Comparative Study of the Origin, Diffusion, and Delusion of Revolutionary Musical Codes," *Journal of Popular Culture* 25.3 (1991): 17–61.

99. Javier Santiago-Lucerna, "Nothing's Sacred, Everything's Profane: Rock Isleno and the Politics of National Identity in Puerto Rico," paper presented at York University, Toronto, March 1995, pp. 16–17.

100. Ibid.

101. Rosemary Hennessy, "Queer Visibility in Commodity Culture," *Cultural Critique* 29 (Winter 1994–95): 31–76.

102. Ibid., p. 52.

103. Ibid., p. 53.

104. Ibid.

105. Ibid.

106. De Genova, "Gangsta Rap and Nihilism," pp. 105–6.

107. Hennessy, "Queer Visibility," p. 33.

108. Cushman, "Rich Rastas," pp. 17–61.

109. Ibid., p. 48. According to Christian Parenti, prisoners are being exploited as cheap labor and their wages are used to pay for their incarceration. He notes that "the California Department of Corrections is also trying to find a niche in Japan's jeans market with its new line of 'Gangsta Blues.' Thus, the much deplored hip-hop culture of African-American and Latino youths—which has embraced the look of denim workclothes—is being imitated, glorified, and sold back to the public by the very criminal justice system that claims to wage war on Gangsta culture" (Parenti, *New Statement and Society,* November 3, 1995, pp. 20–21).

110. Diane Fuss, "Interior Colonies: Frantz Fanon and the Politics of Identification," *Diacritics* 24.2–3 (Summer–Fall 1994): 21.

111. Françoise Lionett, *Postcolonial Representations: Women, Literature, Identity* (Ithaca, N.Y.: Cornell University Press, 1995), p. 10.

112. Homi Bhabha, "Of Mimicry and Man: The Ambivalence of Colonial Discourse," *October* 28 (1984): pp. 125–33.

113. Lipsitz, *Dangerous Crossroads,* p. 62.

114. Manning Marable, "Race, Identity, and Political Culture," in *Black Popular Culture,* ed. Dent, p. 302.

115. Michael Eric Dyson, "Tupac: Living the Life He Rapped about in Song," *Los Angeles Times,* Sunday October 22, 1996, p. 3.

116. Ibid.

117. Ibid.

118. Ibid.

119. Scott Lash and John Urry, *Economies of Signs and Space* (London: Sage, 1992), p. 316.

120. Teresa Ebert, "The Surplus of Enjoyment in the Post-al Real," *Rethinking Marxism* 7.3 (1994): 137–42.

CHAPTER 9

# Battlin' Nihilism at an Urban High School: Pedagogy, Perseverance, and Hope

## David Keiser

The proper starting point for the crucial debate about the prospects for black America is an examination of the nihilism that increasingly pervades black communities. . . . Nihilism is to be understood here not as a philosophical doctrine that there are no rational grounds for legitimate standards or authority; it is, far more, the lived experience of coping with a life of horrifying meaninglessness, hopelessness, and (most important) lovelessness. The frightening result is a numbing detachment from others and a self-destructive disposition toward the world. Life without meaning, hope, and love breeds a cold-hearted, mean spirited outlook that destroys both the individual and others.[1]

What Cornel West and others describe as a culture rooted directly in violence, whose defining principles are homicide, cultural suicide, and social decay, touches many students living in inner cities. Nihilism within urban communities in the United States gravely affects schools. Students bring their lived experiences to school; if students live amid nihilist conditions, their schools will feel the ripples. Students preoccupied with pressing problems such as violence, drugs, and poverty may see school less as a stable social institution than as an additional stress on their lives. Schools need to at least acknowledge these problems, if not make them explicit in curriculum; if students fail to see school as a place where they can grapple with and interrogate their life circumstances, they will be less likely to invest in school.

They may see teachers as indifferent to their problems, and consequently feel alienated and detached from the institution. Some students'

271

alienation may manifest as truancy, defiance, or illicit behavior on school property.[2] Teachers may react defensively, and treat students as unteachable. If students have learning disabilities as well, the problem is compounded, for despite a recent spate of "full-inclusion" rhetoric, many students with learning disabilities or behavioral problems remain ostracized and marginalized within public schools.[3]

## INTRODUCTION

The Corner Campus is a 160 student high school in northern California. It is significantly smaller than other local high schools. The Campus enrolls students who do not succeed in other schools, and, according to the school brochure, "who are looking for or need an alternative to the traditional high schools." While some students face arduous conditions outside school, the policy inside the Campus is to promote critical thinking and agency; even if Campus students live amid nihilist threats, their school tries to provide meaning, hope, and love.

This chapter is about the students of the Corner Campus and the issues they face and make salient in school. The methods used by the Campus teachers and staff in reaching and teaching their students deserve recognition and emulation; my contribution to such recognition is the impetus for this paper. In my first seven months at the school, I noticed a distinctive and intentional critical pedagogy. The teachers make societal inequity explicit, relearn curricula with students, incorporate student experiences, and teach dialogically.[4] Such methodology may counter student nihilism, the loss of hope that school can provide meaning and nurture possibility. Many students see the school as listening to their stories and accepting and educating them despite prohibitive conditions such as gang affiliation, past or present incarceration/probation, and illicit extracurricular activity like drug dealing.

I frame this paper around the collision of critical pedagogy and student nihilism; the possibility that a critical pedagogical perspective may mitigate student attrition and disinvestment in school. In this chapter I ask the following questions: What makes this alternative school work for its students? Given that students can talk freely about their experiences,[5] what do they talk about? What are the problems or frustrations of teaching critically amid violent and impoverished conditions? Lastly, I wonder to what extent teachers can validate student voice without encouraging or condoning illicit behavior? I address these questions through the themes of violence, drugs, and rap music and culture, as manifest both through previously published empirical literature and through student work samples.

## RESEARCH SETTING

The school is centrally located in a busy urban neighborhood. It is located across from an outpatient hospital, and within walking distance of several bus stops. It is surrounded by a parking lot, a rarely used basketball court, and a vacant lot. The actual campus of the Campus consists of the steps in front of the school. A hot dog vendor sells franks and sodas diagonally across the street, and several eateries are within two city blocks.

The regular school day consists of three seventy-five minute periods between nine and one, and tutoring, makeup work, or workshops after school. The extended class periods are almost double those in regular high schools, and provide curricular flexibility and greater time for dialogue between students and teachers. Furthermore, fewer class periods means fewer bells and fewer student transitions between classrooms.

The school is located in an old and spacious school building with twelve classrooms and several offices. Unlike other overcrowded schools in the district, size is not a problem, save the lack of a lunchroom, auditorium, or gym. Behind the school, there are netless basketball hoops amid unremarkable asphalt. The structural problems are leaky, wood-exposed ceilings, walls with chipping plaster, no doors on bathroom stalls, and old gas spigots sticking out of some classroom floors. The hallways of the two floors are partially lined with student writing samples and school murals. On the second floor, a double door is covered with sexy hip hop lyrics and photos from Ebony and Vibe magazines and the acronym LIFE; Ladies in Full Effect.[6] Inside these doors, a part-time school counselor sees students throughout the day, and teaches a class about female empowerment[7] once a week. But the doors themselves connote an urban adolescent spirit bespeaking physical and sexual maturity.

## CORNER CAMPUS KIDS

The school brochure describes the students of the Campus as being

> of all racial, ethnic, and cultural groups. They come from neighborhoods from (this) and other cities in the area. . . . Students come to the Campus for many reasons. Some prefer an alternative to the traditional high school. Some have fallen behind in earning their credits and want to catch up. Others have dropped out of school for personal reasons and now want to resume their studies. They are referred by counselors, friends, and family.

Also in the pamphlet is the rejoinder that all new students must be interviewed by their peers and teachers. Accountability is overt: "Students must also show a commitment to the right of others to learn." Every student agrees to this prior to admission. Thus, the staff expects that students come to school ready and eager to learn, but clearly, this idealistic expectation is mitigated, because some students attend the Campus for reasons ranging from truancy to behavior problems.[8] Some, however, choose the Campus for its small size and pedagogical strengths.

Nina, a fourth-year language arts teacher, posits that while most students attend because they take school seriously, others are persuaded to attend a school cited by the state as a "model dropout prevention program."

> Some come from a small safe environment or 'cuz they've heard its a good small school with an alternative curriculum or they knew somebody who came here. . . . A few people come just cuz they live in the neighborhood. . . . I think 95% of them here think that being in school is important and a step to success—that's reflected in their being here. I think that some of them are under some form of coercion by their parents or their p.o.[9] or something.

## RESEARCH QUESTIONS AND PAPER PARAMETERS

My original research question was 'What makes students invest in the Corner Campus?' But I think that given small classes, caring teachers, and a shorter school day, a better question would ask why some students don't invest. However, I changed my focus when I realized the answer to this question might vary greatly between students. Considering the heterogeneous student populace, my "answer" doubtless would conflate with issues too large for this project.[10] I was still interested in my question but guessed the answer would revolve around the size of the school and the dedication and flexibility of the teachers.

Early in the study I worried about the role of the Campus in its students' lives; later I began to worry about the students. When I got to know the students, and read their work, I became interested in how they made sense of their world verbally and in writing. That is, what were salient themes in their life? In a school clearly focused on student voice, emancipation and agency, what themes emerge?

Rather than simply take notes and interview staff, I taught a basic skills writing workshop, and in seven months, countless themes surfaced, many of which interest me as much as those I chose to write about here. In thinking about nihilism within schools and students, and about the human spirit vis-à-vis education and society, I wonder when and how students decide to sell drugs for a quick profit rather than stay in school for a diploma. I wonder as well, what awaits my students five or ten years from now if they invest in school? And if they don't? From one workshop's worth of student stories, I focus on violence, drugs, and hip-hop culture only because these themes seemed most salient at the time. My title, "Battlin' Nihilism," pays homage to the students and teachers of the Corner Campus who resist the temptation to give up amid drugs, violence, and social and economic inequities. The teachers do this by struggling with critical pedagogy in practice; the students by attending school to obtain a high school diploma.

## CRITICAL PEDAGOGICAL POSSIBILITIES

Critical pedagogy, with its goals of empowering the powerless and transforming social injustice through schooling, represents one strategy for elucidating inequity within a curricular context.[11] All students need to learn to think critically about society and themselves. Human agency is innate, and it is up to schools, among other sites, to nurture student agency, and to inspire students to praxis.[12] If schools and classrooms do not serve as pressure valves from the craziness permeating many urban communities, and if they no longer represent possibilities for change and betterment for students, the nihilist threat will increase. If the pay-off, the result of attending school is meaningless, why go to school? That is, teachers need to better understand and incorporate their students' realities in order to keep student hope alive.

As a former special education teacher, where critical pedagogy is harder to implement, I was excited to do research and work at a school without labels, one which espouses students reading the word *and* the world.[13] Campus teachers learn about students' worlds through dialogic teaching methods, where students' stories become part of the curriculum.[14] Their stories bespeak current urban adolescent realities, several of which are addressed in this paper. Within the Campus, students study current social issues that directly impact their lives. Thus, teachers often focus on issues such as drugs, violence, sex, teen pregnancy, rape, and domestic violence.

## STUDENT TEACHERS AND TEACHER STUDENTS: THE ACTS OF KNOWING AND REKNOWING

Teachers, students, and researchers must be jointly active in the learning process. All must have chances to learn and to construct and revise theories about what and how they know. They must be free to use the language of give-and-take to negotiate ideas, to build knowledge, and to acquire new skills to prepare for lifelong learning.[15]

The above quote addresses critical pedagogy and dialogic teaching, and calls on teachers to learn from students.[16] While many teachers still resist "the language of give-and-take" and maintain "chalk and talk" classrooms, others challenge didactic pedagogy.[17]

In his seminal book *Pedagogy of the Oppressed*, Paulo Freire contrasts the models of banking versus problem-posing education. In the former, students are passive receptacles of knowledge and "accounts" into which teachers deposit knowledge that may be withdrawn for tests, papers, or not at all. The latter model posits teachers and students learning and relearning units of study together, while posing critical questions along the way to gaining knowledge. This problem-posing model assumes both that teachers think their students' knowledge worthwhile, and that they are willing to adapt their teaching style to student needs.

Building on the Freirean model, James Cummins constructed a pedagogical continuum ranging from "reciprocal, interaction-oriented" to "transmission-oriented."[18] Thus, teachers perceive students either as coparticipants in the act of learning or as passive recipients of the instructor's knowledge. Both Freire and Cummins identify the variability of power relations within classrooms. If teachers see students as "bank accounts," or empty vessels needing a "transmission of knowledge," the modes of instruction and themes for analysis will be quite different than if teachers see students as active educational participants or agents of change.

## ONE EXAMPLE OF HOW TEACHERS CAN SQUELCH STUDENT AGENCY

In my work as a special education teacher and supervisor, I saw how teacher expectations and attitudes affect student performance and readiness to learn. I visited schools throughout the Bay Area, and witnessed some demoralizing pedagogical practice. This was manifest through uncreative and demeaning assignments, multiple student expulsions, hostile rapport and even rudeness. But low teacher expectations especially hinder praxis and agency: when students perceive that teachers don't care about their presence or their education, excitement to learn converts quickly to hostility. Students get expelled from class for hours or sometimes days at a time for being loud, or because they are literally misunderstood. They learn that questioning authority may be tantamount to forfeiting opportunities to learn.

For example, the phrase "why ya gotta be bitin' on my caps?" is urban literate;[19] it is neither profane nor disrespectful to the teacher, but I saw a student expelled for two hours for saying that within a middle school classroom. The comment was actually subtle closure to a two to three insult exchange that the teacher missed entirely. But she reacted to what she perceived as threatening, or simply too loud for her class, which had not yet even begun. Antagonism toward students—especially ones already labeled "special" or "at risk" learners—is counterproductive. It affects the other students and their possibilities as well. Pervasive apathy between students, teachers, support staff, and even administration can snowball into complacency and negligence. This chapter concerns an antithetical snowball.

## SOME REASONS WHY STUDENTS FAIL AT OTHER SCHOOLS

While most educators might agree that public schools need help, larger questions are why do they need help? Or, what can be done? We need to examine schools not as autonomous institutions, but as agents of social and academic reproduction.[20] Students learn in school, but also learn to "do" school. Students conforming to expectations of teachers, schools, and society do better in school. But what does society expect from schools? Or from students? In this nexus of student and school expectations, the role of cultural capital is crucial. For the purposes of this chapter, I employ Henry Giroux's definition of student cultural capital: the amalgamation of differing cognitive, linguistic, and dispositional or behavioral attributes that students bring to school.[21]

Dispositional attributes are of course inseparable from their cognitive and linguistic attributes. How and why students behave or misbehave in school may well be related to cognitive and linguistic competence, and especially how this competence is perceived by school and society. Students who do not conform, assimilate, and succeed within schools may be labeled learning disabled, culturally deficient, emotionally disturbed, behaviorally disordered, or simply "too loud." Thus, students learn that resistance is often tantamount to educational exclusion, and may internalize their placement; that is, they belong in special, or alternative, or remedial education.

In addition to behavioral norms, students and indeed their schools, are held to state-imposed curricular standards. One problem with "standardizing" curricula is that schools are not neutral, and knowledge is not objective. Recent revived policy battles over teaching evolution, book banning, sex education, and "multicultural" historical perspectives bear witness. But current educational policy and debate focuses on "the basic curriculum," not on basic human needs of security, safety, and health. Emphasizing curricular standards precludes and prevents treating larger societal ills such as racism and rampant poverty. A 1996 *New York Times* op-ed piece offers this summation on the eve of a second national education summit:

> The public schools offer perhaps the clearest picture of our nation's economic and social health. President Clinton and other leaders are often heard worrying about the poor performance of American students, especially compared to students in other industrialized countries. But they must remember that this poor performance is and always had been partly a symptom of our neglect of the many social crises that afflict our nation.[22]

A critical pedagogy illuminates these symptoms instead of neglects them, because when students bring "social crises" into classrooms, it affects their capacity and desire to learn academic material, and teachers are left between a rock of school bureaucracy and the hard place in which their students exist. That is, schools choose whether "back to basics" means basic human needs or basic academic skills. They need not be mutually exclusive, but teachers must be willing to make social crises and their impact on students an explicit part of curricula and further analyze the "relationship between classroom objectives and cultural capital":

> crucial to the development of progressive classroom social relationships is the opening of channels of communication which allow students to use those forms of linguistic and cultural capital though which they give meaning to their everyday experiences. If students are subjected in the classroom to a language as well as a set of beliefs and values whose implicit message is that they are culturally illiterate, students will learn very little about critical thinking, and a great deal about what Freire has called the "culture of silence."[23]

One manifestation of the "culture of silence" is that students learn that if they don't disrupt the teacher, they will pass the class; if they resist their teacher or their schoolwork, they will handicap their progress. Critical pedagogy opposes the culture of silence, and posits that student experience is the curriculum, and should determine what is prioritized in classrooms. For many public school students, particularly in large urban areas, student experience is laced with violence, but teachers ultimately decide how fully to incorporate such experience into their teaching and curricula.

## VIOLENCE WITHIN STUDENTS' LIVES

In a special issue of *The Harvard Educational Review* on youth and school violence, Pedro Noguera posits that schools need to adapt different approaches to curtailing and containing violence. He criticizes traditional approaches for their over-reliance on punitive measures and institutional controls to ebb violence, and instead calls for a more humane and culturally proactive response:

> The urban schools that I know that feel safe to those who spend their time there don't have metal detectors or armed security guards, and their principals don't carry baseball bats. What these schools do have is a strong sense of community and collective responsibility. Such schools are seen by students as sacred territory, too special to be spoiled by crime and violence, and too important to risk one's being excluded.[24]

While the Corner Campus has neither metal detectors nor security guards, if students fight, they are expelled without exception. The students and staff feel safe for two main reasons: they assume that students come to school to learn, and all agree to the unbendable rule that if you fight, regardless of who started the fight, you will be expelled. For many Campus students, the risk of expulsion outweighs any propensity toward fighting. Teachers identify the one-punch rule as crucial to the success and survival of the school:

> [I]t feels like a safe place. I think the kids feel safe at school. (A student) didn't go to his other school because there were fights every day and drive-bys in the school yard . . . at Corner Campus people feel safe, you know, cuz if you fight you're out, and I think that provides a good basis. (First-year teacher, interview)

> [T]hat school rule—if there's one rule that they know and they know well . . . is that if you start it or finish it, you're gone, you're out of school . . . our students really like that. (Second-year teacher, interview)

While a zero-tolerance policy may have immediate or even lasting effects on a school environment, what about the rampant violence many students face outside school? That is, how can schools deal effectively with violence in their students' lives? Should this task be up to schools? Does continual exposure to violence and death inhibit student readiness to learn? Teachers have used their students' experiences with death as an integral part of their curriculum. Another urban researcher in northern California incorporated student voice and expertise within her classroom, and embodies both sensitivity and critical pedagogy in practice.

> I came to realize that connecting school knowledge with the students' real-life issues is essential in my classroom. . . . Death is one example of students' life experiences that enters the classroom whether a teacher chooses to acknowledge it or not. It is also one of many student experiences that debunk the notion of classroom teaching and education as neutral spaces or endeavors.[25]

This researcher allots nearly half her article to student work samples. This testifies to her commitment to incorporating student voice both in her classroom and within educational research. She raises huge issues in the day-to-day life in urban schools, and inherent subjectivity within teaching and education. She invites teachers to teach holistically, treating the student as an organic whole, not a removed receptor of knowledge.

Teachers need to acknowledge that certain life circumstances outrank academic achievement in their students' lives, and that they can provide a forum for students to express these circumstances. In a recent issue of *English Journal*, Nancy Hudson wrote about the amount of violence within her students' writing. She encapsulates the value of providing a forum for such expression:

> It is partly my job as teacher to understand that this violence exists in almost all my students' lives and seriously affects their socialization and readiness for education. It affects my class, my relationship to my students, and their relationship to each other. We as English teachers must also realize the transformative power of writing and the importance of respecting our students' voices.[26]

Hudson provides a valve for the pressure her students endure living amid violence, and while they may be marginalized by society in terms of access to power, equal opportunity, and money, in her class they speak from places of authority and expertise, rather than from the margins.[27] Thus, violence in their lives is neither ignored nor minimized, but made explicit within scholastic activities.

In the film *Dangerous Minds*, based on the book *My Posse Don't Do Homework*, Louanne Johnson asks her students to analyze death references within the poetry of Dylan Thomas and Bob Dylan.[28] While both Hudson and Johnson promote using classic, or white mainstream literature to get students thinking critically about violence or death, such curricular complacency may be problematic.

Why focus only on white European authors? Why not incorporate voices closer to the students own? After addressing salient and pressing issues, the next step is to incorporate student cultural forms and preferences within curricula. While Johnson points to Bob Dylan's "code words" for drugs and drug dealers in *Mr. Tambourine Man* as a way of getting her students' attention, she uses nothing relating to the rap music her students listen to in and out of her classroom, and she makes little attempt to understand her students' codes and code words. She finds school rules deferring to street codes when she breaks up a fight, and assumes the students will keep their word and not fight again. She is wrong.

## SCHOOL CODES VERSUS STREET CODES

In *The Code of the Streets*, Elijah Anderson explicates the importance of respect and 'juice' to many African-American males living in inner-city communities. His article is about survival amid violence. It compels urban teachers to understand the various obstacles their students must overcome to *attend* school, and to take seriously the nihilist threat in their lives.

> The inclination to violence springs from the circumstances of life among the ghetto poor—the lack of jobs that pay a living wage, the stigma of race, the fallout from rampant drug use and drug trafficking, and the resulting alienation and hope for the future. Simply living in such an environment places young people at special risk of falling victim to aggressive behavior.[29]

At the Campus, student experience is manifest and explored within their curricula; as one teacher told me, "we don't ask them to check their lives at the door." Violence permeates many Campus students' lives, and they are encouraged to deal with it constructively at school through writing, discussing, and acting their experiences. For example, in one English class, *Language Arts through Social Issues*, students choose themes to study each quarter; invariably, they select violent ones. One recent class chose rape, child abuse, and serial killers to write about.

I asked my workshop students to write a few sentences on their feelings about violence, and to differentiate between real and perceived violence. Does violent imagery in media influence student violence? I worry about this relationship, and wonder if students do also; that is, is a gangsta rapper on MTV raping women real or perceived? I hoped we could then critically interrogate societal violence, but soon realized I was perhaps too detached from it to fully understand their perspective. I needed to listen to them before assuming they were as critical of violence as I was.

We talked about proliferation of violence in media and in their communities. I asked how they felt about escalating and incessant violence in society and in their communities especially. Several of their responses to "The way I feel about violence" illustrate nihilism, or de facto acceptance of violence as a normal part of day-to-day life. While student responses ranged from approving. . . .

- I really don't care just as long as it's not affecting me or my family. But if it is we shall retaliate. (Female)
- I can't really talk bad about violent people, because if somebody did something that made me real mad, I would get violent . . . so I see myself as half violent and half nonviolent. (Female)

to abhorring . . .

- I hate that violence happens everyday . . . my cousin was killed and he wasn't violent. (Male)
- I had a friend who joined a gang, he wasn't really violent. . . . He died three months after joining. He got a bullet through the head. (Male)

. . . the consensus was that violence was one means of solving problems, and an inescapable part of life

- [I]t does affect some of the communities because a lot of loved ones get killed or hurt . . . some people think it's a game, but when it comes to losing a life, they find out it's not. (Male)
- Sometimes I feel very brave about violence and other times I feel very scared. (Female)

Unlike other schools, the Campus deals with this reality proactively through academic exercises, discussions, and daily conferences between students and their homeroom teachers. They attempt to at once address and minimize the threat of violence within the school. The student responses indicate both an acceptance and an abhorrence of violence. While some students disavow violence, most realize they might not have a choice. As a follow-up question, I asked whether or not they considered themselves violent. I wondered how living amid violence affects behavior and self-identification. Do my students consider themselves violent?

- Violence is really a thing to be considered by all people so we can stop it. I don't consider myself violent . . . as you know I'm a lover not a fighter. (Male)
- [Y]es, sometimes . . . I see myself being violent when it's needed. (Male)
- I wouldn't hurt nobody unless they started a fight with me. . . . I don't mess with guns because that's an automatic death. (Male)
- I see myself as a violent person when my temper goes off, and that does not take much time . . . other than that, no. (Female)
- I can get a little violent, but I would have to be really mad at somebody. (Female)

These responses illustrate both a de facto acceptance of violence as a reality in day-to-day existence and an encouraging resistance to perpetuating violent behaviors themselves. But even if my students are not prone to violent behaviors, they must deal with the violence of others. Their awareness of violence and need for street smarts is essential for survival in their communities. When I asked one student about nonviolence, or his desire to live peacefully, he offered "Sure, but what's the point? You can't do anything about anything." This is one manifestation of the nihilist threat; loss of hope for a nonviolent world. While letting students talk about violence may not lessen its impact, it shows students that teachers can be responsive and sensitive and may be an incentive for students to attend and invest in their education.

The violence affecting the students of the Corner Campus reflects urban blights such as drugs, poverty, and gang turf wars.[30] When teachers are ignorant or scared of these realities, they may not reach and teach students as effectively. I do not believe teachers need to be from violent areas to relate to students who are, but they do need to listen. In *Dangerous Minds*, Ms. Johnson needed to learn about her students' personal lives before they opened up to her. She then incorporated her students' themes—death and drugs—into her teaching. Teachers can choose whether to allot classroom time to students' life experiences, but avoiding class discussions of violence does not negate its reality for students; if anything it makes it seem shameful, as if it's their fault that violent obstacles distract them from learning in school. Teachers I interviewed identified violence as one of the major obstacles facing the students, and a student teacher at the Campus was somewhat shocked.

> When I was teaching the social issues class last year, we had this unit on gang violence and almost every kid in the class had been affected in some way, not necessarily by gang violence, but some kind of street violence. For all of them, it's touched their lives in some way. You know, they don't feel safe in their neighborhoods or they know someone who's been killed, or you know, that kind of stuff. And that is so foreign to my experience you know I can't even imagine having that kind of stuff hanging over you on a daily basis.

Teachers at the Campus acknowledge that social issues such as violence "hang over" many students on a daily basis, and try to construct curricula which deal with issues proactively. For example, in the aforementioned *Language Arts through Social Issues* class, a unit on rape included excepts from novels, plays, current articles, and a film, and compelling student testimony. Violence in Campus students' lives will not disappear because of empathic instruction, but in acknowledging and incorporating relevant themes, teachers employ critical pedagogy and allow their students to bring lived experiences into classes.

## DRUG USE AMONG STUDENTS

Many young adults use or abuse drugs. Notwithstanding the paternalistic *Just Say No* campaign of Nancy Reagan and others, many high school students continue to use drugs. While some Corner Campus students only use drugs such as marijuana, others deal drugs as well. A recent student poll, published in the quarterly school newsletter, showed that 35 percent of Campus students smoke weed. I asked Ike, a third year teacher at the school, about drug use and abuse among students. His comments both enlighten and frighten:

> One thing that's scaring me, that's really kinda hard to accept . . . is the amount of drugs in their lifestyles and their culture. . . . I found out it's not only them who are abusing it, but their parents . . . they want to quit but they can't because . . . their uncles, their mother, their father, everybody's doing it . . . it's scary . . . here have been a couple of cases where parents have even forced their kids to sell in order to subsidize their income.

During my time at the Campus, I noticed a tacit student acceptance of drug use and drug culture. While not all students use drugs, they acknowledge their classmates using. In fact, marijuana is now seen by many as less a drug than a vice on par with alcohol or cigarettes. The aforementioned poll showed that only 20 percent of students smoke cigarettes, about half the number who smoke weed.

While Campus staff know students smoke, they are sometimes at a loss concerning what to do about it. In drug awareness presentations, teachers acknowledge that students who get high before school are probably "coming down" during class. But the Campus teachers relate to students with language and attitudes that do not seem righteous and alienating to students. While students may not wear pro-drug T-shirts to school, they wear the marijuana leaf icon on earrings, nose rings, caps, and shoelaces. I learned from teacher interviews that dealers and heavy users keep weed referents to a minimum and students who seem preoccupied with "the leaf" do so just to impress others. One day I gave a grammar quiz in which students were to complete sentences with correct subject-verb agreement. Here is one student's paper, with the given grammatical phrase in italics:

> *None of the contestants* won the contest because they smoked bomb.[31]
> *The children and Helen* smoked hella bomb.
> *Everyone in the house* smokes bomb.
> *Margaret and Susan* smoke a lot of bomb.
> *Ellen and Jean, and I* smoked bomb.

A *few of the exercises* involve smoking bomb.
*Either Jim or the twins* have the bomb.
*Part of the movie* showed people smoking bomb.

During a poetry unit, the same student continued his theme in a seventeen-syllable haiku poem:

> I smoke hella bomb
> The bomb is so good to me
> Bomb relaxes me.

This student doesn't care whether his teachers think he smokes weed. But juxtaposed with the teacher's indication that such preoccupation is only a facade, what does the quiz connote? Does it mean the student smokes incessantly, or does it simply reek of indignant disclosure?

Students' feelings about drugs are often more subtle, but equally telling. During a unit on faith and spirituality, I asked my students to write a letter to God, whoever he or she represents to them. While many letters dealt with issues of thankfulness for family and health, one stuck out for its stark honesty and classification of drugs. From teacher interviews I learned that this student comes from a supportive family, but lives in a particularly dangerous housing project, where drug use is rampant. Here is his letter:

> Dear God,
> I have not been doing anything bad. No drugs or anything. I have been going down the right path, but I have been drinking and smoking weed but that is a habit that is hard to break, and I'm not trying to right at this time.

Seeing an opportunity to listen without lecturing, I responded:

> I'm very moved by your honesty—I would say that both alcohol and marijuana are drugs, but this matters less than your awareness that you are trying to do the right thing. Keep trying and do let me know if there's anything I can do.

He never sought my help but he never missed a class. He also wrote a haiku poem about drugs:

> I see his red eyes
> I hear him breathing deeply
> I hate my brother

I think I learned more about my students by allowing them to struggle with unsavory or illegal themes in writing. By accepting street vernacular and illicit stories in writing, I felt as if I was validating student cultural capital, but also wondered to what extent this was in their best interests. I feared that if I mandated proper English usage and forbade drug stories, attendance would fall. Since my class was accredited but voluntary, I thought students would stay and participate more if I eased up on discourse restrictions.

While I agree with Lisa Delpit[32] that students need to learn rules of school and society, I believe that, to some extent, school rules are changeable and should provide a forum for student vernacular. Furthermore, many students know societal rules and disavow them. For example, selling drugs provides an excellent example of a thriving and illegal enterprise that students defend as necessary and worth the risks involved:

- I think it's okay to deal drugs for a while but only if you really need the money. . . . To me it is better and safer to steal and sell what you got than to sell drugs because if you steal the right shit then you make almost as much as you do in drug sales. (Male)
- To a certain extent it is (okay to sell) because I can understand the fact that people are without and they really have nothing to lose. . . . I also feel that most of the people have families to take care of and the $4.25 an hour just is not going to get it. (Female)
- If you can make over $500 a night selling 50 little pieces of rock cocaine, you can become rich. . . . If you was to work at a fast food place it would take four or five weeks just to make $500, and the drug dealer is just taking the easiest way. (Male)
- I think it is okay to deal drugs . . . because people have to support their kids. (Female)

All four of these responses cite money as the reason and redemption for selling drugs. Students sell drugs for pocket money, so they don't have to get a "real" job paying much less money, but many sell to help support their families. Some students, however, felt that dealing was wrong, or at least too dangerous:

- I think that it's dumb to be standing on the corner, many bad things can happen to you out there, and you cannot depend on the people you grind with. (Male)
- No, I don't think it good to sell drugs because you are putting your life on the line and half of the time you got to watch our for the cops or the people you selling with because they could get two face and smoke you in a minute. (Female)

Again, teachers acknowledge this dilemma, and try to empathize with students who either fight the urge to deal drugs, or must contend with parents who do. There was no consensus as to whether dealing or using drugs was desirable behavior; the right of people to choose to sell, however, was defended by all. Drugs are so pervasive as to immobilize most "just say no" arguments. This poignant yet disturbing comment from a second-year teacher illustrates the dilemma many Campus teachers struggle with:

> I think that their dealing is more like an income—subsidizing income—in terms of just survival. I know a couple of kids here who need to sell it in order not to have a job in order to have enough time to study . . . some of our students do sell it just for survival wise. . . . Some kid last year—he came to me and he was all happy and he said "Ike, my dad doesn't make me sell coke now, it's just pot." And I'm like shit, what do I tell him? I'm like "Good for you. Congratulations!" You know? In terms of condoning the behavior . . . it's just so hard to tell because you can't tell them one thing like "it's not right to smoke" and then they go home and their parents and everybody in the world is doing it. Or when we take a trip to the park and see two nurses at the bus stop lighting up. I mean the medical profession just doing it right in public like it was nothing. How can you reinforce your rules here, if they're not enforced as soon as they step out the door?

In terms of rules, then, those of the Campus can be stricter than those of society. Drug use and drug dealing permeate Campus students' lives, and Campus teachers encourage students to stay off drugs and alcohol, but above all, to be careful.[33] Tantamount to understanding the depth of the problem is some familiarity with street vernacular and cultural markers or code words for drugs; that is, rock, bud, bomb, dank, and bammer. Campus teachers make such code words their business, and try to reach and teach in the language of their students. Knowledge of codes shows teacher interest in student culture and may enable teachers to better address student nihilism, as manifest through violence and drug use.

## STUDENTS' CULTURAL CAPITAL

Hip-hop clothing, graffiti tags, and vernacular represent some current urban adolescent markers. A few years before my study, Susan Katz Weinberg studied Latino middle school students in an English as a Second Language class in San Francisco. Her students utilized street slang, nicknames, and graffiti both as handwriting practice and gang affiliation. She explains her students' making sense of their world through nonacademic forms of literacy:

Language and literacy were ways in which students were trying to take control over their lives—to communicate in their own style. Graffiti and tag names represented forms of critical literacy-reshaping written language for one's own purposes. To understand the meanings embedded in graffiti, one must be a member of a particular literacy community. Not everyone can "read" graffiti; you must be taught by an insider who can decipher the codes—the nicknames, the acronyms, the use of Roman numerals. In these ways, Julio and the other students brought the streets into the classroom. They expressed much alienation from school as an academic world. They did not want to read any books that were linked to school in any way, even if a former gang member wrote them. To gain a place for themselves in school, the students created an alternative cultural identity. This identity was based on oral and written language forms from the streets, the world in which they felt included.[34]

Weinberg validated and incorporated her students' gang culture, identity, and indeed literacy into her classroom to increase student participation, but her project begs further questions: How do we validate student culture and voice if that voice is violent or illegal? If we allow students to talk about guns and drugs openly in class, are we simply validating voice, or legitimating licentious behavior? Student language is one front on which this battle plays out.

In Philadelphia, Miriam Camitta studied literate practices among high school students in Philadelphia, and discovered student literary investment outside her curriculum. She found vernacular writing such as love letters, poems, and journal entries happening both in and out of class. Her description of the students' covert behaviors connotes a playful subversion:

In the classroom, vernacular writing flourishes on a surreptitious basis. Here, students write during times when they have finished the assigned work, and sometimes, instead of doing it. Among the one hundred students whom I met daily in my classes, I observed, as in non-assigned student time, that students were writing in their diaries, composing letters, and copying song lyrics into their notebooks.

Thus, private and personal writing, such as diary and letter-writing, can be carried out at the same time as teacher-assigned writing is supposed to be taking place, because superficially it looks the same to the teacher.[35]

Camitta argues for validating adolescent vernacular writing and for recognizing adolescent writers as experts within given literate communities. She analyzes and codifies her students' creations as "patchwork" and "mosaic" compositions appropriating, in part or whole, previously written, recorded, or heard texts in order to recreate an additional text.[36] Students use patches, or samples, both to convey meaning and as status markers of cultural capital. Examples of verbal samples include words, rhythms, and rhymes connoting life in "da hood."[37] Current adolescent slang evolves quickly with popular culture, and meanings change. I usually know what most street slang means, and ask for clarification if I don't. For example, I recently learned the meaning of "bitch made."[38]

Critical teaching demands teachers listen to students, even if their responses are unnerving and irreverent. Current vernacular connotes unsavory themes such as violence against women, but must be interrogated rather than ignored. This is not to say that students should not learn "standard" English needed for scholastic and vocational endeavors, or that offensive language should go unchallenged, but if teachers ask them to code switch from slang to standard English, teachers should as well; that is, using slang in class to make a point, but then translating.

Here is a poem written by a Corner Campus student that conveys the ubiquity and power of current Californian urban vernacular, with translations in parentheses.

*Crazy*

It was a hot sunny day

I was like parlayin (speaking or acting with confidence)

In the muthafuckin' Bay (slang used for emphasis)

About to get sideways (stoned)

to the summer jam. (outdoor concert with several hip-hop bands)

rippin up the mic (rapping or singing smoothly)

wit something tight (lyrics are strong and marketable)

That hit and slam. (and powerful and danceable)

So we hit the high way (unsure if high means on dope . . .)

puffin' on a Phillie (smoking a cigar . . .)

stuffed wit some bomb (with marijuana inside)

That'll have yo ass goin crazy.

## VERNACULAR AS "ALL THAT AND A BUCKET O' CHICKEN"

In current urban vernacular, the expression "all that" is a superlative term for success, proficiency, confidence, or arrogance. It is most often used in the second or third person; for example, "He was all that," or "You thinking you all that." *All that and a bucket o' chicken* is from a play written by a female high school student at the Campus. The phrase in its original context—a dialogue between two female characters—describes a girl's feelings toward a male date, specifically: "He was thinking he was all that and a bucket o' chicken." Translated from vernacular, it means that the girl speaking was quite critical of the boy's arrogance, hence the "He was thinking" preface. Without the preface however, it connotes praise rather than criticism; that is, "You *think* you are special, don't you?" versus "You *are* special."

When the student read her play aloud, the dialogue received laughter and affirmation—similar to an Amen! response. Students praised the playwright for her poignant vernacular usage and for its dialogical context within the story. The female protagonist was out with a man—who thought he was "all that"—and she reported on his cockiness. In one sentence, the writer encapsulated female disempowerment within current urban vernacular. The play was one of several narratives read that day, all written by girls and all depicting rape or murder of young women. The plays were profane, sexually explicit and validated substance use among teens—that is, drinkin' forties and smokin' weed as part of a cool party scene—but also represented hard work such as composing, editing, typing, and performing. In this example, students engaged in literate behaviors demonstrating diligence, perseverance, and courage by reading their prose aloud, but with behaviors and dialogue outside the curricular canon.

The ability of the Campus to go outside "canons" is one of its strengths. Teachers do not use work sheets or many formal textbooks, and encourage students and parents to help plan curriculum. Such openness to student opinion and input yields greater student investment.

## HIP-HOP CORNER: RAP, DAP, AND MAKIN' DUCKETS[39]

Many Corner Campus students come from tough urban neighborhoods, and are encouraged to make sense of their world through schoolwork. For students in rough neighborhoods, respect is often hard-won, and backing down from challenges, whether from teachers or not, is not an option. Saving face far outweighs deferring to authority.[40] Saving student face in urban secondary schools means listening to their stories and language and challenging them to learn school codes as well as street codes. A first step, however, is providing accessible avenues for student participation, such as incorporating rap music into language arts curricula to increase student engagement.

Rap music applies to language arts curricula on several levels: as poetry, where students compose and edit original raps, or analyze previously recorded raps; as resistance commentary, where students discuss and hypothesize about information and messages within the music;[41] and as dialogic teaching and learning, in which students consciously make sense of their world in order to read "the word."[42] Unfortunately, much hip-hop, or rap music elucidates a violent and difficult world. Recent media hype about gangsta rap focused on its anti-establishment lyrics, irreverence, and espousal of drugs, and misogyny. The question is whether artists can ever abridge their first amendment right to free speech, even if their lyrics incite others to act destructively. The rap group *2 Live Crew* won a lawsuit several years ago, after their album *As Nasty as They Wanna Be* was pulled from record store shelves. Most current hip-hop fans don't follow the legal history much; they do, however, listen to and repeat lyrics and themes from current songs and artists. The dilemma for educators is how to incorporate salient themes without promoting or validating negativity or even nihilism.

For example, a recent hit single, *I Got Five on It*, sounds softer and more harmonious than most gangsta rap, and does not espouse violence. It does, however, romanticize the act of splitting a dime bag ($10) of weed from a corner drug dealer. I believe that teachers can frame discussions and analyses around generative themes and genres from students' lives, but we must be ready for difficult dialogue.[43] I have a problem with the proliferation of misogynist lyrics in hip-hop, but I want to hear what my students think and hear when interacting with this medium. In short, I am far less affected by "thug life"[44] than my students. It is in their struggle with this text and with their current reality, that critical thinking can emerge; unlike much standardized curricula, hip-hop media is something popular.

In one classroom, student essays about this lifestyle line the walls. Some essays embrace the lifestyle, others warn to stay off drugs and crack "rocks." The Corner Campus deals with students' experiences proactively, by validating students' voices and experiences, even if they are profane, violent, or otherwise controversial.

## THE CORNER CAMPUS: A CASE STUDY
## IN STUDENT-CENTERED PEDAGOGY

At the Corner Campus, teachers make concerted efforts to "hook" students into school, and to make curricula exciting and relevant to students' lives. In an English class, a teacher solicits generative themes for study from her students; in a history class, the teacher allows students to work together to raise a collective quiz grade; and in a political economy class, a student blames the teacher for passive discussion management and specifies that he would have learned more in class had the facilitation been better.[45] In these three examples, teachers shared their power and control over students to increase student involvement and investment. Whether through thematic choice, teacher criticism, or grading negotiation, the Corner Campus students are encouraged and expected to engage and determine their educational activities.

Such encouragement is one component of critical pedagogical practice—others found at the Campus include dialogic teaching, exposure of societal inequalities, and promotion praxis—reflection and action upon the world in order to change it.[46] This chapter examined salient student issues at a school that employs critical pedagogical practice amid abject nihilist threats. That is, the Campus attempts to hook students' into school by giving them more attention and voice than they would receive in a school five times as large. Most importantly, the school doesn't ask its students to leave problems outside, but rather to critically interrogate them inside. This method may not eliminate threats of violence and drug use, but it doesn't repress them either.

I offered student work samples to illustrate nihilist threats facing students outside school in terms of violence and drug use, but I wish to emphasize that Campus students face difficult situations but usually make the choice to attend school and participate. They persevere within a school that engenders agency and hope, and many do obtain a diploma. For those that do, half choose to attend college. Those that do not face a plethora of futures ranging from entrepreneurship to incarceration. While teachers compel students to stay in school—they can leave legally at sixteen—and get a diploma, many simply cannot or do not make the time. Corner Campus staff work hard to make school worthy of their students' time. Sometimes, however, for varied reasons, they lose students. Still they retain a collective consciousness of hope. Their actions and pedagogies embody their belief that despite it all, Corner Campus students are "all that."

Can student nihilism—loss of hope and absence of meaning—be combatted with critical pedagogy? If student attitudes like "you can't do anything about anything" permeate schools and promote apathy, can teachers reach them anyway? Amid a violent and drug infested urban America, can a small school succeed? After working at the Corner Campus for almost a year, I answer all three questions with cautious optimism. The battle against nihilism and apathy rages in a small alternative high school in California.

## APPENDIX: HOW I LANDED AT THE CAMPUS

I met several Campus teachers and students when they visited one of my doctoral classes. After having an encouraging conversation with one of the visiting teachers, I lined up an interview with the principal. She told me to come to the next staff meeting: if the staff liked me and okayed my involvement there, I could return and if not we couldn't work together.

I chose this site for my research in part because of that screening: to me it shows good judgment, particularly about a full-time graduate student who may extract data and leave. The staff is very tight, and with only nine teachers and two administrators, they work and choose researchers collectively. When I told the principal I taught special education, she told me the school had no special ed kids. That the school eschewed labels attracted me.

For the interview I prepared a one-page list of my interests and experience and schooling, and defended it and myself to a room of committed teachers. After a twenty-minute group interview, I was thanked and told to call back. Thus began a relationship that continues as of this writing. I observed and took notes in classrooms, particularly the two language arts classrooms, for two hours a week for three months. I then began teaching an after school writing workshop two hours a week with ninth and tenth graders. The students receive half the credit of a regular language arts class. Those low in credits or skills are encouraged to take my workshop, but enrollment is voluntary, so I try to make it worth their time. During my first quarter, two of fifteen students were expelled, one eloped and dropped out, and one dropped my class. Eleven others received high school credit.

## NOTES

1. Cornel West, *Race Matters* (New York: Vintage Press, 1993), pp. 22–23.

2. For analyses of how street culture differs from and affects schools and classrooms, see Elijah Anderson, "The Code of the Streets," *The Atlantic Monthly*, May 1994, pp. 81–94; Lawrence Baines, "Fistfights, Guns, and the Art of Teaching English," *English Journal* 84 (September 1995): 59–64.

3. For recent work regarding the ostracization of "tough-to-teach" students, see Lisa Delpit, *Other People's Children: Cultural Conflict in the Classroom* (New York: The New Press, 1995), and Jonathan Kozol, *Savage Inequalities* (New York: HarperPerennial, 1991).

4. For a theoretical explanation of dialogic teaching, see Ira Shor and Paulo Freire, *A Pedagogy for Liberation: Dialogues on Transforming Education* (New York: Bergin & Garvey, 1987).

5. Though the school is legally required to report intimations of violence or crime, students are not discouraged from revealing other illicit realities, such as the need to deal drugs to help support their family.

6. Full effect = thriving in life. This and all subsequent slang translations

emanate from clarifying conversations I had with students, as well as from listening to current radio and reading current hip-hop publications.

7. The counselor was not on staff during the writing of this chapter, because funding could not be found to continue her position. Since I wrote this chapter, I have begun a young men's group, analogous to LIFE.

8. A full explication of the pedagogical implications of this term is superfluous here; in this instance it refers to fighting, not following directions, talking back to teachers, or being loud in class.

9. Parole/probation officer.

10. In this chapter I do not deal explicitly with students' family background, race, ethnicity, previous or current gang affiliation, religious faith, self-esteem, and so on. That is, I address the students, vis-à-vis the issues they brought to my workshop, rather than try to correlate student behaviors with demographic variables.

11. Shor and Freire, A Pedagogy for Liberation.

12. Praxis-reflection and action upon the world. Paulo Freire, Pedagogy of the Oppressed (New York: Herder and Herder, 1970).

13. Paulo Freire and Donaldo Macedo, Literacy: Reading the Word and the World (New York: Bergin & Garvey, 1987).

14. Shor and Freire, A Pedagogy of Liberation.

15. Shirley Brice Heath and Leslie Mangiola, Children of Promise: Literate Activity in Linguistically and Culturally Diverse Classrooms (Washington, D.C.: National Education Association, 1991).

16. Freire and Macedo, Literacy.

17. Jim Cummins, "Empowering Minority Students: A Framework for Intervention," in Transforming Urban Education, ed. J. Kretovics and E. J. Nussel (pp. 327–46) (Boston: Allyn and Bacon, 1986). For a description of critical pedagogy in practice, at the university level, see bell hooks, Teaching to Transgress: Education as the Practice of Freedom (New York: Routledge, 1994).

18. Ibid.

19. It means "you need new lines, you're just copying my insults."

20. See, for example, Henry Giroux, "Doing Cultural Studies: Youth and the Challenge of Pedagogy," Harvard Educational Review 64 (Summer 1994): 278–308.

21. Henry Giroux, Teachers as Intellectuals: Toward a Critical Pedagogy of Learning (Granby, Mass.: Bergin & Garvey, 1988).

22. Stephen O'Connor, "Problems Schools Can't Solve," The New York Times, March 26, 1996, p. A19.

23. Giroux, "Doing Cultural Studies," pp. 292–93.

24. Pedro Noguera, "Preventing and Producing Violence: A Critical Analysis of Responses to School Violence," Harvard Educational Review 65 (Summer 1995): 189–212.

25. J. Alleyne Johnson, "Life after Death: Critical Pedagogy in an Urban Classroom," Harvard Educational Review 65 (Summer 1995): 213–30.

26. N. Hudson, "The Violence of Their Lives: The Journal Writing of Two High School Freshmen, English Journal 84 (Spring 1995): 65–69.

27. Hooks, *Teaching to Transgress*.

28. Louanne Johnson, *My Posse Don't Do Homework* (New York: St Martin's Press, 1992).

29. Anderson, "Code of the Streets."

30. Hooks, *Teaching to Transgress*; Johnson, "Life after Death."

31. Bomb means potent marijuana.

32. Delpit, *Other People's Children*.

33. The campus now has a part-time counselor who takes up these types of issues with students; during this research, however, her position was not funded and is thus not included.

34. Susan Katz Weinberg, "Where the Streets Cross the Classroom: A Study of Latino Students' Perspectives on Cultural Identity in City Schools and Neighborhood Gangs," paper presented at the annual meeting of the American Educational Research Association, San Francisco, March 1995.

35. Miriam Camitta, "Vernacular Writing: Varieties of Literacy among Philadelphia High School Students," in *Cross-Cultural Approaches to Literacy*, ed. B. Street (pp. 228–46) (Cambridge: Cambridge University Press, 1993), p. 233.

36. A current application of patchwork and mosaic techniques can be seen in hip-hop culture. Radio and dance DJs often "mix" a song with another, or personally add verses or emphases during appropriate "beats" and "breaks." In addition, the art of sampling, or appropriating previously recorded songs, verses, or sounds in order to recreate and record new music, has grown increasingly popular over the last decade. Tricia Rose, *Black Noise: Rap Music and Black Culture in Contemporary America* (Hanover, N.H.: Wesleyan University Press, 1994).

37. Rose, *Black Noise*.

38. While I abhor the term "bitch" as derogatory to women, it remains pervasive in hip-hop culture. I thought it meant a man whose success is due to a female presence, but it refers to someone weak and phony.

39. Dap means respect; duckets, a different spelling of ducats (old European coins), means money.

40. Anderson, "Code of the Streets."

41. An example would be the rap group Public Enemy as the self-proclaimed "Black CNN." In effect, many students get their "information" from sources outside school and it behooves teachers to be aware of what and who their students listen to.

42. Macedo and Freire, *Literacy*.

43. Macedo and Freire, *Literacy*.

44. Thug life can be loosely described, at least since the 1980s, as a lifestyle of hustling, violence, and often illegal activity, underscored by the need to be tough and to be feared. For the purposes of this paper, the pertinence lies in the identification many students feel with popular artists, usually rappers, who personify and promote thug life.

45. The student felt frustrated that the pace could not be quicker, and criticized his peers for not reading more, and faster.

46. Freire, *Pedagogy of the Oppressed*; Shor and Freire, *A Pedagogy of Liberation*.

# PART III

# In Conclusion: Reflections on the Dilemmas of Urban Education Reform

CHAPTER 10

# Gaps, Bridges, and Buffers in the Research, Policy, and Practice of Urban Education: A Dialogue

## Theodore R. Mitchell, Carlos Alberto Torres, and Karen A. McClafferty

Hope is the companion of power, and mother of success, for who so hopes strongly has within him the gift of miracles.
—Samuel Smiles

CARLOS TORRES (CT). Let me start by asking you, from the perspective of an educational reformer like yourself, what do you think we need to address in dealing with policy and practice in urban education?

TED MITCHELL (TM). I think that we fool ourselves when we think that the problems of urban education can be solved at a structural level or at a policy level. We direct a lot of attention and energy there. But that's really just superstructural, epiphenomena. The real issues and problems in urban education are issues of race and class and power. And those play themselves out by creating a context of hopelessness. First for kids and parents, particularly kids and parents of color, the underclass who feel powerless. Translates into hopelessness. That hopelessness is also a feature of the environment in which many kids find themselves in urban schools. And while many teachers of kids in urban areas are themselves very hopeful of their futures and have gone into the profession precisely to interrupt the destiny of kids who come from environments of powerlessness and hopelessness, after a time it becomes very difficult to keep that hope alive as a professional working in schools. And that hopelessness moves up the system and really begins to infect the structure and the processes of urban schools. So I think that while structure and policy are important, you can't really change the fundamental modes of living and of the development of the psychology of learning, unless you begin to address and have honest conversations about what it means to work in an environment in which most kids don't have hope.

CT. Now, if this nihilism—which is really the counterpart of hopelessness—is so pervasive, I presume it affects not only parents and children in those conditions, but also the teachers that work with them and the overall structure of urban education, including the administrators who face this nihilism everyday. Yet an element of professionalism in teachers and administrators is, sometimes, to address this nihilism and hopelessness by figuring out some technical remedies that could be implemented and hopefully will do some good. In your experience in Los Angeles, have you seen a strategy of purposive, rational, instrumental reason in implementing technical remedies to solve the problems of urban education?

TM. I think that's a very good question. Yes. I think that the issue of technical remedies has a positive and negative side. And the negative side, I think that technical expertise can sometimes mask a variety of different conflicts and contradictions. So some of the technical fixes for schools in Los Angeles and elsewhere have masked fundamentally underlying problems. This very comforting mantra, that is actually a technical mantra, that all children can learn, is on the one hand quite liberating because it says that children from all backgrounds can learn, but if has an underside that is pointed at the children that says that "You can learn," that doesn't take into account the child's context. So a less technocratic mantra might be, "All children can learn and all children come from backgrounds that compromise their ability to learn in a variety of ways." But I would argue that that's true for affluent kids too, but that gets us off track.

I think that there are some very positive elements to some of the technical solutions that have been in place in Los Angeles, and those have two features: I think in an environment of hopelessness, almost any new idea can be the cause for hope. And so there is, in the organizational, sociological perspective, there is sort of a Hawthorne effect at work in almost any technical reform, that it gives people something to pin the remnants of hope to. And this is going to sound nihilistic in a different way, but in some senses, it doesn't matter what the technical fix is. Just so long as there is a flow of potential technical fixes so that teachers and other professionals can hope that by reorienting their practice, they can achieve a result. And they do, for a short period of time. But those technical fixes that don't get at the root issues of race and class and power aren't ever going to change the structure or the process or the experience of education for those kids. Now, I balance the two poles—the positive that I think I've underplayed and the negative that I may have overplayed. I think that there have been some very positive technical fixes in education in Los Angeles having to do with the reengagement of community with schools. And so the decentralization of some elements of school authority from the central district office to the school community engages parents, engages students, engages some small businesses that may literally surround the school. If the project of making the school a better place for kids, for teachers, a more open place for families and communities—that technical fix has had a profound impact because it has reengaged communities with the schools. It has reengaged, in some senses, parents with their children. And that's had a very powerful effect. And I think a positive effect on schooling in Los Angeles.

CT. And this constructive engagement, it refers to a number of options that would be, one of them, charter schools, perhaps there is some discussion of vouchers, there is also discussion of the partition of the district that is too large and unmanageable, limiting those who are accountable in the educational bureaucracy. But I presume there are some discussions on standards for the schools, standards for learning by students, standards for a knowledge floor for the society, standards for teachers, and I presume there must be some connection of this discussion with the role of universities. Could you comment on all of these issues?

TM. I think that you rightly point out the decentralization comes in a variety of flavors. And those are not merely preferences. They're deeply ideologically rooted. And vouchers, as an example, are not about connecting communities with schools or the educational process. Vouchers are about utilizing, submitting education to the logic of the market. Magnet schools are ideologically rooted to the notion that a superordinate goal—focusing on arts, focusing on science—will sweep aside questions of race and class and power, and bring people together on footing of equal interest. And that too is ideologically rooted. Charters are somewhat in between and I think more communitarian in their focus than either of the other two, really coming out of movements, some of them, religious movements in which groups of parents wanted to create schools that matched their own political or social or religious or educational philosophy or ideology. But they are all brought together by the notion that the large urban bureaucracy does not serve the children. And that can be partitioned in any way. The jury on the research is still out on whether these schools are (*a*) effective for the children who attend them and (*b*) whether they are effective in creating environments of increased equity, increased social mobility, increased understanding of difference. The jury, as I say, is out on that.

And so the question about connections to the university is that they could have a profound one at this moment when there are a variety of natural experiments going on in urban education. Natural experiments going on in Los Angeles. What is the educational experience of kids in charter schools as differentiated from kids in the "normal" public school? How do these different variants of decentralization effect issues of equity? And does choice really empower parents? And does competition between these varieties of schooling really raise the level of performance? All of these are fundamental research questions, and I think that it is incumbent on universities, particularly those like us who are deeply embedded in the context of an urban school system, to be doing the research from which we can know as a people about the differential effect of these educational movements. At a different level I think that it's quite critical that we connect with the profession of teaching, the profession of administration in urban schools so that we can be about the project of helping to build hope, helping to maintain hope, to improve the craft and learn from our colleagues in urban schools, so that in turn our training programs can be more effective in providing people the experiences they need to enter into the profession in the challenging environment of urban schools.

KAREN McCLAFFERTY (KM). It really sounds like you were saying that universities should have almost an inquisitive role and a responsive role, and not at all a prescriptive role. Would you agree with that statement?

TM. I think it's a fine balance. I think that over the last fifty years, one of the university's problems has been its prescriptive relationship with public schools. And in particular, its prescriptive relationship with urban schools. For the most part, the environments in which we teach and work aren't the same or even similar to the environments in which most of the teachers in urban schools work. And yet we have been free—too free—to tell teachers in urban schools how to go about doing their business. And so while I think we certainly have things to say *to* teachers in urban schools, and a perspective and a distance that could be valuable to them, I think we have to have a fundamentally inquisitive cast to our relationship with public school teachers, in which we help them interrogate their circumstances and use our distance and perspective to ask questions and then reflect back on research answers in a way that can be useful to them in their craft.

CT. What about standards—the whole discussion about standards?

TM. You're right, and I apologize for missing the whole theme. It was a Freudian slip. One of the things that we do know—and this could probably even tie in—one of the things that we do know from the research that has been done on these decentralized programs as they've occurred around the country is that equity is most seriously at risk when there are not standards that are uniform across the schools for inputs like resources, like teacher quality, like teacher background. And for outcomes—and I know that that's a loaded term—but outcomes in terms of standards to which students should aspire and standards for which schools should prepare students. I'll give you a great example. The University of California has a very prescribed set of admissions requirements—A through F requirements, they're called. They deal with the number of units that students must take in mathematics and social sciences and language to be eligible for admission to the University of California. There are schools in the state of California where it is impossible to move to the university because they don't offer the full range of A through F courses. That's the kind of standard that needs to be maintained throughout the state, throughout the city of Los Angeles, so that students who are engaged in a charter school in one area or a magnet school in the other can still be assured of opportunities afterwards that are even across the board. And so that kind of standard setting is critical to the success of any school system, but particularly to a school system that is more open to variation, more open to decentralization, more open to local control and to family choice.

CT. There is one question that emerges naturally out of the combination of your point that the problems with urban education are based on conflicts around race, class, and power.

KM. And I would add gender which, although it raises a different set of issues, certainly cannot be separated from a discussion of power.

CT. I would agree with Karen's point: Conflicts around class, race, and gender all have differential implications in terms of the relationship between education and power. Yet the alternative is that when we provide standards—argue some scholars and practitioners—we are providing a level playing field in which everybody could measure up to the same situation. But if the inequities are pervasive in terms of race, class, gender and power, are the standards—by definition—going to equalize or make the level playing field even more complicated?

TM. I think that the standards—equal standards with unequal resource allocation condemn the same people who have always been underserved by the educational system, to being underserved in the future. And that's where I think we often in policy terms have the most difficulty with the standards debate. And it's certainly where we have the most difficulty with resource allocations. And I think that we have to, at that point, recall why it is that we have public education in this country. Public education has been miscast in the last several decades as a private good. It's been miscast as an avenue for individual mobility, whereas in fact, historically, it's quite clear that education—public education—in this country is designed for public purposes. And it's designed, as our friend Horace Mann said long ago, to balance the balanced wheel of society. And from that perspective, an unequal investment in those who have been underserved by the educational system is quite consistent with the American view, the historical view of what the public school is and should do. David Labaree's new book—*How to Succeed in School without Really Learning* (1997)—is a great examination of this idea of the increasing privatization of the notion of public schools. And I think that when we look at urban education policy, we get stuck at this very point, of whether the schools exist to serve the public or whether the schools exist to serve the individual and private needs of those students who attend them.

KM. We've tentatively titled this chapter "Gaps, Bridges and Buffers in the Research, Policy and Practice of Urban Education." Do you see those bridges and buffers and gaps as changing?

TM. It's interesting. And I think my comments on the role of the university were my shorthand description of the ideal state. And I think that between where we are and that ideal state, there are many gaps. There are incredible buffers, and there are few bridges. And I think that one of the things we have to be about in schools of education in urban universities is creating bridges. And some of those bridges need to be between practicing professionals in urban schools and the schools of education, where they become our colleagues in this inquisitiveness. And do teacher-driven research that we can help them do because we have the research infrastructure and we can build the sense of colleagueship. At the same time I think it's important for schools of education to build bridges back the other way to the disciplines in the colleges of letters and sciences, where the renewal of those fields—I'm thinking of my own field of history, for example—the renewal of the field of history in the last twenty years has been dramatic, and has been quite powerful, and I would argue potent for the urban schoolteacher. But the buffers are quite high between the historians at a place like UCLA and the history teacher at Jefferson High School in Los Angeles. And so if we can build sort of the two-tiered bridge—one between us and practice and the other between us and discipline fields—I think we'll be able to achieve a much smoother transition of knowledge and of questions. So I think that there's much to be done, there are sociological buffers in terms of the hierarchy of the profession that for too long teachers and professors have been put apart by the perceived hierarchy between what we do in the university and what teachers do, and that creates an enormous boundary between the two practices. Let's be honest. The style of work is very, very different.

CT. We could have started this conversation arguing back and forth on how deep the problems of urban schools are vis-à-vis suburban schools or rural schools. Is there any problem that you find pervasive throughout urban, suburban and rural schools, particularly in the United States?

TM. I would argue that issues of race and class and power and gender permeate all of our social institutions. And schools happen to be particularly poignant places for the expression of those contradictions and those conflicts. So I would say that those run through all of the schools. But, to put a slightly more professional cast to it, I think that teachers in all of those schools suffer from similar isolation from each other, from the ideas of their fields and from the practitioners research—whether it's pedagogic research or discipline field-oriented research. And I think that one of the things that we can do in the university is to break down that sense of isolation. And it's one of the few places where I see an automatic improvement in the quality of life that can be attributed to technology. That the new technologies do provide us with an opportunity to break down distance, to break down the sense of isolation. To create communities, virtual communities around areas of inquiry that can help teachers and help faculty and help students. But I distrust the impetus to create educational software for kids in classrooms. And trust much more the communication potential of the new technology.

KM. I have such concerns about having faith in technology, which seems to be so unevenly distributed—whether it's rural versus urban or lower-income areas versus higher-income areas. It's not something that everyone has access to.

TM. That's where I would draw a quick distinction between the utility of technology for kids and the utility of technology for teachers. And I think your question has in it a very, very correct assessment that if we depend on technology we will essentially again be advantaging those who are advantaged and disadvantaging those who have always been underserved. And so the application of technology in any type of equal sense to that diverse population is going to increase rather than decrease the disparity and outcomes. I think that it's less of a problem for teachers, but I don't want to extrapolate from our sample, but when we sample the student teachers to our program at UCLA, probably only four or five in a given year don't have access to a personal computer of the type that would be required to exchange email with colleagues. And I've long been a proponent of, for UCLA, to require student teachers to have computers. If we require computers, then we're able to include the price of the computer when we compute financial aid packages. In a counterintuitive way, by requiring the computers, we are advantaging those who otherwise wouldn't be able to afford them. But I think that the root issue is we have to worry very much about all attempted technological solutions. And we have to worry about the disparity of access and we have to, at the same time, think about a technological solution, think about a permanent solution to how to erase the lack of access that certain teachers, certain students, certain families have to the technology that's necessary.

CT. That's very interesting. I posed the question on the similarities across the board because one of my perceptions for the need of a sense of renewal is that we lack the notion of a social movement that could propel the schools to fall into line with emerging democratic social utopias, rather than living in this kind of a game of never-ending mirrors, as you were describing in the beginning. And a social utopia that could have been developed in universities as happened in the thirties and forties with reformers of the quality of John Dewey that we all quote so often. What we don't have across the board is this sense of perpetual stimuli because we don't have the social movements. Perhaps we have even seen a decline in social movements.

I just published a book on Paulo Freire, social movements and educational reform in São Paulo entitled *Education and Democracy*. I am impressed with how, using this very simple and straightforward political and pedagogical methodology of having the schools as a unit looking at the community and the needs of the community and building the curriculum around the perceived generative themes of the community, this project of educational reform in itself becomes a social movement. So the interesting thing about the Freire project and São Paulo experience almost seven years ago was that it started with the premise that the new administration would have a strong political view—it was a social democratic administration—that they will take advantage of the social movements to pursue their own policy agenda. They will take advantage of the progressive teaching in the university to link that with the schools, even in the context of a highly bureaucratic municipal system of education. So that was the premise. But the moment that it moved into having the school as the center of attention, that the school would connect with the community to figure out what the needs are, that moment a social movement that was school-based was created.

So you could have a problem in the school like, say, garbage. So garbage was used as the problem in health sciences, very much so, appropriately so. And the students begin to study the implication of garbage dumped in their neighborhoods for their health. But also it was used for writing essays in language courses. It could be used to figure out ways to deal with mathematics in the school. So the teachers got very much caught up with this thing. The administrators in the municipal system liked the model and they were supporting the model. And of course progressive educators in the university jumped in and said, "I was looking for this all my life!" In a way, what was supposed to be, just to how use or take advantage of the social movements—which were quite prevalent at the time in São Paulo—to infuse the school with a new life, the social movement actually took place in the schools. I see neither the social movements propelling the schools into the kind of social reconstructionism approach like in the thirties, nor the social movements beyond the premise of decentralization that could be part of a much greater democratic accord. But I don't see really social movements fighting for issues of equality in the schools or issues of class, race, gender as we were discussing. So, I may be wrong because you are more connected with the current practices in schools than perhaps I am, but what is your sense in terms of social movements impacting school reform?

TM. I think that you're right, that we haven't had a sense of social movement in education since probably the sixties. And we think about the sixties as a period of activism at college campuses and we think that the great book has yet to be written about the social movements of the time. And I think a part of it has to do with this fragmentation and isolation of teachers who don't have those mechanisms to communicate with each other, don't do it well and are under incredible pressure to just sort of do their work. Second is that I think the fact that the decentralization movement has had this cast of being about individual benefit rather than collective benefit has just put the debate about schools into a box that focuses on individual test scores or test scores in schools. Look at the superintendent in Los Angeles who did a very brave thing in identifying the hundred lowest performing schools. But look at the terms in which he expressed the lowest hundred performing schools. They were test scores. And so again the frame of the debate is very instrumental and it's very difficult without significant leadership to generate a social movement that is not just against the specifics, but against the whole frame of an issue. It says, no, no, we're looking at the wrong target. And I think that universities can be faulted for that. That we have not stood up as we should and say the issues aren't simply about student accomplishment or on one or another test score. The issue is about the social purpose of education. And there I think we can lend, not just support for, but leadership to voices in the public schools. Many, many teachers, and obviously many parents want something very different out of the educational experience. The Freirean notion of schools as communities and as a part of communities is, as you say, very generative and very powerful. And there are isolated experiments going on in Los Angeles and elsewhere. One of my favorites was actually in rural Vermont, where the same kind of education took place, as it turns out, around garbage and waste. And if you can measure it, if you can write about it, if you can find out where it came from, and if you can develop ways of thinking about it artistically, you have an entire curriculum.

CT. But of course you cannot have the standards across the board because every curriculum is tailor-made to a particular school.

TM. On the other hand, you can have sophisticated standards at the other end that say, "Do children know how to solve problems? Can they take data and draw inferences from the data and come up with hypotheses?" And if we could develop those kinds of standards about what kids know how to do at the end, then each approach could vary according to the community and appropriate context could be measured at the end to make sure that students have learned about certain things and how to do certain things. But I think, going back to the notion of social movements, I think you've hit exactly on what is lacking in urban education and the kind of approach that would get us to the fundamental issues of race and class and gender and power that we're unable to address as long as we tinker at the policy level without a real core agreement on what schools are for. That's what I see social movements as doing. They're very different from policy talk. Social movements really start with a serious perspective on how things should be and why. And policy talk too easily gets turned by attractive technical solutions.

CT. Precisely. New social movements—like the civil rights movements— they start out of a gesture of moral outrage. And it works because rather than pursuing a particular specific narrow interest, it essentially looks at the role of welfare of a large number of people. I think one of the sadnesses of my experience as a professor in a university of this caliber in the state of California is to understand that the school, the university itself, has become a marionette, has become the subject of a political game. And therefore we have witnessed in the last seven years an assault on affirmative action. We have witnessed a very serious criticism on immigration policies and the life of immigrants. We have witnessed attempts to manipulate very sensitive issues for specific and narrow-minded goals of specific individuals to promote their political careers. So in a way, the most important decisions being made in education in the last seven years were neither connected with learning per se, nor connected with responses to the moral commitments of social movements, but rather the outcome of the specific goals of the specific individuals promoting specific political ideologies of the Right. I will take this as a very sad note.

TM. I would agree with your assessment of the political environment in which universities find themselves. And it's a terrible Hobson's Choice for universities because the ancient agreement that none of us signed on to was that academic freedom was fine as long as academic findings effected the world only in the very long run. And so the more we try to move our work into the world and to have it be a part of the discussions of policy or leadership of social movements, the more we open ourselves up to the curtailment of traditional freedoms by those who say "You're not playing by the rules. Think what you want, but don't act on it." And I think that it's that narrow fine line that universities find themselves on institutionally, and all of us find ourselves on personally. The question—and this may or may not be relevant for the chapter—but the question of whether I should sit for the interview that was in the *LA Times* was something the *Times* and I went back and forth on for two months because of just this word—What can I say, in the opinion section of the *Los Angeles Times,* that will not compromise my colleagues' ability to do their work in an unfettered way in an environment in which institutions are punished for the defensible or indefensible articulations of their members? And I think it puts us all in a very difficult position when we try to act on not only our beliefs but the research that we've done and the actual product of our scholarly activity.

CT. Let me just pose one more question. Coming back to standards, and thinking of the school of education nested in a university of this caliber, and your comments on standards that are applied unfairly to the school of education, the question is what is the role of a school of education in urban environments? The point is that schools of education do a lot of research and teaching similar to what colleges of letters and sciences do. In addition to that, there is a lot of activity, particularly within methods, that is tailor-made to education, to people who teach teachers with a particular learning approach. To people who really go into the communities and try and figure out ways to do educational work and the appropriate pedagogy and so on. In the case of those professors who resemble more what the College of Letters and Sciences do, it is easier to justify their contributions to university scholarship than in the case of those who are in the trenches seeking practical implementation models of teaching, organization, or administration. Then we are faced with a fascinating dilemma. The training of people who are similar to the Letters and Sciences may not be as controversial as training people who will work on the intervention side. Now, if you are an assistant professor, you don't want to be caught in a debate with evaluators who have said that your research is not the quality or the standard, your research has not had the same impact and support. So we have this dilemma that many people feel that when you're an assistant professor you have to conform to the norm mostly to survive and get tenure. When you get tenure, then you get into another process of complex internal co-optation through which all sort of rewards are given, so you proceed to really reproduce yourself again, and this time going for full professor. By the time you are full professor, which probably will be in your mid to late forties, a lot of the energy that you brought as an assistant professor or an associate professor is not wasted or gone, but is not the same energy. Your status in the profession has changed and therefore you don't have to struggle so much to write the right article to be published in peer review. But you have all sorts of limitations and therefore the challenge changes. And eventually for many the connection with the community becomes more and more remote. But of course it's easier for people to evaluate you around the same standards that everybody else evaluates people in universities, when schools of education do quite different work. By the time you are a very prominent member of the profession, you may have all the freedom in the world to do all the sort of things you want connected with the community, connected with the schools, but very rarely do you use it. Because there is a sense of self-fulfilling prophecy: If you get to that point, just keep doing exactly what you were doing before because the academic rewards don't change. As dean of a school of education, as a concerned reformer in urban education, as somebody who started this interview looking at the issue of nihilism, looking at the issue of the loneliness of utopia in the schools, what kind of answer do you have for that scholarly dilemma.

TM. Go into physics. I got more and more depressed as your question went on. Both remembering what it was like to be an assistant professor and thinking how true this dilemma is.

CT. I posed it in a very Weberian fashion, using an ideal type of the professoriate which is a total exaggeration of reality in order to understand reality. I may not totally agree with what I have just said, but I want to elicit your analysis of this issue of differential academic standards and rewards for a professional school like the school of education, which, almost by definition, is closer to answer the needs and demands of concrete communities than perhaps any other unit on campus.

TM. And in the best Weberian sense, it has enough connection to reality to draw from that experience the poignant elements. I think that education isn't just another discipline. It's not like biochemistry which is both the hybrid of and an advance upon two very strong fundamental disciplines—biology and chemistry. Education is that, where one might draw on political science and philosophy as you have done, Carlos. Or history and economics as I have done. And do enough real history and economics to be credible in those fields and to build on them and do something else when thinking about schools of education. But education is also a professional school in most of the places it's practiced. And certainly in the larger settings, education takes place in professional schools, where part of our responsibility as scholars is to figure out how to take our accomplishments in a pure research environment and translate them into practice. And I think we made a mistake in thinking about that, even for assistant professors, as a luxury, as something that one does after one has published the half dozen peer review articles per year. And one of the things that I tried to do as dean is to build that in as a fundamental requirement, to make those translations while the research is being done, rather than thinking of it as an afterthought or part of public service. And, in our own school, discourse is always critical. And a part of our school's promotion process is to divide the writing of one's record into scholarly activity, teaching, and service. And my push for the time I've been here is to include the work that people do as teachers in the scholarly activity portion of the write-up, rather than in the community service part of the write-up. Because to put it in community service puts it in the same category as serving on the buildings and grounds committee. And if it is that, then it will never be an important and core part of what we do.

Now that sounds good. But in reality, the problem with that strategy is that it simply adds to the responsibilities of the junior faculty member. It doesn't substitute. And so the problem that we're having—and I'll be the first to say that we haven't found our way through these things yet—the problem that we're having is that having accomplished the former, adding these contributions to what we expect in scholarly activity, we have not yet figured out how to reduce or even change what we think of as scholarly accomplishment in the area of peer review articles, in the area of grant production, and in the typical measures, the typical standards of scholarly output. And so I think we, at UCLA, and if my conversations with my fellow deans are any indication, we're all in these first-rate schools of education in urban areas, struggling with exactly this same problem of how to define scholarship in a way that doesn't dilute the rigor of the scholarly work that's done but that does allow people to accommodate the professional work and the pure scholarly work, the sort of pure research production work in the same lifetime.

KM. I can tell you from the research that I've been involved with, service is a very vaguely defined concept. Most often, it's perceived as professional service in the form of journal editing or things like that. It's a struggle to define what we mean by teaching, research, and service.

TM. That's really interesting. That's one kind of problem. The other one is that the category isn't research. Again, the discourse is real interesting. There was a reform a number of years ago that has not affected the discourse at all, which was to change the language from *research*, teaching and service, to scholarly activity. And very explicitly, changing that title was the way in which artists were going to be able to talk about exhibits and musicians were going to talk about shows, and people in professional schools were going to be able to talk about their work in developing professionals or working on policy as a part of scholarly activity. But it hasn't penetrated. If left to our own devices, even within the school, we will still do research, teaching, and service.

CT. You are an historian, and you are working extremely hard on reforming urban education. I presume that when you are involved in making decisions you invariably go back to the history of urban education for the right questions and for the historical answers to a given problem. History continues to be with you and informs your judgment and your understanding and perhaps even keeps you alive as an administrator. And I know that you will not disagree with me because in many ways history has done for you what critical philosophy has done for me. But as an historian, what will be the lessons of history in trying to improve the condition of urban education in this country, particularly in Los Angeles?

TM. I think the first is a historiographical conclusion which is that we tend to think at any point in time that the institutions we have are governed by some sort of natural law. And so the first lesson for me of history is that these institutions we call schools were developed at a particular point in time to meet a particular set of needs. And as crazy as they may appear today, they were functional. Or they continue to be functional. And as a historian, talking to policymakers, the important thing for me to convey to them is first the sense of indeterminacy—we can change these things. There is no natural law of schools that says there is a first grade, a second grade, a third grade, a fourth grade, and a fifth grade. Those were constructs to meet a particular set of demands within a particular ideological context at a particular point in time. If we're convinced that the ideological context has changed, that the historical moment has changed, that the needs of society have changed, we can change these institutions. It doesn't make it easy, but it is historically possible, because these were historical and human creations.

The second and contradictory historical thing that I keep thinking about—and I find myself in this situation all the time—is to see how cyclical the issues are. In Los Angeles today we're talking about issues of moving from a more district-oriented board to a board that's elected at large in the community or a board that's appointed by the mayor. At the turn of the century we did the reverse. We moved from a centrally oriented, centrally dominated board to a district-oriented board. And one finds that if you look at the history long enough, you find that in each reform are the seeds of its undoing. Because there is no perfect system. My mentor David Tyack wrote the wonderful book *The One Best System* in which he talked about the progressive era as a time in which people thought they could really get it right and they could develop the one best system that would be the way in which you could do this forever. Well, there is no one best system. But there are persistent issues and they come up, they go away, they come up, they go away. We do things that bring other issues to the fore.

The internal contradictions inherent to many reforms, they take half a century to finally emerge, but when they do, they sort of return us to facing the contradictions themselves. In this case, the question of centralization versus decentralization is the oldest question, it's the question of what kind of expertise is the best kind of expertise to run a school system. Is it the technical expertise that is more easily expressed in central authority or is it a more diffuse expertise that's about the needs of particular communities and the desires of the local population? And if you think it's the local population and community needs, it's the kind of expertise, well, then, you're going to move toward a local board. But those boards tend to be chaotic. They tend to be indecisive. And if what you're after is direction and decisiveness, and so on, again, I would try to move toward centralization. So the circumstances change, and that's the second lesson, that each area of reform has embedded in it contradictions that arise later and then have to be dealt with.

And I think that what that gives me, and I try to convey to other people, is a sense of calm. That we have been here before. That while there is maybe a sense of critical need and emergency to do something, it's not an urgency to create the one best system, but it's a sense of urgency to meet the needs that are facing us today. And then finally to go back to the beginning to where we started. My sense of history does show me over and over again that these fundamental issues of race, of class, of gender and of power remain with us. Much of the cyclical nature of school reform has to do with our need to address, but never to address at a very deep level, the inherent contradictions in capitalist democratic society in which we talk about equality but have social systems that are geared fundamentally around issues of inequality.

KM. An excellent place to end. Thank you, Ted.

CHAPTER 11

# Memoirs of Urban Education Policymakers: A Dialogue among Three Former Urban School Superintendents

## Harry Handler, Sid Thompson, and Eugene Tucker

### with Carlos A. Torres and Karen A. McClafferty

BIOGRAPHIES OF THE PARTICIPANTS

*Harry Handler* worked for the LA Unified School District for thirty-four years, progressing from substitute teacher to superintendent. He served as superintendent for six years, from 1981 to 1987. He is currently an Adjunct Professor and Special Assistant to the Dean at UCLA in the Graduate School of Education and Information Studies. He has a bachelor's degree from UCLA in mathematics, a master's degree in educational psychology from USC, and a Ph.D. in educational psychology from USC in learning theory, statistics, and measurement.

*Sid Thompson* has been a senior fellow at UCLA since July of 1997. He had retired as superintendent of the Los Angeles Unified School District, a job he held from 1992 to 1997. He has forty-one years of education experience, all of it K–12. He began in the field as a math teacher, became administrator with the district, and then became superintendent. Mr. Thompson graduated from the U.S. Merchant Marine Academy at

Kings Point where he was a math science major. He came to UCLA for postgraduate work and later received a master's degree from Cal State LA.

*Eugene Tucker* is a member of the faculty at UCLA, after working twenty-three years as a superintendent of four different school districts in urban, suburban, and rural settings. His most recent assignment—from 1986 to 1992—was as superintendent of the Santa Monica Malibu Unified School District. He describes Santa Monica as "an edge city that has some urban characteristics." For ten years, Dr. Tucker was superintendent of the ABC Unified School District, a suburban school district with some urban characteristics. He was also superintendent of Coachella Valley Unified School District, a rural school district in Riverside County, California. His first superintendency was in a small elementary school district on the outskirts of the city of Los Angeles in the Santa Clarita Valley. Dr. Tucker received three degrees from UCLA: A B.A. in political science, and an M.A. and Ph.D. in education (curriculum studies, administration, and philosophy).

*Karen McClafferty* earned her Ph.D. from UCLA's Graduate School of Education and Information Studies. Her research focuses on the social role of the educational researcher and the sociopolitical context of the university. She has also done extensive research on urban education and the preparation of teachers for work in multicultural contexts.

*Carlos Alberto Torres* is a professor of education at UCLA, with a particular emphasis on nonformal education and the political sociology of education. His research interests also encompass the new research in the scholarship of class, race, gender, and the state in a comparative perspective, with a special focus on race relations in the United States and Latin America.

## REFLECTIONS ON THE CHALLENGES
## OF URBAN EDUCATION

> Experience is never limited, and it is never complete; it is an immense sensibility, a kind of huge spider-web of the finest silken threads suspended in the chamber of consciousness, and catching every air-borne particle in its tissue.
>
> —Henry James

> You can observe a lot by just watching.
>
> —Yogi Berra

KAREN MCCLAFFERTY (KM). We are delighted to have the opportunity to spend some time with you this afternoon and to get a glimpse into your experiences as superintendents in urban school districts. It is a rare opportunity, indeed, to be able to benefit from so many years of experience. Between the three of you, I believe we have close to a hundred years in the schools. Since we felt very strongly about including not only the voice of research but also the very important voice of practice in this book, we could not resist the temptation to include your insights.

CARLOS TORRES (CT). We entitled this chapter of the book, tentatively, "Memoirs from Superintendents in Urban Education." The book, as you have seen in the documentation, deals with the crisis of urban education. We will start with this very, I think, important question. I think it's also a very provocative question. During the time that you were superintendents, given the role and function, you have to handle all sorts of problems. And sometimes you have to be very discreet, extremely diplomatic. You could not always speak up. You were not able to give criticisms that perhaps, now being in academia, you can do. So, given that situation, that the commitments and the situation that you were in as a policymaker, is not any longer present, what were the critical issues that you handled, what were the critical problems that you found? And now you can really speak about it and discuss in detail. We can start from the criticisms and then we can move into the joys more than the sorrows and we can move into the positive achievements that you made or may have found in the last three decades. And of course if you want to do it chronologically, it would be nice. If you can figure out what is going on now compared to the past, it would be very interesting. The question, then, to be brief, is the following: As former superintendents, what kind of criticisms do you have of urban education, in Los Angeles particularly, and in similar areas?

SID THOMPSON (ST). Well, I'll go, I just came out of some of this. The criticisms that I have relate to the process by which board members are elected. The changes in the types of candidates attracted to the board, compared to the way it used to be, are very pronounced. It used to be, when I first started teaching in the system, that the people who were on the board tended to do the job as an avocation. They had jobs all the way from airline pilot to contractor to book reviewer. They did all sorts of things. We've noticed that that's focused and focused to where it is now a much more politicized process. For example, we used to elect our board members at large, and everybody that came into that job represented all students in the system. Hundreds of thousands of students. But they tended to have a global approach to the system. That was changed some years back to representation from subdistricts. And that was a very significant change. It sounds as if it would be more representative, and in a sense it is, but at the same time, it carries with it a lot of, frankly and bluntly, baggage. It carries with it what happens in ward politics. It becomes a matter of "I'm here, and I have a city council person, I have an assembly person, I have a whatever, that are all related to what I represent as a board member." And so that changes the approach.

It is important to note that during that same period of time, we've had a hardening over the years of the approach by the different bargaining units. They realized that the power was with the board members, and they became very active with money and voting support for individual board members. That's had a very critical impact. It's always been there in one form or another, but it's just much more focused. If you look at the LAUSD now, you have not only three teachers on the board, but you have three administrators on the board. And the administrators are in a sense unionized, and so they have their representatives. And I would submit that it takes away from what we had much earlier. The thing that I missed the most in that job was the fact that we seemed to spend an awful lot of time on everything but instruction. We spent time on adult problems. And when I did instruction, I'd almost say "hallelujah, we're talking about youngsters learning." It just didn't happen enough. It didn't focus enough. And I think it's had an effect.

I would also add two things when you talk about urban education. One is, there's a tendency to deal with it as if it's separate and distinct from where the youngsters come from. We know as a nation, we've not addressed issues in their communities as a total problem, we've dealt with it piecemeal. And the problems that are in those communities are reflected in the way kids come to school. And we talk about their reading scores. Some of these youngsters are fortunate that they can just breathe normally, considering what they go through. And we haven't been able to address that. Secondly, we've had an attitude educationally, when we have dealt with instruction, that talks to the problems these urban kids have. They're poor. And there is a lowered expectation. We talk about remediation as if it's stamped on their foreheads. "Remedial." And we have not, to my way of thinking, in any way sufficiently challenged the majority of these youngsters who do have a brain and are coming from all that I referenced as a problem and yet can learn.

GENE TUCKER (GT). Yes, I'd like to pick up where Sid left off. Even though Los Angeles probably represents the extreme of some on these issues, I agree with Sid in terms of the magnitude, the political climate and other issues involved. But we might indicate for example, that we've seen the growing "politicalization" of school boards. An increase in ethnic politics and changes in the nature of people who choose to run or not to run for school boards are some of the areas in which I've seen a very significant change over time. Power politics by the unions definitely have increased significantly, and in my view, not always for the better. A lot of the union issues are adult issues, as Sid indicated, and not focused on what may generally be considered the educational interest of children.

I would also say that there has been a growing tendency over the last several decades of micro-management by boards. In my earlier days as superintendent, boards were more willing to look at broad policy and leave to professional educators the "how to" accomplish goals. This micromanagement has extended beyond boards to legislatures and to governors. Legislative bodies are taking on or politicizing essentially educational issues. For example, taking stances on the politically correct way to teach reading or a politically correct way to teach mathematics. Again, I think we see a shortage of a clear, long-term vision; statements of goals, outcomes, or purposes; and a surfeit of prescription. I've seen this tendency nationally. Power politics accompany the growth of various ethnic groups in communities. Again, many of the political battles are not so much over the very legitimate concern about the needs of all children and the failure of schools to serve adequately children of color, but the sheer pursuit of personal or group power. I don't think there's any question that schools have not served the children of the poor well. Regardless of the ethnicity of the power structure.

HARRY HANDLER (HH). Sid and Gene have done such an outstanding job, I don't have anything left to say.

GT. Since when? (Laughter)

HH. One thought is that the readers may want to go back and read Michael Kirst's research on whether we should have school boards. He has some publications that I think are worth reading. If I may take a slightly different cut at this, it may be helpful. In trying to answer the question that you sent to us, "What are the key problems in urban education in the country?" I wrestled with four words, four concepts. One is the absence of standards. Standards involved for everyone in the enterprise. And I'm not just talking about standards for the program and student performance; standards for the superintendents' behavior, board members' behavior. Responsibilities of parents, legislators, custodians, community leaders, et cetera.

There needs to be a more intensive dialogue on why do the schools exist. What do we expect students to learn? And what are our moral obligations to see that it happens? So standards would be one concept. The other concepts which—and they go together—are *stability* and *consistency*. If one traces what's been happening over the past thirty years, the rules and the slogans are constantly changing without providing the time and the resources to assess the effect. We're a unique quasi-profession—and I can someday elaborate on that if you'd like me to—in that we can always manage to keep our slogans out in front of our performance. Therefore, the people who are supposed to deliver the instructional program aren't certain what's coming next. Why think any of it is important? Eventually it's just going to change the next year. Examples: homogeneous grouping to detracking; from integrated math to traditional math; from whole language to phonics; from decentralization to centralization to charter schools. Consciously or unconsciously as the superintendent, I kept watching this happen and trying to deal with it. We have these four conflicting values: We believe in equality. We believe in efficiency. We believe in liberty. And I added equity, because equity and equality are not the same to me. We try to maximize the effects of all four and it's impossible. If you really want to emphasize equality, you have to give up some efficiency. I can give other examples. So we haven't really found a way to bring about a balance in terms of the four values.

At a more concrete level, my fourth concept is fiscal responsibility. Yes, the schools need more money; yes, teachers should receive higher salaries. No question! But, yes, policymakers and administrators need to show greater fiscal responsibility. That gets back to long- and short-term planning, as mentioned by Gene, along with establishing priorities, and appropriately funding these priorities. As an anecdote, and Sid will recall this, when I became superintendent of the school district, we didn't have a sixth period. I went through the budgets of every manager in the district and concluded that if every manager of a major operation in the school district would reduce his or her expenditures the following year by 10 percent, we could fund the sixth period. That to me ties to what I'm trying to say about priorities and responsibility.

GT. Let me add on one thing. I think Harry mentioned a point that we probably should talk about. He talked about the whole issue of stability and consistency. I think most of us know that without stability in leadership it's difficult to operate even under the best of conditions. In a rapidly changing environment, with changing demands, it becomes even more difficult. The turnover of urban superintendents is amazing. For Sid and Harry to have been in their positions for five and six years respectively, that's amazing, when in many urban areas, the superintendent stays for two or three years at most.

HH. What's the average now, about two?

GT. Maybe two years.

KM. Because the pressure is so overwhelming?

GT. Again, it's because of the changing political winds. Every time a shift of power takes place after a board election, people want a superintendent who might represent a different point of view, philosophy or political position. And then, you also have turnover among board members. You have two things happening—turnover of leadership and a turnover in expectations and demands. As a consequence, teachers and administrators want to wait you out. Why should they change when they don't know what will be expected by the next set of leaders? By the time one superintendent starts to make a change, the next person or group is in power. The change the previous leader wanted is no longer fashionable, no longer considered appropriate. Therefore, there's a lack of consistency. And then you think of the thirteen-year span a child is in an educational system, and the shifts that have taken place within the scope of that child's experience, it is no wonder that significant progress often eludes us.

CT. Now, the shift takes place in the level of the policy. Does it also affect, directly, the school, or does the school have another dynamic?

ST. Don't forget—and Gene hit it right on the head, we all know this as well—we're talking about change at the top. For urban youngsters, the changes at the school level are just as severe. First of all, you have a lot of teachers teaching in there who aren't regularly credentialed. The problems of teaching in an urban setting, the environment and all that, causes turnover, so not only are you turning over at the top, you're turning over at the site. That youngster, and it's a good way to say it, this youngster in twelve to thirteen years of education not only is going through all of those changes at the top but these are policy changes. He also, or she is getting changes at the school level that are probably more upsetting.

HH. Let me provide another example. In 1983, the LA Unified School District opened school with eight hundred classrooms that didn't have teachers.

CT. So what happened?

HH. Substitutes. But that meant that during that year, thousands of youngsters would have a teacher for a week or two and then a different teacher, a week or two, and then a week where there wouldn't be a teacher and they divided up the class.

CT. So the pedagogical bond is never established.

ST. And the teachers were not fully credentialed.

HH. What were the contributing factors? Salaries were very low, and fortunately the State was able to increase salaries. Let me tell you what higher salaries meant. Instead of paying teachers $13,500, we had enough to pay $20,000 a year. Which made it difficult to recruit. But, the point is that there was policy, and you can see how this went from the board to the school. There was a policy that basically said when the teacher told you what part of the city the teacher wanted to work in, then that's where the teacher was assigned. I went to the board and I received support for what became the "Priority Staffing Program" and basically requested a new policy. People are assigned where we need them. And if not, it's okay, get a job in another district. Well, things worked out well. We opened in '84 with only eighty-four classrooms without teachers. So what does that mean? That one shift in policy had an impact on thousands of youngsters. Eighty-four classrooms that didn't have teachers, versus eight hundred classrooms that didn't have teachers. Markedly different.

CT. One of the arguments that has been used particularly by people like Michael Apple and other people looking at changes in the school board is this notion of the stealth campaign in which some factions of the religious right have been using their board appointments to push for very specific agendas. When you are looking at this—the turmoil at the board level and the more belligerent attitude within the school board members, is this situation also happening in the context that you have studied?

GT. I would say that phenomenon is more likely to occur in suburban, as opposed to urban areas. In urban areas you generally have a much larger, more liberal constituency, and you have more people of color who are voting. They are less susceptible to the agenda of the far right. But our colleagues in suburban areas are the ones who describe this phenomenon quite clearly, and it's quite accurate.

ST. That's why a lot of them have been put out.

GT. With the "wrong" belief system on the part of the superintendent, he or she becomes vulnerable.

CT. If you have mustered enough power in a particular district, then you can have almost your own philosophy being played out in that district.

GT. Especially if you can successfully get your supporters to turn out for school elections. School elections in California can either be held with general elections when a larger percentage of people vote, or they can be held in off years. That decision can be made locally. So, if you have an election on odd-numbered years, the off years, then the percentage of people who vote is smaller. The people who vote will tend to be older, without children in school. And, if you have a very well-organized, well-financed special interest group, they can be very successful at winning elections with a relatively small percentage of the electorate. And that's what frequently happens.

KM. Sounds like an enormously frustrating situation. One that must have made it quite difficult to organize the schools in a way that was best for the students. But in those years you must have had some successes—things that you were able to do which you felt simply *worked*.

## MICRO-VICTORIES IN URBAN EDUCATION

So when you ask about the victories, I think a lot of them are tiny victories. They're micro-victories. Every once in a while a superintendent will get lucky and have a Board of five to seven people who can work together well.

—Gene Tucker

CT. Yes, let us move into the other side of the coin. You have already mentioned some of your successes. It would be nice always to go back to the real successes, to reminisce. Tell us of something that you have witnessed that worked. Something that works in policy and works in practice. I believe there is a lot of rhetoric going on about whether the schools work or don't work. If you take someone like Gloria Ladson-Billings and her book, *The Dreamkeepers*, about teachers of African American students, a bestseller, sold about 40,000 copies, in which she goes back to the classroom and sees these teachers turning out educated products of people that continue and go on.[1] Or Mike Rose's *Possible Lives*, which is a very exciting way of looking at the schools.[2] So I get a feeling that even in the context of persuasions and the criticisms that you outlined, there are success stories. Could you give us some flavor of that?

ST. The one success that I remember most, that hit me most deeply is not a success yet. But it was a beginning. And it was a matter of saying, when I was the superintendent, how little time was being spent on the curriculum and on the kids. I just found myself going absolutely wild with the fact that my time was effectively co-opted by adult issues. So I went after the instructional program, and I determined whether I could get the teachers to teach the subjects or not, because the numbers of emergency credentialed teachers in the classrooms are just enormous. We had to get the core curriculum to the kids. Some of these schools, 30 percent emergency-credentialed teachers are assigned. How do you have a curriculum with that? But I couldn't change it quickly enough. And if I were to sit there and say I'll be the superintendent for the next fifteen years, I still wouldn't see it. So I just determined, the heck with it, I'll just go for it. I'll take a quantum leap, raise the bar, and see what happens.

And so we got into who was taking algebra, who was taking AP courses, who was taking A through F, and you know who they are. And if you go into the urban schools—the barrios, the ghettos, the combinations of them—you get youngsters who will take those courses and who are academically tough. In spite of whatever they face, they're charging. Those aren't the ones you necessarily have to worry about. You have to nurture, but you don't worry. But it's this huge group of so-called C average, that really aren't. They're better than that, many of them. So one of the things that gave me solace, and I think was good, was to take the old system and say, "Okay, no more. I want to get rid of remedial courses." It sounds dumb. "What do you mean, you're not going remediate anymore?" Remediate, yes. But we don't even want to use the term. Remember what I said about remedial on the forehead. That was just a view of the kids.

KM. Like a stigma.

ST. It's a stigma. You're exactly right. If I can just digress just for a second and tell you that I went to a high school graduation in the valley. Valley High School, mixed. At that school, after the graduation where I spoke—I went out, as I did in all graduations, and talked to the kids. "Okay, what's happening to you, where are you going?" I tell this story wherever I go. I spoke to an African American youngster, a young man, and I said "Son, what are you going to do now?" And he says, "Oh, I don't know." He says, "I just don't know. You know, I've got to figure out—I got through this, and I got my diploma." I said, "Well, did you take algebra?" This kid said to me, "No." I said, "Why, why, why, why didn't you try?" He said, "That's for those people." And he pointed to the white kids. Tragedy.

Well I took him around the side of the building and he and I had what could best be described as a down-home, black-black discussion about this perception of his—we had to communicate. I just couldn't let that youngster go off that way. But it shows you where his thinking was about himself. His self image. That he just didn't have the brain. Anyway, I'm going on and on, but I just want to say this. When I switched and went after the curriculum, when I said we're going to have youngsters going into algebra, we're going to require it, you jump 25,000 kids enrolling over the previous figures in one year, and in that group, 60 percent were Cs, Bs, and As. So they reasonably made it. But what it did for me was once again I was going home and sitting up at night about, "Okay, now we're going to do all of this, and what's going to happen, and what are we going to do about teachers." I was worrying about the delivery of the educational program. So that was a major change for me that's carried a lot of impact.

GT. I don't think that the impression we want to give is that it's all negative. There's a very large number of wonderful teachers and a large number of excellent school administrators, caring people who give and give and give. There are good programs in almost every school—band directors who work sixty hours a week to see that kids get a quality music program, drama teachers, coaches, teachers of every subject and grade level. A majority of our nation's educators really do a tremendous amount for children. But a lot of these achievements are because of the individual and not because of what the system is doing. Maybe the system has let them alone, or, at least, created an environment that has allowed them to do good work.

The structure of schools isolates people. If you isolate a wonderful teacher you are likely to get good outcomes. But an isolated weak or poor teacher is likely throughout his or her career to continue offering instruction at a level that is unsatisfactory. So when you ask about the victories, I think a lot of them are tiny victories. They're micro victories. Every once in a while a superintendent will get lucky and have a board of five to seven people who can work together well. During these times we make tremendous progress. For example, changing the nature of collective bargaining, from a very adversarial model of bargaining to interest-based bargaining, which produced better results for schools and the kids. But with a change in the top leadership (superintendent and board members, union president), as occurred in my experience, conditions can deteriorate very quickly. The board changed, the union leadership changed and the superintendent left. In a few short years, they were back to where they were ten years earlier. People liked what they had, but the nature of the structure allowed it to regress to the earlier unsatisfactory conditions.

I agree with Sid. I think there's some very nice victories such as an increased understanding that more money has to be invested in professional development. I've seen that over the years. I think there is a growing recognition on the part of the total profession, and increasingly among some school board members, that we have to invest more in training the people who work in our system. Our schools can't be better than the quality of the people in our classrooms. So I think that's been a long range victory. I think that there's definitely a growing recognition that we need to do a better job with language minority students. Some progress has been made in this area. The current climate in California, however, is causing us some concern about this issue. We're doing a much better job in meeting the needs of children with disabilities. I think there's no question that statewide we're serving children who were not served well before. I think we're developing a better quality of leaders. Many of our new school principals are better qualified and more instruction-oriented.

## RACE AND THE CHALLENGE OF URBAN SCHOOLS

You should be measured by your actions, not your rhetoric.
                                                —Harry Handler

CT. This is really a very useful conversation. Let me pose a question that you have touched upon. There's one area of the conversation to which we're going to move which is one of the concrete interests of Karen about the role of universities in dealing with urban education, but obviously you see a role, since you are here. There are two things I'd like to touch upon before we get into that. One is race relations at the school level. One hypothesis—argued by those such as William J. Wilson—is that the "race problem," put in those terms, the race problem in the U.S. is really a class problem.[3] Not long ago, I think a couple of days ago, I watched a very serious debate at Harvard—Harvard has now recruited perhaps the most outstanding black intellectuals of this country, and all of them were there—and the narrative thread of the seven of them talking at Harvard was what I just stated. The race problem is a class problem.

My question, then, is the following: How would you elaborate on the peculiar "race problem" in Los Angeles, particularly with urban violence associated with that? The second part of the question, which you may want to tackle anyway, is that we have witnessed in the last six years a movement in which the race relations are typically altered because of Proposition 187, Proposition 209, because the affirmative action backlashes and so on.[4] So you were in the trenches, you were really looking at this situation from the inside. What would you say?

HH. You address that in different ways operationally and philosophically. Let me back up a minute so that you understand where I'm coming from. I never saw the superintendency as a person, I saw it as a concept. And I've always felt it a very unfortunate event when people became superintendents and immediately they "owned" the position. Given that philosophic position, perhaps you'll understand where I'm coming from. Number one, you don't deny that there are racial tensions. There are racial tensions. Number two, a number of the efforts to reduce racial tensions have been related to professional development-type activities, focus groups, etc. All of these activities had promise. But they're very limited.

There's no question in my mind that there's such a thing as institutional racism. And institutional racism is not always on the surface. In fact it's the institutional racism which is below the surface that is more dangerous to our society. Did I ever come up with "a solution"? No! Did I have guiding principles that I used in my own personal efforts to try and address some of the issues? Yes. I was the district's principle witness in the desegregation case, and had a number of board members very unhappy with me because I supported integration. But the key point here is, you have to ask yourself, "What do I believe is my role?" You should be measured by your actions, not your rhetoric. You need to accept that whether you like it or not, you are the superintendent. And for the right reasons and the wrong reasons, people take their cues from you.

GT. I would like to comment briefly on racism. It's really interesting, as Sid indicated earlier, you can't separate the child in the school from the child in the community. The community comes into the school, the child brings the community into the school. From my experience, more often than not, students see their schools as safe places. There will likely be some racism in every ethnically diverse group. There will be some territoriality. However, out of a 180–day school year, 178 of those days will be without a major racial incident. My experience has been that when parents hear negative stories, I ask them if they ever visited the campus. They usually have not. Because if they did visit the school, they would see kids pretty much leave school alone. They'll associate with their own friends.

There's not a lot of racial intermixing on most campuses, but neither is there much racial conflict. But when it does happen, it can be very nasty and very difficult. We have to spend a lot of time and energy preparing our administrative and teaching staffs—mostly in high schools and sometimes in middle schools—for potential incidents. Elementary schools are generally free of serious racial incidents.

ST. Yeah, that's what I've found.

KM. So what you're saying—to paraphrase Harry—is that your philosophy or your rhetoric matters little unless the principles are operationalized. And to understand whether or not that's happening, you really need to take a look at what is going on in the schools—the positive and the negative.

HH. I think a key part of that is that you can really see a difference in terms of leadership provided by the principal and the teachers. The bright principal creates activities at the school around common interests. Those common interests—and I'm not just talking about athletics—they bring students together along another dimension. If you're consciously doing that, especially if you're in a high school, it's fantastic the way these young people come together. Now, are you doing something constructive relative to racism? Yes. Are you able to say racism doesn't exist? No. It's there, but now what you're trying to do is every day— that's one of the most frustrating experiences I ever had is when people thought that you could have one period a day for multicultural education and you took care of everything. You create a climate—it's a twenty-four hour a day effort.

GT. Harry is absolutely right. But it's really interesting that most of those opportunities to work with people from mixed groups happen in extracurricular activities. It happens in the athletic program, it happens in the music program, it happens in the drama program. These provide opportunities for youngsters who ordinarily would not interact to work with each other around a common purpose. And today, there's very few administrators who aren't aware of and sensitive to the issue. Where racial interaction is not taking place is in academic classrooms, because of tracking and a whole series of other reasons. Many African American youngsters say "Algebra is not for me" because they don't see many black faces in the algebra classes. And to me that must be one of the next battlegrounds.

ST. I was going to add that as a minority person in the superintendency that one of the great emotional pressures I felt had to do with the African Americans who felt I was "their guy." Now, in the city of Los Angeles as we know, folks live apart. The white population versus the minority population is not a major issue in and of itself except where it's changing in the valley and you have Hispanic movements into many Valley areas. But basically, a more immediate concern right now is the Hispanic/Black. Because there are changes within the neighborhoods where African Americans move out or they see Hispanics moving in and there's a lot of give and take.

And it applies to the superintendency because the pressures I would get were almost daily—"Who are you going to put at that school? I *know* you're going to put an African American, right?" Wrong. Also not just the combination of Hispanic and African American, but you also have the Korean population in Pico Union and west. That's all in that mix. And it's fascinating to see it. Most of the people who live in the greater LA area drive over all that. They're on freeways, never get off. I have one guy who told me, "I didn't realize there was a Koreatown!" I said "Koreatown? That's the largest population of Koreans outside of Seoul!" But the point is that you face on the basis of race, you face not only that from the majority white population—majority U.S. as opposed to our urban schools—but you also face it within ethnic minorities. And so the only way I found I could operate was to work at them and work at them until when they hit me with "You think you ought to make an African American . . . ?" They would apologize, and they would say "Wait a minute, here's what we're saying. We understand that you can't just put blacks in the jobs and all. We know you can't do that. But we want you to at least consider it." Well, okay, that's a start. Because they're coming off of this hard line "you must" to understand the problems. The Hispanics would come to me and they would come in kind of with hat in hand looking at me because they couldn't really fully trust me—they didn't know what I was going to do. After all, he's an African American.

But I made the assignments and I kept that fine balance and I felt, just as Harry had to do and everybody else that's ever thought of this, as you do that, they get to at least understand where you're going to come from. And once they understand that you're not going to play the race role, that you're going to be objective, then they pull back. By the way, Harry, I can't resist. On your institutional racism, it's so true. The African Americans, in that population, you could say the same for the Hispanic populations—going into algebra, when we went into one school we found the vast majority of the African American kids were not taking algebra. When we approached the principal, the principal said, "Well, I know it's tough for the African American kids and the Hispanic kids. They just don't get in there and we haven't enrolled them." But you say, "Let me show you the list. Let me show you these kids who have Bs and As in mathematics prior to the time they could have taken algebra and didn't." And they would immediately say, "Oh, here's John, and here's Mary." If you personalized it, you could just see them with the wheels turning. "Oh my God, I didn't realize it." And then they say to you, "Oh my God, how did that happen? We're not prejudiced!" And I'd say, "No, you're not, but what happens is institutional, with one counselor for six hundred kids, who do they listen to? The middle-class youngster who comes in and says, 'My mom said take algebra, so put me down.' The African American kid, the Hispanic kid? Since they don't raise a ruckus and squeak, they don't get to take it." And the institution tends to accept that.

GT. Maybe this is a segue into another topic. One of the critical issues I see in education is the quality and characteristics of the teaching force. In California our teaching force is a long way from representing the ethnicity of our students. And if you look at who's coming into college now, I don't see in the future teacher pipeline a very diverse population. In urban communities, especially, we're finding an increasingly diverse student population, but still a predominantly white teaching force. And so that suggests to us, that if we think it's important to begin to have a more diverse teaching force, and this speaks to universities, we have to look at how do we do a better job in recruiting and retaining a diverse teaching force. We may need to look at other models for training teachers, ways that are more likely to ensure a more ethnically diverse corps of teachers.

Sid described it beautifully, as did Harry, we have large percentages of unprepared teachers using current training methods—essentially a university model. You get your B.A. degree then you get your teaching credential. The truth of the matter is that people from lower socioeconomic groups cannot defer earning money for that long a period of time. So as a consequence, they're not going into the profession. There's not a lot of evidence to my knowledge indicating that other models cannot also be very effective.

CT. You have any particular hint at what kind of models you are considering?

GT. Yes, I do. I think, for example, we can start looking at what I would call a differentiated staffing model, where people in schools with different levels of training can perform different roles. You might have a fully university-trained person with several years of experience and proven teaching ability who might work with a team that would include people with one or two years of college who would be getting some experience, learning how to perform the teacher's role, working with students or with small groups under the lead teacher's guidance. They would have opportunities to grow and increase their responsibilities over time while they continue their schooling.

If we are thoughtful about it we can create teacher training models that would assure us a more diverse, well-prepared profession. I think that would go a long way to improving our schools and dealing with teacher isolation. Too many unprepared teachers are put in the classrooms. A begin-

ning teacher who comes in unprepared has the same roles and responsibilities as a twenty-year veteran with a proven track record. In an elementary
school, they each have thirty children, they each teach for the same length
of time each day, they each have the same responsibilities. I like a medical
model, for example, which utilizes people in different roles to meet the
needs of the patient. I don't know if Harry and Sid agree, but I see this as
one of the critical issues in education today. I was reading recently that New
York City has 30–40 percent of its teachers who are not fully prepared.

ST. Right, because I think right now, increasingly you hear it takes five
years for youngsters to come through here and get a bachelor's degree, then
another year, or another whatever, for their teacher certification.

HH. Gene, your program now is a six-year program, isn't it?

GT. They work as full time teachers and are paid during their sixth year
while they complete their master's degree.

ST. In my mind, the problem with that system is it takes too long for the
person to end up in the classroom to find out if that's what they really want
to do. If they don't like kids—and there's nothing wrong with not liking
kids, but then they darn sure shouldn't be in front of them. But why should
you be waiting that period of time to find out? In other countries—I went
to school under the British system when I was little and they used what
would be like student teachers much earlier. They still went on to get their
degree.

   We have teaching assistants in classrooms, but for a different reason.
Teaching assistants are in our classrooms because we're providing employment. That really is for the wrong reason. We've been lucky because out of
those we've managed to get some darn good teachers. They find out they
really like this and they go on and get their degree, and we get them back.

HH. We had a period where we hired a large number of teachers who had
emergency credentials. We put together a team of skilled people and had
them go in and observe teachers. They didn't know whether the teachers
had emergency credentials or not. I wanted to know, "What did you
think?" And it was a wash. Which really worried me. Because on the one
hand, we say that the non-credentialed teacher isn't prepared. On the other
hand, we send experts in to observe, and they can't distinguish. So that says
a lot, generates a lot of hypotheses.

   The other thing I want to mention is that, as I listen to Gene, and as
Gene talked about the medical model, and I understand what Gene's saying
and I agree. I know where he's coming from, but it's that kind of problem,
when we discuss it, we have to put another hat on. I tried to put the hat on
of someone who felt very strongly that the system was unfair, that the system is inequitable. And what I had to wonder about is, will Gene's suggestion lead to white people being in the top positions, such as doctors—and
that isn't what you had in mind, but white people being the doctors and the
supporting cast being made up of other than white. But what that really
says, with a slight modification, you could start after two years of junior

college, you could start a career ladder program where people work on their credential, continue to work on their college education, continue to work part time for school districts, and it may take them six or seven years, but then they're fully credentialed teachers.

There's another potential gold mine in the future teacher clubs. There are future teacher clubs in high schools throughout the country, and you can develop curriculum materials in the ninth, tenth, eleventh, twelfth grades. And if you're lucky, you can get out there and get the financial support, you can work with these students to get them financial support while they go to college. If they drop out and aren't in the program, they don't get the financial support. You know you're going to take some losses at the end of the program because some of them aren't going to become teachers. And you can't really say, "I promise you. . . ." But the proportion who do go into teaching is rather rewarding. And it's a small investment. You can really start to prepare people to be teachers and to get them excited about it at an earlier age.

KM. And perhaps in doing that, begin to bring about some changes in the demographic makeup of the teaching force?

GT. Actually, what happens of course in many communities is that the demographic changes are taking place at a faster rate than turnover of teachers. I'll give you some examples. At one time Compton and Inglewood were all white. Within a decade, they became predominantly African American. Within another decade and a half, they became predominantly Hispanic. The power structure remained white for many years after black children were the majority. Now, the power structure is predominantly black, while Hispanics are now the majority. The teaching staff has remained white for a long time, because a teacher's career may span 35–40 years.

So what happens is similar to what occurs at universities. Why are most professors white males? Well, first of all the career of a professor is longer than the career of a teacher. The slow turnover rate provides limited opportunities for women and people of color to enter the professional ranks.

Many people want to see a university staff that reflects the demographic changes. Meanwhile you can't throw out the people who've invested a lifetime making a contribution. Changes will take time. Well, the same is true with the teaching profession. In medicine, for a long time, most doctors were white males. And now, over 50 percent of students in medical school are female. In another decade or two, at least half of the doctors will be female.

Another issue that's important to me in urban education is that given the current structure of schooling, I think that poor, minority children are at a real disadvantage. You think of schooling as primarily being 180 days a year, six hours a day. Children from middle-class families are provided enriched activities in the summertime and supervised activities at the end of the day. Their education continues when school is not in session. Children in urban centers, when not in school, are not likely to be getting rich educational experiences.

ST. TV or the street.

GT. Increasingly, parents are afraid to let their kids play in the street for safety reasons. They keep them at home in front of the television set. So it seems to me that one of the issues we have to think about is the structure of schooling. I think we need to provide rich educational opportunities for more days of the year and more hours per day. Many of these children need more time to accomplish the same high standards that middle-class children in more privileged environments accomplish in less time. So it seems to me that one way of getting at equity is not through equality but by providing more quality learning time and by changing the structure of schooling. Time to learn, that's a critical issue, especially in urban schools.

ST. We're not talking about athletics, per se. But the LA Best program takes an academic approach as recreation—dance, drama—the things they can't do at school normally they do after school. But they also do homework. If the family is disjointed, you might just as well do it where you can do it. And if it's at school, there's nothing wrong with a kindergartner—if I had my magic wand—being two or three more hours in school. What's he going to do? What's she going to do? She's going to be on the street or staring at that tube. Given the option, I'd have them do the after school.

When I was principle at Markham in Watts, right after the riots, they had a federal program, they picked those kids up after school and three busloads of them went to Cal State LA. And out at Cal State LA they had drama, they had art, they had subject reinforcement. When they brought them back at seven o'clock in the evening, those kids only had time to get off that bus and go home. They didn't have time to go off romping in the street. Now I'm not saying it has to be like that, but this LA Best, that kind of approach is very beneficial. I told them in Washington, I said if you're talking about the defense budget going down, why don't you take that money and expand the school day. I said that would be a tremendous support to these kids. Not with games. With true academics and the arts and the kinds of things we'd all like to do. It can be done.

## BOUNDARIES AND BRIDGES IN URBAN EDUCATION: THE ROLE OF HIGHER EDUCATION

We're going to put ourselves out of business if we don't pull this stuff together and start demonstrating that we really know how to bring about improvement.

—Harry Handler

KM. One of the issues we raise in the introduction to this book is the elimination of boundaries or the bridging of them. Ted Mitchell, for example, in a recent issue of the journal *Daedalus* (1997) describes the changing relationship between the university and its environment—the bridging of what were once very clear distinctions.[5] For me, that ties into the issues of how universities relate to public schools. But it also ties into the issue of community involvement in schools. That's come up in certain points during this discussion, but I'm wondering whether you perceive the opportunity for more community involvement, and how that might happen. I'd also like to know how you perceive the university role in urban school reform.

ST. The community to me, whenever a principal would come in fussing and screaming about "She's a big pain in the neck, she's a big community activist," I couldn't take that. I would say, if they're in there, that's a step we want. So I think for most of us, there are a few crazies out there. That's a given. But most of the people that just drove me crazy were also people who really cared about those kids. They just didn't know what to do about it. And I accepted that challenge in all the different jobs I had. The role for the community is there. The question is whether we have more parent involvement. Not with just bake sales and things, but with curriculum. What it is we expect these kids to learn, and how they can help.

I had a parent—a Hispanic, poor lady, had a number of kids—she said to me, "Mr. Thompson, I don't know the first thing about algebra." And in her way she explained, "I can't even spell it." She said, "So, my kids are taking this stuff. What can I do?" And I think I said, "Let me just be simplistic. When she comes in the door, you shut that tube off and have a particular period of time when she's going to work." And you say "I expect you to work. And I'm going to enforce it." And she says, "But I don't even know how to do it." I said, "You don't have to. When she brings the paper, you don't know what they wrote, but you can tell if they're just messing around! You can see it! So say, 'This is junk, go back and work on it,' you're probably right. Take a chance."

But my point is that there is a real need for that. And we would need another whole hour to talk about community, because I believe in it strongly, and I know these guys do. The other thing I wanted to say about service is that we are so stupid in the way that we deliver services to families, it's incredible. Health, anything, name it. We make them go to what I like to call all those gray buildings. And they can't get there. They're afraid of them, they're afraid to go when they can get there. To me, if you want to impact a parent the most, impact them at the center of what concerns them the most. And that's their kid. If you want to work with a parent who's on aid, and all the rest of it, whatever the aid may be, if you want to really work with that parent, work through the children.

As a high school principal I had a probation officer on campus—huge school, 3,800 kids, 4,000 kids—a probation officer on campus, DPSS working on campus. Why? Because 700 of those kids were on probation. Mostly boys. And when those kids didn't come to school, nobody knew it. A probation officer on campus, when he said, "Charlie, I didn't see you yesterday," that was a lot different to principal Sid, typical "Daddy," saying "You should have been in school." No, no. *He* says, "You be here tomorrow, or you have a problem." I can tell you, it was amazing to me. Attendance just went like this (gestures up) with these kids because nobody's playing with them. One kid with many brothers and sisters, his mother died, DPSS on the job, all those kids taken care of in two hours. I would have spent eight hours trying to find out who to call. So I am a firm believer that we need coordinated approaches to support services. Just absolutely need it. But I want to tell you, there's a huge battle because it's turf. And when I left that school, both workers were taken out. Because "We can't supervise them over there."

GT. I liked what you said—coordinated and school-based. One thing about the university during my few years here is that community-based, school-based work is not deeply valued. There's really a disincentive for the faculty to truly be involved. An assistant professor working for tenure and professional advancement knows there's a hierarchy of values. Research is most valued. At the bottom of that hierarchy is community service.

It seems to me that the university needs to think about or explore ways to reward and encourage faculty to become involved with K–12 schools. I think we have faculty who could make very significant contributions to the work of schools, either at the policy or the operational level. I think a lot of research could be centered around that work. My experience has been that it's problematic for junior faculty to get more involved and many senior faculty don't want to leave their comfort zone.

KM. So, rather than trying to "raise the status" of community service, so to speak, we should focus on a more thorough integration of service and research. It seems like a natural goal for any university with a service mission, but an incredibly challenging one, nonetheless.

HH. I jotted down some notes in anticipation of our conversation and I'll probably address your question in them.

This may sound kind of corny, but we still lack public confidence in public schools. You can't go out and generate a lot of support for these kinds of changes without public support. Then I couple that with lack of understanding of the reason they're called the public schools—and this ties to community. They're called public schools because they belong to the public. That may sound kind of weird, but it's something to keep in mind every day of the week that you work with the public. Those schools belong to the public. So public involvement would seem to me natural. Conflicting needs of the multiplicity of special interest groups has been described. I think more people should read Jonathan Kozol's *Savage Inequalities*.[6] How can we address the question of solutions for the future? I think we have to sustain the national interest in the condition of our schools.

This dialogue and this concern has been going on longer than any of us can remember. Usually it was like a sine curve in calculus, where it's a concern today but tomorrow it isn't. This time it has been very consistent and we better keep it up there. You're in an era now where bottom-up is important. So we balance the two, bottom-up and when there is a need for a decision, someone who has carefully gone through the problem and is willing to take risks associated with decisions, we can't walk away from the community. The research community has provided practitioners with far more knowledge and insight than is being utilized. However, within the research community, there is a lack of consensus regarding what to do. The academics and the practitioners need to reach a consensus regarding "What do we know? What changes should be made?" And working together—practitioner and scholar—how are we going to get it done?

For the past four or five years, I've noticed some progress. If I had a magic wand, I'd say "No more research! We've got to stop right now! We need to regroup and agree on what we think we know, and we've got to go do it." Just, "Time out!" It's not that I don't value the research, and I understand the concept of contributing to knowledge. But we're going to put ourselves out of business if we don't pull this stuff together and start demonstrating that we really know how to bring about improvement.

CT. Strong words. And I appreciate that.

GT. You're going to be out of here. You're not going to be invited back. (Laughter)

## THE PASSION OF URBAN EDUCATION

> Your reason and passion are the rudder and the sails of your sea-faring soul. If either your sails or your rudder be broken, you can but toss and drift, or else be held at a standstill in mid-seas. For reason, ruling alone, is a force confining; and passion, unattended, is a flame that burns to its own destruction.
>
> —Kahlil Gibran, *The Prophet*

CT. Kahlil Gibran has described reason and passion as the rudder and sails of the soul—one without the other is useless, and the two together are quite powerful. It's very clear to me that there's a fascinating combination here of passion—and I do appreciate passion—and knowledge or reason. And I think when we are talking about this issue, we are not observing dispassionately, like kind of objective scientists, see how the rats are moving, figure out who is losing weight, who is not. And in fact we are part of the rats. When we are observing, we are part of the rats.

But I have one question. You may think that it's a romantic question—I hope you don't think so. But I have been thinking lately about virtues. I think education is always a very noble profession because people are thought of as instilling virtues. The moral commitment, whatever that is. If you were going to list a couple of virtues of a good superintendent, what would they be? In a way, I'm asking you, if you had to get together with a young colleague who is going to be a superintendent, and you want to pass on the baton, then you look at them and say, "Look, there are a couple of things you should know." The question is open.

HH. I just finished with a passionate statement, so . . .

ST. Well, as I think back on the superintendency, there are certain characteristics a person should have. One of them is energy. Because the job is incredibly demanding, and you can't do it on low energy. So you have to be a person who doesn't require nine hours of sleep a night, because you're not going to get it in that job. Although, I know those who do manage to squeak it out. Not here. The other characteristic that I think you must have, especially dealing with board members, is the ability to bring folks together. You have to work for that. Your responsibility is to bring them together. In spite of what I said about what a pain and what they sometimes represent. You have to work with them. So you have to be a communicator. You have to listen and you have to communicate. Now, there are all sorts of things about organization and budget that I won't go into. But the other to me, for a good superintendent, in spite of the fact that we don't necessarily look for this, is an instructional leader. Somebody that is going to lead the district in instruction.

GT. I would add a couple. I certainly would put intellectual honesty at the top of the list. I think that a good superintendent has to know what he or she believes in and have the courage to stand by those beliefs. I think there are times when all of us are pressed against the wall. We have to make those hard decisions which are not popular, but are the right ones for children. A good superintendent has to be really committed to social justice—a person who truly believes that in a democratic society every child deserves access to quality education and who will work to ensure that happens.

I think that a good superintendent has to have qualities that we often attribute to leadership. He or she should have a vision of what could and should be, have the ability to mobilize and engage others in sharing that vision, and empower the people that he or she works with to achieve the outcomes that have been mutually identified.

HH. Virtue. And I only get to pick one. I want to turn it into a game. I only get to pick one. "INTEGRITY."

ST. It sounds like, "Oh, yeah, of course," but no. It is so important.

CT. I think that's an excellent place to stop. It's been a real pleasure. Karen and I would like to thank you profusely.

## NOTES

1. Gloria Ladson-Billings, *The Dreamkeepers: Successful Teachers of African American Children* (San Francisco: Jossey-Bass, 1994).

2. Mike Rose, *Possible Lives* (New York: Houghton Mifflin, 1995).

3. See, for example, William J. Wilson, *The Truly Disadvantaged: The Inner City, the Underclass, and Public Policy* (Chicago: The University of Chicago Press, 1987), and William J. Wilson, *The Declining Significance of Race* (Chicago: The University of Chicago Press, 1980).

4. In recent years, California has experienced far-reaching backlash against race-related issues such as immigration and affirmative action. Proposition 187 was a voter initiative aimed at denying social services to undocumented

immigrants in the state. Proposition 209 seeks to end affirmative action in education and hiring. Both were passed by voters.

5. Theodore R. Mitchell, "Border Crossings: Organizational Boundaries and Challenges to the American Professoriate," *Daedalus* 126.4 (1997): 265–92.

6. Jonathan Kozol, *Savage Inequalities: Children in American Schools* (New York: Harper Perennial, 1992).

# THE CONTRIBUTORS

*Michael W. Apple* is John Bascom Professor of Education at the University of Wisconsin, Madison. A former elementary and secondary school teacher and past president of a teachers union, he has worked with educators, unions, dissident groups, and governments throughout the world to democratize educational research, policy, and practice. He has written extensively about the relationship between education and power. Among his most recent books are: *Official Knowledge* (1993), *Education and Power* (1995), *Cultural Politics and Education* (1996), and *Power, Meaning, and Identity* (1999).

*Anthony Gary Dworkin* is Professor of Sociology at the University of Houston and holds the Ph.D. degree in sociology from Northwestern University. He is past chair of the Department of Sociology at the University of Houston. He is the author of nine books and numerous articles on teacher morale and burnout, student achievement, racial, ethnic, and gender stratification, intergroup relations, and ethnic stereotyping. He is past president of the Southwestern Sociological Association, has served in several elected and appointed positions in the American Sociological Association and other professional associations, and serves on editorial boards and grant review panels in sociology and education. He currently serves as editor of a book series entitled "The New Inequalities," published by the State University of New York Press. Most recently, Dr. Dworkin served on a task force for the Texas Higher Education Coordinating Board, addressing the issues of higher educational access for disadvantaged populations and the maintenance of cultural diversity. He served as principal investigator on the U.S. Department of Education Urban Community Service project described in his chapter.

*Pamela Fenning* holds a master's and doctorate in School Psychology from the University of Wisconsin, Madison. She has completed a clinical internship at the Devereux Foundation (Pennsylvania), and has worked as a school psychologist with students who evidence significant emotional and behavioral difficulties. Her research and clinical interests involve developing appropriate services for youth who have serious emotional disturbances, evaluating mental health and educational programs within public schools, and implementing discipline policies within school and residential settings.

*Harry Handler* worked for the Los Angeles Unified School District for thirty-four years, progressing from substitute teacher to superintendent. He served as Superintendent of Schools for six years, from 1981 to 1987. He is currently an Adjunct Professor and Special Assistant to the Dean at UCLA in the Graduate School of Education and Information Studies. He has a bachelor's degree from UCLA in mathematics, a master's degree in educational psychology from University of Southern California (USC), and a Ph.D. in educational psychology from USC, in learning theory, statistics, and measurement.

*David Lee Keiser* teaches and writes in Berkeley, California. He is currently completing his dissertation at the Graduate School of Education at the University of California at Berkeley while teaching undergraduate courses in multicultural education and poetry. He has published several dialogues about the retraction of affirmative action, in *Social Justice* and *Bad Subjects*, as well as poems in several anthologies. His dissertation, *Stokin' the Fire: Writing Empowerment at an Urban High School*, follows three years of high school teaching, and expands upon the chapter published in this volume.

*Karen McClafferty* received her M.A. and Ph.D. from the Graduate School of Education and Information Studies at the University of California at Los Angeles. She has worked as a researcher with Children's Television Workshop, developing educational television programming for at-risk youth. Dr. McClafferty is the co-author of several articles on the preparation of teachers for urban schools. Her current research focuses on the sociology of education, with special attention to the social and political context of educational research and the role of higher education in the improvement of urban schools.

*Peter McLaren* is Professor of Education at the University of California, Los Angeles Graduate School of Education and Information Studies. He has authored, edited, and co-edited over thirty books and monographs on topics that include critical pedagogy, the sociology of education, critical ethnography, critical literacy, and Marxist social theory. His work has been translated in eleven languages. His most recent books include *Schooling as a Ritual Performance* (3rd edition, Rowman and Littlefield, 1999), *Critical Pedagogy and Predatory Culture* (Routledge, 1995), *Critical Multiculturalism* (Westview Press, 1997), and *Che Gue-*

*vara and Paulo Freire: An Introduction to the Pedagogy of Liberation* (in press, Rowman and Littlefield). Professor McLaren's current interests include globalization, neoliberalism, and Marxist social theory.

*Roslyn Arlin Mickelson*, a former public high school social studies teacher, is Professor of Sociology and Adjunct Professor of Women's Studies at the University of North Carolina at Charlotte. She received her Ph.D. from the University of California, Los Angeles in 1984. Prior to coming to North Carolina in 1985, she completed a postdoctoral fellowship at the University of Michigan, Ann Arbor's Bush Program in Child Development and Social Policy. Her primary research examines the political economy of schooling and the ways that race, class, and gender shape educational processes and outcomes. Her current research, supported by the National Science Foundation and the Ford Foundation, explores the academic and equity implications of corporate involvement in school reform.

*Theodore R. Mitchell* is currently serving as Vice President of the J. Paul Getty Trust and Professor of Education at University of California, Los Angeles. He has also served as Vice Chancellor and as Dean of the Graduate School of Education and Information Studies at UCLA. His own research has been in examining educational organizations in an historical perspective. His particular interest is in exploring the ways educational organizations in the United States have resisted or embraced change. He is the author of numerous essays and articles, and is currently completing a book entitled *The Republic for Which It Stands: Liberty, Order, and the Development of Public Schools in America*.

*Raymond A. Morrow* is Professor of Sociology and Adjunct Professor of Educational Policy Studies at the University of Alberta, Edmonton, where he has taught since 1984. A co-author with Carlos A. Torres of *Social Theory and Education* (SUNY Press, 1995), he has also published extensively in other aspects of social and cultural theory, including a book on *Critical Theory and Methodology* (Sage, 1994) which outlines what is termed an interpretive structuralist research program based in part on the work of Anthony Giddens and Jürgen Habermas.

*Marianela I. Parraga*, M.Ed., born in Bolivia, is bilingual (Spanish/English) and also has a strong background in French. As a graduate student of Loyola University of Chicago's doctoral program in School Psychology, she has been actively involved as a student representative and as a graduate research assistant. Recently, she was awarded a regional minority scholarship through the Illinois School Psychology Association. Her research interests are in addressing parent-professional communication, developing school discipline policies, and evaluating programs for students in special education. She looks forward to beginning her career in an inner-city school in Chicago.

*Margaret K. Purser* holds an M.A. degree in sociology from the University of Houston and is president of M. K. Purser Consulting. She is a professional demographer and geographer who built many of the models utilized in the Urban Community Service project described in the chapter and served at one time as a co-principal investigator on the project. School districts, local and regional governments, and businesses rely upon her forecasts for planning and community development.

*Ayman Sheikh-Hussin* received his Ph.D. degree in economics from the University of Houston and served as the computer specialist on the Urban Community Service project described in the chapter. He is currently in charge of information technology in the Houston office of Communities in Schools, a social service agency working with at-risk youth.

*Sid Thompson* has been a senior fellow at UCLA since July of 1997. He retired as superintendent of the Los Angeles Unified School District, a job he held from 1992 to 1997. He has forty-one years of education experience, all of it K–12. He began in the field as a math teacher, became administrator with the district, and then became superintendent. Mr. Thompson graduated from the U.S. Merchant Marine Academy at Kings Point, where he was a math science major. He came to UCLA for postgraduate work and later received a master's degree from California State University, Los Angeles.

*Laurence A. Toenjes* was educated at the University of California at Berkeley (B.A. and M.A., economics) and Southern Illinois University at Carbondale (Ph.D. in economics). Dr. Toenjes has extensive experience in state level education budgeting (Illinois) and school finance analysis (several states, including Texas). During the past three years, while at the University of Houston as a Research Professor in the Department of Sociology, he has participated in projects involving extensive data collection and analysis for many of the school districts in the Houston metropolitan region. He has also worked with numerous state agencies, educational interest groups, task forces, and private groups on education related issues. He served as co-investigator on the Urban Community Service project.

*Carlos Alberto Torres* is Professor of Education at UCLA's Graduate School of Education and Information Studies and Director of the Latin American Center. He holds a Ph.D. in International Education and Development from Stanford University. He has published numerous books and articles focusing on education in Latin America, with a particular emphasis on nonformal education and the political sociology of education. His research interests also encompass the new research in the scholarship of class, race, gender, and the state in a comparative perspective, with a special focus on race relations in the United States and Latin America.

*Eugene Tucker* is a member of the faculty at UCLA after working twenty-three years as a superintendent of four different school districts, both urban, suburban, and rural. His most recent assignment—from 1986 to 1992—was as superintendent of the Santa Monica Malibu Unified School District. Dr. Tucker received three degrees from UCLA: A B.A. in political science, and an M.A. and Ph.D. in education (curriculum studies, administration, and philosophy).

*Amy Stuart Wells* is an Associate Professor of Educational Policy at UCLA's Graduate School of Education & Information Studies. Her research and writing has focused on the role of race in educational policy making and implementation. More specifically, she studies school desegregation; school choice policy, including charter schools; and detracking in racially mixed schools. She received her Ph.D. from Columbia University in Sociology of Education—a joint program between Teachers College and the Graduate School of Arts and Sciences—in 1991. She is author of several journal articles and books, including *Time to Choose: American at the Crossroads of School Choice Policy* (Hill & Wang, 1993); first author with Irene Serna of "The Politics of Culture: Understanding Local Political Resistance in Detracking in Racially Mixed Schools," *Harvard Education Review* (Spring 1996); and first author with Robert L. Crain of *Stepping over the Color Line: African American Students in White Suburban Schools* (Yale University Press, 1997). In 1995, she began a two-year study of charter schools in ten school districts in California funded by the Ford Foundation and the Annie E. Casey Foundation.

*Geoff Whitty* is the Karl Mannheim Professor of Sociology of Education and Dean of Research at the Institute of Education, University of London. He ran the Urban Education Program at King's College London and was later Dean of Education at Bristol Polytechnic and the Goldsmiths' Professor of Policy and Management in Education at Goldsmiths' College, University of London. He is author of *Sociology and School Knowledge* (Methuen, 1985) and co-author of *The State and Private Education* (Falmer Press, 1989), *Specialisation and Choice in Urban Education* (Routledge, 1993) and *Devolution and Choice in Education* (Open University Press, 1998).

*James D. Wilczynski* received a M.A. in Clinical Psychology at Xavier University of Ohio. He is currently completing his Ph.D. in School Psychology at Loyola University of Chicago. He previously worked in the Department of Psychiatry at Cook County (Illinois) Department of Corrections. Current areas of interest include working with students with emotional and behavior disorders, developing and evaluating alternatives to suspension programs for regular and special education students, and violence/gang prevention strategies for school settings. He is currently a school psychologist for the Lockport Area Special Education Cooperative in Illinois.

# INDEX